D1195531

THE SOCIAL FRAMEWORKS
OF KNOWLEDGE

EXPLORATIONS IN
INTERPRETATIVE SOCIOLOGY

GENERAL EDITORS

PHILIP RIEFF
Benjamin Franklin Professor of Sociology
University of Pennsylvania

BRYAN R. WILSON
Reader in Sociology, University of Oxford
Fellow of All Souls College

Also in this series
MAX WEBER AND SOCIOLOGY TODAY
Edited by Otto Stammer
Translated by Kathleen Morris

Forthcoming
LUCIEN LÉVY-BRUHL
Jean Cazeneuve
Translated by Peter Rivière

THE CARNETS OF LÉVY-BRUHL
Translated by Peter Rivière

FALSE CONSCIOUSNESS
Joseph Gabel
Translated by M. A. and K. A. Thompson

THE SOCIAL FRAMEWORKS
OF KNOWLEDGE

GEORGES GURVITCH

Translated from the French by
MARGARET A. THOMPSON
and
KENNETH A. THOMPSON

With an Introductory Essay by
KENNETH A. THOMPSON

A TORCHBOOK LIBRARY EDITION
HARPER & ROW, PUBLISHERS
NEW YORK, EVANSTON, SAN FRANCISCO, LONDON

Contents

Introduction

PART ONE
Microsociology of knowledge

PART TWO
Particular groups as social frameworks of knowledge

PART THREE

Social classes and their cognitive systems

PART FOUR

Types of global societies and their cognitive systems

Contents

Supplement

Introductory Essay

by Kenneth A. Thompson

A scholar of extraordinary erudition, the author of numerous important works in philosophy and in general and special sociologies, and a successor to Durkheim's chair at the Sorbonne, Gurvitch (1894–1965) developed his empirico-realist dialectic sociology into one of the most original and significant sociological systems of our time.[1]

Although Gurvitch was the author of at least thirty books on various topics in sociology and philosophy,[2] and played a prominent role in French sociology, his works are still not widely known in Britain and America. And yet, both in his commitment to the development of theories which did full justice to the complexity of socio-cultural life, and in his awareness of the interdependence of sociology, philosophy and history, he stood closer to the founding fathers of modern sociology than most of his contemporaries.

Born in Russia in 1894, his political and social thought was much influenced by the creative ferment evident in the early stages of the Revolution of 1917, although he subsequently left Russia in 1920 when he became convinced that there was little prospect of his hopes being realized for a truly pluralistic state based on decentralized, collectivist democracy. The experience of social revolution left several indelible traces on all his subsequent theorizing about social structure. As he later explained:

In observing, in living through, the various reactions of the different milieux, groups, classes, syndicates, cells, committees, old and new organisations, and in witnessing the almost total explosion of the old global social structure, I had several ideas which later guided me in

[1] Pitrim A. Sorokin, *Sociological Theories of Today* (New York, Harper & Row, 1966), pp. 464–5.

[2] Only four have appeared in English: *Sociology of Law* (1942), *The Bill of Social Rights* (1946), *Twentieth Century Sociology* (ed. by Wilbert E. Moore, 1946), and *The Spectrum of Social Time* (trans. M. Korenbaum and P. Bosserman, 1964).

ix

my sociological studies: (1) social law springs up spontaneously, completely independent of the state and its legal order, and can relate in various ways with the law of the state. (2) The depth levels of social reality, whose hierarchy and relationships may be completely reversed, at times contradict each other and at other times interpenetrate. (3) The group is like a microcosm of the forms of sociality. (4) The global society and social classes are like macrocosms of groups. (5) The possibility of collectivist planning outside of state control rests on a pluralistic democratic economy and federalist ownership.[1]

The result of these experiences, and his study of various dialectical theories, including those of Proudhon, Emil Lask, Fichte, and the Marxists, was that Gurvitch's own theory of social structure was of a dynamic kind, stressing the radically dialectical process involved in structuration, which is no more than a precarious equilibrium of several variable hierarchies of social phenomena.

Another major influence was the phenomenological philosophy of Husserl and Scheler, and the intuitionism of Henri Bergson.[2] It was phenomenology, as we shall see, that provided some of the insights by which Gurvitch was able to overcome shortcomings in Durkheim's sociology of knowledge; in particular, it was the phenomenological concepts of 'intentionality' and the 'open consciousness' that enabled him to provide a dialectical theory of the relationship between society and individual consciousness. However, whilst freely adapting such concepts to his own use, he believed that as a sociologist he had to renounce commitment to any

[1] Georges Gurvitch, 'Mon itinéraire intellectuelle' (originally prepared for publication in 1958, this autobiographical article was later revised by Gurvitch; an English translation by Janine Chaneles was published in *Sociological Abstracts*, vol. XVII, no. 2 (April 1969), i–xx, p. iv).

[2] Gurvitch's lectures on 'Current Tendencies in German Philosophy' in the late 1920s, which were published in 1930 as *Les tendances actuelles de la philosophie allemande*, played a large part in introducing phenomenology into France. From the point of view of the development of his interest in the sociology of knowledge, the most significant aspect of the book is that the largest section was devoted to Scheler and not to Husserl. (Cf. Herbert Spiegelberg, *The Phenomenological Movement*, 2 vols. (The Hague, Martinus Nijhoff, 1960), vol. 2, p. 402.) Gurvitch later expressed a rather rueful view of his part in spreading phenomenology. He commented, 'I was taken for a protagonist of phenomenology, and even of the existentialism of Heidegger. Actually, I had written as objective an exposé as possible, concluding with some sharp criticism of each author. I was clearly favouring the realists who were not phenomenologists—such as Lask and Nicholas Hartmann—and I stressed my criticism of the later works of Fichte' ('Mon itinéraire . . .', op. cit., p. vi).

single philosophical position (although it is not altogether clear how his own 'dialectical hyper-empiricism' escapes this). Two errors that he found in many other sociological theories, and which he sought to avoid in his own theory, were: first, the tendency to fall in with some kind of idealist philosophy, such as that of the neo-Kantians, which influenced many French sociologists and anthropologists from Durkheim to those of the present day; and second, that of emphasizing a single, predominant factor, such as the 'collective conscience' in Durkheim's later works, and the economic substructure in the work of Marx. Gurvitch constantly stressed that in his own 'dialectical hyper-empirical' theory, relativism and realism should be pressed to their limits, and variations should be expected in the hierarchies of different social factors from one group or society to another.

The purpose of this introduction is to provide an explanation of some of the main elements in that theory, so that the reader will be spared the task of making such a prior investigation before being able to appreciate the use to which Gurvitch puts his theory in sketching the outlines of a systematic sociology of knowledge. I would also like to suggest in passing how this theory might make a contribution to the task of bridging the gap between those theorists who have been concerned with the relationship between society and individual consciousness (such as G. H. Mead, American symbolic interactionists, phenomenological analyses of the *Lebenswelt*, as begun by Alfred Schutz and continued in part by ethnomethodologists) and the dialectical theories of structure provided by Marxist scholars, which lack a theoretical grasp of the 'mediations' between structural processes and individual consciousness.[1]

Gurvitch follows Marcel Mauss in taking as the subject matter of sociology the 'total social phenomenon', which demands that any aspect of social life be viewed in the context of social reality as a whole, so that the distortive reifications of 'abstract culturalism', sociologism, or psychologism may be avoided. In order to integrate

[1] Peter L. Berger has pointed out that G. H. Mead and American symbolic interactionism, whilst contributing to an understanding of the relationship between society and individual consciousness, lack a theoretical grasp of social structure; whereas Marxism has concentrated its sociological interest on structural problems, leaving the explanation of individual consciousness to a purely mechanistic type of psychology. Cf. Peter L. Berger (ed.), *Marxism and Sociology* (New York, Appleton-Century-Crofts, 1969), pp. ix–x.

the various aspects of social reality, sociological theory must provide
a systematic account of the dialectical interrelations of micro-social
processes, groups, classes, and societies, and their interpenetration
at different levels of social reality.

In view of these considerations Gurvitch's sociology rests on two
precepts:

(a) 'It always takes into account *all the levels* of social reality
simultaneously, viewing them as a whole.'
(b) 'It applies to the study of social reality *the typological method*.'[1]

Social reality, or the total social phenomenon, is differentiated
along two main axes, one vertical and one horizontal, corresponding
to the two aspects—depth levels of social reality and social types.
The types differentiate social frameworks (*cadres sociaux*), which is
the generic term for categories along the horizontal axis. All social
types (social frameworks) should be analysable according to all the
depth levels.

The depth levels, which constitute the vertical axis of the conceptualized total social phenomenon, can be related in part to
degrees of spontaneity or rigidity of different elements of social
reality—ranging from the deepest level, that of collective consciousness, to the surface level of social morphology and ecology.
In his early work on the sociology of law he favoured a phenomenological method in explaining the depth levels:

The best approach to problems of the sociology of the noetic mind
(or of human spirit) and to the determination of its exact place among
the various sociological disciplines, would seem to be via the levels- or
depth-analysis of social reality. This type of analysis is inspired by the
'method of inversion' (Bergson) or 'phenomenological reduction'
(Husserl), i.e., an immanent downward reduction through successive
stages towards whatever is most directly experienced in social reality.[2]

In his later work Gurvitch renounced this phenomenological basis
because it was too value-laden and he preferred a more empirical
and dialectical approach. His new criterion for ordering the depth
levels was their accessibility to direct, external observation; the
lowest levels were those that required the greatest effort in order to

[1] Gurvitch, *La vocation actuelle de la sociologie* (Paris, Presses Universitaires
de France, 1950), pp. 7 and 49. A useful commentary on Gurvitch's theoretical
framework is Phillip Bosserman's *Dialectical Sociology* (Boston, Porter Sargent,
1968).
[2] *Sociology of Law*, p. 42.

grasp them and study them scientifically, and even on such a basis the order or hierarchy could vary from one social framework or situation to another. Apart from the changing rationale for the ordering of the depth levels, the origins of this approach to social reality from a sociological viewpoint are to be found in his discovery of five such levels in the work of Durkheim: (1) the geographic and demographic basis of society; (2) institutions and collective behaviour; (3) symbols; (4) values, ideas and ideals; (5) states of the collective mind.[1] Gurvitch went on to distinguish ten depth levels, in his own theory:

1. *The Morphological and Ecological Surface.* This is the most superficial and usually the easiest to observe level of social reality; it includes the geographic and demographic phenomena. However, it is social in that it is penetrated and transformed by human action, as in the case of those material objects that become 'property'. This points to the dependence of this surface level on deeper levels of social reality—hence Mauss's insistence that sociology must study the total social phenomenon.

2. *Social Organizations.* These are pre-established collective patterns of behaviour that are regularized, ordered and centralized in a more or less rigid manner. They are one of the modes of social control, both over their participants and over the more spontaneous 'infrastructure' of social life. The spontaneous total social phenomena remain subjacent to the organized 'superstructure', and can never be fully expressed or contained in it. Organizations are only partial expressions of social structures, just as social structures are partial expressions of the total social phenomenon. In any social situation we are likely to be involved in one or more forms of social organization; at a wedding ceremony, for example, we are subject to both ecclesiastical and legal organizations.

3. *Social Patterns or Models.* These are the more or less standardized images of expected collective behaviour, the signs, signals and rules that give regularity to collective behaviour. They extend beyond particular domains of organizations and are more flexible; hence they constitute a depth level between organizations and collective behaviour extraneous to any organization. Both technical and cultural models are included in this category—from

---

[1] Ibid., pp. 31–2.

mundane aspects of daily life, such as cooking recipes, economic techniques, to models that reveal the character of the religion, art and education of the society. Collective signals and signs are a particular case of social models; they differ from symbols in that they express fairly completely whatever signification they are intended to convey, which is not the case with symbols.

4. *Regular Collective Behaviour not Confined to Social Organizations.* This is subjacent to the social models and is expected to realize those models, but it often deviates from them to varying degrees. This more or less regular behaviour can be ranked according to the amount of spontaneity it exhibits:

(a) Ritual and procedural behaviour, based on rigorously regulated traditions, e.g. religious rites, jural procedures.
(b) Practices, mores, routines, folkways.
(c) Fashions and fads.
(d) Behaviour that is insubordinate and non-conformist in relation to the social models.

5. *The Web of Social Roles.* These are more spontaneous and flexible complexes of behaviour than the previous levels because they depend so much on individual creative performance. However, Gurvitch stresses that a role only exists as part of a social matrix, and the social drama of role performance involves groups and not just individuals.

6. *Collective Attitudes.* It is at this level that we begin to encounter the spontaneous 'infrastructure' of society. They are dispositions which urge groups and even whole societies to react in common, to behave in a particular way and assume certain roles, but they are never entirely realized. Gurvitch believed that the social character of attitudes had been lost sight of by public opinion pollsters, who failed to distinguish between the faltering and artificially elicited answers to questions directed to the so-called 'average individual', and the real attitude of the group, which is an indissoluble whole.

7. *Social Symbols.* These are extremely variable and pervasive in almost all aspects of social life. They operate as a kind of fluid and omnipresent social cement, preserving some unity in the total social phenomenon by filling in the gaps and separations that occur. Their task is to beckon or urge the perceiver to participate in the full meaning of that which is symbolized; but it is a principal

characteristic of a symbol that it is an inadequate vehicle and cannot fully express that which is symbolized: 'One of their essential characteristics is that they reveal while veiling and veil while revealing, and that while pushing towards participation, they also restrain it.'[1] Because of this fundamental ambiguity, a society's symbols are always in danger of becoming fatigued and breaking down. Such a situation is an indication of a social system in transition or in the process of collapsing. Gurvitch thought that some theorists, such as G. H. Mead, tended to over-emphasize the role of symbols to the point where all social experience and relationships could be explained in terms of symbolic communication. In some circumstances, however, social symbols play only a minor role. Certain collective intuitions[2] can go beyond symbols and realize full participation. The last three depth levels reveal this tendency.

8. *Spontaneous, Innovative, and Creative Collective Behaviour.* This is collective behaviour that not only stands outside the crystallized and standardized models and symbols, but also seeks to replace them. It changes the meanings of established models and symbols, and upsets their heirarchy. In periods of crisis, revolution, religious reformation, great reform, migrations, and discoveries, this kind of unprecedented and unforeseen behaviour plays a decisive role, so that established models and symbols offer no guidance. However, it is not limited to such extreme situations, but is always appearing and challenging the more rigid and crystallized levels of the total social phenomenon. The influence of Fichte and Bergson on Gurvitch's thought is evident in his discussion of this depth level.

9. *Collective Ideas and Values.* Beneath all forms of collective behaviour, attitudes, organizations, patterns, signs, roles, and symbols, there exists a sphere of collective ideas and values, which supply the fundamental orientations that these other levels only express in piecemeal fashion.

10. *Collective Mentalities (or Collective Consciousness).* This is the

---

[1] *The Spectrum of Social Time*, p. 3.

[2] Gurvitch uses the term 'intuition' not in any metaphysical sense, but in the phenomenological sense of an immediate experience, or direct apprehension of what is immediately given to consciousness, as opposed to reflection, or the application of categories and judgements to the data of experience. For an application of this distinction to different modes of perception of the Other, see the research report presented in the Supplement at the end of this book.

most profound level with regard to spontaneity and immediacy. It is concerned with intersubjectivity and the non-symbolic inter-penetration of individual and group consciousness through the immediate and direct route of intuition. It is here that Gurvitch's familiarity with phenomenological philosophy enabled him to preserve the positive aspects of Durkheim's notion of collective consciousness whilst eliminating some erroneous elements, such as Durkheim's tendency to slip into cultural idealism by giving the collective consciousness a totally transcendent character and to restrict it to a single, static entity, rather than viewing it as plural-istic and dynamic. We will return to this subject when discussing Gurvitch's microsociology.[1]

Turning from the vertical axis of depth levels to the horizontal axis of typologies of social frameworks, Gurvitch distinguished between three general categories: forms of sociality,[2] groups, and global societies (or inclusive societies). The forms of sociality are the simplest and most irreducible elements of every collective unit—analogous to electrons, waves and quanta in physics, and cells in biology. They are described by Gurvitch as 'the ways of being bound to the whole and by the whole'. These social bonds are the basic and elemental forms of social framework. They are extremely dynamic and complex; at the same time they are the most abstract of the social frameworks and do not in themselves re-present real social structures. Because they are frequently in a state of unstable equilibrium and indeterminacy, Gurvitch used the analogy of microphysics and calls this part of sociology micro-sociology.

The second type of social framework is the group, and groups are more concrete and directly observable than forms of sociality. They are social frameworks that are structurable, and sometimes even organized. Their stability depends on the maintenance of some degree of equilibrium among the forms of sociality. Accord-ing to Gurvitch's definition, the group is a real social unit, but it is

---

[1] Cf. for a full discussion of these depth levels, *La vocation actuelle de la sociologie*, pp. 49–97.

[2] It should be explained that *'sociabilité'* has been variously translated as sociality or sociability. Sociality has the advantage of being more generic and less subjective than the more familiar sociability. However, it will be noticed that in this Introduction I refer to the *forms* of sociality, whereas in the rest of the book they are termed *manifestations* of sociality; the first term is more familiar, but Gurvitch changed to the second term in his later works because he was being inaccurately described as a sociological formalist.

only partial—it is never completely independent, but is always a part of a third social framework, a global society.

Global societies are macrocosms of groups, and have a certain stability in so far as they maintain some equilibrium among the different constituent groups. The predominance of a particular kind of group in a global society is one of the criteria that determines how it is classified among the different types of global society. Gurvitch distinguishes several types of group and several types of global society, as follows:

GROUPS

Gurvitch has given fifteen criteria by which groups can be classified, but in this book he uses only two: *mode of access* (open, conditional, closed), and *function*.

Of the groups distinguished according to the criterion of mode of access, he mainly deals with groups with conditional access, such as professional groups, as these are the most significant as centres of knowledge.

Among the groups distinguished according to their functions he concentrates on three fairly small, multi-functional groups— the family, the small-scale locality group, and the factory; two large-scale, multifunctional groups—States (which are not to be confused with the global society, such as a nation), and Churches (Roman Catholicism, Eastern Orthodoxy, and Protestantism); and finally, the suprafunctional, social classes (peasants, bourgeoisie, proletariat, and techno-bureaucrats).

GLOBAL SOCIETIES

1. *Archaic Societies*

Four sub-types are discussed: tribes with mainly a clan basis; tribes incorporating varied and relatively unhierarchized groups; tribes organized on the basis of military divisions, families, clans; organized monarchic tribes, which partly retain clan divisions.

2. *Historical (or Promethean[1]) Societies*

Six types from the past are discussed: charismatic theocracies (like ancient Egypt and Imperial China); patriarchal societies (as

[1] 'Promethean' because there exists some collective and individual consciousness of the capacity of human intervention to change society.

B

described in the Old Testament, the *Odyssey* and the *Iliad*);
feudal societies (such as existed in Europe from the tenth to the
fourteenth centuries); city-states in the process of becoming
empires (like the Greek *polis* from the seventh to the fifth century
B.C., and the Roman *civitas*, from the fifth to the first century B.C.);
societies of emerging capitalism; democratic–liberal societies of
developed, competitive capitalism (such as those in Europe and the
United States at the end of the nineteenth century and the beginning of the twentieth century). To these are added four types that
are still in competition: the managerial society of organized
capitalism (the United States, Japan, West Germany, France, and
to some extent Britain); techno-bureaucratic fascist societies
(Italy from 1922 to 1944, and Germany, 1933–45); centralized
collectivism (the U.S.S.R. and China); decentralized, pluralistic
collectivism (this type has not been fully realized as yet, but
Yugoslavia and certain other countries in Eastern and Western
Europe exhibit such tendencies).[1]

The global society has its own symbols, patterns, hierarchical
criteria, and other characteristics, which penetrate all the constituent groups; in fact it only expresses itself and is structured in
and through the organized groups. Thus the state is only an
organized political grouping within the nation, which is a global
society. The global society is the best expression of the total social
phenomenon.

Whereas the forms of sociality are the subject matter of microsociology, groups and global societies are the observable collective
units studied by macrosociology. Microsociology is concerned
with the most abstract, general, and repeatable social frameworks;
groups occupy an intermediate position in that they are concrete
social units which are also susceptible to a certain amount of
abstraction, generality, and repeatability; global societies are the
most concrete and least repeatable social types, and so most nearly
approach the status of historically unique entities.

All of these social frameworks interpenetrate each other at the

---

[1] Gurvitch made no secret of his own preferences among these types, and it
would be unrealistic to expect otherwise from one who spent much of his life
promoting ideas and causes that he thought were vital for the development of
real participatory democracy. However, the fact that he was *engagé* should not
be allowed to obscure the fact that in his discussion of types of knowledge and
global structures his intention was to offer hypotheses and not simply value
statements.

different depth levels, and the constant flux or dialectic in this interpenetration is Gurvitch's most emphatic corrective to other sociological theories. He is most concerned to emphasize this aspect where it concerns the subjective side of social reality—the active participation of the individual consciousness in collective consciousness, and the nature and degree of reciprocity of perspectives. The interpenetration of the various social frameworks and depth levels will be discussed later, but first we need to look at the kinds of relationships Gurvitch sets out to discover between the social frameworks and different types and forms of knowledge. He made extensive use of typologies because he was sceptical about the amount of abstraction and generalization that could be attempted in sociology without distorting social reality, especially in dealing with the deeper levels of the total social phenomenon (symbols, values, collective consciousness, etc.), where quantification would risk destroying their specific content. He therefore limits himself to the task of discovering functional correlations between such entities as types of knowledge and types of social framework, although in cases of disjunction between such entities he suggests that it might be possible to establish a causal relationship (even though it could only be a singular causality, limited to a given framework and social conjuncture).[1] His caution in limiting the possibility of causal explanation to single cases derives from his view of the variability and complexity involved in the interpenetration of social frameworks and depth levels in each social conjuncture. Generalized predictions cannot be made because there are not enough sufficiently similar cases to permit valid induction:

Between the antecedent and the consequent there is a margin of uncertainty too intense to permit the elaboration of generalised predictions on the repetition of the same causes and the same effects. This repetition of causes is never sure nor complete; and the production by

[1] Cf. for a discussion of Gurvitch's position and the issues involved, N. S. Timasheff, 'Order, Causality, Conjuncture', in Llewellyn Gross (ed.), *Symposium on Sociological Theory* (New York, Harper & Row, 1959), pp. 145–64; also G. Gurvitch, 'La crise de l'explication en sociologie', *Cahiers Internationaux de Sociologie*, XXI (1956), 3–18; and 'Le concept de structure sociale', *Cahiers Internationaux de Sociologie*, XIX (1955), 3–44; where 'conjuncture' is defined as the copresence, or conjunction, of relatively independent causal chains. Timasheff points out that causal explanation refers to the intersection of two causal chains, and that, whereas the unfolding of every chain is covered by the postulate of order, their intersection is not (p. 152).

them of identical effects is still less sure or complete because of the evolution and unceasing fluctuation of circumstances and social conjunctures.[1]

This book is largely devoted to analysing different types of knowledge and social frameworks, and on the basis of these typological descriptions it suggests hypotheses as to the functional correlations that might exist between them. The types of knowledge discussed are: perceptual knowledge of the external world (space and time, etc.); knowledge of the Other, the We—groups, classes, and societies; common-sense knowledge; technical knowledge; political knowledge; scientific knowledge; philosophical knowledge. The forms of knowledge can be viewed as five dichotomies with regard to the form taken by each of the types of knowledge or the overall cognitive system of a social framework. They are: (a) mystical knowledge and rational knowledge; (b) empirical knowledge and conceptual knowledge; (c) positive knowledge and speculative knowledge; (d) symbolic knowledge and concrete (or adequate[2]) knowledge.

DEPTH SOCIOLOGY AND MICROSOCIOLOGY

We have seen that Gurvitch's theory can be traced along two axes—the horizontal (forms of sociality, groups, and global societies), and the vertical (depth levels). The vertical and horizontal constantly intersect, but his theory is perhaps most original and daring where the intersections concern the deepest of the depth levels (those layers of social reality that are least rigid and most spontaneous) and the least structured social frameworks (the forms of sociality, which are the subject matter of microsociology).

Although in his later statement of his general theory in *La vocation actuelle de la sociologie* Gurvitch turned away from phenomenological philosophy and towards a more empirical and dialectical method of discovering the hierarchy of depth levels in any situation, he originally developed them under the influence of the Husserlian method of phenomenological reduction—the successive 'bracketing' of different layers of experience in order to

---

[1] *La vocation actuelle de la sociologie*, p. 46.

[2] The use of the term 'adequate' probably derives from Husserl's *Adäquation*, which refers to that property of a conscious experience by which an object is presented so fully that no improvement of presentation can be conceived.

reach 'the immediately given in experience'. It is not necessary to discuss this genesis of the depth levels here, but one aspect of it is significant for the sociology of knowledge, and especially with regard to Gurvitch's relation to Emile Durkheim's sociology. The difference can be related to three things—knowledge, symbols, and collective consciousness. Durkheim's basic assumptions are expressed in an important passage in his book *The Elementary Forms of the Religious Life:*

. . . the collective consciousness is the highest form of the psychic life, since it is the consciousness of the consciousnesses. Being placed outside of and above individual and local contingencies, it sees things only in their permanent and essential aspects, which it crystallizes into communicable ideas. At the same time that it sees from above, it sees farther; at every moment of time, it embraces all known reality; that is why it alone can furnish the mind with the moulds which are applicable to the totality of things and which make it possible to think of them. It does not create these moulds; it finds them within itself; it does nothing but become conscious of them.[1]

Gurvitch's criticism of this was that Durkheim, by tending to see the incarnation of reason in the collective consciousness, passed from the sociology of knowledge to an epistemology with a sociological basis that sought to reconcile empiricism with a Kantian apriorism. Durkheim thus lapses into 'cultural idealism' by giving the collective consciousness a transcendent character, and identifying it with an *a priori* reason. Gurvitch agreed with Durkheim's emphasis on the irreducibility of the social and the fact that it is more than simply the sum of its parts. They both wished to assert that social reality is not simply based on relationships between individual minds. However, Gurvitch believed that Durkheim's lack of a social psychology[2] ironically forced him back into just such a dilemma—on the one hand there is the transcendent collective consciousness, and on the other hand there are isolated

[1] Emile Durkheim, *The Elementary Forms of the Religious Life*, trans. J. W Swain (London, Allen & Unwin, 1915), p. 444.
[2] Robert K. Merton has also suggested that the lack of a social psychology lies at the basis of the flaws in Durkheim's sociology of knowledge: 'The most serious shortcoming in Durkheim's analysis lies precisely in his uncritical acceptance of a naive theory of correspondence in which the categories of thought are held to "reflect" certain features of the group organisation. . . . Durkheim's sociology of knowledge suffers from his avoidance of a social psychology' (Merton, *Social Theory and Social Structure* (New York, Free Press, 1949, 1968 edn.), pp. 533–4)

individual minds that can only enter into a relationship by way of symbolic communication. Gurvitch asked, 'How is communication possible between individuals, since the symbols must have the same meaning, and is this same meaning possible without a union, an interpenetration, a partial fusion of the minds, which underlie all symbolic communication?'[1]

The difficulty in Durkheim's position derives from his 'classical' conception of the individual consciousness as closed up within itself, in contrast to the phenomenological view of it as 'open' and intuitive, and involving a 'tension' towards that which is beyond itself. This is based on the phenomenologists' concept of 'intentionality': consciousness is consciousness *of* something, it involves intending something heterogeneous to itself and so it is implicitly presentative. Gurvitch uses this concept of intentionality to link the interpenetration, or immanence, of individual and collective consciousnesses, with social frameworks. He distinguishes degrees of intensity of fusion of individual consciousnesses on the basis of intentionality, and it is this reciprocal participation or immanence that provides him with the criteria for a typological description of the forms of sociality. We will see that this also has significance for relating these most fluid and abstract social frameworks to the deepest depth levels of social reality—those below the level of symbols.

Gurvitch was much influenced by Max Scheler in his discussion of reciprocal participation as the basis of collective consciousness. However, he thought that Scheler tended to exaggerate the emotional aspect and neglected the intellectual and volitional.

Though Scheler is right when he insists on the important role of the collective intuitions in social life, he seems to us to fall into unquestionable exaggerations ignoring . . . the fact that collective mental acts may consist of experiences and judgements, or finally the fact that collective intuitions do not need to be exclusively emotive but can be also volitional and intellectual, or combine the three.[2]

Certainly Scheler provided some suggestive descriptions of emotive collective intuition, as in the case of shared psychic suffering, which differs from physical pain or pleasure in not being a purely individual phenomenon—as in his example of the 'feeling-

[1] Gurvitch, *Essais de sociologie* (Paris, Sirey, 1938), p. 123.
[2] *La vocation actuelle de la sociologie*, p. 218.

in-common' shared by two sorrowing parents standing beside the dead body of a beloved child.[1] We have seen, however, that Gurvitch maintained that there is also collective intellectual intuition, otherwise there could be no effective symbolic communication which leads him to assert that there is always a pre-existing intellectual 'We'. One argument in favour of this is to be found in the fact that we have difficulty in communicating with a psychotic even though he speaks the same language and has an intense psychological life in his 'closed' mind.[2] Volitional intuition would occur in acts of creativity, choice, or decision, when the 'tension' experienced by consciousness as it meets an object (or obstacle) is transmuted into an effort to go beyond or destroy the obstacle.

Thus collective intuitions—affectual, intellectual, and volitional —go beyond symbolic communication in enabling fuller participation in that which is apprehended. Gurvitch defines symbols as: 'Signs which express only partially the contents they signify and are the mediators between the contents and the agents, collective and individual, who state them and to whom they are directed; this mediation consists in a drive toward the mutual participation of the agents in the contents and of those contents in the agents.[3] However, symbols are ambiguous in that they also veil that which they seek to disclose, and so hinder participation in it. Gurvitch believed that the depth levels below the symbolic—such as spontaneous, innovating and creative collective behaviour, collective ideas and values, and collective consciousness—have a tendency to transcend the symbolic sphere and to be closer to collective intuition and hence full participation. Durkheim, and in a different way G. H. Mead, tended to equate all relations between Ego and Alter (both individual and collective) with symbolic communication. In fact, according to Gurvitch, this is unduly restricting, as it limits the focus to interpersonal relations, to relations with the Other, and ignores the character of the 'We' which is ontologically prior to every relation with the Other.[4]

[1] Max Scheler, *The Nature of Sympathy*, trans. Peter Heath (New Haven, 1954), pp. 12–13.
[2] Cf. John Vincent Martin, 'Depth Sociology and Microsociology: A Critical Analysis of the Basic Concepts of Georges Gurvitch', unpub. Ph.D. thesis, Harvard University, 1957, pp. 127–8.
[3] *La vocation actuelle de la sociologie* p. 77.
[4] He maintained that this over-emphasis on interpersonal relations appeared

In explaining the solution offered by his own microsociology to this problem (which is also his solution to Durkheim's problem of the relation between individual consciousness and collective consciousness), Gurvitch poses the question in terms of a dialectical process by which a 'reciprocity of perspectives' is arrived at between three 'poles' within the total psychic phenomenon—the 'I' (individual), the Other (interpersonal), and the 'We' (collective).

The *I*, and *Other*, and the *We* are but three opposing poles, inseparable from all conscious psychic life. The *I*'s communicate with the *Others* principally through the medium of signs and symbols of which the only possible basis is the *We*, which gives them effective validity. To wish to separate the I, the Others and the We is to desire to dissolve or to destroy consciousness itself; indeed consciousness cannot but consist in precisely the tensions between these three terms and in their various combinations. As a matter of fact, there does not exist in the flow of psychic life, when effectively experimented with, either individual consciousness, consciousness of the Other, or collective consciousness. What does effectively exist are accentuations of I which can be constructed as a direction towards individual consciousness. There exists an accentuation of the communication between I and the Others which can be constructed as an intermental process, and there exists an accentuation of the We, which can be constructed as a direction towards collective consciousness or collective mentality. These three poles have a sense only as long as they are indissolubly linked. The I and the Others are inherent in the We and the We are inherent in the I and the Others. Obviously they must be confronted on the same level of depth. . . . The situation can also be expressed as follows: *Consciousness is a dialectical relationship between I, Other and We, which partially interpenetrate each other and partially converge through opposition.*[1]

This discussion of the relations between individual and collective consciousnesses is the key to understanding both the deeper levels of Gurvitch's depth sociology and also the first type of social framework, the forms of sociality, which constitutes the subject matter of his microsociology. The 'relation with Others' involves mutual awareness, and is a form of social bond; as an abstract type it is concerned with degrees of opposition, ranging from at most repulsion, to at its least rapprochement. In the case of the 'We' as

also in sociometry, which had not 'effectively overcome the exclusively intermental point of view of interpersonal relations' (Gurvitch, 'Microsociology and Sociometry', *Sociometry*, XII (Feb.–Aug. 1949), 1–31).
[1] 'Microsociology and Sociometry', op. cit., p. 13.

a type of social bond, we are concerned with the degree of mutual participation of different individual consciousnesses in the same mental acts or mental states. The 'We' can take different forms depending on the degree of fusion; Gurvitch differentiates three basic types:

Partial fusion among minds opening to each other, and among behaviours interpenetrated in a 'we', may appear in different degrees of intensity and depth. When the fusion is very weak and only integrates superficial layers of consciousness which open only at the surface and remain closed with regard to what is more or less profound and personal, sociality is *mass*. When minds fuse, open out, and interpenetrate on a deeper, more intimate plane, where an essential part of the aspirations and acts of personality is integrated in the 'we', without, however, attaining the maximum of intensity in this integration, sociality is *community*. When, finally, this most intense degree of union of 'we' is attained, that is, when the minds open out as widely as possible and the least accessible depths of the 'I' are integrated in this fusion (which presupposes states of collective ecstacy), sociality is *communion*.[1]

Gurvitch also discusses the degree of fusion represented by mass, community and communion, in relation to pressure, volume, and attraction. With regard to pressure he notes that, 'The intensity of fusion in the "we" and the pressure felt by its members, far from going together as some would think, are in inverse ratio of proportionality.'[2] Thus in the mass, the individual's personality, his deeper self, is not greatly involved, and so the 'I' experiences social life as exerting pressure on individual spontaneity. In contrast, where the personality is deeply engaged, as in a communion, and

---

[1] Gurvitch, 'Mass, Community, Communion', *Journal of Philosophy*, XXXVIII (Aug. 1941), 485–96, at p. 489. We might note at this point a parallel in Alfred Schutz's phenomenological analyses of the social world where he gives examples of different degrees of fusion and interpenetration in a 'We': 'Both sexual intercourse and a casual conversation are instances of the We-relation in which the partners are face-to-face. Yet what a difference in the degree of directness which characterises the experiences in these relations! Very different depth-levels of the conscious life of the partners are involved. Intensity and degree of intimacy vary radically. But not only *my* experiences *in* these relations differ in all the aforementioned aspects. We may say that differences in the "degree of directness" are characteristic of the We-relation proper' (Alfred Schutz, *Collected Papers*, 3 vols. (The Hague, Martinus Nijhoff, 1962), II, 28).

[2] *La vocation actuelle de la sociologie*, p. 125.

individual and collective consciousnesses are deeply interpenetrated, with complete mutual participation, then social life is not experienced as external pressure. In the community, there is a tendency towards equilibrium between the 'I' and the 'We', and a balance is sought between pressure and attraction. Attraction, therefore occurs when the personality is deeply engaged in the 'We' and when there is a high degree of participation; here we find attraction and intensity of fusion in the 'We' are in a direct ratio of proportionality. In the case of volume or size, there is once again an inverse ratio of proportionality with intensity of fusion; the greater the number of members, the less intense will be their union, provided no other factors intervene.

This account of the degrees of fusion of mass, community, and communion, has clear significance for the sociology of knowledge. Because a community tends to attain a better balance as a form of sociality, it favours regular collective behaviour and the functioning of models, signs and symbols, which are relatively more refined and well-grounded than in masses, and more varied than in communions. Communions depend on collective intuitions, and masses manifest crude symbolic images; communities are wider in their field of vision, and actualize a variety of mental states and mental acts, particularly those based on reflection, such as conceptualizations and judgements. Masses and communions are less stable and more short-lived than communities, and they appear sporadically; for example, large groups frequently display the mass form of sociality, especially when they lack contiguity (as is usually the case with social classes and publics), whilst religious sects, at least in their originating, evidence the sociality of communion. In periods of war and revolution, however, global societies can proliferate communions and masses rather than communities.

One further distinction in Gurvitch's microsociology has significance for his sociology of knowledge: it is that between passive sociality and active sociality. This cuts across the two basic forms of sociality—partial fusion in a 'We' and partial opposition between 'I' and the Other. He explains the difference as follows:

Sociality is relatively passive when the affective coloration appropriate to the mentality and attitude it implies, predominates over volitions and actions which could arise in it. Sociality is relatively active when the volitional coloration appropriate to the mentality and attitude it implies, predominates over affectivity and intellection which accompany it. The active character of a form of sociality manifests itself especially in the affirmation of a common task to be accomplished, which is more clearly evident when it concerns a 'We' than when it concerns relations with an Other.[1]

It follows that masses, communities, and communions can be either active or passive. The distinction is similar to that which he makes between 'mental states' (memory, representations, affectivity, etc.) and 'mental acts' (judgement, intuitions, etc.). In this way Gurvitch relates the forms of sociality to intentionality by following Bergson in differentiating various degrees of tension of consciousness. According to Bergson, conscious life manifests an indefinite number of different planes, ranging from the plane of action to the plane of dream, and each of these planes is characterized by a specific tension of consciousness—the plane of action showing the highest, and that of dream the lowest degree of tension.[2]

This theory of microsociological processes can be related to the macrosociology of knowledge, despite Gurvitch's caution and pessimism about the possibilities for generalization in sociology, in that it does provide the elements for an explanation of the dynamics of the filter process by which different groups develop a reciprocity of perspectives among their members. It could explain some of the deeper aspects of group consciousness, those by which the attention and focus of individual minds are made to coincide, not only at the level of symbolic communication (so well explained by Mead), but also at the deeper and ontologically prior levels that must provide the foundation for any epistemic community.

It is in dealing with these questions that Gurvitch's early exposure to phenomenological philosophy causes him to adopt a position so similar to that of Schutz (although Gurvitch was in some ways the better sociologist, especially when it came to developing appropriate classificatory typologies, such as, in this

[1] *La vocation actuelle de la sociologie*, p. 159.
[2] Cf. for a discussion and application of Bergson's distinctions, Schutz, op. cit., I, 212 f. Schutz suggests that tension of consciousness is highest in the wide-awake, working self (concerned with action in the outer world based upon a project and characterized by the intention of bringing about the projected state of affairs by bodily movements), which is most attentive to life and its requirements. It is the degree of tension of consciousness that determines the form and content of our stream of thought, especially the space and time dimensions in which the working self experiences its own acts.

case, that of mass, community, and communion). Gurvitch's criticisms of Mead in this book are similar to those made by Schutz in his essay 'Making Music Together: A Study in Social Relationship'. Schutz discusses Mead as one of those who tended to identify meaning with its semantic expression, and to consider language, speech, symbols, significant gestures, as the fundamental condition of 'social intercourse as such'.[1] Mead's explanations only appeared to remove difficulties connected with the basic issue of whether the communicative process is really the foundation of all possible relationships, or whether it might not presuppose the existence of some kind of social interaction which is essential to all communication, but which does not enter into the communication process itself. Schutz describes this as the 'mutual tuning-in relationship'. It is upon this alone that all communication is founded and, 'It is precisely this mutual tuning-in relationship by which the "I" and the "Thou" are experienced by both participants as a "We" in vivid presence'.[2] Gurvitch's contribution is to show how the character of this tuning-in relationship can vary from one social framework (or epistemic community) to another, especially with regard to two of the types of knowledge he examines—perceptual knowledge of the external world (particularly in the perception of space and time), and knowledge of the Other and the We, and variations in the forms of knowledge emphasized.

Let us examine his discussion of perceptual knowledge of the external world as it concerns space and time dimensions. Gurvitch's typology of different times can be compared with the distinction made by Bergson between the spatialized, objective or cosmic time, and the inner time or *durée* (duration). Bergson did not sufficiently develop a theory of the multiplicity of times, however,

---

[1] This difference between Schutz and Mead is not brought out in one of the most successful recent works on the sociology of knowledge, which otherwise draws heavily on their theories—that of Peter L. Berger and Thomas Luckmann, *The Social Construction of Reality* (New York, Doubleday, 1966). See, however, the critical discussion of Mead's theory by Maurice Natanson, especially with regard to Mead's failure to clarify the nature of the 'social' and 'social' relationship. Natanson comments, 'A first step toward such clarification would involve a study of the fundamental "being-with" relationship. To "be-with" others is to be part of a complex set of relationships which includes space and time elements among others. To "be-with" another is to share certain typical assumptions, certain relevances, certain typical expectations concerning behaviour' (Natanson, *The Social Dynamics of George H. Mead* (Washington, Public Affairs Press, 1956), p. 65).

[2] Schutz, op. cit., I, 161.

Introductory Essay xxix

according to Gurvitch. Duration, which Bergson linked to tensions of consciousness, is the inner time in which present
experiences are connected with the past by recollections and re-
tensions, and with the future by anticipations and protensions. In
Gurvitch's view, one of the reasons why Bergson failed to develop
a theory of the multiplicity of times was that he did not study the
possible variations in emphasis on past, present, or future; nor did
he sufficiently develop his own observation that 'one can easily
imagine different rhythms, which are slower or more rapid,
measuring the degree of tension or of relaxation of the consciousness. . . .'[1] Gurvitch says that the characteristics of time must be
understood dialectically with regard to continuity and discontinuity; past, present and future; quantitative and qualitative;
homogeneity and heterogeneity; stability and change. He discusses eight types of social time[2] and relates these to the different
depth levels and social frameworks. On the basis of this analysis he
is then able to posit certain likely functional correlations between,
for example, forms of sociality, depth levels and particular social
times.

To give just one example: whilst masses favour the depth level
of attitudes (often unconscious), and communities favour rules,
patterns and symbols, communions emphasize the level of collective
ideas and values (sometimes combined with symbols), and time at
this depth level often entails an intense struggle between advance
and delay. Communions tend to oscillate between time in advance of
itself (sometimes going to the point of becoming an explosive time
of creativity) and cyclical time; active communions (such as
revolutionary groups) are more likely to live in the former time,
and passive communions (such as mystical groups) are dominated
by a cyclical time, like that of ceremonies and periods of feasts or
fasts.

[1] Henri Bergson, *Matière et mémoire* (Paris, 1896 and 1910), p. 231; quoted
in Gurvitch, *The Spectrum of Social Time*, p. 21.
[2] The eight types of time are: (1) enduring time, of slowed down long duration; (2) deceptive time, giving an appearance of long and slowed down duration
and yet subject to discontinuity due to sudden crises; (3) erratic time, of
irregular pulsation between the appearance and disappearance of rhythms;
(4) cyclical time; (5) retarded time, where anticipated occurrences are always
overdue; (6) alternating time; (7) time in advance of itself, always pushing
forward to the future; (8) explosive time, where past and present dissolve in the
creation of the immediately transcended future. (Cf. *The Spectrum of Social
Time*, pp. 31–3.)

In the case of perception of space, Gurvitch notes that it differs from time in its variability in one important respect—whilst both are subject to diverse conceptualizations, time varies from one sphere of reality to another, even independently of consciousness; whereas the space in which the external world exists in reality can only be a single space, even though there are diverse perceptions, symbolizations, and conceptualizations of it. However, perceptions of space vary according to two basic criteria: (a) its relationship to the subject (both the individual person and the collectivity), which can cause space to be perceived in a way that is autistic, egocentric, projective, or prospective;[1] (b) characteristics attributed to the form of space, which can cause space to be viewed as diffuse, concentric, or expanding and contracting.

Using the example of communions again, we find that Gurvitch characterizes their perception of space as essentially autistic, egocentric and concentric; in other words they tend to identify the world with their own membership, and their shared rites, models, signs and symbols. Because of this inherent tendency towards imbalance of the centripetal forces over the centrifugal (in contrast to the more even balance in communities), communions are less favourable centres of knowledge than communities, or even masses. As a form of sociality, therefore, communion is a kind of collective solipsism as far as knowledge is concerned in the long term. This is borne out in the case of knowledge of the Other and

---

[1] Gurvitch was influenced by Piaget's classification of the perceptions of space corresponding to the stages of child development. In his book *La représentation de l'espace chez l'enfant* (Paris, 1948), Piaget distinguished between: (a) autistic space, which is identified with the subject; (b) egocentric space, limited to the immediate environment of the subject; (c) projective space, which broadens considerably and permits of a differentiation of components, but in which emotivity continues to predominate; (d) the gradual passage from projective space to euclidian space, i.e. quantified space.

Gurvitch changed the last type to *prospective* space, because in Piaget's formulation euclidian space inevitably entailed conceptualization and quantification, whereas he did not wish to so limit it. Prospective space allowed for direct apprehension, without conceptualization, and also, it could be projected in different directions and so relates more closely to real space.

Whereas Piaget used the French word *espace*, Gurvitch preferred the term *étendue* because it did not carry the same connotation of quantified space. In English the problem does not arise, although some translators seek to stress the distinction by rendering *étendue* as 'extensity'. Cf. for the discussion of Piaget's distinctions and his own, Gurvitch's article 'Les variations des perceptions collective des étendues', *Cahiers Internationaux de Sociologie*, XXXVII (1964), 79–107.

the We: knowledge of the We is egoistic and knowledge of the Other is at a minimum (once again in contrast to communities). In a sense it might seem inappropriate to select the communion form of sociality as an example of the connections Gurvitch makes between microsociology, the depth levels, and some of the types of knowledge. He himself devotes much more space to discussing communities, because they represent a form of sociality more conducive to most types of knowledge than either masses or communions; they tend to appear more frequently than masses and communions within groups, classes and global societies; and they are more stable and so favour the regular functioning of models, signs and symbols. All of which creates a 'halo of rationality' around communities. However, the dynamic aspect of Gurvitch's sociology of knowledge (as with his whole theory) is only preserved by the constant emphasis on the fluid, precarious equilibria in each totality, and the incessant processes of structuration, destructuration and restructuration. He insists that communities, like all forms of sociality, remain spontaneous and fluctuating, despite their tendency to maintain a balance. This is why communities themselves are not identical with groups; they only induce the structuration of groups to the extent that they predominate over mass and communion.

MACROSOCIOLOGY

Despite the originality and great potentiality of Gurvitch's microsociology of knowledge, he was anxious that its importance should not be over-emphasized relative to that of the macrosociology of knowledge. Microsociology has an important part to play in providing operational frameworks for the study of the dialectical processes by which macrosocial collective units are structured by maintaining a precarious equilibrium between multiple hierarchies of depth levels, forms of sociality, social regulations, and the types and forms of knowledge. However, he considered that the microsociology of knowledge would only attain significance if it facilitated the study of relationships between systems of knowledge and macrosocial frameworks.[1]

[1] He was somewhat sensitive to the charge that he gave priority to microsociology—perhaps because he had made his way into sociology from philosophy and felt that his interest in the reciprocal immanence of individual and collective

He accepted the usual assumption of the sociology of knowledge that its most fruitful task lies in exploring the correlations between cognitive systems and particular types of macrosocial frameworks—especially social classes and global societies. It is clear that for much of the time and in most circumstances the cognitive system of the global society will tend to predominate over the cognitive characteristics of forms of sociality or groups. However, there are circumstances in which this predominance declines or breaks down, as for example in periods of crisis or upheaval, when the forms of sociality and particular groups can exercise great influence on the encompassing social frameworks. Such extreme cases only serve to highlight the constant dialectic between the partial and global social structures, and in the structuration process itself, based as it is on a precarious equilibrium between the various hierarchies.

Gurvitch places great emphasis on the role that knowledge and various cultural works play in cementing or binding the structures so that they do attain some stability. But he rejects all sociological theories that invest culture (particularly the types and forms of knowledge) with a greater independence and primacy than it in fact possesses in the complex web of social reality. He designates such theories as 'abstract culturalism' (a disguised form of idealist philosophy), because they neglect so many other aspects of social reality in their over-emphasis on the given-ness of a 'system' or 'form' of culture. He complained that the only role left for real groups and societies in such theories was to perform according to a score that had been orchestrated in advance, and the score was the 'system' or 'form' of culture.[1]

consciousnesses caused him to be regarded with suspicion by sociologists. He ruefully commented that in one of his first works on sociology he had set out the distinction between microsociology and macrosociology, but, 'Unfortunately, I had been imprudent in developing in detail only the microsociological typology (specifically: Mass, Community, Communion), without studying as fully the typology of groups and the typology of global societies. This caused me to be wrongly identified with the idea that I was giving priority to microsociology, while, in truth, I was inclined to give the priority to types of global societies, while continuing to stress the dialectics of the three scales'. 'Mon itinéraire intellectuelle', p. vii.

[1] Gurvitch (ed.), *Traité de Sociologie*, 2 vols. (Paris, Presses Universitaires de France, 1957 and 1960), I, 7.

It is only within this context that one can fully appreciate the reasons for Gurvitch's severe criticisms of Lévi-Strauss's structuralist theories of culture. The section of this book devoted to the cognitive systems of archaic societies was written mainly to counter Lévi-Strauss's tendency to minimize the differences between knowledge in archaic societies and that of modern societies.

The main danger of 'abstract culturalism' is that it tends to blur the distinctions between culture, structure, and social reality (the total social phenomenon). The difference between Gurvitch's theory and that of 'abstract culturalism' can be illustrated by two analogies (or, more technically, the typical referents of their 'as if' statements): the 'abstract culturalist' is likely to compare his structuralism to structural linguistics, and to speak of the 'grammar' of culture; Gurvitch, in contrast, constantly evokes the picture of structure as a 'balancing act' or precarious equilibrium. For Gurvitch there is a constant dialectic not only between structure and all those social phenomena extraneous to it (the subjacent total social phenomena), but also between the forces of destructuration and restructuration inherent in the components of structure. Thus his types of global social structures are classified according to the particular precarious equilibria that they establish with regard to: (1) the heirarchy of groups; (2) the combination of forms of sociality; (3) the tendency to accentuate certain depth levels; (4) the stratification of modes of division of labour and accumulation of goods; (5) the heirarchy of social regulations or social controls; (6) the cultural works; (7) the scale of social times; (8) the ranking of various social determinants.

Disjunctions can occur within a global social structure and between that structure and elements in the subjacent total social phenomenon. His purpose in the sections of this book dealing with particular groups, social classes, and global societies, is to suggest the functional correlations that might exist between the types and forms of knowledge and other components of structure. On a more

According to Gurvitch, Lévi-Strauss's claim that there exists a universal logical structure at the base of every society is nothing but a return to the position of Kant and the belief in a 'transcendental consciousness'. In particular, Gurvitch defends Lévy-Bruhl's distinction between modern and archaic conceptions of the relation of symbol to reality: for modern man a symbol is merely an external sign characterizing the reality, but distinct from it; for the primitive mind no such separation exists. In the latter case, according to Lévy-Bruhl's 'law of participation', the symbol becomes united to the reality and is completely at one with it. (Cf. Gurvitch, 'The Sociological Legacy of Lucien Lévy-Bruhl', *Journal of Social Philosophy*, 5 (1939), 61–70, at p. 70.)

Lévi-Strauss dismissed Levy-Bruhl's theory as unfounded in his book *The Savage Mind* (London, 1966), p. 268. He replied to Gurvitch's criticisms of his own views in an extensive Postscript to chapter xv of his collection of essays entitled *Structural Anthropology* (New York, Basic Books), 1963.

Gurvitch's original criticisms of Lévi-Strauss appeared in 'Le concept de structure sociale', *Cahiers Internationaux de Sociologie*, XIX (1955), 3–44.

general level, he seeks to analyse the nature of the dialectical process by which equilibrium is maintained with regard to different hierarchies in the components of each structure. Having suggested functional correlations, tendencies towards regularity, and the way in which the parts are integrated into the social whole, he is able to focus on possible disjunctions within structures, and between structures and the subjacent total social phenomena, where these disjunctions concern knowledge. One example of such a disjunction within a global social structure is that where two cognitive systems enter into conflict, such as happens when a social class attains an equilibrium among the forms of sociality that favours the as-cendance of the community form, and so lays the foundation for the development of a cognitive system that can rival that of the global structure.[1]

For an example of a disjunction between the structure and the total social phenomenon the reader is referred to the chapter in this book dealing with charismatic theocracies and their cognitive systems (e.g. Ancient Egypt and Imperial China), where the established structure is shown to have been ill-adjusted to other powerful elements in the total social phenomenon, such as tenden-cies towards economic rationalism, and the presence of large masses of non-integrated conquered peoples and slaves. Where such disjunctions can be discovered (and in the sociology of knowledge we are mainly interested in disjunctions between cognitive systems and social frameworks) there is then a pos-sibility of establishing a causal relationship—although it can never be more than a singular causality, limited to that unique total social phenomenon.

One of the most fruitful parts of Gurvitch's sociology of know-

[1] His objection to Marxist interpretations of social class was that they minimized the complexity of classes as sources of knowledge, by considering only their political knowledge, and also by not viewing them as macrocosms of groups and in relation to the forms of sociality. In this respect Gurvitch's sociology of knowledge is more thoroughly dialectical than that of many Marxists. It provides a conceptual framework that brings together consideration of the connections between individual and group consciousnesses (including class consciousness), and the dynamics of structuration (including class struc-ture); as such it has much to offer in the systematic analysis of the relationship between substructure (*Unterbau*) and superstructure (*Ueberbau*), which Marx hoped to promote. Cf. for Gurvitch's analyses of social class: 'Groupement sociale et classe sociale', *Cahiers Internationaux de Sociologie*, VII (1949), 2–42; and 'Avant-propos: les classes sociales dans le monde d'aujord'hui', *Cahiers Internationaux de Sociologie*, XXXVIII (1965), 3–11.

ledge for empirical research is that which deals with the cognitive systems of social classes and particular social groups. Social classes we have seen are especially important because they are social macrocosms incorporating other groups; they are partial social worlds which are aspiring to become total social worlds, and so they represent frameworks of knowledge that rival that of the global social structure. Particular groups and their cognitive systems are also important 'middle-range' areas for empirical research in the sociology of knowledge. They too have to be viewed in terms of their dialectical relationships of reciprocity of perspectives, polarization, ambiguity, mutual implication, and complementarity, both with regard to the microsocial forms of sociality, and with the cognitive systems of the encompassing social classes and global society.[1]

The research project described at the end of this book provides an example of the kind of empirical investigation that might be carried out on the basis of Gurvitch's theoretical framework. It addresses itself to the different forms that knowledge might take with regard to perception of the Other by particular groups. It distinguishes between two modes of perception: an intuitive, direct apprehension of the Other, and a reflective knowledge based on the elaboration of systematic images of the Other and the exercise of judgement based on the group's shared criteria. The two modes of perception can be viewed as being engaged in a dialectical process,

---

[1] Gurvitch believed that one of the errors of most dialectical theories was that they tended to reduce all dialectical operational procedures to simple *polarization* (or antinomy), or else in the case of modern science to *complementarity*. In order to grasp the dynamic processes involved in the construction of social reality, five different operational procedures of dialectic should be used: (a) the dialectic of complementarity discloses that two terms or elements that seem to be mutually exclusive could not exist or be understood without each other— they dialectically complement each other; (b) the dialectic of mutual involvement consists of those terms or elements that at first sight appear to be opposite or heterogeneous, but in fact overlap or partially interpenetrate or are immanent to each other; (c) the dialectic of ambiguity (or ambivalence) denotes such relationships as those where there is both attraction and repulsion, agreement and disagreement, love and fear, existing at the same time; (d) the dialectic of polarization is the classic dialectic of thesis, antithesis and synthesis; (e) the dialectic of reciprocity refers to tensions which result in neither identification nor separation of forces, but in a mutual immanence which produces parellelism or symmetry in their separate manifestations. Cf. Gurvitch, *Dialectique et sociologie* (Paris, Flammarion, 1962); also the critical discussion in Pitrim A. Sorokin, *Sociological Theories of Today* (New York, Harper & Row, 1966), pp. 464–96.

like that which exists in the movement between the three poles of the 'I', the Other, and the 'We', and in the interpenetration of groups, social classes, and global societies. Social classes and global societies are seen as limiting factors on the emergence of images of the Other autonomous to the particular group, just as groups to varying degrees inhibit spontaneous and direct apprehension of the Other in individual consciousness. The report presented here provides only part of the analysis that was carried out on the data collected, but it is enough to establish the central hypothesis that positive correlations exist between forms of knowledge and their social frameworks, and that the degree of interpenetration of different social frameworks varies significantly.

It was suggested earlier in this introduction that perhaps, Gurvitch's unique contribution to the sociology of knowledge might be found in his microsociology, which could supply some of the missing elements for a social psychology of knowledge. However, the microsociology can only attain its full significance when it is combined with his macrosociology in the development of a systematic sociology of knowledge. His theoretical insights into the dialectical relations between the individual and collective consciousnesses, and his radically dialectical theory of social structure, offer a much-needed framework for such systematization.

Preface

This book, despite some necessary changes, elaborations, and developments, essentially reproduces the course of public lectures which I gave at the Sorbonne during the academic year 1964–5. This work is the result however, not only of a whole series of lectures, but also of thought and effort begun as long ago as 1944, and made more difficult by misgivings about the feasibility of encompassing a subject as vast as the 'sociology of knowledge' in a single volume, or even in several volumes by a single author.

Indeed I gradually realized that the number of problems which a 'sociology of knowledge' or even, more modestly, an 'introduction to the sociology of knowledge' must address, required the efforts of a whole team of researchers specialized in the various branches of this new sociological discipline.

Laborious, intellectual experiment led me to the conclusion that it was wiser to concentrate my efforts on only one branch of the 'sociology of knowledge', but one which seemed essential because I saw it as the foundation of all others, or, to put it another way, as the necessary starting-point for all specialization and research in this field.

The key problem involves the *social frameworks of types and forms of knowledge* and the *hierarchies* of various manifestations of knowledge, when pre-eminent macrosocial units such as states, churches, social classes and global societies are concerned: in other words, the problem is concerned with *cognitive systems*.

With regard to my previous work, my position has changed on only one point, but one which seems fundamental. Whereas in my earlier writings I may have dwelt on the impossibility of going beyond the study of functional correlations between the social frameworks and knowledge, I have finally arrived at the conclusion that relationships of causality, be they unilateral or reciprocal,[1]

---

[1] In both cases it is, of course, a question of a 'singular causality', and not 'causal laws'; cf. on this subject my *Déterminismes sociaux et liberté humaine* (2nd edn., 1963), pp. 63–75.

should be considered both in cases of rupture or of very strong tension between superstructures and the total underlying phenomena.

I am the first to realize that this book risks appearing too abstract and too schematic, particularly to the uninitiated. Obviously more abundant material could have been used. But if this work is limited to using certain choice examples, it is because it aims, not to be complete, but to indicate new directions for research, that have so often been neglected or unappreciated by its predecessors. In other words, it aims *to formulate an original plan of research, rather than to present definitive results.*

In this respect I have often felt that I was entering virgin territory, in spite of the existence of a fairly copious literature, and predecessors of merit.

As in all my earlier sociological works I have attempted to bring out the great multiplicity and infinite variability of the social frameworks as well as the corresponding manifestations of knowledge. Here again my efforts are inspired by the firm belief that 'relativist empiricism' is the necessary conceptual tool for a truly scientific sociology of knowledge, i.e. for a sociology of knowledge free from prejudices and preconceptions.

My hopes would be more than fulfilled if the orientations which I should like to give to this new sociological discipline were to find an extension in the work of younger colleagues, even if they arrive at different conclusions from my own.

G.G.

Introduction

CHAPTER ONE

The Problem

Of all cultural works, knowledge would seem to be the most detached from social reality. Does it not seem to lay claim to universal validity and to be founded on sound judgements, which are usually considered to be the prerogative of individual consciousness? Undeniably religion, moral life, education, art,[1] and especially law, maintain more directly observable and, at least in theory, more intense and intimate relationships with the social frameworks.

In addition, according to a long tradition coming from classical antiquity, to speak of knowledge is to mean first and foremost, if not exclusively, philosophy and science, and so it is not surprising that the very term 'sociology of knowledge' has provoked concern among lay-people as well as scientists and philosophers. They wonder, with a certain amount of irritation, whether the placing of knowledge in a sociological perspective might not be a new form of *scepticism* and *nihilism* which would invalidate all knowledge. This confusion is increased still more by the fact that, from Bacon to Pareto, social correlates of knowledge have been interpreted as *idolae fori*, 'derivations', or emotive residues, which

---

[1] However, I would maintain that certain types of art, such as 'belles lettres', and particularly the novel and poetry, and the theatre on the other hand, are more influenced by variations of knowledge than all other aesthetic manifestations. (Does not social life itself sometimes take on a theatrical character not only under the guise of official or unofficial parades, but also in spontaneous social totalities, especially certain unorganized groups such as household families, for example? Cf. on this subject my article, 'Sociologie du théâtre', in *Lettres Nouvelles*, no. 35 (1956), pp. 203 ff.) This is why the 'sociology of the theatre', brilliantly studied in two remarkable books by Jean Duvignaud (*L'acteur. Esquisse d'une sociologie du comédien* (Gallimard, 1965), and *Sociologie du théâtre. Essai sur les ombres collectives* (Presses Universitaires de France, 1965)), along with many essays by various authors on the 'sociology of literature', depends as much on 'sociology of knowledge' as on 'sociology of art'. They can therefore serve as intermediaries between these latter two branches of sociology. Cf. on this subject, Georges Lukačs, *Le Roman Historique* (French translation, Payot, 1965), and Lucien Goldmann, *Pour une sociologie du roman* (Gallimard, 1964), as well as his article 'Matérialisme dialectique et histoire de la littérature', in *Revue de Métaphysique et de Morale*, no. 3 (1950), pp. 283–301.

3

dominate society and obscure knowledge. This misunderstanding has not entirely been dispelled either by Comte or Marx. Both had a high opinion of the sociology of knowledge, Comte in identifying all sociology with it, and Marx by linking it with the problem of ideology and alienation.[1] Both, however (returning each in his own way to Condorcet's ideal), dreamed of freeing knowledge from its roots in the social frameworks, so that in the final phase these social frameworks might be governed by knowledge. More recently, Karl Mannheim, with his *freischwebende Intelligenz*—the socially unattached intelligentsia—succumbed to the same temptation and, without even waiting for the advent of the classless and disalienated society, naively fixed his hopes on the intellectuals and 'universal education'.[2]

Emile Durkheim,[3] basing his approach on Saint-Simon (who first saw the mutual involvement of modes of knowledge and social frameworks),[4] and on Condorcet and Comte, but going beyond the prejudices of both of these, was the first to discard

[1] Cf. my 'Sociologie de Karl Marx', in *La vocation actuelle de la sociologie* (1963 edn.), vol. II, ch. xii, pp. 247, 253 ff., 260–5, 285–8. Cf. similarly my brief critical summary in *Traité de Sociologie*, vol. II (1964), ch. ii, pp. 109–12.

[2] Among the numerous works of K. Mannheim, see especially *Ideologie und Utopie* (Bonn, Cohen, 1929), the English translation of which, *Ideology and Utopia, An Introduction to the Sociology of Knowledge* (London and New York, 1936), has been particularly successful (the text of this translation has moreover been considerably extended by the author), and *Essays on the Sociology of Knowledge* (posthumous), edited by Paul Kecskemeti (London, Routledge & Kegan Paul, 1952). Beginning with Marx, Mannheim combined several fairly heterogeneous influences in his development, such as those of Scheler, Max Weber, John Dewey, and also Georges Lukačs to some extent. It is probably this modernist eclecticism which, in spite of its patent confusion, has made his thought so appealing, particularly in Great Britain and even more so in the United States. Cf. my critical summary of the 'Sociologie de la connaissance de Mannheim', in *Traité de Sociologie*, vol. II, ch. ii, pp. 115–19.

[3] Cf. my address to commemorate the centenary of Emile Durkheim's birth, reproduced in the *Annales de l'Université de Paris*, no. 1 (1960), pp. 36–8; and my summary, 'Le problème de la conscience collective chez Durkheim', in *La vocation actuelle de la sociologie*, II (1963), 46–53, and my brief account in the *Traité de Sociologie*, vol. II, ch. ii, pp. 105–7.

[4] Cf. C.-H. de Saint-Simon, *La physiologie sociale, Œuvres choisies*, Introduction and Notes by G. Gurvitch (Presses Universitaires de France, 1965), pp. 5–6, 14–16, 47–51, 68, 82. We should note particularly Saint-Simon's affirmation that 'the production of ideas occurs within the structure of every society', which is a reference to the variations of systems of knowledge according to the types of society, or, as he puts it, according to the different 'régimes'. This conception is already clearly expressed in *l'Introduction aux Travaux scientifiques du XIXe siècle*, vols. I and II (1808–9), and in *Le travail sur la gravitation universelle* (1813).

the belief that placing knowledge in a sociological perspective would compromise its validity. He maintained that to relate knowledge to social frameworks *was not to debase it or diminish its value.* But Durkheim had to pay for this progress by tending to see the incarnation of reason in the collective consciousness, and by passing from the sociology of knowledge to an epistemology with a sociological foundation, which would reconcile empiricism and a Kantian *a priori-ism*.[1] In fact, he found in social reality only the philosophical preconceptions he had previously introduced.

Considerable progress was made by Lucien Lévy-Bruhl, who did not entertain the possibility of drawing philosophical conclusions from his work on primitive mentality. By contrasting the knowledge and experience of primitive peoples with that of civilized races, Lévy-Bruhl emphasized that consciousness of time and space, the category of causality, the concepts and experiences of the Self and the Other, of the external world and society, are different in the two cases.[2] In the process he discovered that in the same type of society several types of knowledge were apparent (knowledge of the external world, knowledge of the Me and the We, technical knowledge, mythologico-cosmogonic knowledge, etc.) with differing degrees of mysticism and rationality.[3] He was most at a loss when it came to distinguishing the plurality of systems of knowledge that would correspond to the different types of society. Their diversity does not permit reduction to the simple quality of the archaic and the civilized.[4]

[1] Cf. Durkheim in *Les formes élémentaires de la vie religieuse* (1912), Introduction, pp. 18–28 and Conclusion, pp. 617 ff., 635 ff. My commentaries are to be found in the *Traité de Sociologie*, vol. II, ch. ii, pp. 106–7, and in *La vocation actuelle de la sociologie*, II, 46–53 already quoted.

[2] Cf. particularly Lucien Lévy-Bruhl, *La mentalité primitive* (1922), 15th edn. (Presses Universitaires de France, 1960); *L'âme primitive* (1923), 3rd edn. (Alcan, 1927); discussion on the primitive mind in the *Bulletin de la Société française de Philosophie*, no. 29 (1929), meeting of 1 June, pp. 105–39 (with several participants, including F. Boas, L. Brunschvicg, M. Mauss, P. Rivet, E. Meyerson).

[3] Cf. L. Lévy-Bruhl, *Le surnaturel et la nature dans la mentalité primitive* (Alcan, 1931); *La mythologie primitive* (Alcan, 1935); *L'expérience mystique et les symboles chez les primitifs* (Alcan, 1938). Cf. also L. Lévy-Bruhl, *Morceaux choisis* (Gallimard, 1936).

[4] Cf. on the subject of the contribution of Lévy-Bruhl, my remarks in *Traité de Sociologie*, vol. II, ch. ii, pp. 107–9. The great and much-lamented ethnologist Maurice Leenhardt (whose conceptions were founded on empirical research carried out in Polynesia) was able to do justice to Lévy-Bruhl. Cf. his main work *Do Kamo* (Paris, Gallimard, 1947), and his article 'Les Carnets de Lucien

Max Scheler, a completely different kind of philosopher, was the first to discover and bring to light a *plurality of types of knowledge* in our contemporary society. The emphases and combinations of these types of knowledge vary according to the social frameworks. Scheler observed that the intensity of the connection with social frameworks was differentiated both as a function of the types of knowledge and of the frameworks themselves. But this move towards relativism in the sociology of knowledge was compromised by the philosophical preconceptions of Scheler, who went so far as to assert a stable hierarchy of types of knowledge, disposed according to the static scale of values which he attributed to them. Thus Scheler was driven to establish an *a priori* order of knowledge, an order crowned by theological knowledge, followed closely by philosophical knowledge. Third in the order would be knowledge of the Other (the specificity of which was strongly maintained by Scheler). Knowledge of the external world would occupy a lower position. The last two places would be occupied by technical knowledge and finally scientific knowledge. Variations in the positions and emphases of these different types of knowledge would concern only what he called 'the subjective *a priori*', or the symbols appropriate to each social framework, and not 'essences', which would remain static, as would the reality studied, and the unique scale of values.[1] The

Lévy-Bruhl', in *Cahiers Internationaux de Sociologie,* Cahier vi (1947), pp. 28–42, an article later developed in a preface of 21 pages in the same *Carnets* (Presses Universitaires de France, 1949). However, with great finesse, Leenhardt distinguishes between the 'mystical' and the 'mythical', regretting the fact that Lévy-Bruhl did not sufficiently distinguish between them. To take Leenhardt's thought to its conclusion, it must be said that the theogonic–cosmological myths of the archaic peoples can be mystical, but are not always so, and conversely, the mystical (be it in archaic society or in civilized society) does not necessarily imply the mythical. It seems undeniable that Lucien Lévy-Bruhl somewhat exaggerated the 'mysticism of the primitive mentality'. This does not in any way give the right to certain analysts, such as C. Lévi-Strauss, to dispute the important discoveries of a great master of French ethnology, or to reduce all archaic mythology to rationality, and rationality to 'universal reason'.

[1] Cf. the following works of Max Scheler: 'Problem einer Soziologie des Wissens', in *Versuche zu einer Soziologie des Wissens,* published under his direction (München Duncker und Humblot, 1924), pp. 15–146; *Die Wissensformen und die Gesellschaft* (Leipzig, 1926), one part of which is composed of the study entitled *Erkenntnis und Arbeit,* pp. 233–486, and the other is a 2nd edn. adaptation of the 1924 study, pp. 1–229. For greater convenience the reader is referred to volumes VI and VIII of Max Scheler's works: (VI, *Schriften zur Soziologie und Weltanschauungslehre;* VIII, *Die Wissenformen und die Gesellschaft*); cf. also *Philosophische Weltanschauung* (Bonn, F. Cohen),

Platonism and Augustinianism of Scheler limited his sociology of knowledge, the final goal of which was to help the 'intellectual élite' detach all aspects of knowledge from social frameworks, by re-establishing the essential order between types of knowledge, essences, and modes of reality.

In the case of Sorokin—the author of *Social and Cultural Dynamics* (New York, 1937–41, vols. I–IV), who devoted the second volume of his work to *Fluctuations in Systems of Truth*—spiritualistic philosophical preconceptions were much more clearly evident than in Scheler's work, despite the accumulation of empirical materials of an exceptional richness. He developed a cyclical conception of human knowledge, which passes through ideate, idealistic, and sensate epochs, consonant with the types of societies, the first of which he obviously preferred and hoped would return, though at the risk of contravening Auguste Comte's Law of Three Stages. In other respects he limited the sociology of knowledge to the single study of philosophical knowledge, of which science and technology seemed to him to be merely applications.

*

We consider it advisable, therefore, to look for one of the main reasons for the difficulties encountered previously in the sociology of knowledge in the philosophical preconceptions which have been introduced, whether consciously or not. For, in spite of the unquestionable interest that it continues to inspire, the sociology of knowledge has given rise to a certain disenchantment. It has even undergone a period of decline in the last 20 years.[1] It was with the intention of giving it a fresh start that at the 5th World Congress of Sociology (meeting under the auspices of UNESCO, at the beginning of September 1962, in Washington) a 'special committee for the development of the Sociology of Knowledge' was set up. It will be required to provide the first evidence of its

p. 158. To these books we must add the communication by the same author: 'Wissenschaft und Soziale Struktur', in *Verhandlungen des vierten deutschen Soziologentages, 1924, in Heidelberg* (Tübingen, J. C. B. Mohr, 1925), pp. 118–212. For a deeper analysis of Scheler's sociology of knowledge, see my critical summary in *Traité de Sociologie*, vol. II, ch. ii, pp. 112–14, and my more detailed account in *Les tendances actuelles de la philosophie allemande*, 2nd edn. (1949, Vrin), pp. 113–17 and 129–34.

[1] One of the most recent publications in this field, W. Stark's book, *The Sociology of Knowledge* (London, 1958), has practically nothing new to say.

effectiveness at the 6th World Congress (which will take place at Évian in early September 1966). In 1957, I myself organized a 'Laboratory for the Sociology of Knowledge' in France, with a view to stimulating research and empirical enquiry in this field. Some work has been effectively carried out and published,[1] whilst some is still in progress.

But, in recent decades, it is only the sociology of technical and scientific knowledge, along with the sociology of the diffusion and communication of acquired knowledge (by radio, television, cinema, and, more recently, by paperbacks), which have succeeded in attracting wider public attention and have stimulated numerous publications. As a sign of the times, this situation undoubtedly reflects certain tendencies in the cognitive systems corresponding to types of contemporary social structures, especially those of directed capitalism.

However, we believe neither that the above-mentioned tendencies are exclusive, nor that the framework of directed capitalism is immutable. It may in fact have the least chance of surviving much longer. . . .

Furthermore, the deeper causes of the present crisis in the sociology of knowledge seem to lie elsewhere: in too close a dependence, even servitude, of the sociology of knowledge on what is explicitly or implicitly a basically philosophical orientation. We have been compelled, in several publications, to point out just how many philosophical preconceptions—both unconscious and conscious—could be harmful to sociology. At the same time, it has been necessary to emphasize the fact that of all the human sciences (leaving aside the exact or natural sciences) sociology is the least separable from philosophy, as certain areas are common to both:[2] such as that of the totality, or rather

[1] Cf. 'Enquête sociologique sur la Connaissance d'Autrui', in *Cahiers Internationaux de Sociologie*, XXIX (1960), 137–56; 'Bibliographie de la sociologie de la connaissance', XXXII (1962), 135–70; 'Bibliographie de la sociologie de la vie morale', XXXVI (1964), 135–84; 'Enquête sur les attitudes morales des groupements', XXXVII, 149–59; cf. also the special number of the *Cahiers* devoted to 'La crise de l'explication en sociologie', vol. XXI (1956); Les cadres sociaux de la connaissance sociologique', vol. XXVI (1959), and finally 'Signification et fonction des mythes dans la vie et la connaissance politiques', vol. XXXIII (1962).

[2] Cf. *Dialectique et Sociologie* (1962), and in particular, pp. 221–39, as well as *Philosophie et Sociologie*, ch. xvii, 1963 edn., vol. II of *La vocation actuelle de la sociologie*, pp. 482–96. Cf. also my article 'Philosophie et Sociologie', in *L'Encyclopédie française* (director Gaston Berger), vol. XIX, 1951. It is interesting to note that during recent years one can notice a revival of interest in the problem

'totalization' which is manifest in the 'We', groups, classes, and in each of those who participates as a 'Me';[1] so also the field of 'action' which can, at a higher level, become an *act*[2] and, at its most developed, a *creative act*.

of the relationship between sociology and philosophy. As an example one might quote a special issue of the *Revue Internationale de Philosophie* (Brussels), (1950), no. 13; *Filosophia e Sociologia*, works of the Congrès philosophique de Bologne (1954); Maurice Merleau-Ponty, 'Philosophie et Sociologie', in *Cahiers Internationaux de Sociologie*, X (1951), 50–69, reproduced in his post-humous book *Les signes* (1964); and lastly the book of Edward A. Tiryakian, *Sociologism and Existentialism* (Boston, 1962). Is it perhaps the result of the recent philosophical movement in which certain orientations have converged and brought about a fruitful encounter between the different interpretations of the dialectic and effective pluralistic empiricism? These orientations are concerned with enlarged and multiple experience, realism, the multiplicity of operative frames of reference, and transcendence of the artificial alternative between 'existence and science', 'comprehension and explanation', etc. Let us hope so, but let us also remain on our guard, in order to avoid a return to a 'social philosophy' or any sort of philosophical preconception, whatever it may be. . . . Furthermore we must not forget that the most animated philosophical discussions during the last quarter of a century have rather been within the 'natural sciences' and, even more so, the 'exact sciences'—mathematics, physics, and biology. These were conflicts between 'idealists' and 'realists', determinists and indeterminists, continuists and discontinuists, 'mechanists' and 'vitalists'. This has in no way compromised the 'maturity of these sciences'. Why should it be otherwise for sociology, which deals more closely with 'the human condition'? In this regard, sociology emphasizes 'meanings' as well as the tendency for the 'act' to predominate over the 'product', and the total effort over partial, and differentiated, actions and activities.

[1] In fact, the problem of the 'total man', so differently interpreted by Marx (who projects it towards the future) and Mauss (who rather transfers it back towards the past, even the most distant past, i.e. to archaic societies), presents itself in reality for each 'Me', because each 'Me' inevitably participates in the most diverse social wholes. These provide their members with criteria for arriving at a relative and varied integration of the contrary or complementary tendencies of each human person.

[2] Cf. for the distinction between 'conduct', 'attitude', 'action' and 'act', so often confused (in which the American 'theorists' of the T. Parsons school and their French proselytes excel) my analysis in *La vocation actuelle de la sociologie*, I (3rd edn.), 76–115. In so far as it concerns knowledge, we must insist particularly on the opposition between 'mental states' and 'mental acts', collective and individual. In the cognitive sphere, acts are the 'experiences which are more or less immediate' (the borderline cases of which are intellectual intuitions by which one participates directly in reality) and judgements—both constituting the most intense manifestations of the 'open consciousness'—particularly when they lead to a mutual implication. 'Mental states', even intellectual ones, such as representations, memory and 'opinions', in contrast to 'mental acts', are manifestations of the 'barely open consciousness'. (These 'opinions' are still very tentative and uncertain, despite the exploitation in both politics and advertising of so-called 'soundings of public opinion', which is a vague and imprecise term encouraging all kinds of false pretences on a large scale, since

We had occasion in our *Déterminismes sociaux et liberté humaine*, to describe the different degrees of intensity of actions and collective acts, particularly *innovatory conception* (of rules and symbols), *choice, decision,* and *collective creation*;[1] through which *human liberty* manifests itself in *historical societies* i.e. *Promethean societies*.[2] We have come to the conclusion that *sociology is as much a science of human liberty as of social determinism.* It is obvious that here sociology and philosophy share a common field.

The same holds true with regard to signs, symbols, ideas and values.

Finally, it is in the special branches of sociology, such as the sociology of knowledge, sociology of moral life, sociology of art, that the *common ground of philosophy and sociology appears in maximum relief.* In fact, to study the variations of knowledge, morality, or art, in relation to partial or global social frameworks, it is necessary first of all to agree on what 'moral life', 'knowledge' and 'art' mean. In other words it is necessary to define them in terms of specific cultural products and social facts. But to avoid this preliminary definition becoming arbitrary, confused, or dogmatic, a philosophical analysis is indispensable. So that this in its turn does not also become dogmatic, i.e. dependent on a preconceived and often unconscious position, it is necessary to realize that the sociologist and the philosopher, while frequently meeting on the same ground, do not use the same method to explore it.

Thus the sociologist of knowledge must never pose the problem of the validity and value of signs, symbols, concepts, ideas, and judgements, that he meets in the social reality being studied. He must only ascertain the effect of their presence, combination, and effective function.

On the other hand, the philosopher must be concerned with the justification of the validity and value of the above-mentioned elements. He thus makes an effort to integrate as many as possible of the various aspects of partial knowledge in an infinite global

in fact collective and individual opinions in this case become 'public' only through the intervention of opinion poll investigators.) Obviously tendencies towards a more open consciousness or, on the contrary, towards relative closure, can involve almost infinite degrees, which will require a new concrete examination in relation to each social framework and conjuncture.

[1] Cf. *Déterminismes sociaux et liberté humaine* (2nd edn., revised and corrected, 1963), passim, and in particular, pp. 1–13, 95–104, 221, 246–324.

[2] Ibid., pp. 220–1, 246–7, 324.

totality, wherein each would find its place. The contribution of
the sociology of knowledge, by uncovering a great variety of
cognitive systems, complicates the task by enriching the contents
of philosophy and especially that particular branch known as
epistemology, or 'philosophy of knowledge'.

If collaboration, negative as well as positive, is established
between the sociology of knowledge and philosophy, the domination of one over the other is excluded. To deduce an epistemology
from the sociology of knowledge would be as ill-fated as to link
the fate of the sociology of knowledge to a particular philosophical
position. Besides, from all points of view, it is essential for the
development of the sociology of knowledge that it learn to remain
modest and renounce inordinate pretensions.

*

This for several reasons:
To begin with, in the sociology of knowledge, *explanation* must
never go beyond the establishment of functional correlations,
regular tendencies, and direct integration into social frameworks.
The search for causality can occur in this field only in certain
cases of precise disjunction between social framework and knowledge, a disjunction which can only be established by a preliminary
dialectical analysis of the given situation. Before specifying this
consideration we must emphasize these two facts: (a) one cannot
assert that knowledge is a simple projection or an epiphenomenon
of social reality without undermining or denigrating it; (b) normally, every type of knowledge and every cognitive system is a
part of the network of a social framework only as an aspect, stage,
element, of the total social phenomenon, and in particular of its
manifestation in a social structure, where knowledge plays a
cementing role concurrently with other cultural products (morals,
law, religion, magic, education, etc.).

*

Dialectics of polarization, ambiguity or complementarity can
arise between a social framework and knowledge, although usually
they are found in dialectical relationships of mutual involvement
or reciprocity of perspectives.[1] These two relationships are equally

[1] Cf. for the distinction of different turning points of the dialectic movement,
both real and methodological, my book *Dialectique et Sociologie* (Paris, 1962)
pp. 189–220.

D

dialectical, because they can become strained just as symmetry can be broken, or even turn in opposite directions. This is why, as a general rule, the disjunctions between social reality and knowledge, which alone render possible the intervention of causality between the two terms, can be more easily studied by beginning with the first kinds of dialectic. Thus a social structure that is backward in relation to its underlying total social phenomenon can resist upheaval, temporarily at least, by virtue of an advanced system of knowledge. This was the case with the City-States of ancient Greece and of the 'Ancien Régime' in France, and of Russia in the nineteenth century and the beginning of the twentieth century.

Advanced knowledge can become a cause of backwardness in the evolution of the structure, whilst facilitating its eventual upheaval. However, the structure and the underlying total social phenomenon become in their turn the causes of a particularly abstract orientation of knowledge and of its limitation to the élites. In the opposite case: a social structure that is relatively advanced compared with the system of knowledge can be the cause of the change in orientation of that system. This phenomenon comes to mind in the case of the U.S.S.R. after the revolution. It can also be observed in the United States after the advent of organized capitalism, which tends towards the domination of technical knowledge over all other kinds of knowledge. Here the causality is always singular and, for this reason, limited to specific cases.

*

The 'social correlate' corresponding to each type and system of knowledge, which is placed in the foreground by the sociology of knowledge, should not be considered as an obstacle to knowledge. Certainly awareness of this correlate, or the 'placing of knowledge in a sociological perspective' can reveal the inefficiency of systems of knowledge ill-suited to the social frameworks in which they are maintained, just as they can help to a certain extent in 'bracketing' this correlate by reducing its importance. But the sociology of knowledge cannot serve to invalidate false knowledge, 'demystify' it, or 'disalienate' it, as Marx wanted to do. First, it is not its function to decide on the veracity of the content of knowledge, for it does not claim to take the place of epistemology; secondly, the 'disalienation' of knowledge, understood as the freeing of all ties between knowledge and social framework, even if it is projected as something possible only in the future, can represent for the sociologist *only an intellectualist utopia of disincarnate knowledge.*

*

The sociology of knowledge must give up the scientific and philosophical prejudice that all knowledge is dependent on philosophical and scientific knowledge,[1] which are the types of knowledge relatively most detached from social frameworks, and so are the most difficult for sociology to study. It is particularly true for the *sociology of philosophical knowledge*, where the same positions reappear centuries apart. The sociology of knowledge must attain greater maturity before being able to deal with the sociology of philosophy with any hope of success.

The sociology of knowledge must first of all concentrate its efforts on the types of knowledge which are most deeply involved in social reality and the network of its structures, such as: *the perceptual knowledge of the external world, knowledge of the Other, political knowledge, technical knowledge, and common sense knowledge.* These are the areas where research and empirical investigation can be carried furthest. At the moment the sociology of knowledge has particular need of this research as well as concrete historical investigations.[2]

*

The sociology of knowledge must relinquish the very widespread prejudice that *cognitive* judgements must possess a universal validity. The validity of a judgement is never universal, for it is attached to a precise frame of reference. Now there exists a multiplicity of frames of reference, often corresponding to the social frameworks. If truth and judgements were always universal,

---

[1] Given that in modern societies science becomes increasingly dependent on laboratories and other research organizations, both public and private, the sociology of scientific knowledge, understood as the study of the frameworks of its organization and its means of diffusion, finds here significant points of reference. But in the majority of cases, this does not lead to penetration into the deeper character of this knowledge's orientation.

[2] These considerations have guided the choice of subjects studied by 'The Laboratory for the Sociology of Knowledge' (under our direction).

one could not establish a distinction either between particular sciences or between types of knowledge; yet even the most dogmatic sociologists and philosophers distinguish two or even three types of knowledge—philosophical knowledge, scientific knowledge, and technical knowledge. For our part, we consider that there exists a much larger number of types of knowledge, which the sociology of knowledge as well as epistemology must take into consideration, and each of these types acts as a frame of reference, thus eliminating the dogma of the universal validity of judgements.

Furthermore, the sociology of knowledge cannot assert itself unless it admits that collective knowledge is in a dialectical relationship with individual knowledge. The history of civilization bears witness to the fact that collective knowledge exists, and that it is based on collective judgements which recognize the veracity of collective experiences and intuitions. The abandonment of the concept of the self-contained consciousness (the closed consciousness turned in on itself), in favour of the open consciousness in a close and constant relation with the world, has made it possible to acknowledge that the interpenetration of consciousnesses and their partial fusion are as real as the individual consciousness. Thus, all consciousness appears to involve a dialectic between the 'Me', the Other, and the 'We', and the objections to the possibility of collective knowledge are concentrated on *acts of judgement*, which are related to reflection and the spoken word, and might seem to be individual.

Now, what does to reflect mean, if not to debate the pros and cons, to contrast *arguments*, i.e. to participate in a *dialogue*, discussion, or debate? But in that case, reflection, far from being the prerogative of the individual consciousness, has a bearing which is so clearly collective that one could say that *in personal reflection there appear different 'Me's which argue amongst themselves.* In other words, it is at least partly a question of a projection of the collective in the individual. In passing from the act of judging to the criteria of judgement, it would be easy to show that the criteria of *formal coherence* and *formal correctness* of judgement are always collective, even though the *criteria of veracity* can be either collective or individual.

Thus, to claim, for example, to have been present in several places at once or to have communicated with spirits will be judged coherent in certain primitive societies and incoherent in others. If we turn from formal coherence to formal correctness we arrive at the same conclusion. Let us take as an example the following declarations: 'There's an inhabitant of another planet!'; 'There's a spaceship!'. Formerly they would have seemed obviously incorrect, whereas they no longer seem so today. As for the veracity of judgement, its criterion is clearly collective in matters that concern the perceptual knowledge of the external world, knowledge of the Other and the We, political knowledge, and even, in large part, technical knowledge. Only scientific knowledge and philosophical knowledge rely on criteria of veracity which in some cases are collective and in others individual.

It is only the act of speaking that is always individual. Utterances can be collective, and not only when they are repeated in chorus. As for the rest, an individual judgement can be expressed by a collective utterance, just as collective judgements can permit an individual *verbal expression*. In short, the whole discussion of the possibility of collective judgements shows that it is in fact a false problem.

CHAPTER TWO

Definition of the Sociology of Knowledge

Before defining the sociology of knowledge and enumerating its many tasks, there remains one basic objection to be answered. It will perhaps be said that the differentiation of the types of knowledge to be dealt with in this book seems artificial, since the various types of knowledge exercise a reciprocal action upon each other, thus constituting an irreducible whole. First of all it should be noted that in this area we are concerned with questions of fact. The different types of knowledge can just as well oppose and contradict each other as unite and interpenetrate. This is a matter of complete relativity and the problem itself requires the sociology of knowledge. Secondly, to establish variable hierarchies of types of knowledge, and to state that the predominant types vary according to the diverse types of global or partial social structures, is in no way to dispute the tendency of these types, pre-eminent in a specific social framework, to influence and penetrate the other types of knowledge which are below them. On the contrary, this allows a place for flexibility and empirical observation in explaining the specific network of interpenetrations and influences between the different types of knowledge. When one establishes, for example, that in present-day societies technical and political knowledge hold first place, one is not surprised to see that the knowledge of the Other, the perceptual knowledge of the external world, scientific and even philosophical knowledge are strongly technicized and politicized. This objection therefore seems without foundation.

*

What do we mean exactly by the term 'sociology of knowledge'? It is primarily *the study of functional correlations which can be established between the different types, the differently emphasized forms within these types, the different systems (hierarchies of these types) of knowledge, and, on the other hand, the social frameworks, such as global societies, social classes, particular groupings, and various manifestations of sociality (microsocial elements). Of the social frameworks, the partial, and particularly the global, social structures constitute the central nucleus of these studies, though they are facilitated by the role that knowledge can play, along with other cultural products and social controls, in a structural framework— this delicate balance of many hierarchies.*

Once its principal task is accomplished, the sociology of knowledge should study the following in detail:

(a) the relationship between the variable hierarchy of the types of knowledge and the hierarchy—also a variable one—of other cultural products and different social regulations (called 'social controls');

(b) the role of knowledge and its agents in the various types of societies;

(c) the different modes of expression, communication and diffusion of knowledge, though again inasmuch as they are functionally related to the collective subjects—both receptive and expressive;

(d) the regular tendencies of the various types of knowledge, corresponding to the types of global societies, classes and even particular groupings, to become either differentiated or combined; (this might constitute the first chapter of the 'genetic sociology' of knowledge);

(e) finally, the specific cases of *disjunction* between the social frameworks and knowledge in their relations with each other, created by polarizations, ambiguities and dialectical complementarities. This requires research into the effective but singular causality which sometimes operates in the direction of the social frameworks' influence on the orientation and nature of knowledge; at other times in the opposite direction of knowledge's influence on the maintenance or disruption of social frameworks; and sometimes manifesting itself in reciprocal causality. This causal study would form the subject matter of the second chapter of the 'genetic sociology' of knowledge, and would be closely related to historical research.

CHAPTER THREE

Sociology of Knowledge and Epistemology

Before concluding these preliminary statements, it is necessary to specify the relationship between the sociology of knowledge and epistemology. All notions of unilateral dependence of the one upon the other have been dismissed. However, they do have common ground that is studied by both, though in a different manner. This brings them into close contact and thus enables a reciprocal contribution—both negative and positive—and therefore joint collaboration between these two otherwise irreducible disciplines.

The existence of collective knowledge presents new problems to epistemology:

(a) that of collective entities, the validity of their cognitive acts, and the value of these in relation to individual knowledge;
(b) that of intellectual social symbols (subject to various conceptualizations) and the extent of their validity;
(c) that of non-symbolic, cognitive social signs (subject to all kinds of tests) and their effectiveness.

Wherein lies the positive contribution of epistemology to the sociology of knowledge? First, in the collaboration between epistemology and this branch of sociology: in its efforts to differentiate knowledge as a social fact distinct from other social facts, and in its attempts to differentiate the types and forms of knowledge. Secondly, epistemology helps the sociology of knowledge to pose the problem in terms of functional correlations (and, if necessary, in terms of singular causality), by permitting this discipline to have a sociological perspective of knowledge which does not entail debate on the validity of knowledge. Thirdly, epistemology, by means of the concepts of totality, infinity, multiplicity, plurality of perspectives and frames of reference, including the generality of the latter, opens the way to a sociological explanation of the orientations of knowledge, which is not to be confused with the problem of its 'distortion'.

It is not difficult to see that this positive contribution of epistemology to the sociology of knowledge does not involve any particular epistemological doctrine and does not require at any time the espousal of some philosophical position. In theory there can be $n+1$ philosophical justifications for the collaboration of these two disciplines.

In its turn, the positive contribution of the sociology of knowledge to epistemology consists in placing at its disposal a wealth of concrete, empirical material accumulated in the course of investigations into the variations of:

(a) the hierarchy of the types of knowledge;
(b) the emphasized forms of knowledge within each type;
(c) the relationships between systems of knowledge and other social controls, i.e. the variations in the effective role of knowledge in different types of social structures.

By proposing to settle the problem of truth and falsity or, in other words, to offer a justification for the validity of knowledge, epistemology is forced to respond in an increasingly subtle and flexible way to the questions posed by the sociology of knowledge, and to avoid all facile solutions.

Moreover, the sociology of knowledge poses to epistemology the problem of the validity of an almost infinite number of perspectives of knowledge. It is up to epistemology to resolve in its own way the question of knowing whether these perspectives (be they 'ideological', 'utopian', 'mythological', etc.) are all equally valid, or whether some of them are less so than others.

It is therefore a question of joint collaboration between the sociology of knowledge and epistemology which, though remaining irreducible, render mutual service. 'Imperialism could not occur between them: they observe each other and each incites the other's endeavour. It is a disturbing but fruitful confrontation. Here co-operation and a policy of openness are essential. This does not exclude the possibility of fusion and confusion between these two disciplines, though they must remain autonomous.'[1]

*

In this preliminary overview of the problems facing the sociology of knowledge, we have tried to be as brief as possible in order

[1] I take the liberty of quoting the text of my own study, 'Philosophie et Sociologie', in *La vocation actuelle de la sociologie*, II, 496.

to arrive at the concrete study of the relationships between social frameworks and the types and forms of knowledge. We have thought it necessary, therefore, to sacrifice the history of the sociology of knowledge, of which a brief critical summary can be found in our study entitled *Les problèmes de la sociologie de la connaissance* (Problems in the sociology of knowledge).[1] Moreover, we are preparing a *History of Sociology in the Nineteenth and Twentieth Centuries*, in which an important place will be given to the sociology of knowledge.[2]

[1] *Traité de Sociologie* (2nd edn., 1964), vol. II, ch. ii, pp. 103–20.

[2] Here is the list of my own publications prior to the present work and dealing with the same subject (excepting obviously my contribution to the *Traité de Sociologie*, vol. II, quoted in the preceding note): *Initiation aux recherches sur la sociologie de la connaissance*, copy 1 (Paris, 1948), mimeographed, C.D.U. (out of print), p. 165; 'La sociologie de la connaissance', in the *Année sociologique* (3rd series, 1949), pp. 463–86; 'Structures sociales et systèmes de la connaissance', in *La notion de structure et structure de la connaissance*, XXe Semaine de Synthèse (Paris, 1957, A. Michel), pp. 291–342; 'Structures sociales et multiplicité des temps', in *Bulletin de la Société Française de Philosophie* (Paris, 1958), no. 3; 'Les cadres sociaux de la connaissance sociologique', in *Cahiers Internationaux de Sociologie*, XXVI (1959), 165–72; 'L'effondrement d'un mythe politique', in *Cahiers Internationaux de Sociologie* (Paris, 1962), XXXIII, 5–18; 'La multiplicité des temps sociaux', in *La vocation actuelle de la sociologie*, II (2nd edn., 1963), 325–430; 'Les variations des perceptions collectives des étendues', in *Cahiers Internationaux de Sociologie*, XXXVII (1964), 79–106; 'Sociologie de la connaissance et épistémologie', in *Transactions of the Fifth World Congress of Sociology*, V (Washington, 2–8 September 1962), (1964), 63–202; 'La sociologie de la connaissance', in *Revue de l'Enseignement supérieur*, nos. 1–2 (1965), pp. 43–52.

CHAPTER FOUR

Types and Forms of Knowledge

It is impossible to start our research into the concrete relationships between knowledge and social frameworks (whether these be manifestations of sociality, particular groups, aggregates of such groups in states and churches, social classes, or global societies of different types), without undertaking, as a preliminary, a precise and detailed analysis of the *types of knowledge* and their interconnection with the *forms of knowledge*. So far in this introduction we have hardly mentioned either of them, or the cognitive systems which they constitute when structured social frameworks are involved.

In order to study the varieties of knowledge by placing them in 'sociological perspective', it is necessary at the outset to analyse the types and forms of knowledge which have appeared up to the present.[1] This is why we consider it necessary to devote the most important chapter of this introduction to it, even at the risk of boring the reader with such an apparently abstract analysis.

Concerning the types and forms of knowledge that we intend to study, it might be objected that the problem has meaning only in relation to global societies, or, just possibly, in relation to social classes. Indeed one might be tempted to agree that no valid conclusion could be arrived at by studying the appearance of types and forms of knowledge as a function of the manifestations of sociality, or particular non-structured groupings, since they are themselves so variable, and their effects on knowledge are so diverse. These objections are, however, much less convincing than they might appear.

Nor is it denied that it is necessary first to enquire whether or

---

[1] Other types and forms of knowledge could certainly arise in the future. From this point of view our distinctions are not at all exclusive, given that they recognize, in principle, the possibility of $n+1$ types and forms of knowledge, each of which should be noted each time that it appears in a social framework. This is simply a question of the points of departure for an effectively relativistic and realistic sociology of knowledge, i.e. corresponding to the exigencies of any sociological study that aims to be truly scientific.

not the integration of microsocial or group elements within larger social macrocosms might modify their characteristics, including, in this case, their cognitive aspects. The following facts should not, however, be forgotten. In favourable circumstances (such as civil and international wars, revolutions, large-scale popular movements, etc.) the manifestations of sociality and non-structured groups can, in their turn, act upon the encompassing social frameworks, by affecting the cognitive aspect as much as any other. *Thus the general rule of all sociology is borne out in the sociology of knowledge, according to which well-executed micro-sociology leads ultimately to macrosociology,* and inversely, the latter cannot do without the help of the former when it takes into consideration details, concrete situations and circumstances. The dialectic of mutual implication occurs here with particular intensity.

*

Certain types of knowledge, most particularly the perceptual knowledge of the external world, but also knowledge of the Other and the We, groups, classes, etc., political knowledge, certain branches of scientific knowledge arising from the natural sciences (astronomy, physics, biology, etc.) or human sciences (including history and sociology), involve the study of the specific space and time in which their objects move.

Consequently, a sociology of these various branches of knowledge of necessity touches on the sociology of space and time. One might be tempted, therefore, to begin with this latter. However, space and time themselves manifest a variety and complexity appropriate to each type of knowledge, and appear in each case in a specific light. This occurs in such a way that their study, wherever it is possible, requires a special sociological perspective. Furthermore, it seems preferable to conduct the study of space and time separately for each type of knowledge, although the perceptual knowledge of the external world seems to occupy a special position.

Our intention is not to initiate a different sociology of knowledge for each type of knowledge that can be distinguished: such an enterprise would from the outset be doomed to failure as soon as we approached the study of social frameworks as vast and rich as social classes and, particularly, global societies, to which corre-

spond entire cognitive systems.[1] In effect, as soon as social frameworks of major importance are concerned, there is no doubt that
the types of knowledge range themselves in an hierarchic system.
And in this variable hierarchy the predominant type or types
penetrate all the others, as we have already implied. For example,
in Ancient Greece, philosophical knowledge and perceptual
knowledge of the external world, which held first place, penetrated
all the other types of knowledge—as did scientific knowledge in a
competitive capitalist system. Under organized and directed
capitalism it is technical knowledge and political knowledge which
dominate and impregnate all the other types.

Let us now specify in detail the distinctive characteristics of
different types of knowledge.

1. *The perceptual knowledge of the external world postulates a
coherent ensemble of images, placed in concrete and specific space and
time; the ways in which they may be perceived, and the possibilities
of conceptualizing and quantifying them, are very variable.* This
knowledge presupposes collective perceptions and judgements on
the veracity of the combination of space and time as well as on
their content. Before giving an idea of the relative importance
which this kind of knowledge can assume within a hierarchic
system, one single example must suffice: that of feudal society.
Perceptual knowledge of the external world was there relegated to
last position (the absence of perspective in art, towns and villages
turned in on themselves in their architecture and arrangement,
are sufficient proof of this).

As a social fact, perceptual knowledge of the external world
presupposes first of all the collective perception of space and time
wherein the world is situated. The collective subjects (the 'We',
groups, classes, global societies), like individual subjects, constantly encounter obstacles which obstruct their course, activities,

---

[1] The problem of types of knowledge isolated from each other could only be
posed in specific circumstances, such as those of intense destructuration of
global structures undergoing violent upheaval in an encounter with heterogeneous structures, such as those of colonizers as they dominate the colonized
(e.g. Indians dominated by the French, the British, and the Dutch in North
America). Sometimes a tendency towards isolation of types of knowledge is
produced as a function of the intensity of the 'We' as it asserts itself as an esoteric
communion, and when particular groupings show a propensity towards becoming closed collective units. Cf. infra, 1st Part, Chapter 4, pp. 55–56, and
2nd Part, Chapter 2, pp. 60–64.

and aspirations. Space and time are among these obstacles. It is by struggling against them and trying to dominate them that the subjects become aware of them. In this struggle an initial selection is made, as appropriate for each perception, and dependent on frames of reference that tend to coincide with the social frameworks. For this reason, a considerable number of perceptions, even individual ones, are controlled and prompted by collective criteria. How could it be otherwise? Would not an individual perception, isolated from collective criteria, run the risk of becoming illusory? A man who had an exclusively individual perception of space and time would be aberrant, lost in the external and social world, and therefore incapable of finding his bearings there. He would be at the boundary, beyond which his perceptions of space and time would become those of a state of madness, or at least a psychopathological state.

Bergson defined concrete space, as distinct from quantified space, as being composed of extensions in opposition to tensions, which characterize different degrees of qualitative duration. If one can define time in a purely descriptive way as 'a co-ordination or disjunction of irreversible movements which have their duration in succession and their succession in duration',[1] one could say of space that it is 'a co-ordination or disjunction of juxtaposed points, extensible and reversible, which co-exist simultaneously'.

We must draw attention to another essential difference between time and space. It is that the multiplicity of times concerns not only social life, but every kind of reality outside the human, for it is imposed independently of all awareness of time. There are as many times as there are spheres of reality, and in each sphere several times can enter into competition. This is not so with the plurality of space. The space wherein the external world and the social world are placed, as a *reality* independent of all consciousness, can be only a *single* space. Any other interpretation would introduce a mystique of several visible and invisible worlds, which would be acceptable only in an archaic society. The diversification of space occurs only as a result of diverse perceptions, symbolizations, conceptualizations, etc. This does not mean that different types of space are devoid of all reality, but only that it is not then a question of the total reality of space so much as the perspectives wherein various states of consciousness place it.

[1] *La vocation actuelle de la sociologie*, II (1963), 329.

These perspectives are not illusions, in as much as they constitute different ways of approaching the one real space.

This is why the types of time, particularly social time as defined in our earlier works, could primarily be considered independent of the way in which they are perceived, whereas types of space are inseparable from the different ways in which they are perceived, both in social space and the space of the external world. In both cases the varieties of space are but different approaches to the one real space.

But whether it is a question of space or time, one's perception of them is of a collective nature. Even so, it discloses a multiplicity of characteristics, hence the variety of images of the external world in different social frameworks, despite the selection which collective judgements make between perceptions, whether true or false.

Perceptions of space vary according to two essential criteria:
(a) That of relationship to the subject, collective and individual. It is possible to establish the following distinctions:

1. *'autistic'* space, which is identical with the subject;
2. *'egocentric'* space, penetrated by the emotivity of the subject;
3. *projective* space, which gets progressively wider the further away it is from the subject, but still involves the subject's activity (for example, the morphologico-ecological space spoken of in sociology, or the space relevant to organizations, models and symbols, and therefore limited in its scope);
4. *prospective* space, the most distant from the subject and the nearest to real space.

(b) The second criterion is a function of the very nature of the perceived space. It serves to establish other distinctions such as:

1. Diffuse space without precise outlines;
2. Concentric space turned in on itself;
3. Space which expands and contracts without difficulty. It should be noted that often prospective space overlaps with space that expands and contracts, and that *autistic* space is at the same time concentric. However, these relationships are not inevitable. Hence, in our epoch, due to new techniques, the means of communication triumph over diffuse space and also concentric space, but prospective space is, to a certain extent,

bound up with the technical facilities, so that it has a tendency to become concentric again, cut off from diffuse space.

Time is even more diversified than space: to the various types of awareness of time is added the multiplicity of real time. In considering the spectrum of social time alone, we believe it possible to distinguish eight types of real time. If one simply calls to mind the realities of the external world and the times wherein they move—excluding all projections clearly falsified by the emotions—one discovers a considerable variety of times in combination with space. Perceptual knowledge of the external world sets in motion a complex dialectic between diverse space and times, both perceived and real. It should be noted here that the coherent image of the external world, the object of this knowledge, involves space and times which can combine with each other, even unite, as well as clash with each other and enter into conflict; they can just as easily become polarized as complementary, etc., but their relationships always remain strained and ambiguous.

If one takes account of the fact that the criteria for measuring space and time, like those of the actual coherence of the external world, change often from one society to another, one class to another, one group to another, one cannot fail to recognize the extreme variety of the images of the external world which confront the sociology of perceptual knowledge. And one is led still more to regret that neither this knowledge, nor its relationships with the social frameworks according to which it varies, have until now attracted the attention of sociologists. Consideration is given to this problem in the general exposition. But first another type of knowledge must be discussed.

*

2. *Knowledge of the Other, the We, groups, classes, and societies, perceived as real and verified by conscious judgement, represents a particular type of knowledge.* This has been realized only fairly recently, and more so in philosophy than in sociology. This paradox has a three-fold origin. One cannot imagine any social framework (microsocial, groupal, global) where this perception and knowledge would not be produced, because they are a constitutive element of social reality itself; however, they are more often *implicit* than *explicit*. At the same time, there is variation from

one social framework to another in the reciprocal intensity, importance, and character of the role played by the physical appearance of the Other, his facial expression, overt behaviour, gestures and words, social attitudes, and his desire or refusal to communicate. Likewise, in the knowledge of the Other, there is variation in the criteria, models, and symbols suggested by different groups, classes and global societies for conceptualized images of the Other. As an example, we will quote criteria of the Other and the We from global societies. They may expand and contract depending on the situation (thus they would not include the foreigner, the slave, nor even the serf—since none of these could be considered capable of being an Other or part of the We). Or, on the contrary, they may expand (to the extent that a man is taken as representative of humanity in general and loses his particular individual traits). Moreover, in certain social frameworks and circumstances, the Other as object of perception or knowledge may take the form of father or brother, friend or enemy, companion or rival, comrade or adversary, inferior or superior, protector or oppressor, centre of attraction, repulsion or indifference. It may also assume an ambivalent character by combining opposing traits.

Finally—and this is the third source of the aforementioned paradox—knowledge of the Other has played a considerable role only in patriarchal or feudal types of societies, particularly the trade guilds and monastic orders of the Middle Ages; it occurs also in certain small groupings (household families, internship systems, etc.). Perhaps it could become of major importance in types of societies organized according to principles of decentralized and pluralist collectivism based on worker control.

In any case, we will have to consider this type of knowledge as being particularly bound up with social frameworks.

*

3. *Common sense knowledge*, which could also be designated by the fashionable term 'knowledge of everyday life', is a particular type of knowledge. It consists of a combination of knowledge of the Other and the We; of perceptual knowledge of the external world (the most closely related to a 'We' or a group); certain simple forms of technical knowledge—physical techniques; polite manners, and maintaining reserve and distance. It tends to favour traditional knowledge, that of older and experienced people, and

E

savoir vivre, which neither children, nor more generally, the younger generations possess.

The younger generations are often reminded of 'common sense' by their elders, who flatter themselves that they can teach them how to cope with the difficulties of everyday life and to avoid mistakes. But the success of this transmission of common sense knowledge is more problematical in modern industrial societies: the conditions of life there change at a baffling rate, imposed by continual transformation of techniques. In the face of this perpetual upheaval of daily life, each generation, even each part of a generation, must work out its own common sense knowledge, and it is this which detracts from its importance in present day systems of knowledge. It should be noted that the more highly cultured a society is, the less is the role of common sense knowledge; the more illiterate the society, the more important is its role.

However, there exist certain small-scale groups where common sense knowledge continues to predominate, such as household families, small hamlets or isolated villages. Moreover, certain professional bodies, such as the army, the Bar, the medical profession, and even faculties and other organizations of higher education, in spite of the specific knowledge which they disseminate, confine themselves in their inner life and functioning to a simple common sense knowledge. This is evidence that this is certainly a specific type of knowledge.

4. *Technical knowledge* is not simply knowledge of the means employed to attain ideal goals, as certain spiritualistic philosophers make believe, nor an applied scientific knowledge, characterized by formulation and transmissibility, as crude positivism asserted. Technical knowledge is a type of knowledge *sui generis*, irreducible to any other. It is imbued with the desire to dominate the world, to control, manipulate, and order it. It is a constituent part of the *praxis* (in the sense that Marx understood it) and it is directly integrated with the 'productive forces'.

However, it would be false to limit technical knowledge to the sole knowledge of the manipulation of matter and, even more so, it would be wrong to identify it with technology. On the one hand, technical knowledge is both explicit, in as much as it is transmitted, and implicit, in as much as it is involved in practice, skill and dexterity. On the other hand, technical knowledge has a much wider domain than the manipulation of matter. *It is that knowledge which is concerned with every kind of effective manipulation—artificial and subordinate, but tending to become independent and valued as such—precise, transmissible, and innovative, its acquisition is inspired by desire to dominate the worlds of nature, humanity, and society, in order to produce, destroy, safeguard, organize, plan, communicate and disseminate.*

The degrees of technical knowledge, both explicit and implicit, vary widely within the same type of society, and range from the expert and those who hold technical secrets, to the executor of authorized orders, and even the amateur handyman and the ordinary citizen.

The distinct character of technical knowledge can be verified by reference to well-established facts concerning its varied and sometimes unexpected importance in diverse types of global societies. From a very rudimentary level in the ancient cities and empires—in spite of the considerable development of scientific knowledge—technical knowledge attained a relatively high level of development in theocractico-charismatic societies (e.g. in Ancient Egypt). In feudal societies it reached an even higher level but without a corresponding development in science.

Again, at the beginning of capitalism, technical knowledge developed not as a function of scientific knowledge but directly in the mills and factories. The conjunction of technical and scientific knowledge was not effectively accomplished until the twentieth century, and then only in the limited sector of technology, at the higher level of experts and engineers. During the course of the last decades technical knowledge has begun to dominate scientific knowledge and to assign to it a subordinate role, not only in the natural sciences but also in the human sciences. Present-day psychology and sociology offer examples of this domination by techniques; this movement can only continue to gather momentum at the risk of undermining their very foundations in the long term.

But this is not all. We have arrived at a period in which techniques influence social structures, especially in those types of societies which gave birth to them. Now the history of techniques shows that until the present time technical knowledge had never created social frameworks, but that on the contrary it was social frameworks which gave rise to techniques. It can be stated that in so far as partial or global social structures are cemented by cultural works, the latter have always guided and dominated technical knowledge.

Today, however, we are witnessing a striking disjunction between, on the one side, social structures and their non-technical cultural works, and, on the other side, techniques. Unfettered technical knowledge escapes domination and control. Technical knowledge, at an advanced level, reveals its destructive forces, and the technocrats—those sorcerer's apprentices—declare themselves unable to control the forces which they unleash. Technical knowledge is swept along as if by a flood, and it is as if a race were developing between it and society. This situation only renders the sociology of technical knowledge more interesting and makes one regret that nothing significant has as yet been attempted in this field.

*

5. *Political knowledge* must be carefully distinguished from 'political science'[1] and 'political sociology',[2] which study (by different methods) political régimes, the organization and functioning of elections, political parties, etc.—in short, everything which concerns the state, the *politeia* (to use the term introduced by Aristotle)—Plato spoke only of the *republic* and, in a later dialogue, of the *politique*, i.e. the 'politician'—all of which is designated by *politics* in English. Political knowledge must also be distinguished from 'political doctrines'[3] or 'political philosophy', which justify present or future régimes, and sometimes have the purpose of systematizing acquired political knowledge.

Thus political knowledge, as defined here, is fairly close to the Anglo-Saxon concept of *policy* (as opposed to *politics*), yet extending into the following two areas: (a) the 'strategy of social action', which may or may not deal with the functioning of the state; (b) the spontaneous and reflective knowledge which orients this strategy. The latter, therefore, penetrates every aspect of action affecting the politics of the state (policy).

---

[1] Taught in France at *L'École des Sciences Politiques* and at *L'École Nationale d'Administration*, and in part at *La Faculté de Droit et des Sciences économiques* in order to complete the study of 'constitutional law'.

[2] Taught at the *Faculté des Lettres et Sciences humaines* as optional entrance subject for the *Certificat de Sociologie générale*, constituting one of the certificates for the *Licence de Sociologie* (Soc. degree).

[3] Taught mainly at the *Faculté de Droit et des Sciences économiques* for the same degree as political science.

Thus, we are consciously using the term 'political knowledge' in a sense distinct from science, including that science which studies what directly or indirectly concerns the actions of the state. We are concerned with a spontaneous and reflective knowledge extraneous to science, which is forged directly in a social struggle in which the stakes are varied. It is above all a *partisan knowledge*, in which militants and leaders ('political men') are infinitely stronger than scholarly men who have been brought up on 'political science' and even 'political sociology'. This political knowledge does not presuppose the existence of the state or its political action. In fact, it is already apparent in the different types of archaic societies by the struggle of clans and tribes, by rivalries between clans, and by the combats which 'male initiation houses' engage in. 'Political knowledge' is also observable in patriarchal societies (which belong to the category of historical societies without constituting 'states'); this knowledge is then expressed in struggles between the eldest son and the younger brothers (involving their mothers, their followers and supporters), or again in the intrigues between 'adopted children' and 'natural born descendants', etc.

Political knowledge is most evident in actions, intrigues, and struggles, in which groups, classes, and parties, directly confront each other. Today it can be studied more easily in the resolutions of trades union congresses and various political parties, than in their programmes or doctrines. Although a combination of value judgements and judgements of fact, this political knowledge nevertheless could not be reduced to a profession of faith, *since it is first and foremost knowledge*: a very precise and realistic knowledge concerning opposing forces and the setting in which such action occurs. Political knowledge implies, therefore, clear awareness of difficulties to be overcome, and an acute sense of the action to be taken in any social situation. Accordingly, it will, therefore, inspire either revolutionary extremist action or at least assertive action, or in other circumstances bring about compromise, calculated delay ('in order to get second wind', according to Lenin's famous expression at the inauguration in the U.S.S.R. in 1922 of the policies of the N.E.P.),[1] and even withdrawal.

There exists something of an arcane element in the character of

---

[1] The New Economic Policy, which for some time allowed the free market of certain agricultural products.

political knowledge, which justifies its inclusion in the cognitive sphere. This lies in the fact that it is a specific combination of faith in an ideal and the knowledge necessary for circumventing obstacles,[1] and for seizing opportunities as soon as they arise. Here, technical knowledge applied to the manipulation of men, partisan groups, and sometimes large masses, plays a not unimportant role: it is becoming increasingly important in our age. . . . Thus, from one point of view, political knowledge is made up of a *combination of several types of knowledge*: knowledge of the Other and the We, common sense knowledge, technical knowledge, and direct knowledge of the economic and psychological aspects of social reality as manifested in global conjunctures. However, it is not simply a question of the summation of these types of knowledge, but it involves their *indissoluble fusion* in a type of knowledge *sui generis*, which is itself irreducible and unique. This is substantiated by the observation that political knowledge in certain cognitive systems, especially those which correspond either to directed capitalism or centralized communism, shows itself to be capable of dominating and penetrating all other types of knowledge.

*

Certainly political knowledge is the most ideological sort of knowledge. Nevertheless, and it is important to state this, no knowledge completely escapes the influence of ideology. Indeed it permeates the perceptual knowledge of the external world, knowledge of the Other and the We, common sense knowledge, technical and scientific knowledge in varying degrees, and philosophical knowledge very strongly.

We have just characterized the different aspects of political knowledge, which in a way brings us back to the task of delimiting it in relation to the other types of knowledge.

In order to define it more precisely, we must emphasize that in essence political knowledge consists of a *particular network of spontaneous and reflective statements on the present, future, and sometimes past, situation of a social structure or conjuncture. This knowledge is the most directly committed, i.e. it has first and foremost*

---

[1] Better still, this knowledge sometimes succeeds in setting obstacles against each other, i.e. in manipulating them so that they are overcome by being destroyed. . . .

a partisan character. This is why it is usually impervious to opponents' arguments (or even those of direct competitors). This tendency, which we have already indicated, is not incompatible with its capacity for uncovering even the most well-hidden obstacles, and arriving at accurate assessments of actual conditions and circumstances favourable to the partial or total realization of intended goals. Thus, as we have seen, in different circumstances political knowledge can inspire refusal to compromise, 'total separation',[1] absolute intransigence, or tactical retreat and moderation.

It is permeated not only by ideology, but also by utopias and 'myths' in the Sorelian sense of signal-images calling for action. Finally, within cognitive systems it tends to be raised to a higher position in societies where group conflicts are acute, class antagonisms are strong, or when, as at present, several different types of global structures enter into a desperate competition, the results of which are frequently uncertain.

*

6. *Scientific knowledge* is a type of knowledge which tends towards disinterestedness ('neither laughter, nor tears' according to Spinoza), openness, accumulation, organization, a balance and conjunction of the conceptual and the empirical. It springs from what are essentially constructed, operative frameworks, which are justified by the results obtained, and themselves often require experimental verification. Except in the ancient city, where science was not completely differentiated from philosophy, scientific knowledge has occupied a predominant position in the hierarchy of knowledge only in certain types of capitalist structures, especially competitive capitalism. Since the advent of industrial society it has entered into competition with philosophical knowledge, which, as a result, has had to give way to it.

In spite of its pretensions to be 'above the melée', i.e. detached from social frameworks, scientific knowledge has but a relative independence, and the great error of positivism was to take these pretensions literally. In all scientific knowledge social correlates intervene, and the more developed the knowledge, the stronger the correlates.

[1] Proudhon's term in *De la capacité politique des classes ouvrières*, 1865 (edn. Rivière, 1859). Cf. on this subject p. 237 of the Rivière edition: 'The separation which I recommend is the very condition of life. To be separate and distinct is *to be*; just as to intermingle and to be absorbed is *to be lost*.'

If we consider first of all the exact sciences and the natural sciences exclusively, we can see them affected in four ways by social correlates.

(A) First, this knowledge is based on experience and experimentation, which are always *essentially human* and subject to human influence. Epistemologists of different schools—Leon Brunschvicg, author of *L'expérience humaine et la causalité physique*, 1922, and Gaston Bachelard, for example—have sufficiently demonstrated it in their numerous works.

(B) Second, all science is based on a conjunction between an operative conceptual framework of reference, experience and experimentation: in every science the conceptualizations, which are sometimes backward but most often in advance of their operative effectiveness, also evidence the appearance of social correlates in scientific knowledge. Thus, each new hypothesis, whether justified or not, bears the imprint of the structure of the society in which it was formulated. We have seen Darwinism take up in biology the principle of competition—at work in the capitalism of those days—clearly revealing its ideological nature. This is also present, though less apparent, in quantum physics. Present-day microphysics unconsciously reflects the limits of the amount of atomic energy that the global social structures in conflict in contemporary societies are able to release.

(C) Third, more than all others, the exact sciences need laboratories, research organizations and experimentation on a vast scale, i.e. international as well as national. In the age of atomic energy and electronics, planning of scientific research is necessary. Until public planning attains the necessary extension, it will be a question of competition between private organizations of scientific research, linked to international and national industrial trusts.

(D) Fourth, a connection between sciences and social reality—whether the latter dominates the former due to the 'productive forces' in which they are integrated, or whether social reality is dominated by the sciences—is established by the fact that scientific knowledge requires appropriate means for the dissemination of its results. In teaching, popularization, paperbacks, radio or television, wide-ranging sociological problems arise concerning the ways in which scientific knowledge might be disseminated and controlled. This problem has been tackled in the works of B.

Barber.[1] Also, a well-informed British physicist, J. D. Bernal, has considered all the aspects of the organization and diffusion of the exact sciences in modern societies. A quarter of a century ago, he devoted a very interesting book to their functioning in modern society—*The Social Function of Science*, 1939.

*

The sociology of scientific knowledge is even more interesting if one considers the human sciences, and particularly two of them: history and sociology, the duumvirate destined to crown and guide the sciences of man. Less committed and ideological than the other human sciences, which systematize with practical ends in view, sociology and history cannot, however, be freed from some ideological elements which the sociology of knowledge is able to distinguish. Social frameworks intervene in two ways: first in connection with the growing organization of research, and with the even more relativistic composition of the operative conceptual apparatus, and on the other hand, in connection with the very subject to be studied. Indeed, societies, classes, groups, and the 'We', are involved in dialectical processes and are imbued with human meaning. Nowhere is the claim of scientific knowledge that it remains 'above the melée' less feasible than in this field. If, therefore, the sociology of scientific knowledge is an important part of the sociology of knowledge, the sociology of history and sociology is doubly so.

7. *Philosophical knowledge.* To end this analysis of the types of knowledge as social facts within the realm of sociology, philosophical knowledge remains to be examined.

Being a second-order knowledge, it is grafted retrospectively on to other kinds of knowledge (as on to non-cognitive mental acts), and it strives to integrate these partial aspects into infinite totalities, so as to validate them. In theory this type of knowledge is *exalted, remote, esoteric,* and *élitist.* Although it issues from a dialectic between detached and committed knowledge, *individual knowledge* here predominates over *collective knowledge*; hence the famous 'ivory tower of philosophers'. But, even here, the situation

---

[1] *Science and the Social Order* (1952); (with Hirsch) *The Sociology of Science* (1962).

is paradoxical. Philosophy is crystallized into sharply contrasting doctrines; various schools are formed which are reminiscent of churches and are in perpetual conflict. Moreover, it should be noticed that the relationship between philosophical knowledge and scientific knowledge remains complex, long after the period when the predominance of the former seems quite indisputable.

All science has a need for a refined, operative conceptual tool, which is constantly being renewed as a function of research. From this point of view, it cannot dispense with epistemology and, consequently, philosophy. And this does not only apply to the human sciences. It is precisely within the natural sciences and particularly the exact sciences, in mathematics, physics and biology, that during the last quarter of a century the most lively discussions have occurred (conflicts between intuitionists and those who favour the predominance of conceptual constructions, determinists and indeterminists, continuists and discontinuists, mechanists and vitalists). But these conflicts have not in any way compromised the 'maturity' of these sciences.

In fact, philosophy and science have common methodological ground: the need for the preliminary eradication of mummified operative frameworks, the suppression of ossified concepts and dogmatized experience. The rigorous test of dialectical hyper-empiricism frees both science and philosophy from preconception. At the same time, this dialectic establishes relationships between philosophical knowledge and scientific knowledge which are either complementary, polarized, ambiguous, mutually implicated, or sustain a reciprocity of perspectives. Everything depends on the question posed at the particular moment of a science's interaction with philosophical knowledge.

Here one begins to get an idea of how much more difficult the sociology of philosophical knowledge will be than the sociology of scientific knowledge. Furthermore, the crystallization into philosophical doctrines and schools, which sometimes reappear hundreds and even thousands of years apart in completely different types of societies, indicates a need for caution on our part. The re-interpretation of these doctrines, the modification of their meaning, can obviously be seen in a sociological perspective. It is a sign of the immaturity of the sociology of knowledge that it experiences difficulty when confronted by the history of philosophy. It is this which particularly attracted the attention of the Marxist writers, whilst the sociology of other types of knowledge, though much more accessible, has so far been of little interest to them.

Analysis of the variations in the hierarchy of the types of knowledge as a function of types of societies leads us to the following conclusion: philosophical knowledge occupied first place only in the ancient city, and in societies at the beginning of capitalism, where it was the basis of the Enlightenment. In modern times, it is obviously supplanted by technical and political knowledge.

Before directly relating the types of knowledge to social frameworks, we have still to undertake a final, more abstract analysis, and to meet a criticism.

We have already pointed out in the introduction that within the types of knowledge one could pick out various emphasized *forms of knowledge*; these are also modified as a function of social frameworks and can, if need be, serve to characterize both the variable systems of the types of knowledge, and each one of these types in its relation to the social frameworks.

Here are the five dichotomies of the forms of knowledge which are differently emphasized within each type of knowledge:

1. Mystical knowledge and rational knowledge.
2. Empirical knowledge and conceptual knowledge.
3. Positive knowledge and speculative knowledge.
4. Symbolic knowledge and concrete knowledge.
5. Collective knowledge and individual knowledge.

Since all knowledge is a dialectical combination of experiences and judgements, and since this combination itself can assume different characteristics (arising from complementarity, ambiguity, polarization or mutual implication), the forms of knowledge only rarely appear in a relatively pure form; they are more likely to appear as tendencies or colorations.

Nevertheless, to avoid any misunderstanding, we shall comment on each of these dichotomies.

1. *Mystical knowledge and rational knowledge.* The mystical element, i.e. the supernatural, can originate in judgement or experience, but usually it is experience which comes under its influence. It is only in archaic societies—those with what Lévy-Bruhl called 'primitive mentality', which permits the affective nature of the

supernatural to predominate—that mystical knowledge, originating in experience and judgement, triumphs over all the other forms. Its mystical nature diminishes in relation to its conceptualization into theogonic–cosmogonic myths. It also diminishes in magical knowledge: the rational element in magic—the desire to dominate nature and the Other—is usually opposed to mysticism or else is combined with it.

In all other societies, the mystical or rational form of knowledge depends as much on the types of knowledge as on the social frameworks and circumstances. Apart from theology, where mysticism and rationality are always combined, philosophical knowledge and political knowledge, depending on their orientation, may be consciously directed towards either the mystical or the rational. On the other hand, the perceptual knowledge of the external world, knowledge of the Other and the We, technical knowledge and common sense knowledge, in their way of combining mysticism and rationality, are entirely influenced by the environment of the society in which they develop. Perhaps one might place scientific knowledge apart from all the other types of knowledge, since it is unquestionably the least subject to mystical coloration. Obviously this is a borderline case. A few exceptions should be mentioned: was not the mystique of Pythagorean numbers one of the sources of mathematics? Did not astrology give birth to astronomy, and alchemy to chemistry?

2. *Empirical knowledge and conceptual knowledge.* This new dichotomy, which in no way impinges on the case already considered above, is a much more relative dichotomy. All knowledge presupposes both experience and conceptualization, although this is a question of degree. The types of knowledge which tend towards the strongest conceptualization are philosophical knowledge, scientific knowledge, and high-level technical knowledge. On the other hand, the perceptual knowledge of the external world inclines rather towards empiricism. The knowledge of the Other and the We, political knowledge and common-sense knowledge, which are particularly variable in this respect, are also the most interesting to study in relation to social frameworks.

However, within scientific knowledge, the struggle between the conceptual and the empirical evolves not only as a function of the phases through which the different sciences pass, but also as a function of the social frameworks in which they occur. Thus, sociology, which in theory ought to maintain equilibrium, between the empirical and the conceptual, in practice bifurcates towards one or the other, as a function of the struggle necessary for its growth, but also as a function of the society in which it exists: in the United States there is an exaggeration of the empirical form; in the U.S.S.R. an exaggeration of the conceptual form; in France there is an attempt to balance the two.

3. *Positive knowledge and speculative knowledge.* We should be committing a grave error if we were to regard positive knowledge as the same as empirical knowledge, and speculative knowledge as the same as conceptual knowledge. In favourable conditions, empirical knowledge may become speculative, and conceptual knowledge may also appear to be positive. It required the positivist philosophy of the first half of the nineteenth century to make the claim that scientific knowledge, summoned to replace every other type of knowledge, should only be positive. Rather it is common-sense knowledge and the perceptual knowledge of the external world which tend towards the *positive* in the sense of fidelity to traditions, stereotypes or established practice.

Let us be clear: if by positive one means the refusal to risk new hypotheses, or to venture outside the beaten paths, one will say that cautious, conformist knowledge is positive. In this case, speculative knowledge would be defined on the contrary by its ability to assume new initiatives or to advance in unknown directions. If one examines the history of science one finds that all the great scientific discoveries have been made as a result of risky speculations, which were later verified. Not only philosophical knowledge, but also technical and scientific knowledge, favour the speculative form rather than the positive.

Such is not the case for the other types of knowledge (knowledge of the Other and the We, political knowledge, the perceptual knowledge of the external world, etc): their variations with regard to the positive and speculative form require a special study.

4. *Symbolic knowledge and relatively concrete knowledge.* This dichotomy in the forms of knowledge is particularly relative, since there are no grounds for thinking that we could arrive at a completely concrete knowledge. In all that concerns this form of

knowledge, it can therefore only be a question of degree. However, we must not confuse signs and symbols nor inordinately extend the domain of the symbolic. Signs are expressions which serve as substitutes for meaning and fulfil the function of intermediaries between this meaning and the individual or collective subjects called to comprehend it. For example, an arrow indicating the route to be taken to get to a certain place is a sign whose meaning is: here is the shortest way to reach the place you want. This raises a question: is there a specific type of knowledge or even a system of types of knowledge which might content itself with signs? This seems highly doubtful to us, provided that one does not confuse signs and symbols.

Symbols (as we have already defined them in our earlier works)[1] *are the signs (i.e. substitutes invoking absent things) which only partially express that which is absent, and serve as mediators between the real (or unreal) contents that go beyond the collective and individual consciousness that formulates them and to which they are addressed. This mediation, among other things, promotes the mutual participation of the agents in the contents, and the contents in the agents.*

One of the essential characteristics of symbols is that they reveal while veiling and veil while revealing, and promote participation, while preventing or restraining it, yet nevertheless encouraging this participation. . . .

The whole of social life is filled with symbols of different kinds,[2] but since knowledge as a social fact interests us, we shall dwell more on the symbols which are *predominantly intellectual*: those which consist of representations, measures, various concepts of time and space; logical categories; great mathematical concepts which evoke the idea of the infinite (differential and integral calculus); symbols serving as the basis of the conceptual apparatus of the different sciences.

One speaks of symbolic knowledge mainly when symbols tend to create concepts or schematic ideas of the contents that they are called upon to express. On the other hand, one could designate as relatively concrete that knowledge in which contents clearly predominate over symbols. Thus, political knowledge, knowledge

---

[1] Cf. *La vocation actuelle de la sociologie*, vol. I (3rd edn., 1963), pp. 89–98, and *Déterminismes sociaux et liberté humaine* (2nd edn., 1963), pp. 143–51.

[2] *La vocation actuelle de la sociologie*, pp. 93–4.

of the Other and the We and common-sense knowledge have a marked tendency towards the symbolic form. This is so much more marked in these types of knowledge that the emotive coloration of symbols forcefully intervenes to limit considerably their intellectual character. Technical knowledge tends rather towards concrete knowledge, except in archaic societies where the techniques are linked to magic. Finally, the perceptual knowledge of the external world, scientific knowledge and philosophical knowledge, depending upon their orientations, social conjunctures and types of society, oscillate between the two poles of this dichotomy. This brings us to one general consideration: the emphasized forms of knowledge should always be studied through the types of knowledge and their systems. Thus we are brought to the primordial search for functional relationships between social frameworks and types of knowledge.

We are thus forewarned against any temptation to establish too direct a functional correlation between the types of social wholes and the forms of knowledge. If, for example, we analyse as rich a social framework as social classes—peasantry, bourgeoisie, proletariat, or technocrats—we realize that each of the four is the source of many fluctuations with regard to the emphasized forms of knowledge. Mystical or rational knowledge, empirical or conceptual, positive or speculative, symbolic or relatively concrete, collective or individual, are evident (or have been evident) forms of knowledge depending on the various global structures and conjunctures, and depending on the types of knowledge which prevail or have prevailed.

One can therefore establish this general rule which is equally valid for all the levels of social frameworks to which we shall relate knowledge (microsocial and groupal frameworks, social classes, and global societies): *the forms of knowledge serve only to characterize the fluctuations in types of knowledge and in cognitive systems*; they constitute reference points necessary for a study of the functional correlations between knowledge and social reality, but to relate them directly to the social frameworks most often leads to erroneous conclusions.

*

We are now in a position to specify the main divisions of this book.

In the *first part*, we shall study the types of knowledge as a function of manifestations of sociality; in other words, we shall try to establish a *microsociology of knowledge.*

In the *second part, we shall relate the types of knowledge* and, in certain cases, the cognitive systems, *to certain particular groups* which seem especially suitable as frameworks of knowledge. We shall limit our choice to groups which are noted for their *mode of access* and their *functions*, restricting ourselves to a few examples.

In the *third part*, we shall study the types and systems of knowledge related to social classes.

Finally, the *fourth* and perhaps the most important part, seeks to relate cognitive systems to types of global societies. This part appears to be the most significant because it allows us to verify the success or failure of the preceding sections: indeed, the correlation of knowledge with manifestations of sociality, certain particular groups, and social classes attains its full significance only if it facilitates the study of relationships between systems of knowledge and global social structures.

PART ONE
Microsociology of Knowledge

CHAPTER ONE

Preliminary Considerations

In approaching the microsociology of knowledge, we shall begin by responding to an objection which is frequently raised; one which we have already implicitly dismissed in the introduction: is the microsociology of knowledge possible and useful? We have already shown that the correlation of cognitive systems with types of global structures of society seemed to be the most attractive and fruitful task of the sociology of knowledge. Can it be accomplished without the help of a microsociology and a sociology of groups viewed as frameworks of knowledge? As a general rule, it seems as impossible to undertake microsociology without considering groups and global societies as to attempt macrosociology without considering microsociology. If the analysis is conducted properly, macrosociology must be rediscovered through microsociology and vice versa; likewise, to begin with the sociology of groups, necessarily leads to either microsociology on the one hand, or global sociology and sociology of social classes on the other. This is as true for the real social frameworks as for their conceptualization in the social types at different levels. The manifestations of sociality, groups, and social classes change their character as a function of the global societies in which they exist; inversely, global societies are modified at all levels under the influence of the changing hierarchy and orientation of the forms of sociality. There is therefore a dialectic between the partial and the global, which assumes the character of complementarity, mutual implication, polarization, or reciprocity of perspectives—a dialectic which is characteristic of the whole of social life.[1]

However, concerning cultural products and especially the types and forms of knowledge, the objection to which we are responding rests on an implicit, entirely dogmatic, presupposition: that knowledge and the collective mentality which serves as its basis should only be related to global societies and social classes, given

[1] Cf. *Dialectique et Sociologie*, pp. 189–220.

45

that these social frameworks have such a strong influence on the knowledge of the groups and the knowledge corresponding to manifestations of sociality that they completely modify the cognitive tendencies of these social frameworks.

This objection implies a rather widespread preconception which attributes a much greater independence and effectiveness to knowledge (and all cultural products in general) than in the complex web of social reality they in fact possess. In completely rejecting *'abstract culturalism'*[1] (which is nothing but a disguise for an idealist philosophy), we do not want either to neglect or to exaggerate the importance of the microsociology of knowledge (which is not more than the study of relationships between particular groups and knowledge). As we have already said many times, we recognize that the usefulness of these studies will only be finally brought out by the correlation between *systems of knowledge* and *global societies*—these macrocosms of classes, groups, and manifestations of sociality.

*

We shall now return to our definitions of the microsocial frameworks which we shall correlate with the types and forms of knowledge.

The manifestations of sociality represent the many forms of integration into a whole or by a whole. They compete, complement or combine with each other to different degrees in each real collective unit. They are total social phenomena, but of a fluctuating, unstable, mostly spontaneous, even astructural nature; nevertheless, they are used by the real macrosociological collective units in their process of structuration.

We have taken the opportunity in our various works to stress the distinction between 'sociality by partial fusion' and 'sociality by partial opposition'; the first is manifest in participation in the

[1] Cf. on the subject of 'abstract culturalism', my polemical discussions in the *Traité de Sociologie*, vol. I (2nd edn., 1963), ch. i, pp. 7–8. Also see *La vocation actuelle de la sociologie* I (3rd edn., 1963), 50 ff. As representatives of 'abstract culturalism', one can quote German theorists—from Rudolph Stammler to Max Weber—and particularly the American ethnologists and sociologists with their 'cultural anthropology'. Of the American sociologists, the work of Talcott Parsons—that incarnation of the sclerosis of American sociological theory— merits a special mention *as a frightful example of the vacuity* to which 'abstract culturalism' leads.

'We', the second in relationships with the Other, which can be either inter-personal (Me, You, Him) or inter-groupal.

To attain our ends it will be sufficient if we confine ourselves to sociality through partial participation in the 'We', and to classify the aspects of it according to the measure of its intensity. This is because, with regard to cultural products in general and knowledge in particular, the 'We' are infinitely richer social frameworks than the 'relationships with the Other'. In fact, fusion into the 'We' is not only an awareness of its relative unity, but also that of a whole world of meanings which are otherwise inaccessible. On the other hand 'relationships with the Other', even the most restricted ones, are confined to the rather limited horizons of 'partners' and for the most part are restricted to reproducing the collective judgements, ideas, symbols and signs of a 'We', a group, a class or a global society.

The three degrees of intensity of the 'We' are the Mass, the Community and the Communion.[1] The *mass* constitutes the minimum degree of *participation* in the 'We'; the whole exercises on its participants the strongest *pressure* and the weakest *attraction*. Its size allows for the possibility of an almost unlimited expansion. By *community* we mean the medium degree of intensity in *participation* in the 'We', accompanied by a medium *pressure* and a medium *attraction* exercised by the whole on its participants; its size therefore admits of only a limited expansion. Finally, in *communion* one sees the maximum degree of intensity in participation in the 'We'; it is accompanied by very weak *pressure* and very strong *attraction* exercised by the whole on its participants; its size tends to diminish in order to maintain the strength and depth of the fusion.

[1] Cf. for a detailed analysis, *La vocation actuelle de la sociologie*, I (3rd edn., 1963), 116–245, particularly pp. 143–78.

CHAPTER TWO

Masses as Social Frameworks of Knowledge

Masses are especially prominent as social frameworks of knowledge when they appear in social classes, and global societies, or at least in large-scale groups, such as the state, the church, political parties and trades unions (and much less so when they appear in families, local groups, factories, etc.).

The perceptual knowledge of the external world and political knowledge claim first place when related to masses. Scientific and technical knowledge can sometimes be perceived here, but at a rather low level of popularization and diffusion. Other kinds of knowledge—philosophical knowledge particularly, but also knowledge of the Other and the We, and even common-sense knowledge—are obviously not favoured. If their presence is sometimes observed in masses, it is essentially through the intermediary of political knowledge inasmuch as it allows itself to be guided by slogans, utopias and myths.

We shall begin with the perceptual knowledge of the external world. For passive masses,[1] the known external world is placed in autistic, egocentric space, which is often diffuse and sometimes limited by the adequacy of the models current in the social frameworks into which the masses are integrated. Thus, the mass of the unemployed place the external world in extensions related to their most urgent needs: a job, assistance, food. That mass of people who speak and read the same language, beyond national frontiers, divide the external world according to the validity of their language patterns. The world known by passive masses is placed in diffuse and arhythmic time of irregular pulsations. It fluctuates unexpectedly, but tends to be time of long duration or 'retarding' time, or, though more rarely, 'dance in place', i.e. cyclical, time. Space clearly predominates over time, which is still barely perceptible.

The situation changes considerably when the masses become

[1] Cf. on the distinction between 'passive sociality' and 'active sociality' my *Vocation actuelle de la sociologie*, I, 178–86.

active. Their knowledge of the world is then strongly oriented as a function of their action, their impatience and their initiative. This applies to discontented masses, revolutionary masses or ecstatic masses. Time and especially future time, as well as discontinuity of succession, then begin to prevail over the space in which the external world is placed. In the knowledge of the active masses, 'time in advance of itself' may predominate, which leads to the external world being divided into hostile or friendly zones, favourable or unfavourable to this time.

As for the forms of knowledge, the masses' knowledge of the external world inclines towards the symbolic, speculative and collective forms. When masses become active, the conceptual form takes precedence over the empirical.

Let us now consider the masses' political knowledge; all that has just been said is here confirmed. This knowledge, implicit in passive masses, becomes explicit as soon as active masses appear.

Passive masses give hardly any evidence of political knowledge except negatively, i.e. through indifference—paradoxical though that may seem—or even through abstention in certain circumstances, in anticipation of a more favourable moment. This abstention of the passive masses is, then, only superficial. It is dictated by a partisan knowledge which is committed and tactical—it is often only half-conscious, though, at its best, it is fully comprehended.

In active masses, political knowledge assumes a conceptual form. On the one hand political symbols are conceptualized and formulated as myths appealing for action; on the other hand, the means of effectively and rapidly attaining the objectives implied in the symbols and myths are also conceptualized. This two-fold conceptualization constitutes what is called either the 'programme' of a political party, its 'declarations' or its 'resolutions'. Conceptualized in this way, this knowledge is less the product of the masses than of the macrosocial frameworks (parties and social classes) where it occurs. However, the success or failure of the programmes is most often a function of their congruence or lack of congruence with the action and the direct political knowledge of the masses.

In conclusion we must point out a final characteristic of the active masses as social frameworks of political knowledge: their tendency to make political knowledge dominate all other kinds of

knowledge. Thus, knowledge of the Other and the We is transformed into recognition of adversaries and allies, and the perceptual knowledge of the external world turns to the investigation of
opposing sides. Common-sense knowledge, technical and scientific
knowledge are also politicized when they depend on active masses
as frames of reference. However, it should not be forgotten that
this tendency of the masses can be radically modified by the
groups, classes and societies in which they are integrated and
embodied; it can also be counterbalanced by other manifestations
of the We: communities and communions.

CHAPTER THREE

Communities as Social Frameworks of Knowledge

Communities are distinct from masses and communions in that they are particularly conducive to knowledge. Perhaps this is the reason why certain sociologists, and particularly French followers of the late Emmanuel Mounier, believed it possible to attribute a greater value to communities than to masses and communions. But knowledge is obviously not the only criterion for establishing a hierarchy between mass, community and communion, and so an abstract, *a priori* hierarchy remains impossible. The relative importance of communities depends on the macrosociological structures where they occur, and their cognitive contents (types and forms of knowledge) or their moral and aesthetic contents.

Communities are manifestations of the most balanced form of sociality and, for this reason, the most durable; they appear most frequently within groups, classes and global societies. This is why, all other conditions aside, they tend to favour rather regular behaviour, and more or less pre-established and stereotyped functioning of models, signals and symbols. This, in the majority of cases, creates a halo of rationality around communities, and an atmosphere conducive to all types of knowledge, with the possible exception of philosophical knowledge. When it assumes the character of a school or a philosophical trend, philosophical knowledge is much more favoured by the communion than the community. This is not so for the other types of knowledge, especially for the perceptual knowledge of the external world, or knowledge of the Other, common-sense knowledge, political knowledge and technical knowledge. But science alone creates teams of scholars and researchers, springing directly from communities.

Communities, whilst being the most common and durable microsocial phenomena, at least in theory, cannot be considered identical with groupings[1] (i.e. partial macrosociological collective

[1] The error to which we refer, which is very widespread, results largely from

units), which will be studied in relation to knowledge in the second part of this book. This applies even when communities are active (which is not always the case). Indeed, communities, like all manifestations of sociality, remain spontaneous and fluctuating, despite their tendency to maintain a balance. This is why communities as such have no specific structure of their own, but adopt the structure of the groups in which they succeed in dominating the mass and the communion. This is also why there can be no question of searching for *cognitive systems* corresponding to communities. It can only be a matter of pointing out the types of knowledge which operate in communities rather than ordering them in a precise, relatively stable hierarchy.

Concerning the *perceptual knowledge of the external world*, communities are much more *extroverted* than the other 'We'. In this knowledge, *prospective space* combined with *projective* space take precedence, whilst autistic and egocentric space become blurred. In the same way, space widens and contracts without difficulty, losing its concentric nature. The external world is placed in a fairly continuous time, where present, past and future, advanced

the vocabulary used. 'Community' recalls to mind the 'commune', as a small-scale local grouping, or conversely 'the national community' and even international communities ('The Community of the French Union' or the 'Coal and Steel Community' leading to the 'Common Market'). It is obvious that in these latter cases, one is speaking of macrosocial units such as Nations—'Global Societies' in our terms—or of even larger collective units that one would like to see emerge. All this clearly has no relationship with the 'Community' as the medium degree of the intensity of the 'We' conceived as a microsocial element which can appear in any sort of group. Moreover, the term 'Community' has produced real havoc in American sociology. The works of R. M. MacIver, beginning with his book, *Community*, have introduced a striking confusion between local groupings of various sizes, and sociality as '*mutual understanding*' ('*entente*') which goes beyond simple 'relationships with the Other'—Tönnies' 'Gemeinschaft' type, as opposed to 'Gesellschaft', though partly freed from its semi-instinctive, semi-mystical nature. On this confused and imprecise foundation a series of works by American sociologists has been constructed, such as those of R. D. Makensie, *The Metropolitan Community* (1937); Dwight Sanderson, *The Rural Community* (1938); C. Zimmerman, *The Changing Community* (1938); and W. L. Warner and P. S. Lunt, *The Social Life of a Modern Community* (1941). We quote these works merely to show that our conception of the community as a microsocial element has nothing to do with these American-style 'Community-Studies', where the term community has been applied to the 'most heterogeneous groups' (P. Sorokin, *Society, Culture and Personality* (1947), pp. 242–3) and, as another American critic said: '*The community remains (in the United States) one of the vaguest sociological concepts*' (L. Wilson, 'Sociographie des groupements', in *La sociologie au XX*e *siècle*, under my editorship, vol. I (French trans., 1947), p. 109).

and retarding time tend to be in equilibrium. This is why, *in knowledge of the external world, when communities are the source, time and space lend themselves to conceptualization, measurement and even to quantification.* All these elements emanate either from large-scale groups (churches, states), or from global societies into which communities are integrated and within which they stimulate this tendency. Thus we can observe that in societies where communities have predominated—ancient city-states, the free towns of the Middle Ages, Renaissance societies, and societies corresponding to competitive capitalism—the perceptual knowledge of the external world was clearly favoured, and assumed a rational, somewhat concrete form, balancing the speculative and the positive.

Knowledge of the Other also occupies a special position in communities; yet we must specify what we mean by the Other in groups and global societies where communities exist. Keeping to our former example, in the ancient cities, the Other is the fellow-citizen, not the alien and certainly not the slave. Until the present time, knowledge of the Other played an important role only in societies of a feudal and patriarchal nature. Other types of global societies have in fact always impeded the tendency of communities to favour this type of knowledge. Doubtless it would be quite different in a decentralized collectivist society, based on workers' self-management.

As a rule, communities as such encourage *common-sense knowledge*, for they favour models and rules and give them a rational colouring. It is the communities which, inasmuch as they are preserved in families, small-scale local groupings, etc., enable common-sense knowledge to survive in our society, which is rather hostile to this kind of knowledge. This shows once again with what difficulty the 'We', as community, poorly withstands the global or partial structures in which it exists.

When communities are dominant in a group, class or global society, they rationalize political knowledge to a certain extent. They liberate it from exaggerated symbolism, mythologies and utopias. Under their influence it tends to become more positive than speculative. We have already seen that masses have the opposite effect on this type of knowledge, and we shall see that with communions this is again the case.

As *frameworks of technical knowledge*, communities, which

favour models and stereotypes, help to maintain existing technical knowledge at a certain level; on the other hand, when this knowledge results from team work (factory, office, laboratory, etc.) communities can contribute to the improvement or even the discovery of new technical knowledge. This has happened fairly often, notably at the beginning of industrialization. But, in the present phase of industrial society, the innovative role of communities of workers has become minimal, due to the extreme complexity of technology.

CHAPTER FOUR

Communions as Social Frameworks of Knowledge

With few exceptions, communions are much less favourable to knowledge than are communities and even masses. Whether they are active or passive, they tend to turn in on themselves, to enclose themselves in their own world in a sort of collective solipsism. By thus characterizing communions, we are not concentrating solely on their mystical character, which is not at all necessary, since communions can be rational (as for example between philosophers or partisans of a political doctrine) or be based on socio-political action. What we are concerned with is the tendency of communions of all kinds towards division and limitation: a communion in fact has no means of resisting the threat of rupture between its intensity and its extension, except by sacrificing extension to division.

Of the types of knowledge, communions usually favour only knowledge of themselves, i.e. their We, political knowledge and cosmothoeogonic knowledge; the perceptual knowledge of the external world is also acknowledged, although distorted. Other types of knowledge are hardly ever found here, except in a few quite exceptional cases: for example, a communion of researchers at the time of a great scientific discovery, or a communion of experts stirred by a philosophical revelation of universal significance.

Their knowledge of the 'We' is egotistic, and this has a two-fold sense. 'Outsiders', whether they are other 'We's' or individual non-participants, are unappreciated or even despised. Now, the communion subjects these reluctant or indifferent outsiders, who are not susceptible to its appeal, to the maximum of pressure in contrast to the amount applied to its members, which is minimal.

Communions tend to move in a time in advance of itself, a propulsive time. But, given their introverted character, their 'celebrations of the future' are easily transformed into a cyclical movement, a kind of dance in place, from which time in advance of itself offers no escape. To tear communions from their isolation requires exceptional circumstances, such as large-scale strikes, victorious revolutions or the beginning of great religious movements.

Political knowledge, which communions favour, is less dependent on tactics than ideals; it is characterized by a strong emphasis on the symbolic form, intensified by the predominance of either myth or utopia, or a combination of the two.

In archaic societies, it was probably the communions which acted as sources for mystical experiences, rationalized in cosmotheogonic myths. But in historic societies, it is difficult to establish direct links between the communions of believers and the dogma formulated by the theologians.[1]

With regard to the perceptual knowledge of the external world in communions, we must note that, for them, the space in which this world is placed, is identical with their members and the shared rites, models, signs and symbols. Therefore space is essentially autistic, egocentric and concentric. The time of communions about which we have already spoken is that time in which they place the external world: it is, beneath the apparent urgency, the cyclical time of the eternal round.

*

These brief reflections on certain aspects of the microsociology of knowledge may seem rather schematic and therefore somewhat disappointing. We must not forget, however, that we are involved in pioneer work, and that this microsociology will become more concrete when we take the macrosocial frameworks of knowledge as reference points: particular groupings, classes, and, of course, global societies. It is here that it will be justified and effective.

---

[1] One might quote as an exception the Quaker sect whose trust is placed in communion based on silence.

PART TWO

Particular Groups as Social Frameworks of Knowledge

CHAPTER ONE

Preliminary Considerations

We now intend to study the primary manifestations of microsocial frameworks: *particular groups as sources of knowledge.*

In order to be able to talk about a *group* it is essential that, in a partial social framework, centripetal forces predominate to a certain extent over centrifugal forces; it is also essential that the convergent 'We' prevails over the divergent 'We'. The unity of the group cannot be reduced to the plurality of manifestations of sociality. In effect, *every particular group* is already a *microcosm of the manifestations of sociality*, just as classes and global societies are in turn macrocosms of groups.

In our earlier works we defined particular groups thus: 'The group is a real but partial collective unit, directly observable, based on continuous and active collective attitudes, having a common task to accomplish, a unity of attitudes, tasks and behaviour, which constitutes a structurable social framework, tending towards a relative cohesion of the manifestations of sociality.'[1]

---

[1] Cf. *La vocation actuelle de la sociologie*, I (3rd edn., 1963), 305, and more generally, ch. v, pp. 284–357.

CHAPTER TWO

Groups Distinguished by their Mode of Access and Knowledge

According to the criterion of mode of access to a group one can distinguish: (a) open groups; (b) groups with conditional access; (c) closed groups. Among the open groups, besides actual groupings such as different publics, age groupings, etc., we should mention crowds, demonstrations, meetings, rescue teams, certain philanthropic groups, etc. It is clear that open groups do not generally represent specific sources of knowledge, with the exception of groups of young people or the elderly, to the extent that they constitute real collective units. Thus, elderly people as a group can, in certain types of global social structures, make their cognitive system predominate over all other knowledge in their society. It is then considered to be a group of 'wise men'—sole bearers of esoteric knowledge as well as knowledge accepted for general diffusion—which is the case in patriarchal, or simply traditional, societies. The most curious fact here is that the 'open groups' of old people imperceptibly become transformed into closed groups.

From this point of view, closed groups are easier to study as social frameworks of knowledge. Closed groups have been very widespread in types of society other than our own; today they are the exception. Examples are certain trusts and cartels, the famous 'two hundred families' of pre-war France, groups such as the nobility or the *haute bourgeoisie*, which recruited only by birth or heritage. Here again it is a question of social frameworks which are not very favourable to fundamental knowledge.

It is clear that every organized group is also structured. However, a group may not only be structurable, but also structured, without also being organized, nor even capable of being expressed in a single organization (such as social classes, which are a patent example of this). Further, when organization enters into the equilibrium of a structure, it is no more than one element, and not even an indispensable one at that.

Structured groups clearly offer more precise and more easily utilized reference points in the study of the types and forms of knowledge than non-structured groupings. In fact, in structured groups, knowledge, like other cultural works, acts as a cementing element in the structure.

We shall, therefore, be content to deal with structured groups. The general schema of the classification of groups that we suggested in our earlier works included fifteen, often interrelated, criteria;[1] we shall be concerned only with distinct groups: (1) according to their *mode of access*;[2] (2) according to their *functions*;[3] (3) within the latter, the blocs of *multi-functional groupings*, such as *states* and *churches*, which often claim to be 'suprafunctional', that is to say incarnating the global society—in which respect they are always mistaken. . . .[4]

For each of these three cases, we shall limit ourselves in the following section, to a few examples.

We shall retain only one of these characteristics: that of the 'structurable, if not structured, framework'. Structure is always a precarious equilibrium of multiple hierarchies. The structurable character of a group arises first of all from the fact that its unity is realized through the setting up of a kind of special cohesion between the manifestations of sociality, and the collective attitudes, actions, acts, common tasks and their expression in more or less regular collective behaviour. Second, it arises to a large extent from the emergence of equilibrium between a multiple hierarchy of depth levels, social rules, temporalities, mental colorations, etc. Finally, this same structurable character of the group comes also from the fact that its integration in a social class or in a global society tends to be manifested in the accommodation it reaches in its relations with the other groups, and in the role and place that it occupies in the particular hierarchy of groups that are characteristic of a given global society.

Briefly, the term 'structurable' as applied to groups designates a tendency to establish an internal system of multiple hierarchies, and a tendency for the group to be seen externally in terms of its position, role, and relationships. If this tendency reaches fruition,

---

[1] *La vocation actuelle de la sociologie*, vol. (3rd edn., 1963), 308–57.
[2] Ibid., pp. 327 ff.
[3] Ibid., pp. 333 ff.
[4] Ibid., pp. 338 ff.

and if this precarious equilibrium is attained, the group is structured, which is not to say that it is organized. Thus old people,
groups of young people, certain professions, are structured groups
at the present time, but they are usually unorganized, even though
they can sometimes be partially represented in different organizations. Conversely, various publics, ethnic minorities, producers
and consumers, industries, age groups or 'generations' (with the
exception of those that we have mentioned), are structurable
groups that are, however, only rarely structured.

In so far as cognitive systems appear here, they are reduced to
certain political, technical, and common-sense types of knowledge,
combined differently according to the character of the closed
groups and the circumstances in which they are situated. The
emphasis of this knowledge varies, moreover, according to the
types of global society in which the closed groups are integrated.
But whether they are a caste of priests, a feudal group, the military
or civil nobility, the highest strata of the bourgeoisie, national or
international trusts or cartels, their specific knowledge, as opposed
to that of the global society, is small and shows a tendency towards
the hermetic and esoteric, even when the rational form triumphs
completely and leads to the improved calculations of complex
financial accounting. . . .

Among groups that are distinguishable by their mode of access,
those which have most to offer the sociology of knowledge in its
present state, are the groups with conditional or even restricted
access—for example, the privileged professional groups, which
demand of their members qualifications that are obtained through
competition (*agrégation,* for admission to the teaching profession;[1]
law degree, for the bar and the magistrature; diplomas bestowed
by the *École des Sciences Politiques* or the *École Nationale d'Administration,* for top level diplomatic or administrative careers). Some
of these professional groups are subject to organized control. Thus,
the community of doctors and the community of lawyers have the
right to forbid any members judged unworthy to practise their
profession.

The same applies with regard to the careers of university professors and the *Grandes écoles techniques* (including *l'École Polytechnique, l'École des Mines, l'École des Ponts et Chaussées,* etc.).

[1] *Translators' Note: agrégation*—competitive examination conducted by the
state for admission to posts on the teaching staff of the *lycées.*

In theory, establishments of higher education recruit their members by co-optation, whether or not supported by diplomas, and competitive election (doctorate with honourable mention, and inscription on the special aptitude list, for the faculty of letters; *agrégation* following two doctorates, for the faculty of law, etc.). However, there exist establishments of higher education based exclusively on co-optation, e.g. the *Collège de France, l'École Pratique des Hautes Études*, etc.

We shall deal more fully with the case of the Faculties (Letters, Law, Medicine, etc.) and other similar establishments. Depending on their specializations and their professorial chairs, all these institutions are sources of scientific, technical or philosophical knowledge. Their aim is to develop, teach or disseminate it. Other types of knowledge occupy a minor place. Nevertheless, certain types play a role in the functioning of these establishments; in particular, 'political knowledge' in administration, as well as common-sense knowledge, and even in certain cases knowledge of the Other and the We. In this cognitive system, perceptual knowledge of the external world, being limited, remains in the background.

Before continuing this analysis of the incidence in universities and similar establishments of types of knowledge other than those which are the subject of research and teaching, it is important to note that the scientific, technical and philosophical knowledge of the university are all characterized by emphasis on the same forms of knowledge. The conceptual, symbolic, positive, collective, and rational predominate, so much so that knowledge as conceived and taught in the universities remains partly esoteric, hermetic, and traditional, if not ossified.

Here the sociology of knowledge reveals a paradoxical situation. It is clear that these are the groups called upon to stimulate and further the progress of these most important types of knowledge, and yet, without any deliberate intention, but simply by their very functioning, they often halt its advance and retard or limit its diffusion. This defect of university education is, however, corrected to a certain extent by the competitive spirit that exists between the universities, faculties, and various schools of thought. Nevertheless, it is true that innovation is brought about very slowly, and is undertaken with the utmost caution.

If we consider the other types of knowledge which occur in the internal life of establishments of higher education and their functioning, such as strategic (or political) knowledge, and common-sense knowledge, we note with surprise that they rarely correspond to the level of the knowledge being taught. This apparently paradoxical phenomenon is no less explicable: in fact the professors who are rightly considered to be the most eminent scholars are not necessarily those whose authority is dominant in the faculty meetings and other contexts, when administrative questions are under consideration, for qualities and *knowledge of quite a different type* are required. Finally, knowledge of the Other and the We (i.e. colleagues and students) occurs in the university only if the community succeeds in predominating over the mass and the communion; and this presupposes, among other things, small universities, which are increasingly rare today.

*

In dealing with groups as social frameworks of knowledge, we will pass from groups with more or less limited access, to *groups distinguished according to their functions.*

Here again *we shall limit ourselves to three examples*: the family (Chapter 3), *small-scale local groups* (Chapter 4), and *factories* (Chapter 5). All three are multi-functional groups, whose importance with regard to knowledge, however, is incomparably less than that of states (blocs of local groups), and churches, to which we shall devote the succeeding chapters (Chapters 6 and 7).

CHAPTER THREE

Families and Knowledge[1]

The family as a group naturally changes its character according to the type of global society in which it is integrated and the class to which it belongs. In order to arrive at some precise idea of the family as a source of knowledge, we must start with its most concrete manifestations.

Let us consider a present-day French family, where the wife remains at home and raises several children. If there is harmony we shall see that the *knowledge of the Other and the We* predominates over all other kinds: knowledge between husband and wife, parents and children, and between the children. But let any kind of disharmony or trouble occur in the family, and its members cease to understand each other. They are then divided into opposing camps: parents against children, or one of the parents allied with one of the children against the others. Such a situation is obviously the kind in which knowledge of the Other is obscured. It is in this way that some children remain misunderstood and unappreciated in their own family. This can also happen between the parents.

Another kind of knowledge that tends to play a role in the family when it is functioning normally is *common-sense knowledge*, which the parents are expected to transmit to their children and to apply themselves in order to maintain the smooth running of the family. But, in contemporary life, this type of knowledge seems to be more limited in global societies and social classes. As a result, influences contrary to the *savoir vivre* present in the family are exercised on the parents from the outside (from involvement in work, participation in unions, etc.) and on the children (schools, and the friends that they meet there). Only families from certain backgrounds (the middle classes and peasants) continue to cultivate this kind of knowledge.

[1] The expression *household family* would be scientifically more exact. However, in this chapter, where we shall consider the present-day family—the French family for example, we thought it permissible to use the more common expression 'family'.

It cannot be denied that the functioning of the family requires *political knowledge*, if by that we mean parents' knowledge of the strategy that they must use in the education and upbringing of their children, and likewise, knowledge on the children's part of the means for obtaining the maximum freedom from their parents.

On the other hand, if one takes political knowledge in its most general and usual sense, which implies primarily the adoption of a strictly political position, and knowledge of strategic rules to be followed in the global society, it is less certain that it now holds as important a place in the family group as it did previously, when the family was subject to a long and continuous tradition. Doubtless this was due to the much lower mobility in the class situation of families. We know that mobility is greater today, and that, for a given social stratum, the continuity of political knowledge in the general sense is often broken. By the end of the nineteenth century and the beginning of the twentieth century it was not uncommon to see the sons of the most famous Conservative families in Great Britain change over to the Labour Party, and sometimes even become its leaders. In France, too, sons of orthodox bourgeois families were observed developing into militant socialists and anti-clericals, just as in the reverse case, descendants of socialist families adhere to *l'Action française*.

It seems, therefore, that we are witnessing a progressive decline in the influence of the family on the general political knowledge of its members and descendants; however, this process, despite its development, particularly in the twentieth century, remains limited.

Finally, one can discern the increasing importance of a certain *technical knowledge*, though at a rudimentary level, in the functioning of the family. Thus the handling of household equipment and motor-driven machines requires at least a minimum of information.

The other types of knowledge, particularly scientific and philosophical knowledge, are obviously not encouraged by familial social frameworks. As for perceptual knowledge of the external world, it arises only in certain considerations of a practical nature, concerning the setting-up of the home, its situation and particularly the area, as well as the distance that members of the family must travel to work. It is therefore primarily egocentric.

The most favoured types of knowledge in the contemporary family emphasize particularly the empirical and positive *forms*, whilst the other forms are mid-way between the symbolic and the concrete, allowing for different combinations of the collective and individual, the mystical and rational.

As a source of knowledge, the family is not characterized by great richness; consequently it has no great attractiveness for the sociological study of knowledge. This derives from the fact that, today at least, this group is usually too susceptible and too subject to the cognitive influence of the classes and global societies in which it is integrated.

CHAPTER FOUR

Small-scale Local Groups and Their Knowledge

The situation is somewhat different in 'small-scale local groups' (hamlets, villages, etc.). Their tasks are not only always multi-functional, but can also be precisely delimited. For example, among the 'tasks to be accomplished' which permit of an obvious differentiation are those of keeping order and controlling neigh-bourhood relations, of carrying out economic and administrative activities, and of regulating relationships with other similar local groups, etc. These groups normally tend to favour the growth of communities to the detriment of masses and communions. Whence in part arises the previously mentioned error of most American sociologists, who confuse small-scale local groups with communi-ties, whereas these groups, at certain moments in history and in certain circumstances (wars, revolutions, liberation movements, etc.), cannot avoid the development of communions, or the dissolution of the community into a mass. It would therefore be erroneous to apply directly our conclusions about communities—for example their openness to the perceptual knowledge of the external world—to local groups. Many other factors are operative here, such as their structure and organization.

Nevertheless, leaving aside the influence of social classes and global societies, small-scale local groups are sources of a *specific perceptual knowledge of the external world*. The space in which the world is placed is primarily egocentric and concentric: that of flower and vegetable gardens, fields, forests, roads and communica-tion routes with neighbouring villages and small towns where markets are held. The external world tends to expand but, at the same time, it risks being placed in a diffuse space when it concerns relations with the large towns, the state and its capital (where the centres of administrative and political organization are).

The time in which the external world moves, and the time of which the small-scale local groups are aware, is primarily seasonal (and even cyclical) and time of long duration, which are combined. However, we must acknowledge that local groups apply to these times and to their own familiar space the conceptualizations and measures which come to them from states and churches, or, more generally, from the global societies into which they are integrated. They then see themselves as forced to suppress their concrete, qualitative space, to which they nevertheless remain attached.

These small-scale local groups are also sources of a *common-sense knowledge* which is adapted to their way of life and existence. In the turbulence of present-day life, where common-sense knowledge is being diminished or may even be disappearing, it is often in these groups that it finds its last refuge, since it gradually ceases to have a role within families.

It might be supposed that small hamlets and villages, where neighbourly relationships are very close, might be the source of a profound knowledge of the Other and the We. In fact, recent research invalidates this hypothesis. The Other appears similar to the subject who knows him; the alleged knowledge that he has of him is based on his resemblance to the subject and on his likeness to stereotypes, which usually originate in the global society.[1] It is obviously rather difficult to judge whether this is because of the decomposition of the intellectual and moral intimacy in hamlets and villages (where, for example, television and radio play a part), or whether the relationships of common neighbourliness, characteristic of these groups, are particularly unfavourable to the knowledge of the Other.

Hamlets and villages function also as sources of *technical knowledge*. It is mainly a question of the adaptation of the technical knowledge of agriculture to the specific needs of particular areas. The introduction of other techniques, such as fertilizers and tractors (which are becoming more common), must be attributed to the influence of the global society.

Political knowledge, whether it concerns the tactics to be used in maintaining good relations with neighbours, or participation in the political life of the country (municipal elections, legislative elections, etc.) appears even in local groups; this might serve as a starting point for what is called 'electoral geography' which is often conceived too narrowly. It is not necessary to emphasize

---

[1] Cf. *Enquête sociologique sur la connaissance d'Autrui*, carried out under my supervision by Jean Cazeneuve, P.-H. Maucorps and A. Memmi, *Cahiers Internationaux de Sociologie*, vol. XXIX (1960), especially pp. 151–3.

the fact that small-scale local groups do not serve as sources of scientific or philosophical knowledge.

Of the forms which materialize in the types of knowledge engendered by rural groups, the rational, empirical, and positive are seen to predominate; the presence of these forms makes them akin to families in this respect, but the strength of the symbolic and the collective distinguishes these groups from the family.

CHAPTER FIVE

Factories and Knowledge

We shall discuss *factories* and *workshops* as *social frameworks of knowledge*[1] only very briefly (sometimes the factory is composed of several workshops). We shall consider only *one of their aspects*, that is, groups of workers, irrespective of whether they are qualified or not, whether they use automatic or manual machines, or whether they work on an assembly-line or co-operate on the same job.

In these groups, *technical knowledge*—however low its level—is adapted to machine work, and to attempts to avoid industrial accidents and difficulties in co-operation between members of a team. This type of knowledge tends to predominate in these situations.

Immediately following is *political knowledge*, understood primarily as tactics of adaptation to the moods of team-mates, foremen or engineers. In this respect, it comes close to a *sort of common-sense knowledge* related not to tradition but to the specific environment of the factory. This specialized political knowledge can sometimes enter into conflict with political knowledge at the proletarian and national level and consequently with the attitude of the unions and organizations of worker representation. However, between these two aspects of 'political knowledge', a third is interpolated: the way of expressing discontent, fatigue, and spontaneous opposition to the authoritarian régime in the factories. This kind of political knowledge contributes to the reconciliation and combination of the other two.

[1] In spite of extensive literature devoted to 'industrial sociology'—of a very uneven quality it is true—this is one aspect of a 'new branch' of sociology which has never been very searching. This is because most of its American representatives, like their French rivals (who tend to imitate the Americans) are exclusively concerned with showing that the conflicts which occur in factories and workshops under a capitalist régime will resolve themselves, through . . . the political wisdom of the employer in improving work conditions. Cf. the denunciation of this point of view by Alain Touraine in De l'ambiguité de la sociologie industrielle américaine', in *Cahiers Internationaux de Sociologie*, XII (1952). But neither there nor elsewhere has the problem of the factory as a *social framework of knowledge* been raised.

The perceptual knowledge of the external world is equally specific.
It concerns the external world of the workshop, the factory, and
the enterprise. Its objects are the premises, the machines, the
offices—including those of the directors and engineers—which are
so near and yet so far from the workers; the concrete space and
specific time in which the work and life of the members of the
work-team occurs, whether or not they work on assembly-line
production; and finally the distances to be covered by the workers
to meet their bosses and to get to their machines, and the time
taken up in travelling from home to work.

The quantification of space and time, derived from the corresponding global society, occurs with particular intensity in this
last aspect of the perceptual knowledge of the external world
among groups of workers in the factory.

In this cognitive system *knowledge of the Other and the We* comes
in last place because of the workers' subservience to machines, the
administration of specialist technicians and factory directors. It is
essentially knowledge of the behaviour of comrades at work,
sometimes their conduct in relation to the union—or unions if
there are several of them, or even, should the occasion arise, their
behaviour during a strike. Obviously under a régime of worker
self-management and decentralized collectivism, knowledge of the
Other, in the person of team-mates working on the same job, could
assume very great importance. It has only relatively little importance under the régime of organized capitalism.

*

In the types of knowledge found in the factory, the forms most
emphasized are the concrete, the rational, the empirical, the
positive and the collective. The only exception is political knowledge, at the level of spontaneous opposition to authoritarian
management of the workshop factory, and at the level of union
and proletarian struggle against the global structure of society
under a capitalist régime at whatever phase of development. The
forms of this political knowledge can be characterized by a
relatively strong emphasis on the speculative, the symbolic, and
even the mythological, yet without losing their rational, calculative
and concrete aspects.

CHAPTER SIX

States and their Cognitive Systems

States, although composed of local groups, are not supra-functional, but remain multi-functional like local groups. They are much richer and more varied social frameworks for the different types and forms of knowledge than those dealt with thus far. Nevertheless, they are not identical with global societies which in modern times are composed of nations. Being somewhat less than total social phenomena, states are political societies which are expressed in particular structures, upon which is superimposed an organized apparatus exercising unconditional constraint, known as political sovereignty. Neither the political societies, their structures, nor their organized apparatus possess a universal power, even when they claim to do so. Their power, however great it may be, is ascribed to them by the global society, which alone possesses juridical sovereignty and seeks to maintain its social sovereignty.

Yet, since the birth of industrialization, states have tended to become the instruments of class domination. This is why they always exist in a very tense atmosphere, heavy with internal conflicts (quite independent of international links and participation in alliances, whether legal or factual, which have come to be designated by the term international blocs)[1]: witness the State's struggles with local groups of various sizes (including large towns and regions), tensions between the public services, or between the population as a whole and the army, antagonisms between the legislative, administrative and judicial organs. Another aspect of this resides in the difficulties which arise between the state and economic groups, unions, churches, and especially those difficulties brought about by the social classes which are not in power.

To this complex situation must be added variations in the form of the state in terms of the diverse political régimes. The more open the organized apparatus is to penetration by the structures

---

[1] I would have preferred the term 'international societies', particularly since there are always several of them.

of the political societies, and the subjacent global societies through their spokesmen, the more democratic is the régime. A patrimonial monarchy, absolute monarchy, constitutional and parliamentary monarchy, liberal democracy, popular democracy, bureaucratic technocracy (often related to fascism), centralized collectivism, decentralized collectivism based on worker self-management all serve to orientate the cognitive system of the state in different directions. In the fourth part of this book, devoted to the types of global societies and their corresponding systems of knowledge, we shall discuss the problem of the role that different political régimes play in relation to knowledge. However, since the state is being considered here as one particular group, it seems necessary to give immediately some characteristics of the cognitive systems corresponding to the social frameworks called 'states'.

Being primarily a collection of territorial groups, opposed to other states and jealously guarding its own frontiers, the state accords a primordial importance to *the perceptual knowledge of the external world*. Because its base is the territory that it occupies, it places this in autistic space (which is emphasized particularly in the case of 'isolationism'). Inasmuch as it is opposed to other states, it places the external world in egocentric space. Lastly, when it allies itself with other states, or when it enters into one of their 'blocs', or, on the other hand, when it is opposed to them, the external world that it knows is placed in both projective and concentric space. This is verified by military activity which, in former times, required the building of fortresses and fortified lines, and today encompasses the construction of aeroplanes, the production of atomic bombs, and the launching of intercontinental or interplanetary missiles and satellites.

Certainly the state is coming to perceive the external world more and more from the economic point of view: sources of raw materials, fertile regions, or regions particularly favourable to industry (whence comes the problem of 'territorial planning') or tourism. The same is true for commercial exchange, 'peaceful competition', or the 'common Market' (if one day it were to materialize).[1] In this context, the space in which the external world is placed is so loosely knit that it becomes prospective.

---

[1] I believe that the 'Common Market' could materialize only under a *decentralized collectivist régime*, if this were to succeed in being set up in all the West and East European countries. It seems clear to me that this prospect is

The state as a source of knowledge therefore gives rise to *a specific perceptual knowledge* of the external world and the space in which the world is situated. This is a particularly complex knowledge which is complicated still further by the multiplicity and variation of the technical means of communication which the state sets up and uses in its territory. Add to this the variations in the dominant social time, and its projection in the known external world.

In the state's perceptual knowledge of the external world, it is normally the time which is related to the present and the near future which predominates. The state resorts to quantification of the space and time in which it struggles, both for the purpose of assuring the regularity of its functioning and for remedying the complexity of its knowledge of the external world. It thus establishes different standards of measurement which result in 'spatio-temporal references' and calendars.

The emphasized forms in this type of knowledge are especially the symbolic, conceptual, collective, positive and rational, except in charismatic theocracies, where the last two are replaced by the speculative and mystical forms.

The second type of knowledge which plays an essential role in the cognitive system of the state is obviously *political knowledge*. The holding and exercising of political power necessitates the use of tactical means to manage the susceptibilities, and to satisfy the requirements of different regions, different public services, different groups, and particularly different social classes (when they exist), and political parties (when they are allowed to express themselves). Even under authoritarian, dictatorial régimes, the rulers need a certain 'political knowledge' to maintain their position and consolidate their power. The forms emphasized within this knowledge vary according to the régime.

Common-sense knowledge may or may not figure in the state's cognitive system. It can either combine with the *political knowledge* of the rulers, or strengthen that of the opposition to a given political régime. Today, both in the global society and in a large number of particular groups, *common-sense knowledge* about the

not for tomorrow. But until this is realized, all the palaver about 'Europe' and the 'Common Market' is either pure utopianism or a mask under which new forms of economic imperialism by certain members of the so-called 'Common Market' are hidden.

H

machinery of the state resides in certain *particular public services* and *corporate bodies*. There is, for example, much more common-sense used in the decisions of the Council of State—The Supreme Administrative Court in France, or the Supreme Court in the United States (whose power is considerably greater than that of the French Council of State)—than in governmental administrative decisions. However, when it appears in public services the jurisdiction of which is very limited (for example, P.T.T.,[1] S.N.C.F.,[2] etc.) common-sense knowledge is often changed for the worse by bureaucratic routine and the bureaucratic mentality.

Technical knowledge usually plays an important role in the state. This means not only knowledge concerning the manipulation of matter (particularly of productive forces), but also the control of men and societies. From their inception, states have had ultimate control of the instruments of destruction and the armies which possess them. Added to this is the control of commercial navigation (ancient cities), agriculture (theocratic–charismatic states, patrimonial and feudal states), industrial manufacture (states at the beginning of capitalism), and today, planning and utilization of land (states corresponding to organized, directed capitalism). It also involves the control of the state's enormous techno-bureaucratic apparatus, which is more widespread and powerful than ever. Certainly, the emphasized forms of technical knowledge in the state are extremely varied.

It would seem at first glance that the other types of knowledge, even the knowledge of the Other and the We, and particularly scientific and philosophical knowledge are not directly related to the state. But this first impression is misleading. . . .

We have already seen that political and common-sense knowledge imply knowledge of the Other and the We (including groups and social classes, when they exist). But there is much more. *Philosophical knowledge*, without necessarily corresponding to the state and political régime which is dominant at the time, may either be influenced by the state or, on the contrary, bring influence to bear on the state. Thus, socio-political philosophies may serve to justify political régimes or, conversely, contribute to their

---

[1] P.T.T. is Poste–Télégraphe–Téléphone.
[2] S.N.C.F. is Société Nationale de Chemins de Fer Français (French Railways).

demolition. It is undeniable that liberal, democratic, socialist, communist or fascist philosophies may influence the political régimes which are most opposed to them, by provoking violent reactions or crises, and even, in favourable circumstances, their collapse. Here knowledge may have its revenge on the social framework in which it appears; the functional correlation of knowledge and the corresponding social framework is broken in favour of knowledge.

We must not forget that the state may consciously intervene in the development of scientific and philosophical knowledge (as in technical knowledge or rather, in this case, 'technological' knowledge), by taking initiatives concerning the running of educational establishments, the diffusion of knowledge, the organization of new scientific research, and the foundation of new pedagogical institutions imbued with a more modern spirit. This is what happened at the beginning of capitalism, at the end of the seventeenth century, and in the eighteenth century, when the state had to take steps to combat the Catholic Church's control of the three levels of education—all dominated by rhetoric and scholasticism which had long since passed out of general social life. The intervention of the state in modernizing education had already begun in the sixteenth century with the foundation of the 'Collège de France', responsible for introducing the spirit of the Renaissance into university life, competing with the Sorbonne which lay dormant under the weight of scholasticism. This example was followed in the seventeenth century, due to the initiative of Richelieu, by the foundation under Louis XIII of the *Académie française* in 1634. At Colbert's insistence, during the reign of Louis XIV, the following were founded: in 1663 the *Académie des Inscriptions et Belles-Lettres* and, in 1666–9, the *Académie des Sciences*. These two Académies served as centres for spreading Cartesian philosophy first of all and later the philosophy of the 'age of enlightenment'. At the same time the schools of higher technical education (Écoles de l'Enseignement Supérieur Technique) were founded: 'L'École des Mines', 'L'École des Ponts et Chaussées', 'l'École Navale', 'l'École d'Artillerie', etc. The secularization of all public education and the separation of church and state, particularly in the area of knowledge, its diffusion and propagation, proclaimed by the French Revolution, in fact merely completed something that had already been begun under the

Ancien Régime. The revolutionary state itself founded an important section of the existing *Institut* in 1795: 'L'Académie des Sciences Morales et Politiques'. 'L'Académie des Beaux-Arts' which was also a creation of the Revolution started in the same year.

Obviously in these cases that we have just cited, the state did not intervene as a framework of traditional knowledge, but as a creator of new centres charged with promoting a new cognitive system.

These suggestions as to the role of the state with regard to knowledge are but brief ones; they take on a more concrete form in the fourth part of this book when we consider as frameworks of knowledge different types of global societies, societies and structures with differently organized states, whose various régimes play specific roles as social frameworks of cognitive systems.

CHAPTER SEVEN

Churches and their Cognitive Systems

We cannot end this part of the book without dealing with those blocs of multi-functional groups which, in historical societies, are often more widely-encompassing than states. These are churches, representing universal religions, such as Christianity, Islam, Buddhism, and Judaism.[1] In considering churches as a source of cognitive systems, we shall leave aside matters concerned with the relationship between church and state (relationships which can range from identification, as in theocracies, to total separation as in liberal or planned democracies, and centralized or decentralized collectivist régimes).

As social frameworks of knowledge, churches always depend firstly on the nature of their revealed dogmas, their beliefs, and the rites and practices in which their members participate; secondly, they depend on the strength of the mystical communions that they contain; and finally, they rest on the structures and organizations that correspond to their dogmas, beliefs, rites, and practices. We will limit ourselves to the examples provided by the three Christian churches: the Catholic Church, the Orthodox Church, and the Protestant Church, and we will be brief, since this field is not our main concern.

The cognitives systems that correspond to these three social frameworks are far from being identical, as we shall try to show in the following analysis.

(A) THE CATHOLIC CHURCH AND ITS COGNITIVE SYSTEM

It is theologico-philosophical knowledge which predominates in the cognitive system corresponding to the Catholic Church, where it attains its highest degree of elaboration and consistency. This is

[1] Brahmanism is still not a universal religion, for in effect it does not extend beyond India. This is equally true of Confucianism and, even more so, its rival Taoism (whose founder was Lao-Tseu); these do not extend beyond China and the regions under its influence, unlike Buddhism, which has spread into the major part of Asia.

due to the fact that it affirms dogmas the specificity of which, compared with the other two Christian churches, consists of an emphasis on the *absolute transcendence of the Holy Trinity*,[1] a strong emphasis on the rational, conceptual, and collective forms of knowledge, whilst the mystical, speculative, and symbolic forms of knowledge are somewhat reduced. This tendency is combined with a particularly stable structure and an extremely rigid organization, characterized by an intense drive for universality. In other respects, this knowledge remains pre-eminently the preserve of the clergy and its complex hierarchy. In the Middle Ages, for example, it was the prerogative of the universities, at that time ecclesiastical establishments. Even today it hardly touches the simple believers. This observation is confirmed by the fact that the more the Catholic Church emphasizes its tendency towards universality, the weaker become its communions in their efforts to expand into communities and even into masses of believers.

The second type of knowledge that can be seen to play a major role in the cognitive system deriving from the Catholic Church is *the perceptual knowledge of the external world, centred in the Vatican.* The common saying that was so widespread in the Middle Ages: 'all roads lead to Rome', expressed a fact that is still valid today— *the Catholic Church places the world in projective and prospective space converging on the Vatican.* It is space corresponding to the extension of the church, the validity of its dogmas, rites, symbols, practices, and also its prospects—previously it was the prospect of converting the infidels, today it is that of reintegrating the Orthodox and Reformed. Knowledge of time appears only in a fairly relative manner, since it is the cyclical time of religious rites and calendars that predominates.

In third position, *political knowledge* also plays a considerable role in this framework. The functioning of the Catholic Church, through its vast organization, the complex hierarchy of its clergy and the equally complex relationships that exist between the

[1] In this respect, the placing on the Index of the first work of Maurice Blondel, *L'action*, and the works of Fr. Labertonnière, is very characteristic. In fact, they were condemned for their supposed 'modernism' and their subtle concessions to the partial immanence of the Holy Spirit in the world through creative action (a position which recalls somewhat the inspiration and theological interpretations of the Orthodox Church). I have not studied sufficiently the writings of Fr. Teilhard de Chardin to discover and evaluate the place of 'modernism' in his thought, which is enjoying such success in various philosophical and religious circles today.

different orders, presupposes appropriate tactical knowledge, which is often more implicit than explicit. Moreover, this knowledge is made necessary by the many conflicts which, through the ages, have opposed the Catholic Church to the state and to other secular groups, and especially its relations with other Christian bodies, which have been rather strained, although today they are oriented towards mutual understanding.

In feudal societies certain aspects of this political knowledge have been formulated in well-known political doctrines.[1] Again it must not be forgotten, in this connection, that in the middle of the nineteenth century and in the twentieth century, many current doctrines have been influenced by the church's political knowledge— whether it be the counter-revolutionary doctrines of a Bonald and a Maistre, or even socialistic doctrines imbued with Saint-Simonism, like those of Buchez[2] and Leroux, or even the much more conservative conceptions of Frédéric Le Play,[3] and the more advanced and modern social catholicism of Marc Sangnier's *Sillon*, and the recent 'worker priest' movement. These are all efforts to maintain a connection between modern politico-social doctrines and the spontaneous political knowledge of the Catholic Church.

It is surprising to find here that neither appropriate tactical knowledge, nor the various political doctrines inspired by the Catholic Church, emphasize a mystical or speculative form, and that, on the contrary, they remain manifestly rational, conceptual, and even rather positive. This is certainly not so in the Orthodox Church.

Knowledge of the Other and the We is not directly discernible in the Catholic Chruch as a whole; it is limited to monasteries and, more strictly, to the different orders. The same applies for *technical knowledge*, understood in the sense of the manipulation of matter, of which the monasteries and the religious orders of the Middle Ages were sometimes the initiators. But if one includes in technical knowledge the manipulation of men—which is one of the aspects

---

[1] Beginning with Marsilius of Padua, who was the first to proclaim the principle of 'the sovereignty of the people' as a source of secular power, with the obvious intention of applying it to papal power.

[2] Cf. on Buchez the thesis of François Isambert, some extracts of which have been published in *Les Cahiers Internationaux de Sociologie*.

[3] Cf. on Frédéric Le Play, the article by Andrée Michel, 'Les cadres sociaux de la doctrine morale de Frédéric Le Play', in *Cahiers Internationaux de Sociologie*, XXXIV (1963), 47–8.

of political knowledge—then the Catholic Church, by its very functioning, offers a striking example.

The other types of knowledge (common-sense knowledge, scientific knowledge, philosophical knowledge in the proper sense) are completely absorbed into the preceding types.

(B) THE ORTHODOX CHURCH AND ITS COGNITIVE SYSTEM

When we pass from the social framework of the Catholic Church to that of the Orthodox Church, the cognitive system changes considerably.

Theologico-philosophical knowledge still occupies first place, but it is oriented quite differently. It tends to assert that *the creation of the world by God is not ended*, but is continued under *the aegis of the Holy Spirit*; the latter 'raises Humanity and Society to a participation in the divine creation of the world and of themselves'. This tendency, intermediate between affirmation of the transcendence or of the immanence of God in relation to the world and society (that is to say between theism and pantheism) dispels the rigidity from the structure and even from the organization of the Orthodox Church.

It allows for various forms, ranging from a democratic administration by the assembly of all believers (or at least all ecclesiastics) to patriarchy and even Byzantine cesaro-papalism, with elected or nominated synods as an intermediate form.

In any case, the theologico-philosophical knowledge appropriate to the Orthodox Church—knowledge in which the mystical form is strongly emphasized—can influence *simple believers* as well as the clergy of all ranks. As, for example, the widespread belief among Russian peasants that the land which they cultivate 'belongs only to God', but 'must be managed by those who work it'. Under the Ancien Régime this belief led to denials of the legality of land-owners' rights, and under the present Soviet régime it may lead to refusal to attribute agrarian ownership to the centralized collectivist state, and may favour tendencies towards self-management of the 'kolkhozes' in the direction of decentralized collectivism.

Political knowledge occupies second place in the framework of the Orthodox Church, both from the tactical point of view and from the point of view of the realization of socio-political ideals. It intervenes not only in the complex relations between church and state, in the varied and fluctuating functioning of the ecclesiastical powers, or between the many Orthodox churches, but also in the political orientation of believers, despite slight differences.

Thus for the Orthodox Church, the *revealed theological dogma is in no way incompatible with extreme left positions,* to the extent that the society, under the aegis of the Holy Spirit, is believed to be called to help God in His work of continuous creation of the world, particularly the social world. It is perhaps this which explains the survival of Orthodoxy in Communist countries for large sections of the population. However, it must be recognized that this has never prevented the Orthodox Church and its faithful in various countries from taking positions on the right or the extreme right, or from displaying a total socio-political indifference, depending on the various circumstances.

Perceptual knowledge of the external world occupies only the third and last place in the cognitive system corresponding to the social framework of the Orthodox Church. In fact, this church, in contrast to the Catholic Church, does not show any tendency to proselytism. Moreover, according to Orthodox belief, *the dimension of the external world should be minimized in the face of faith.* Knowledge of the external world is justified only to the extent that humanity and society, directed by the Holy Spirit, participate in the continuing creation of this world by God.

In other respects, the widespread dispersion of Orthodoxy and its independent churches throughout the world, serves to place the external world in diffuse space. Moreover, knowledge of the time wherein the external world and human societies move, plays a much more important role here than spatial knowledge, due to the fact that the dogma of the Holy Spirit inspires a particular interest in that time which is concerned with participation in the creation of the world and society, as well as for time in advance of itself.

The other types of knowledge are in the same position here as in the Catholic Church, the only considerable difference being in the forms emphasized: in effect one sees here the pre-dominance of the *mystical, speculative,* and *symbolic* forms of knowledge.

(C) THE REFORMED CHURCHES AND THEIR COGNITIVE SYSTEMS

Examination of the various Protestant Churches as social frameworks of knowledge leads to quite different results from those to which the study of the other two Christian churches led us. First, Protestant dogmatics do not aim at constituting a system of faith, and certain Protestant groups, such as the Quakers, which are widespread in the United States, deny in principle the usefulness of all theology. In other respects, the cult of the purely internal faith, the belief that God is accessible only to the individual conscience, or sometimes even that He is immanent in it, in the same way that paradise and hell are immanent in conscience, make Protestant churches less favourable sources for a specific system of types of knowledge.

It seems that in this social framework *political knowledge* must be placed in the forefront, at least under its tactical guise, such as it appears in certain relationships: pastors and the faithful, pastors among themselves and with the administrative councils elected by the members (the consistories), the relations between the many Protestant churches and with the state, as well as with other Christian churches, and finally, their relations with political parties.

Exegetical knowledge of scripture replaces theologico-philosophical knowledge, though not without involving the taking up of specific philosophical positions. It would occupy second position in this cognitive system.

The Protestant Churches do not provide a place for any specific knowledge of the external world. Being both secular and profane, the external world is not recognized by them as a worthy object of knowledge; this conscious refusal to even consider the external world leads to the predominance in the church of a knowledge of the external world based on standards imposed by the state and the global society.

On the other hand, the Protestant churches do encourage *philosophical knowledge*, as well as *scientific knowledge* and *technical knowledge*, about which Marx and Max Weber made similar observations. Unfortunately these two granted too much importance to those theological inspirations of a bourgeois origin which favoured the development of capitalism, and did not dwell sufficiently on the structure and organization of the Reformed churches.

With regard to their philosophical positions, these churches have particularly encouraged idealist subjectivism and its various expressions (Kant, Schleiermacher, Kierkegaard). The closed consciousness, turned in on itself, which has been placed in the forefront by these churches, *has not favoured knowledge of the Other*. From this point of view the ideas of Kierkegaard are characteristic: individuals can neither communicate nor understand each other without doing it through the intermediary of Christ. Common-sense knowledge in this framework has no specific place and is mixed with that of the bourgeois class, with which we will deal later.[1]

We shall not dwell on the fact that the emphasized forms in the types of knowledge which constitute the cognitive system appropriate to the Reformed churches are usually the rational, conceptual, symbolic (very slightly), and individual forms. Only philosophical knowledge, particularly that of Kierkegaard, allows a certain mysticism to appear.

[1] Cf. below, the third Part of this book, Chapter 3.

PART THREE

Social Classes and their Cognitive Systems

CHAPTER ONE

Preliminary Remarks

When we move on from particular groups—even such large-scale, strongly structured and organized groups as states and churches—to social classes as frameworks of knowledge, we are faced with cognitive sources which are extremely complex, varied and often very forceful. This is because rising social classes are partial social worlds which are aspiring to become total social worlds as exemplified by global societies. The social classes in power often identify with these global societies; social classes which are declining or have been dispossessed are filled with the memory of a glorious past and are incapable of facing the prospect of their own demise.

There is no doubt that social classes, to the extent that they exist, are in mutual conflict; now these conflicts, differing in intensity according to the types of structure and the circumstances of the society in which the classes evolve, have a strong influence upon states and churches, and other specific groups. It is this which would seem to justify the Marxist thesis that in the area of the sociology of knowledge, social classes are much more important sources than the specific groups. But here we must guard against the temptation to be dogmatic.

Social classes in the strict sense (and Marx seems to admit it, especially in his historical works) arose only with capitalist societies or, in a more general way, with industrial societies. The 'class consciousness', which Marx sees as one of the elements necessary for the constitution of a class, along with participation in production and distribution, cannot be equated, as he claims, with the 'ideology' of this class. For him this term assumes extremely varied meanings (from that of illusion or distortion to that of 'cultural works of a social class', from that of justification of a political position, to that characteristic found in all human science which has not been imbued with Marxism).

Class consciousness is first and foremost a manifestation of collective psychical life; this extends far beyond its mere cognitive

aspect. Besides, the cognitive system of a class is not absorbed
by its ideology which expresses only one aspect of it. The
characteristics which the Marxists present tend to reduce the
complexity of social classes as sources of knowledge; most Marxist
representatives consider them—without deliberate intention—only
in terms of their implicit or explicit 'political knowledge'.[1]
Besides, a Marxist interpretation of social classes does not
sufficiently reveal their richness as macrocosms of groups (within
which could be appropriately integrated the various 'social
strata', among other things) and as microcosms of manifestations
of sociality; neither does it illuminate the variation in the relationships between classes and their varying importance in the global
society.

In trying to give a sufficiently wide and flexible definition of the
concept of social class which takes into account the multiplicity of
its concrete historical forms, we arrived at various formulae, some
condensed, others more detailed. Here from amongst these definitions is the one which we consider to be the most acceptable:
'*social classes are large-scale macro-groups, representing macrocosms
of particular groups, macrocosms whose unity is based on their tendency
towards supra-functionality, elaborate structuration, resistance to
penetration by the global society, and incompatibility with other
classes*'. All these statements serve to emphasize only the *tendential
characteristics of classes* which admit of several degrees of intensity:
in fact, neither the supra-functionality, nor the recalcitrant nature
in relation to the global society, nor the incompatibility with other
classes are elements which are given once and for all. *They permit
of an infinite number of emphases.*

Again we fail to understand how certain critics could have re-
proached us for having wanted to 'resolve the problem in advance',
instead of choosing a formula which does not 'prejudge the answers'.[2] Doubtless, this arises from a misunderstanding of terms,
which are perhaps not sufficiently subtle, rather than from the

[1] Cf. my works: *Le concept de classe sociale de Marx à nos jours* (mimeograph,
1st edn., 1954; 3rd edn., 1960, Paris, C.D.U.), and the Introduction in *Œuvres
choisies de C.-H. de Saint-Simon: La physiologie sociale* (1965, Presses Universitaires de France), pp. 17–21, 29–30, and *Proudhon* (1965, Presses Universitaires
de France), pp. 5, 9–10, 12–13, 32–3, 34–5, 43, 45, 61–70; *La vocation actuelle
de la sociologie* (3rd edn., adapted, 1963, Presses Universitaires de France), I,
357–402, and II, 452–61; and see also my *Dialectique et Sociologie* (1962,
Flammarion), pp. 118–56.
[2] R. Aron, *La lutte des classes* (Paris, 1964), pp. 64 ff., and 91 ff.

fundamentals of the question, since, by putting the emphasis on the extreme variation in the degrees of intensity of supra-functionality, the resistance to penetration by the global society, and the incompatibility, we think that we have arrived at the most relativist definition of social classes which has so far been given, especially since we have also pointed out that the number and hierarchy of strata are different in each one.[1]

Yet we want to emphasize that in taking social classes as social frameworks of knowledge, we are well aware that the cognitive systems that we shall discover are more likely to be implicit and spontaneous than explicit and formulated. The correlation between social classes and knowledge is therefore complicated by the fact that it is not always direct, but sometimes indirect. This does not at all lessen the interest in the problem. Finally it should be noted that social classes can influence organized groups such as states and churches and, through their mediation, their systems of knowledge.

The various industrial societies, past and present, according to their types and circumstances, have given rise to a much larger number of social classes than those normally considered.[2] Marx himself made the same observation: each of his historical works analyses from six to eight classes, certain ones sometimes being described as 'fractions' of classes. However, to make our task easier, we shall keep to the three classes which are the most easily distinguished—the peasant class, the bourgeois class, and the proletarian class—and also the incipient 'techno-bureaucratic class', which is so much at issue today.

[1] Cf. my Introduction to the published works of the Fifth Colloquium of 'l'Association Internationale des Sociologues de Langue Française', a Colloquium devoted to social classes in the world today, in *Cahiers Internationaux de Sociologie*, XXXVIII (1965), 4–9.

[2] This is the most important observation of all the participants at the aforementioned Colloquium, and this despite the differences in tendencies and interpretations. The same conclusion can be drawn from their concrete descriptions of the 'class struggles', i.e. the nature of the conflicts which set them in opposition. The variety of conflicts is almost unbelievable. Cf. vols. XXXVIII and XXXIX of the aforementioned *Cahiers*, reproducing the entire proceedings of the Colloquium in Quebec on 'Social Classes in the World Today'.

I

CHAPTER TWO

The Peasant Class and its Cognitive System

It must be remembered that the peasant class is not identical to the rural population. Whereas in France today the rural population seems to be divided into several burgeoning classes, and in Great Britain and the United States there undoubtedly no longer exists a peasant class, nevertheless in certain collectivist countries such as the U.S.S.R., China, Yugoslavia, Poland, even though they claim to have abolished social classes, the peasant class shows such vitality that it is impossible to ignore its role in the evolution of these régimes. In Latin American countries, Brazil in particular, the peasant class, whilst breaking up into several very distinct fractions, gives indisputable evidence of its survival, despite the tendency of certain elements to leave the countryside for the large towns.

The specific form of agrarian ownership is not always of much help in describing the concrete characteristics of the peasant class. It is mainly defined in terms of direct work on the land, the technical means used, and the rather limited area of available land, to which is attached a particular ideology.[1] This ideology often develops mistrust of the large towns and their unrest, suspicion of the state, whose expenditure is deemed to be largely unproductive, and resentment towards the other classes: the bourgeoisie because of the exorbitant price of industrial products, the many intermediaries, the food merchants, and particularly the livestock merchants who are even more strongly disliked. In collectivist countries, the bourgeoisie has given way, in the consciousness of the peasant class, to the techno-bureaucracy, the planners, other officials of the régime, or even the representatives of the nearest town's administration, in controlling the delivery of agricultural products sold in the markets and the prevailing prices.

*

(A) In the cognitive system corresponding to the peasant class,

[1] Sometimes this 'ideology' is diversified, as in Brazil, according to the fractions of the peasant class, one part of which remains nomadic or attracted by as yet uncultivated areas.

the *perceptual knowledge of the external world* must be placed in first position. The space and time in which the world is placed are apprehended, perceived, conceptualized and mastered in almost the same way as in the knowledge of small-scale local groups. Space is egocentric and diffuse. Time is mainly seasonal, of long duration and slowed down. Attachment to technical patterns and traditional symbols hinders modernization. The 'community' which occurs within the peasant class or its fractions is inclined to take on a passive and even unconscious character, which tends to bring that community closer to the 'mass' element.

One of the traits which differentiates the perceptual knowledge of the external world of the peasant class from that of small-scale local groups is that the peasant's knowledge is usually much more imbued with emotive colour, more suspicious of other collective units and organizations, more favourable to diffuse space and retarding time, and less capable of mastering real and social space and time, except that space and time where agricultural labour is dominant and where the daily life of the peasants is lived.

Only religious or civil wars, political and social revolutions, national wars, epidemics, disastrous harvests, etc. (apart from the usually slow penetration of new techniques, for example, tractors, or chemical discoveries which increase the fertility of the soil) can shake the peasant class from its torpor and get it to modify its cognitive images of the external world and the social world. But when such turmoils are over, the knowledge of the world of the existing peasant class tends to turn in on itself, as in all its modes of knowledge and living, and to ensure the continuity of its own tradition.

(B) *Common-sense knowledge* would occupy second place in the peasant class's cognitive system. Indeed, when it persists, it can attain a depth and penetration which takes on a philosophical tone, sometimes termed 'peasant wisdom', as well as a political propensity to 'self defence' and a certain 'peasant cunning'. But today common-sense knowledge is hardly discernible in the knowledge of the peasant class, except to the extent that this class is forced to defend itself against the threat of disintegration weighing upon it, a threat which is felt particularly strongly in centralized communist countries.[1]

[1] In advanced capitalist countries, especially the United States and Great Britain, the peasant class disappeared a long time ago.

(C) *Political knowledge*, which is related to common-sense knowledge, plays a much greater role in the peasant class's cognitive system than one is normally led to believe. This is because this type of knowledge, not only as a strategy, but also as the affirmation of an ideal, is only very rarely crystallized (in Western countries at least) into a doctrine, or even slogans or programmes. Thus, the peasant class is rarely represented by a political party which speaks directly in its name. However, one can quote exceptions. In France, under the Third Republic, it was the radical-socialist party which best embodied the spontaneous political ideal of the peasant class: the three generations are represented by the peasant grandfather, the father who might be an elementary-school teacher and secretary to the mayor, or a teacher in a *lycée*, and the grandson who might be a minister or president of the Council. But just when the peasant class finally gained access to power it began to disintegrate as a class, leading in the process to the decomposition of the Third Republic itself.

The situation is different in Eastern Europe. One might quote the case of the populist party in Russia (*narodniki*), subsequently called 'revolutionary socialist', which, not without reason, claimed to represent the Russian peasant class. Indeed, the results of the vote in the 1918 elections to the Constituent Assembly showed that even at that time the majority of the population under the communist régime favoured this party. Despite the almost immediate dissolution of the Constituent Assembly, which completely satisfied the peasant class's demands for the confiscation of all private agrarian properties, the 'redistribution of land', and the re-establishment of the former Russian 'mir' under the new form of Soviet 'kolkhozes', the peasant middle class proved to be rather suspicious of the régime. Its present-day political aspirations are far from clear: they are evident only in its loyalty to the Soviet régime and the Orthodox Church, as well as in its predominant influence over the Red Army.

Except in unusual circumstances, therefore, the political knowledge of the peasant class is characterized by cautiousness, suspicion, a tendency towards ambiguity, and, contrary to what one might have supposed, this class is little inclined to the mythological element characteristic of the political knowledge of other social classes.

(D) *Knowledge of the Other*, which is accorded only the penultimate place in this cognitive system, appears in two forms. On the one hand, it appears to be suspicious, not only of people from other classes, but also of neighbours belonging to the same class and, in a way, of everyone. Conceptualizations of the Other are based mainly on stereotypes—rather a striking fact, given the intimacy of daily peasant life. On the other hand, knowledge of the Other tends to become empirico-intuitive as soon as it concerns members of the family, agricultural workers engaged to live in and work for the family, and particularly participants in the same co-operatives of collective agrarian production (kolkhoze). In the latter cases particularly, this is knowledge of the concrete individuality of each comrade-team mate.

Thus, in the peasant class's knowledge of the Other, there is great complexity, even a certain ambiguity which sometimes goes as far as being contradictory. . . .

(E) Although we mention the *technical knowledge* of the peasant class last, this does not mean that it is always in last position; but its effectiveness and nature are highly variable. When it becomes identified with traditional knowledge, it is generally integrated into the perceptual knowledge of the external world and common-sense knowledge. But where new and modernized techniques are concerned, it often meets with resistance. To be successful in introducing it, requires strong insistence from the global society, with or without the assistance of the reorganization of agrarian ownership and production, as well as from the régime to which the latter are subject. In summary, technical knowledge plays a minor role in the 'class consciousness' that contributes to the structuration of the peasant class.

As for the forms emphasized within the types of knowledge in this cognitive system, it should be noted that, for the most part, the mystical and rational form, the conceptual and the empirical, the positive and the speculative are combined, but that symbolic and collective forms clearly predominate over the concrete and individual.

CHAPTER THREE

The Bourgeois Class and its Cognitive System

The bourgeois class is much easier to define and study than the peasant class, although in particular periods and circumstances it has played different roles: first, it played the role of revolutionary avant-garde, then gradually it became moderate and conciliatory, and then later conservative or reactionary, and at the present time, where it is dominated by a great fear of social revolutions, it is fascist to varying degrees.

Certainly ownership of the means of production, sources of raw materials, and financial capital, remain significant, along with the tendency to dominate home, colonial, international or 'common' markets, as a constitutive element of the bourgeois class. However, this class is largely open to all prosperous groups, and, along with employers, finance and business magnates at a certain level, should be included the liberal professions, high-level civil servants, and the administrative and technical bureaucrats of industry, banks, trusts, and cartels. All of these 'fractions' play a major role in the life of the bourgeoisie in the period of organized and directed capitalism.

At the time when the bourgeois class flourished, in the nineteenth century, the 'great patrons', who were good organizers and calculators, and shrewd, generous, philanthropic entrepreneurs, were also representative of the most wealthy strata of the bourgeoisie. Before its present day degeneration, the bourgeoisie had an optimistic class-consciousness, characterized by confidence in an unlimited 'technical and economic progress', in the harmony of the interests of all, in the universality of the benefits of capitalism and urban civilization. In contrast to the peasant class-consciousness, which was turned in on itself, bourgeois class-consciousness claimed to lend itself to universal diffusion. It was for a long time attracted to the most 'rational' and the least 'emotive' of class ideologies.

(A) Seen in this light, the bourgeois class appears as a particularly favourable source of knowledge in general and most of its particular types. The cognitive system corresponding to this class is characterized by, first of all, the tendency to interpenetration and parity of three types of knowledge: *scientific knowledge, technical knowledge*, and the *perceptual knowledge of the external world*. It was the advent of the bourgeoisie which brought about progress in the sciences—the natural and exact sciences in the first place—both directly and through the intermediary of the state and its educational establishments. It was the bourgeoisie who, by dominating the state, imposed the strongest and most effective quantification of space and time ('time is money'), a quantification which linked together perceptual knowledge of the external world and scientific knowledge by combining them. It was also the bourgeois class which created the conditions favourable to narrowing the gap between the scientific knowledge of nature and technical knowledge. Before the ascent to power of the bourgeois class, at the beginning of industrial society, technical knowledge was rather inclined to develop outside the sciences, directly in the factories and their work practices.

We can illustrate this interpenetration and tendency towards combination of the three types of knowledge mentioned in relation to the bourgeois class by discussing the perceptual knowledge of the external world. We observe immediately that the external world is placed in prospective space, which is favoured because it corresponds to the immediate interests of the entrepreneurs—economic expansion and technical development. Now, this prospectiveness is impossible without the intervention of technical media, and the technical media can develop at a sufficient rate only with the aid of scientific knowledge. Thus it is that the prospective and projective space in which bourgeois knowledge places the external world, have especially been linked in part to the conquest of new markets, particularly those of colonized countries (or those to be colonized), as well as with the search for manpower and natural resources (minerals, oil, coal, hydro-electric power, etc.), and with new investments of capital, and national and international industrial organizations (including trusts and cartels).

This space easily contracts and expands due to better means of communication, and combines with time fixed by the circulation of capital and investments, the productivity cycle of enterprises, and the duration of work and exchange. In this knowledge of the external world of the bourgeois class, therefore, space and time are oriented in the same direction, and tend to be combined and measured according to the same quantitative standards.

Certain developments were necessary before the bourgeois class, embittered and troubled by a great fear of its own decline, began to place the familiar external world in more egocentric and turbulent space and time—space and time which do not lend themselves to quantitative measures, and are as resistant to scientific studies as to purely technical solutions. These requirements were: stronger resistance from the proletarian class—its trades union and political movements—as well as the difficulties provoked by increasingly more serious economic crises, the decolonization wars, and also the advent of collectivist régimes born of social revolutions.

Thus it is that the external world as known by the contemporary bourgeois class seems to be placed in diffuse space on the one hand, and in concentric and projective space on the other. The former is derived from uncertainties about the fate of capitalist social structures, and the latter are related to membership of 'blocs' which are in conflict or 'peaceful competition'. Likewise, there is fierce competition between the time alternating between advance and retardation, and the time of irregular pulsations, which are prevalent in capitalist societies; and these are projected into the very knowledge of the external world, divided as it is into blocs. Is there any need to add that the measures of time are here revealed to be as impotent as those of space?

(B) These observations lead us to the *political knowledge* of the bourgeois class. In theory it occupies a lower position than the other three types of interpenetrated knowledge just discussed. Since its inception in the seventeenth century and up to the present day, the bourgeois class has always evidenced a very effective political knowledge, as much with regard to tactics as in assertion of an ideal. This political knowledge, specific to the bourgeoisie, has been crystallized many times into formulated doctrines (from Hobbes, Spinoza, and Rousseau, to neo-liberalism and solidarism at the end of the nineteenth century).

What appears striking about the political knowledge of the bourgeoisie, whether spontaneous or systematized, is that until the first decades of the twentieth century it was able to remain fairly moderate,[1] depending on myths of peace, 'equality of

[1] One of the exceptions is represented by the violent reaction against the Commune of 1871.

opportunity', unlimited technical progress, equality of the interests of all, and of 'abundance'; yet this appeal was made with prudence and reserve. This was because the bourgeoisie has always sought to avoid getting involved, despite the revolutions and counter-revolutions that it was able to profit from, and the role it could play in colonial, international, and even civil wars. Over the centuries it has remained a cautious political force, even in periods of great turbulence. This is because ultimately it has always had more to lose than to gain from any crisis or revolution; primarily it fears losing its wealth and consequently its very existence. Since it is always ready to compromise and make concessions wherever possible, the bourgeoisie easily becomes cautious and conservative wherever its economic interests are not seriously threatened and its existence is not brought into question. This situation changed only after the social revolutions of the Eastern European countries; the great fear of the communist threat, before and after the Second World War, gave fascist tendencies to the political knowledge of the bourgeoisie, which are strengthened today by the influence which the techno-bureaucratic stratum exercises in its midst.

(C) Among the other types of knowledge we can eliminate *common-sense knowledge*, which has played a role only within bourgeois family life. *Knowledge of the Other* does not have a very great importance either—it is reduced in the bourgeois cognitive system to the generic concept of the human person, identical for every individual (of which the Kantian interpretation has been the most adequate expression).

(D) Only *philosophical knowledge*, which is highly favoured by the bourgeois class, deserves a special mention. The combination of rationalism and voluntarism in Descartes, of rationalism and empiricism in Bacon, and particularly the philosophies of the 'Age of Enlightenment' (and, under a different form, as we have pointed out, the thought of Kant and the neo-Kantians) most clearly bear the imprint of the bourgeois class.

We shall not enter into detail, because we do not think the time has yet come for studies in depth of the sociology of philosophical doctrines. But to avoid misunderstanding, we are keen to emphasize at this point that most of the philosophical doctrines formulated from the end of the nineteenth century and in the twentieth century, no longer bear any trace of a direct link with the bourgeois class.

The emphasized forms in the types of knowledge associated with the bourgeois class tend on the whole towards the rational and the empirical, rather than the conceptual, towards the concrete rather than the symbolic, and the individual rather than the collective. Only the speculative and positive forms appear to be almost equal, or at least in close competition. Certainly it is only a matter of tendencies, for many variations seem to be possible, depending on the phase of capitalism—competitive or organized and directed—and on the particular circumstances.

CHAPTER FOUR

The Proletarian Class and its Cognitive System

The working class or proletariat, which occupies a disadvantaged position in capitalist industry because its members do not own the means of production and exist only by their labour (whether qualified by occupational training or not), has been slow to organize itself and develop self-consciousness. This is due to the heteroclite origins of this class, arising as it did from the poorest section of town population, ruined craftsmen, and the lower, disintegrated strata of the peasantry.

The proletariat's class-consciousness dates only from the beginning of the nineteenth century; it appears in various socialist and collectivist doctrines, among which the various kinds of Marxism later became dominant. Of course the collective mentality and the collective consciousness of the proletariat extend beyond what is properly called its 'class-consciousness'. They imply, in addition to aspirations towards a better future and social revolution, the awareness of poverty, successive oft-experienced disappointments, weariness, anxieties concerning the intensity of internal divisions, and sometimes even prolonged indifference. The proletarian class can enter into conflict with its own organizations, be discouraged by internal struggles, or feel crushed and betrayed by the new bureaucracy which controls its organization.

Variations in the intensity of class struggles (which involves change in the emphases of the elements 'mass', 'community', and 'communion', as well as in the importance of the groups within the proletariat), and in the forms which these struggles take, and more recently the tendency to form 'fractions', or to splinter into several 'working classes', considerably complicates the problem of the proletariat as a social framework of types and forms of knowledge.

Contrary to what occurs in the bourgeois class, in the past the hierarchy of groups included in the working class was established less by reference to economic levels (e.g. electrical workers and printers—the best paid, dockers and porters—the worst paid) or skills, than it was to the role of certain groups acting within the proletariat in its struggle against the other classes (trades union elites, worker delegates, 'activist minorities'). According to the results of recent enquiries the hierarchy of groups in the working class has become still more complicated during the last decades. In fact, the proletarian strata possessing the technical skills particularly important for the operation of machines (e.g. maintenance mechanics for automated machinery) benefit not only from their privileged economic position and direct influence on the administration of the enterprise, but also from the possibility of resorting to new and specific strategies in the struggle for their own interests and for those of the working class as a whole, including the trades unions and their organs of control in the enterprise. New problems are thus posed concerning the effective unity of the proletarian class today, although no definitive conclusion can be offered.

But, until proved otherwise, it is difficult to allow that these 'privileged fractions of the proletariat' are losing their class-consciousness, which unites them to all the other proletarian groups and strata. We believe, therefore, that we can deal with the working class as the *single source of a cognitive system*, whilst recognizing certain nuances related to internal variations in this social framework.

*

(A) Clearly the predominant type of knowledge in the cognitive system of the proletarian class is *political knowledge*, both spontaneous and implicit as well as formulated, explicit, and crystallized into various doctrines. This is concerned with strategy and also the ideals they hope to attain in the near or distant future. For the proletarian class, never having been in a privileged position, under either capitalist régimes or centralized communist régimes (which, while claiming to speak on its behalf, nevertheless keep it in a subordinate position) is a discontented class which aspires to a better future and the satisfaction of hitherto unsatisfied needs.

A knowledge of the tactics of struggle is therefore necessary—struggle with the government, the directors of factories and businesses, other classes, and with the trades union and political organizations which, while claiming to represent it and speak in its name, are either hostile or, more often, betray it. It is also concerned about a better future and a régime which would more effectively fulfil its promises. In this regard what is involved may be either an ideal image capable of rapid realization, or a myth (in the Sorelian sense of a call to action). In both cases the proletariat's political knowledge can take either an empirico-intuitive form, arising directly out of its experience of conflict, or in contrast it can crystallize in conceptualized (even rigid and sometimes imposed) doctrines. Furthermore, a dialectic[1] between the empirical and conceptual forms in the proletariat's political knowledge, is just as likely to lead to their polarization as to their interpenetration. This possibility should not be ignored. . . .

Depending on the contributions of the different fractions and strata within the proletariat, this political knowledge can become either opportunist or revolutionary, realist or utopian, rational or mystical. But whatever its guise, it is always present, and its orientation does not depend solely on the proletariat or its various strata and groups, but also on the circumstances (revolutionary, counter-revolutionary, peaceful, aggressive, etc.) in which the global society—the field of action and struggle for all classes—exists.

(B) *Second place* in the cognitive system of the proletariat is occupied by *technical knowledge*. Obviously this concerns the active part of the proletariat, that section involved in the productive process, i.e. those who can properly be called workers, not members of their families who are simply dependents. The character of this technical knowledge varies according to the fractions and strata which make up this class. As occupational training becomes more widespread, particularly that devoted to dealing with repairs and breakdowns of automated machinery, technical knowledge plays an increasingly more important role in the productive activity of the working class. Whereas at the beginning of capitalism it was a spontaneous knowledge acquired on the job, which remained rather superficial and at the level of dexterity and manual skill, today, despite the extreme complexity of machines, this technical knowledge can function as a basis for the constitution of a special category of workers. What distinguishes this category of workers, who are selected for their skill at a particular job, from engineers, is that their technical knowledge is still not connected with scientific knowledge. It is this

[1] Cf. on my idea of the dialectic and the multiplicity of its manifestations and processes, my book *Dialectique et Sociologie*, pp. 179–220.

disjunction between the two types of knowledge which constitutes the vulnerable aspect of even the most qualified workers and keeps them in the ranks of the proletariat.

(C) In *third place* in the working class's system of knowledge is *perceptual knowledge of the external world.* This is much more subjective and emotive than in the bourgeois class, since the proletariat has difficulty in detaching itself from the work-place and its conditions, from the area delimited by the distance between work and home, from the kind of transport necessary to cover that distance, and from the actual living conditions of the home, etc.

In other respects the perceptual knowledge of the external world of the working class is also distinct from that of the peasant class which, as we have seen, is essentially egocentric, turned in on itself, and suspicious with respect to everything unfamiliar. The working class, on the contrary, is open to knowledge of all aspects of the external world, present and future, and also to the situation of classes in foreign countries, just as much as in its own. Thus it is the externalization of their own class which particularly attracts the attention of the workers, wherever it occurs.

The space and time in which the *external world* is placed have a specific character. The fatigue, disappointment, lassitude, and indifference of the workers disposes them to perceive *egocentric* and *projective* space. The space relevant to proletarian organizations—trade union and political—when combined with time in which the future often dominates the present, shows a *prospective* tendency. As for concentric space—diffuse and loosely-knit, it varies depending on whether it concerns the proletariat itself, hostile classes, or the future society. In other respects, knowledge of the external world and the space in which it is placed, fall deeply under the influence of knowledge of time in which the distant future predominates over the present and the past; time in advance of itself, and in certain periods creative time, tend to prevail over knowledge of space.

The working class seems little attracted to common-sense knowledge, which usually intervenes only through political knowledge, particularly where tactics are concerned.

(D) As for *knowledge of the Other and the We*, it deserves a special analysis in the framework of the proletarian class. Knowledge of the concrete Other is limited to members of the same trade union and political cell, or to those in the same work team. The character of the Other is seen in a favourable light when it exhibits militancy. But if knowledge of the Other is very limited, that of the 'We', of groups, and classes, on the other hand, is very intense. Whether it is a question of the proletarian class and its subdivisions (special cases), or of hostile, neutral, or intermediary classes, knowledge of collectivities plays an important role in the actions and consciousness of this class. This is not a matter of vague protests or simple prejudices, but of what is quite often a penetrating knowledge, bound up with historical memories, long experience of trade union and political struggles, and visions of a better future.

(E) This leads us to an examination of an assertion made by certain nineteenth-century sociologists, which is of some interest, but which contains an error clearly revealed by the cognitive situation in the twentieth century. Proudhon and Marx on the one hand, and August Comte on the other—the latter, however, antipodal to the first two—invoked the proletariat as the decisive renovator of *philosophical knowledge*. Proudhon, in the *Système des Contradictions économiques* (1846), and in *De la Justice dans la Révolution et dans l'Église* (1858; study vi on 'Work' and study vii on 'Ideas') asserts that the proletariat, which he compares to Prometheus, by disalienating work, will cause *philosophical knowledge* to triumph as a practical demonstration that 'the idea with its categories is born out of action and must return to action, or the agent will suffer loss'.[1] Marx, in his 'Theses on Feuerbach' (Introduction to *The German Ideology*, 1845), considering the proletariat as the incarnation of practical social activity, asserted that it would be inspired by a new philosophical knowledge.[2] 'The question whether objective truth can be attributed to human thinking is not a question of theory, but is a practical question' says Marx (vol. VI, edn. Costes, French translation by Molitor, pp. 141–2). 'The materialist doctrine of bringing about changes in conditions and education forgets that the conditions are changed by men and *that the educator himself must be educated*. The coincidence of the change in circumstances and the change

[1] Cf. for discussion of Proudhon's philosophical ideas my book *Proudhon. Sa Vie, son oeuvre* (Presses Universitaires de France, 1965), pp. 15–31.
[2] Cf. the summary of the philosophical ideas of Marx in ch. xii of *La vocation actuelle de la sociologie*, II (2nd edn., 1963): 'La sociologie de Karl Marx', 220–70.

in human activity can be grasped and rationally understood only as revolutionary practice' (p. 142). 'Philosophers have simply interpreted the world in a different way, *it is a question of changing it . . .*' (p. 144).

In summary, Proudhon and Marx present the working class as being called to develop a *new philosophical knowledge*, later designated as *pragmatic philosophy*. This philosophy has been particularly successful in a capitalist country *par excellence*, the *United States of America*, where, from William James to John Dewey, pragmatist philosophy has triumphed without being of the slightest interest to the proletarian class.

Auguste Comte in his sociological analyses hardly ever discusses class divisions and still less often the existence of the proletariat. His sociological concepts are opposed to those of Marx and Proudhon (whom he ignored, moreover, and who were both very hostile towards him). However, in his *Discours sur l'ensemble du positivisme*, which dates from 1848, and was to be included in the first volume of his *Système de politique positive* (vol. I, 1851), he does not hesitate to appeal to the proletariat 'as bearer of a new philosophical knowledge', which he identifies naturally with his own positive philosophy! He declares, more particularly and somewhat surprisingly: 'The complete social regeneration required by positivism is feared almost as much by the various middle classes as by the upper classes; *this is why positivism can obtain strong collective support only within the proletarian class*' (pp. 134–40). There exists, therefore, he states, 'an affinity between positive philosophy and the proletariat' (pp. 136–7). He does not base these statements on any proof, and forgets them in the other three volumes of his *Système de politique positive*, which is concerned exclusively with reactionary autocrats.

After Marx's death, dogmatic Marxism, represented particularly by Engels, Kautsky and Plechanov, and which Lenin (in spite of his voluntarism[1] and his implicit empiricism, as well as

---

[1] This voluntarism is clearly seen in Lenin's book *The State and the Revolution* (1917), and in the speeches given during the later years of his life. Knowledge of French revolutionary syndicalism could have played a role in the development of his thought, but it is not certain. It might seem surprising that I should be alluding to the 'implicit empiricism' in Lenin, since in his book *Matérialisme et empiro-criticisme* (1st edn. in Russian, 1909) he violently condemned the concepts of Mach and Avenarius, and those of their Russian disciples, Bogdanov and others, who attempted to effect a reconciliation between empirico-criticism and Marxism.

his very acute sense of the uniqueness of Russian history) never succeeded in throwing off completely, assigns to the proletariat, among other 'historical missions' (such as the 'total disalienation of man and society') that of *becoming the principal support of a particular philosophy—'dialectical materialism'*. This is a term which Marx never used[1] and which no longer has any meaning, for the concept of 'matter' changes ceaselessly with the development of science, particularly the development of contemporary physics. What connection is there between today's 'quantum physics', emphasizing the 'quanta of energy', and 'matter' in all its various meanings?

Thus the term 'dialectical materialism' only serves to confuse the interpretation of the 'dialectic' in the sense that Marx had effectively defined and applied it, by talking about humanistic realism and vitalism. Moreover, Marx distinguished *real dialectical movements* (in different global societies, different social classes, different groups, etc.) and strongly insisted on the distinction between the *real dialectical movement* and the *dialectical method applied to* its study.

In my recent book, *Dialectique et Sociologie*, I have tried to show that the non-dogmatic dialectical method can only be empirical, and that true empiricism, which does not confine itself to the

However, it must not be forgotten that there were *two different periods in Lenin's thought*. Moreover, all historians of philosophy know that there exist almost infinite variations in the interpretations of empiricism, ranging from the dogmatic sensualism of Locke and Condillac to the 'dialectical empiricism' whose principles I have sought to defend (cf. *Dialectique et Sociologie* pp. 177–220).

In other respects, when I refer to the 'implicit empiricism' of Lenin, I am alluding not to his theoretical statements but to their concrete applications— for example, his statement that social revolution can be victorious in technically underdeveloped countries (termed 'the Third World' today), where the proletarian class has hardly begun to develop. This has been equally true, in part at least, for Russia, where, at the time of the October Revolution the proletariat, despite its revolutionary spirit and powerful clandestine organizations, represented only 6–7% of the total population. Lenin brought out forcefully in his later writings that 'the conditions for victory of social revolutions' were extremely variable from one country to another. . . . And this was not the least of his merits as a thinker, as well as man of action.

[1] He spoke only of 'humanistic realism' and later of the dependence of consciousness on social life. When Marx mentions 'the new materialist historiography' he is thinking rather of the method of research than of the material infrastructure of the society and the historical reality which is the most important part of it. And this has not the slightest connection with 'materialist philosophy'.

K

surface of things, can only be dialectical (whence the term 'dialectical hyper-empiricism' which I coined). According to this interpretation, the dialectical method is simply an exercise in the expurgation of mummified concepts, an expurgation preliminary to all scientific and philosophical knowledge, and particularly necessary in human science, of which sociology and history are the two main branches.[1]

As for the proletarian class, whether it be in the position of an exploited class, or of a class whose leaders are supposed to be in authority (wrongly supposed usually) *it has never yet woken from its philosophical sleep and torpor.* What will it become in the future? We shall try to show in the chapter devoted to the cognitive system of societies planned according to the principles of decentralized collectivism,[2] based on self-management by all the interested parties, that philosophical knowledge combined with knowledge of the Other has the opportunity to occupy first place. But this rightly presupposes the disappearance of the proletariat and the formation of new classes. In any case, we are in a position to state that to consider the proletarian class as the source of philosophical knowledge rests on *beliefs and myths.*

Now, if this is chimerical, where do such ideas come from? First perhaps from the supposition that the political knowledge of the proletarian class conceals an implicit philosophy. Secondly, from the fact that the thinkers who nourished such a hope found nothing constructive or satisfying in the philosophical knowledge of their time. Their need for consolation was revealed, among other things, in expectation of a new philosophy emanating for the first time from the proletarian class. But so far nothing has corresponded to this expectation. None of the philosophies formulated in the twentieth century, not even Bergsonism nor different kinds of phenomenology, realism—absolute or relative—or existentialism in its diverse interpretations, can be attributed to the proletarian class, or have evoked the slightest response in it. Today, when technical knowledge, increasingly imbued with scientific knowledge, predominates, it is rather scientific knowledge which, even though not popularized, exercises a stronger attraction for the upper levels of the proletariat.

[1] Cf. the discussion of Marx's dialectic in my book *Dialectique et Sociologie* (1962).
[2] Cf. below, part IV, ch. 12.

In the types of knowledge associated with the proletarian class, i.e. political knowledge, technical knowledge, the perceptual knowledge of the external world, and the knowledge of the 'We', the *collective, symbolic, and speculative forms clearly predominate.* A mystical tendency sometimes reduces the rational form, and the conceptual and empirical forms balance each other.

CHAPTER FIVE

The Quasi-class of Techno-bureaucrats and its Cognitive System

The quasi-class of techno-bureaucrats possesses an uncontrolled power over decision-making, which makes their exceptional technical resources independent of the goals which they should serve. Their strength lies in their omnipresence, which extends from large industrial enterprises to high State administration, organs of public and private planning, and headquarters of modern armies. They are particularly strong in trusts and cartels under an organized, directed capitalist régime. This omnipresence of the developing techno-bureaucratic class is revealed and intensified in its tendency to invade the 'apparatus' of various political parties, regardless of their positions, and particularly workers' (alas!) and employers' organizations. This tendency of the techno-bureaucracy to be omnipresent represents a threat everywhere, and from all points of view: in the different international organizations such as the United Nations, UNESCO, NATO, the different institutions of 'Europe' and beyond.

It is not restricted to directed capitalist régimes,[1] but represents an essential aspect of fascist régimes[2]—their logical outcome—which, though destroyed in Germany, Italy and Argentina, threaten to reappear in new guises, even within certain countries of the 'decolonized Third World'. Technocratic tendencies can even appear under communist régimes in certain phases of their development, particularly in centralized collectivism.[3] It is seen in their efforts to compensate for their backwardness in the field of production techniques. However, the threat of technocracy has never been great here, and it is now more likely to be avoided, due to a more vivid recollection of economic democracy, being the basis on which the Soviet revolution was founded. It is also due

---

[1] Cf. below, part IV, ch. 9.
[2] Cf. below, part IV, ch. 10.
[3] Cf. below, part IV, ch. 11.

to Yugoslavia's example, and that of Poland to some extent, since these two countries are moving towards a decentralized collectivism based not only on 'worker control' but on workers' self-management in the factories, and on participation by representatives of all interested parties in the councils of regional or central planning organizations.

Nevertheless, there is no doubt that the existence of a techno-bureaucratic class, whether already formed or in the process of formation, involves serious dangers and unpredictable consequences in most of the régimes that are in conflict today. The *cognitive system* which would correspond to this class seems to be of some importance and deserves a certain amount of attention.

*

Technical knowledge is obviously in *first place* and *attains its most advanced stage of development.* The techno-bureaucratic class holds the major technical secrets which permit the manipulation of nature, and, through its mediation, of other men, groups and societies. Atomic energy and atomic bombs, intercontinental (and interplanetary) missiles, automatic and electronic machines, etc. exercise a real or potential influence in all fields. There is no doubt that this knowledge gives to its possessors—individuals and groups—the desire and possibility to abuse their power. Global social structures, as well as the non-technical cultural works which bind them, face the prospect of being overwhelmed and threatened by the unleashing of the techniques that the technocrats claim to control. But in reality the technocrats, far from succeeding in mastering these all-powerful machines, most often find themselves outstripped by the forces which they themselves have set in motion, thus playing the role of sorcerer's apprentice. Their power is therefore reduced to an authoritarian, uncontrolled domination over the members of the different organizations dependent on these techniques.

Second place in this cognitive system should be given to *scientific knowledge* which is combined with high-level technical knowledge. Scientific knowledge itself becomes more and more technicized as the techno-bureaucracy inclines towards the often abusive technicization of all science.

The techno-bureaucratic class serves as a framework for implicit and explicit *political knowledge,* which occupies *third place.*

Such knowledge is necessary for finding a basis for reconciling the five opposing groups which make up this class, namely: (1) the expert technicians; (2) the planners; (3) the 'organizers' or managers of the vast economic enterprises, trusts and cartels, as well as the political parties and occupational associations; (4) the bureaucrats—top civil servants of the public services; and (5) military technicians. The interests, ideas, the rather confused ideology,[1] and the political orientation of these five often conflicting groups, are not identical. In order to have some chance of being structured into a single class, it is therefore necessary for them to have recourse to a skilful political strategy.

A formulated political doctrine, putting forward the necessity for the power of 'ruling élites' on the grounds that they possess exclusive skills which will enable the society to attain a completely dehumanized 'technical civilization', *is, in effect, propagated in capitalist countries,* where it may assume different nuances. In collectivist, communist countries, such a doctrine (at least an explicit one) is rendered impossible, since the founding of an industrial democracy, based on self-management and the triumph of a profound humanism (which remains the ultimate goal), is imposed upon even the most privileged groups of managers in the various branches of industry, officials of the 'party machine', and military experts.

In fourth place comes the *perceptual knowledge of the external world,* which this cognitive system situates in very specific space and time. In this case space is identified with the spread of technical devices and the organizations which have them at their disposal (whilst at the same time being dominated by them).

In theory these spatial extensions are primarily *prospective,* because they are directly related to the unrestrained techniques, which have become independent of the social structures that produced them. Furthermore, these spatial extensions are characterized by their capacity to expand indefinitely.

---

[1] Nietzche's oft-quoted 'Superman' is a far cry from racism (whether or not it is explicit) and the deep contempt for an inferior neighbour, or the kind of narcissism which arises from success based on exceptional skills. This is one of the manifestations of the confused nature of technocratic ideology. However, despite all the variations and disguises, it remains profoundly anti-egalitarian and hostile to democracy. To talk about 'liberal technocracy' (as do certain people in France today) is to make a play on words which is a contradiction in terms. Technocracy, in all its forms, is the *modern manifestation of tyranny, and subtle tyranny can sometimes become much more terrible than outright tyranny. . . .*

But in reality these technically based spatial extensions are related to the aggressiveness of the techno-bureaucratic groups which, while controlling them, are overwhelmed by the forces that they have unleashed, and end up being enslaved by them. To the extent that this space remains linked to these groups of 'sorcerers' apprentices', it is influenced by an element which is both ego-centric and projective.

The time in which the techno-bureaucratic class places the external world is the time which it attributes to its own activity, i.e. the time-in-advance-of-itself of the technical devices, and the time of long-term planning. Sometimes it is the explosive time of newly created devices or new uses for them. Such times strengthen the prospective and aggressive nature of the spatial extensions wherein the developments which this class claims to have brought about in the external and social world are manifested.

Yet, the techno-bureaucratic class, in its perceptual knowledge, is the victim of an illusion: its members are in fact the first to be enslaved by the technically based time and space extensions which they hope to control when they accede to power, but which lead society towards self-destruction. In the face of such a prospect, this class finds some alleviation of its *unconscious anxiety* (which its pretentious bravado merely disguises) to the extent that its members (from any group) always eagerly support the dissolution of concrete space and time into a *total spatio-temporal quantifica-tion*, even though their own knowledge of the external world reveals this quantification to be very relative. . . . This is therefore the source of a new obstacle to the structuration of this class, an obstacle which it can overcome only by an aberrant, aggressive frenzy.

Up to the present time the techno-bureaucratic class has not given rise to any philosophical doctrine in the strict sense, but it is not impossible that it may do so in spite of all the obstacles that we have mentioned (the contradictory ideology, the unconscious anxiety of the techno-bureaucrats in the face of their impotence when dealing with the technical devices at their disposal, the conflicts which divide the mentality in the different fractions of this class). One cannot deny, however, that some implicit philoso-phical orientations can be discerned in the attitude of this emer-gent class which lie half-way between cybernetics, a pragmatism devoid of humanism, and the ambiguous inspiration of a Heidegger

—the only authentic philosopher to have accepted the Nazi régime and later to have retracted.[1]

In the techno-bureaucratic class's cognitive system, neither the *knowledge of the Other* nor *common-sense knowledge* play a specific role. Distrust of others, particularly of those in inferior positions, is too great to permit even the slightest realization of the knowledge of the Other.

With regard to the emphasized forms of knowledge, the rational and the mystical, as well as the individual and collective, appear to be in equilibrium, whilst the conceptual, symbolic and speculative predominate.

As with all other classes, the integration of the techno-bureaucratic class into the different types of directed capitalism or fascism has repercussions on the nature of the corresponding cognitive system, as we shall see in the fourth part of this book.

[1] Heidegger was appointed rector of the University of Freiburg under pressure from the Nazi government, after having denounced the 'Jewish character' of phenomenological philosophy in his interpretation of his master, Husserl—the founder of phenomenology. All his official speeches at this time were full of praise for Hitler; moreover, the members of his family, his wife and children, were enrolled in the Nazi party. . . . The fact that Heidegger then withdrew from political activity and made honourable amends even in his philosophy, reformulated in the *Holzwege*, does in no way change the ambiguous nature of his philosophy, nor his conduct, about which the French public is rarely informed.

PART FOUR

Types of Global Societies and their Cognitive Systems

Preliminary Remarks

It now remains to relate the types and forms of knowledge to *global structures* and the different types of *subjacent total social phenomena.* The hierarchy of types of knowledge, which has already been established in certain structured groups (we have stressed the example of states and churches) and particularly in the social classes, becomes more marked here and is a richer field for study. The emphasized forms within each type of knowledge are also more stable and measurable.

Global societies, it will be recalled, are total social phenomena which are the most extensive and important, the richest in content and influence in any given social reality. They surpass in richness and authority not only the functional groups and social classes, but also their conflicting hierarchies. These 'macrocosms of social macrocosms' possess a juridical sovereignty restricting the power of all the groups which are integrated therein, including the state, the juridical sovereignty of which has always been relative and subordinate, in spite of all appearances to the contrary.

Global societies also exercise a certain social sovereignty over all the collectivities of which they are composed, i.e. they enjoy a *de facto* predominance. A global society is not only structurable, but is always structured. Various organizations participate in these precarious equilibria which the structures represent. But neither the structures (whether they are global or partial) nor the organizations completely represent the total global social phenomenon, not only because it is supra-functional, but also because it is the most changeable and fertile of all the possible infra-structures. There is always more ebb and flow in the total global social phenomenon than in its structure. Independently of the fact that a global structure, to avoid its disintegration, maintains its equilibrium only by countering the tendency towards destructuration with a constantly repeated effort of restructuration, there is always a marked disjunction between the life of the global structure and that of the subjacent total social phenomenon. Concerning the

problem of the relationship between types and forms of knowledge, this can sometimes raise the question of whether the
manifestations of knowledge associated with the global structure
and the underlying total phenomenon are always identical, and
whether there are not occasions when two cognitive systems can
enter into conflict or even contradict each other in a global society.

It is impossible to establish types of global societies without
approaching them through their structures, and it is also abso-
lutely necessary to go beyond the global structures to arrive at the
total social phenomenon itself. The social structures can be classed
by types according to a certain number of criteria: (1) the hierarchy
of groups; (2) the probable combination of the forms of sociality;
(3) the tendency towards accentuation of certain depth levels;
(4) the stratification of modes of division of labour and accumulation of goods; (5) the hierarchy of social regulation or social
controls; (6) the system of cultural works, and (7) the scale of
social times.

In summary, and before establishing the types of societies and
global structures which will serve as frameworks for our study of
the various corresponding cognitive systems, it should be remembered that the concept of the global society deals with *complete
and sovereign total social phenomena, which are essentially supra-
functional, always structured, but which are never completely
represented by a single organization. They seek the ascendancy over
the social classes which form within them. They predominate over the
macrocosmic groups, the depth levels, the forms of sociality, the
different social regulations, the modes of the social division of labour,
and the diverse social times. The 'cohesion'—the precarious equilibrium—of these structures is cemented by one or several cultures in
which they participate, although they are sometimes overwhelmed by
them.* This is because the global structures are always both
creators of cultural works and their beneficiaries. The accentuation
of these two elements permits of an almost infinite number of
variations, but even in borderline cases where cultures are derived
from others, their adaptation to situations, or to relatively heterogeneous or disparate social frameworks, presupposes a creative
element on the part of the total global social phenomena. Indeed,
to 'adapt' a derived cultural work to 'new circumstances' is to
recreate it in some way.

*

In our investigations into the functional correlations between cognitive systems and different types of global societies, we shall compare the structures of 'archaic societies' and the structures of 'historical' or promethean societies. Among the latter, we shall distinguish between those of the past and those of the present (which today are in conflict).

CHAPTER ONE

Ethnology and Approaches to Philosophical Anthropology

We believe that the study of archaic societies as social frameworks of knowledge involves great difficulties, beginning with the one that the non-participant observer in the total social phenomenon experiences (this is so both for the ethnologist and the ethnographer) when he goes beyond the structure to what is subjacent. Other difficulties, all equally real, arise from the fact that in this type of society, the cultural products are not sufficiently differentiated. In such conditions of extreme uncertainty, the sociology of knowledge might, if need be, restrict itself at least temporarily to studying historical or, as we have proposed describing them, promethean societies, and to postpone the study of archaic knowledge to a time when the sociology of knowledge is more advanced.

Archaic societies as social frameworks of knowledge are emphasized here principally in protest against the tendency of Lévi-Strauss to minimize (with the exception of a few modes of expression), the difference between the knowledge of archaic societies and our own. In *La pensée sauvage* (1963), *Le totémisme aujourd'hui* (1962) and *Le cru et le cuit* (1964), Lévi-Strauss maintains that there exists a universal logical structuralism at the base of every society.[1] He appears to disregard the remarkable work *La mentalité primitive* by Lucien Lévy-Bruhl, which brought out the difference between the knowledge found in archaic societies and that of societies that used to be called 'civilized', but which are more appropriately termed 'historical'.

Lucien Lévy-Bruhl, who accumulated materials of the utmost importance about knowledge in archaic societies, nevertheless omitted both to differentiate among them and to bring out their

---

[1] Cf. *Anthropologie structurale* (1958), particularly pp. 303 ff., and my critique in *Traité de Sociologie*, I (2nd edn.), 211 ff., and in *La vocation actuelle de la sociologie*, I (3rd edn., 1963), 420–3.

subtle distinctions. He sought rather to reduce all these societies to a single type, and to characterize their corresponding knowledge by a single emphasis on the mystical form, arising from the strength of the 'affective category of the supernatural'[1] as is reflected in the title of one of his works. (He himself suggests several types of knowledge: the perceptual knowledge of the external world, knowledge of the Other, technical knowledge, mythologico-cosmogonic knowledge.) Since there exist numerous types of archaic societies and even more of historical societies, his remarkable analyses over-simplified the problem of archaic knowledge or, to be more exact, they merely posed the problem rather than resolving it.

Thus Lévy-Bruhl's works appear to rule out any return to the prejudices of the eighteenth century and the belief in a transcendental, universal consciousness. Yet Lévi-Strauss seems to be effecting such a return.

Lévi-Strauss has waited a long time before acknowledging his primary source of inspiration, having previously chosen to refer to his American mentors—Boas or Kröeber. Yet, in his latest book, *Le cru et le cuit*, stimulated by Ricoeur's statements, he could not avoid acknowledging that in 'the search for mental constraints, my problem is the same as that to which Kant addressed himself'.[2] He appears to think that by subscribing to Ricoeur's opinion (who describes his thought as 'Kantianism without a transcendental subject') he strengthens his position, forgetting that for Kant there was no opposition between 'transcendental subject' and 'transcendental consciousness', acknowledged to be '*identical in everyone*'.

In any case, the analysis of myths—derived from the Indians of Latin America or Central America, and subjected to somewhat

[1] *Translators' Note*: Gurvitch provided an explanation of the 'affective category of the supernatural' in an article on Lévy-Bruhl's work, in which he stated, 'Granted that the entire life of primitive people is permeated with a profound mysticism, it does not follow that it is impossible to distinguish within the primitive mentality a sphere where this mysticism is particularly intense, where, so to say, it acquires a privileged character. This is the affective character of the supernatural which is allied to the intensity of fear. . . . He maintains that the problem is one of different degrees of intensity of fear and hence of affective category. Where this intensity is at its highest we find a privileged sphere of the immediate mystical experience, the foundation of which is the supernatural', Gurvitch, 'The Sociological Legacy of Lucien Lévy-Bruhl', *Journal of Social Philosophy*, V (1939), 61–70, at pp. 68–9.

[2] *Le cru et le cuit*, p. 18.

repetitive analysis—could not serve to prove the existence of a 'transcendental consciousness'. On the contrary, in *Le cru et le cuit* Lévi-Strauss reveals the difference which exists between these myths and the myths of other archaic societies. Even then, for any unprejudiced mind, the cognitive systems of the different capitalist or collectivist societies have nothing to do with the myths which concern Lévi-Strauss. When he tries to explain the sexual taboos and the marriage prohibitions between descendants of the same clan as arising from the necessity of keeping intact merchandise intended for exchange (in *Structures élémentaires de la parenté*) he projects the concept of *merchandise*, which is more appropriate to a capitalist structure, into archaic societies where this concept is not applicable. Thus he repeats the errors of the founders of classical political economy such as Adam Smith and Hume— errors which were denounced by Rousseau.

Instead of demonstrating the manifestations of the transcendental consciousness by identifying the content of myths, Lévi-Strauss restricts himself to reducing the opposition between 'nature and culture' to that of 'the raw and the cooked', which does not prevent him from talking about a 'dialectic between the two'.[1] But here he misuses the term 'dialectic'. It would be fruitless to look for a real dialectical movement, either in the raw or the cooked, since the dialectic can only be found in the *passage*, or in 'the way in between' two phenomena. Thus, according to Lévi-Strauss's thesis, it might be found either in the fire, which brings about the change from raw to cooked, or in the rotting of either or both, which is, in effect, what Lévi-Strauss claims.[2] Even if one broadens the elementary opposition between 'nature' and 'culture' to encompass the permanent penetration of nature by human action (Saint-Simon's society 'in action') and the resulting cultural works, which are in turn subject to the force of nature's resistance, one must recognize that nowhere does this dialectical movement appear more impoverished than in the 'raw and the cooked'. It is on this point that Lévi-Strauss concludes his last book, which ought to permit him to carry out an effective analysis of archaic knowledge since this is the least dialectical of all knowledge.

[1] Op. cit., pp. 140 ff.
[2] Ibid., p. 152.

CHAPTER TWO

Archaic Societies and their Cognitive Systems

As we see it, archaic societies (or non-promethean societies) are
alien to us. Essentially these societies lack all awareness of the
possibility of changing structures by conscious effort and, *a fortiori*,
they are deficient in both collective and individual human will and
liberty.

This situation is partly revealed in *theogonic, cosmogonic* mythology concerned with the origins of both the world and the society,
the members of which are considered simply as beneficiaries. Such
a mythology pervades all the types of knowledge that appear in
these societies, especially as the types of knowledge are not clearly
distinguished: indeed, not only are scientific and philosophical
knowledge missing, but common-sense knowledge, perceptual
knowledge of the external world, knowledge of the Other and the
We, and political knowledge, tend to fuse together.

*The theogonic and cosmogonic myths permeate all types of know-
ledge*, so that they cannot be considered as a separate and distinct
type of knowledge. All that one can say is that they tend to act
with particular intensity on the perceptual knowledge of the
external world possessed by archaic societies. Thus, when Lucien
Lévy-Bruhl suggests that the space and time in which this world
is placed cannot be quantified, because space is full of occult
obstacles and time is divided into good and evil times, it is a case
of myths directly affecting the collective perception of space and
time.

But this general characteristic includes many nuances and
variations as soon as one begins to distinguish between the different
types of archaic society. We shall confine ourselves to only four
of them[1]—not that this number cannot be increased in keeping
with the type of research undertaken—because we consider it
sufficient in order to study variations in the cognitive systems in
question, and the fluctuation of the forms within the corresponding
types.

[1] Cf. my *Déterminismes sociaux et liberté humaine* (2nd edn., 1963), pp. 222–45.

Here, then, are the types of structures and global societies which we intend to single out as social frameworks of knowledge:

(1) *Tribes with mainly a clan basis, co-operating in familial bands,* examples of which are found—or used to be found—in Australia and among the South American Indians;

(2) *Tribes incorporating varied and relatively unhierarchical groups* (clan, magical, familial, local, military, and occupational groups, etc.), whose cohesion rests on submission to a chief possessing mythical power (ethnologists such as Malinowski, Williamson, Lehmann, and Maurice Leenhardt have found various examples of these alongside other types of archaic societies, in Polynesia and Melanesia);

(3) *Tribes organized on the basis of military divisions, domestic and conjugal families, and sometimes clans, which have been largely wiped out* (the American ethnologists Boas, Lowie, Eggan, Hoebel, and others, and in France, Durkheim, followed by Mauss and Davy, found traces of these types of society in the extreme north of the United States, among the Cherokee and Kwakiutl for example);

(4) *Tribes which still maintain some clan-based divisions, but find organized expression in a monarchic state, supported by local groups which predominate over other groups,* and by an elaborate theogonic, cosmogonic mythology, which directly affects the functioning of the social structure (Evans-Pritchard, Fortes, Herskovits, Baumann, Westermann, Tempels, Griaule, Radcliffe-Brown, and Dariell Forde, have studied the structures of certain small tribes in black Africa that correspond, entirely or in part, to this type, which is only one of many types of global structure to be found in black Africa).

I. TRIBES WITH MAINLY A CLAN BASIS

With regard to the first type, that of tribes with mainly a clan basis, co-operating in familial bands, we must emphasize the predominance of the morphologico-ecological base, the division of labour in society based exclusively on age and sex, the absence of a technical division of labour, and the lack of clarity and intensity as far as myths are concerned. In these conditions the importance of tradition and routine is obviously not reinforced by these myths. Traditional and routine patterns are seldom predominant over rites, signs, and symbols. Moreover, social regulations are only slightly differentiated and not very clearly formulated. It might seem, therefore, that in this type of society, 'totems', which are always images of animals or vegetables, make up for more abstractly formulated and precise signs, symbols, and rules, which are lacking.

Furthermore, this question presents us with an opportunity to insert some brief remarks dealing more generally with the problem of 'totemism'. In fact it appears in various degrees of importance and intensity in most archaic structures, from the most simple (with which we have commenced this account) to the most complex (including the great Negro monarchies, which occupy a position somewhere between archaic societies and historical societies).

Certain interpreters have linked 'totems' to 'hunters' magic', and others to the pictorial expression of deeply rooted traditions, or rather to their symbols. Ethnologists of an earlier generation, led by Frazer and Durkheim, attributed to 'totems' a primary significance (we think exaggerated) for the very existence of 'clans' and 'tribes'.

Thus Durkheim saw in the totems a symbolization which bore witness to archaic society's self-deification. He took delight in quoting the claim of the Bororo Indians (Southern Latin America), who identified themselves with the arara—the most beautiful parrots in the world. According to Durkheim, the arara were not considered as gods, but as their symbols, just as they symbolized the Bororo tribes. He saw in the arara, therefore, an example of the intermediaries that guided actual human collectivities towards a direct participation in the divine. Finally, according to Durkheim, totems projected social reality into a divine transcendence, which resulted in the self-deification of society, first begun in these archaic societies.

During the last 40 years a strong reaction has taken place among Anglo-Saxon ethnologists and ethnographers against the exaggeration of the importance of totemism in archaic societies. We have noticed that, despite the many efforts at interpretation, the people actually involved attribute the most diverse meanings to the significance of their totems. Thus, many scholars have been led to wonder whether it might not be better to eliminate all attempts at a single interpretation of totemism, and recognize $n+1$ possible meanings, with regard to which a purely descriptive ethnography might compile a partial inventory.

However, what remains of totemism in clan-based tribes involves a real dialectic between 'classification' and 'participation', which presupposes 'complementarity', or mutual implication, or ambivalence. This does not appear in Lévi-Strauss's *Totemism*, where he tries to avoid difficulties rather than resolve them. When he is compelled later to demonstrate a connection between the 'logical principle of classification' of totemism and that of 'modern science', according to which they would both represent 'quantified thought', his sole intention is to prove that mystical participation and affectivity were always absent from the knowledge of archaic societies, and that any differentiation between 'primitive thought' and our present-day knowledge (however scientific it may be) is not possible. This profession of rationalism and agnosticism has as its goal, therefore, the elimination of all trace of differentiation between classification of and participation in reality, as far as knowledge is concerned. But Lévi-Strauss does not even seem to realize that in this way he is falling into an extreme idealism, which, moreover, is at the root of his 'axiomatic structuralism'. If, in *Le cru et le cuit* (*The Raw and the Cooked*), he returns to a primitive materialism, from which not even the 'dialectic of rotting' can save him, one is forced to observe that his none-too-subtle arguments succeed in making clear the untenability of his position, when he finds himself denying that any difference exists between the cognitive systems of the various types of archaic society, let alone historic societies.

*

Let us now return to the cognitive systems of societies where the relationship between clans and totems is dominant. We arrive at the following list.

(A) *In first place among the types and forms of knowledge found here is perceptual knowledge of the external world.* The space in which the external world is placed is essentially autistic and egocentric. The 'hunting grounds' are distinguished from the rest of the universe. Time is cyclical and seasonal. To the extent that space and time are tinged with a certain mysticism, or have either a close or more distant connection with the myths, it is a question of opposition between the pure and impure, good and evil.

Common-sense knowledge is directly integrated with that of the external world. It is concerned with pathways, natural routes, rivers that can be followed or serve as guides on a journey. It has often been emphasized that archaic people have a prodigious memory for those long routes that they consider to be free from physical or mystico-mythological dangers. It is particularly in this type of society that such a memory plays a role.

Perceptual knowledge of the external world also includes relationships between clans—each one having its own territory, as well as relationships of the clans with the whole tribe—the existence of which is hardly ever given prominence, especially if the clans are nomadic.

(B) *In second place* comes *technical knowledge*—improvised, implicit, spontaneous, dealing mainly with hunting, husbandry, and agriculture. We believe that Malinowski was right, as opposed to Lévy-Bruhl, although he may have generalized too much (for he also spoke about archaic societies in general), when he stated that techniques become mystical only when they are connected with dangerous activities.

(C) *In third place* would come a combination of *political knowledge, knowledge of the Other and the We*, and *common-sense knowledge*; the first occurs particularly in relations between clans or between clans and tribes.

As for the emphasized forms within these types of knowledge, the mystico-mythological form, and also the speculative form, appear to be somewhat attenuated; on the other hand, the empirical and, naturally, the collective forms predominate.

Finally, let us stress the fact that in this type of archaic society it is not possible to discover one particular group that could claim to be the guardian of knowledge, whether it be knowledge of myths or magic. It is highly debatable whether the witchdoctor– shaman even exists here.

II. TRIBES INCORPORATING VARIED AND RELATIVELY UNHIERARCHICAL GROUPS

These are clan, familial, magical, occupational, military, and local groups, whose relative cohesion is assured, however, by a chief possessing a somewhat mythological power. These different groups find themselves on an equal footing; the Mana (in this case, Mana Tangata), an immanent supernatural force, assures them of collective and individual success, victory, and prestige. This potential for successful action in social relationships—which serves as a basis for magic, whether exercised by professionals or private individuals, on the occasion of risk-laden work and taboo infringement—seems to penetrate the whole global structure. It plays an important role both in the system of social regulation and in the organization of economic exchanges (Kula, Sagali, Kere-Kere) by assuring the circulation of goods according to the principle of reciprocity.

To this plurality of magical activities based on the 'Mana Tangata', is opposed the uniqueness of the myth of cosmo-theogonic-social origin, of which the chief, particularly the king–chief, is the guardian and custodian. 'The chief', says Maurice Leenhardt in *Do Kamo*, 'is not the war chief, he is the head of a myth. He has no governmental function and he does not rule; son and heir of the ancestors, he is guarantor of the perman-ence of their blessings; he presides at the distribution of great prestations, he encourages any reciprocal offering and accepts offerings as homage.' Malinowski gives similar characteristics for Melanesian societies.

In this type of archaic society, mythology, religion, and magic, play a much greater role than in the first type we considered; the types and forms of knowledge are here quite different in their order, combination and emphases. Another difference is in the very clear social division of labour between several occupational groups: pearl fishers, hunters, farmers, dancers, soldiers, merchant middle-men, priests, and magicians. On the subject of religion, it should be noted that its boundaries are uncertain: indeed it exhibits pantheistic elements which could combine with magic, from which it diverges, however, by its attachment to the cosmo-gonic myths and the chieftainship rather than the clans. Usually the chief delegates the religious cult to priests: these cultic activities occur at the birth or marriage ceremonies and in funeral rites. On the other hand, magic intervenes in everyday work and exchanges, permeating all techniques, and all intergroup and inter-personal relationships.

(A) Thus, in this type of archaic society it is appropriate to put in first place *mythologico-theological knowledge*, which is supported by the chiefs and priests. It tends to approach closely perceptual knowledge of the external world, although the latter includes many other elements, such as magical vitalism.

In mythologico-theological knowledge, the conceptual, symbolic, positive, mystical, and collective, forms are accentuated.

(B) In second place is *technical knowledge*, although it can be at quite a low level (except that which concerns pearl fishing). But because magic enters into many occupational groups and their work, and because of the presumed penetration of Mana into inanimate objects (particularly pearls), plants, and animals, technical knowledge plays a considerable role in the system of knowledge of this type of archaic society. This *magico-technical* knowledge is semi-mystical and semi-rational; on the whole it is empirical, positive, concrete, and can be collective as well as individual.

(C) *Perceptual knowledge of the external world* comes only in third place, in spite of the support provided by cosmogonic myths and religion. This is because the external world appears to be so imbued with different kinds of magical Mana that it seems to be subordinate to technical knowledge combined with magic. The result is that the space in which the external world is placed is less egocentric than projective, and slightly prospective; on the whole it is more diffuse than concentric. Time, in combination with space, is a time of long duration, which is supported by myths, but a time of irregular pulsations is also experienced, issuing from magic, techniques, and exchanges. The forms of this knowledge are identical with those of technical knowledge.

(D) In fourth place comes *political knowledge, knowledge of the Other and the We*, and *common-sense knowledge*, which in this case tend to be identical. Indeed, in a global social framework where the different groups are relatively unhierarchical, but very active, political knowledge with regard to strategy for relationships between these groups is indispensable; but, being quite instinctive, it is confused with the common-sense knowledge of each group. Moreover, they cannot co-exist without a certain knowledge of the Other, as well as of their own members. Obviously, this knowledge of the Other and the We, based on magic and Mana, accompanied by mutual fear but also by an element of competition, even if it is only mystical, does not culminate in a profound knowledge. However, it cannot be ignored. The forms emphasized are the empirical, speculative, mystical, and collective, whereas the symbolic and the concrete tend to limit each other.

What appears from this brief analysis of the cognitive system of the second type of archaic society is that, whilst it resembles what Lucian Lévy-Bruhl called the mystical character of primitive mentality, it also reveals traits and nuances which entail different degrees of intensity of the 'affective category of the supernatural'.

III. TRIBES ORGANIZED ON THE BASIS OF MILITARY DIVISION, DOMESTIC AND CONJUGAL FAMILIES, AND CLANS

Boas and his students described the Potlatch among the Cherokee and Kwakiutl. Their work inspired two disciples and successors of Durkheim—Marcel Mauss and Georges Davy—who, while interpreting this phenomenon in a different way, emphasized the aspect of competition (challenge and response), which is part of the network of these societies. Since then, Lowie, Eggan, Bowers, E. A. Hoebel, and many more, have developed a more subtle and complex picture of this type of archaic society. It can be noticed that in this type of society the division into clans and sub-clans has declined. Neither do local groups any longer play a very important role. It is now a case of encampments of some sort, even when the originally nomadic tribes have become settled. The tribal councils are composed of leaders of military groups, or by the leaders of domestico-conjugal families (and sometimes a combination of the two). The leaders of military groups, which can be entered only after a person has undergone certain tests, are selected by their predecessors. These groups are in competition with each other; moreover, within each of them, an important role is given to competition in exploits by individuals and groups. They exercise a police function on particular occasions, such as at ritual dances, seasonal hunts, transmigrations, wars, etc.

Among the other groups, the most important are certainly the dance societies—sun dance, pipe dance, tobacco dance, bison dance. They have much more of a religious than a magical character: shamanism, the magic of hunters and farmers, is often exercised outside these dance associations, which are sources of mythologico-cosmogonic knowledge. Religion has a clearly pantheistic character; its rites can equally well be observed by each believer or group leader, independently of the dance societies, which makes it rather difficult to distinguish between religion and magic.

The mentality of the North American Indian tribes seems less coloured by emotion and mysticism than that of all the other archaic societies; this is shown very clearly not only in the tendency towards competition, but also in the joking-relationships, and in an element of juridical regulation maintained by arbitration tribunals. These aspects of the structure of the societies we are now discussing have raised doubts among some American ethnographers: consideration has been given to the possibility that this might be a phenomenon produced by decomposition due to the influence exercised over three centuries by the colonizing society. Ethnographers such as Barnett and Garfield have even formulated the hypothesis that the famous *potlatch* might only be a simple mutation of the markets and fairs of the colonizers. Not being a specialist on this question, I shall abstain from taking up a position in the debate, which in itself seems rather characteristic of the uncertainties of ethnology.

We intend only to give a list, naturally *hypothetical*, of the types and forms of knowledge likely to correspond to this type of archaic society.

(A) In *first place* we should put *political knowledge*, combined with *common-sense knowledge*, and *knowledge of other groups which make up the tribe*. Indeed, the competitive nature of these societies could contribute to the primacy of these three types of knowledge in combination. As for the forms of knowledge, the mystical and symbolic seem to be limited by the rational and concrete, but the collective predominates over the individual, although not without difficulty.

(B) In *second place* would come a combination of *mythologico-cosmogonic knowledge* and *perceptual knowledge of the external world*. The myths of the creation of the universe and the tribes (Old Man Coyote), take on precise outlines and are related to the external world. The space in which this world moves is both concentric and projective; the corresponding time is rather cyclical, which does not rule out within the tribe the presence of a time of irregular pulsations, and a deceptive time in which, beneath a time of long duration, there is hidden time in ferment. As for the forms of knowledge, the mystical, symbolic, speculative elements are more strongly emphasized than in the types of knowledge in first position, whilst the collective form predominates without challenge.

(C) *Technical knowledge,* particularly that concerned with the cultivation of tobacco, the rearing of horses, and hunting, occupies last place. The emphasized forms are the same as in the preceding types, except that magic makes the mystical form more active here than in mythologico-cosmogonic knowledge.

We now arrive at the last type of archaic society whose knowledge we have selected for examination.

IV. ORGANIZED MONARCHIC TRIBES, WHICH PARTLY RETAIN CLAN DIVISIONS

In the past the monarchies of Black Africa have provided good examples of such tribes.

Certainly one finds a great variety of types of society in Black Africa. There is no need to dwell on the fact that, in many of the global societies and structures of these regions—themselves divided into many areas of civilization (Bantu, Zambezian, Congolese, Upper Niger, Sudanese, not to mention the composite areas and the Pygmies of the equatorial forests)—the state not only did not exist in the past, but does not even exist today. We are only concerned with a single type of archaic society among all those that have existed in Black Africa—that which has been examined by Fortes and Evans-Pritchard in their work *African Political Systems,* and further discussed in the works of the late Griaule and his collaborators based on the Sudan.

Now the two characteristics which seem to have particularly impressed all the ethnologists who have examined this type of society are: the existence of a political state, organized as an authoritative monarchy, and the marked relationship between a widely developed mythologico-cosmogonic knowledge and the functioning of the social structure. Griaule, for example, has shown that the social structure of these societies exactly reproduces their cosmogony and their theogony, on both the small-scale and the large-scale, to such a point that the mythological and religious order, the order of the universe, and the social order, all correspond. This is not so clearly the case in any of the other types of archaic society that we have considered. Moreover, it could be that we are dealing with a reproduction which is not unilateral, as was thought by Griaule and his school, but is in some way reciprocal. Or more precisely, we could be dealing with a parallelism resulting from mutual implications. In any case, recent interpreters insist on the fact that the disposition of land, the distribution of inhabitants in the village, and even the arrangement of furniture within the houses, correspond to the contents of myths, and that a profusion of symbols express these myths, whilst at the same time participating in their creation.

Despite the strength of the clans and tribes, the very highly developed hierarchy in these societies depends less on them than on the collective use of land, local groups and the rank of their leaders in relation to the king—who holds responsibility for all the land—as well as on the wealth and position of the corresponding polygamous, domestico-conjugal families.

But this hierarchy sees itself in competition with a series of important groups, such as the priests (in theory, under the king's authority, but in fact independent of the political organization), the professional magicians (rain-makers, witchdoctors, specialists in increasing productivity and fertility, magico-economic specialists—according to Evans-Pritchard's expression), the male initiation houses, age and sex groups, clubs and secret societies, groups of craftsmen (especially blacksmiths and woodcarvers); all these associations to some extent possess the character of magic fraternities, wearing their masks and performing rites. The secret societies occasionally degenerate into bands of brigands; sometimes (and most frequently), they are called upon to constitute the king's entourage, in which they form the personal guard, the police (often exercising their functions masked, and at night), the army, and the judiciary (in secret tribunals).

The king himself possesses important magical prerogatives. He is a thaumaturgical king, endowed with both magical and religious power. Consequently, it is possible for him to become jealous of the professional magicians and banish them from the country, as did Chaca, the all-powerful king of the Zulu.

One might, therefore, advance the hypothesis that these black monarchic states in some way represent a prefiguration of the first type of historical society—the 'charismatic theocracies' with which we shall deal in the next chapter. Due to the victory of certain magical fraternities over all other groups, the leaders of the fraternities with magical and economic power might have become kings. But, although victorious, the magical fraternities soon found themselves prisoners of the vanquished: starting with the king himself, they were placed in the service of religion, the priesthood, and the traditional theogonic-cosmogonic mythology. In these black monarchic states it is as if a double reciprocal annexation of magic by religion, and religion by magic, had occurred simultaneously; the foundation of the royal power is both mythologico-religious and magical, and because it is magical it is also economic.

With regard to the cognitive system of this type of society we think it possible to formulate it in the following manner:

(A) In *first place* would come a combination of *mythological knowledge, political knowledge*, and *technical knowledge*. It is no accident that in these societies mythology is essentially vitalist and puts the emphasis on the perpetual renewal and increase of fertile forces—cosmogonic, social, political, and economic. The primordial importance of magic only serves to reinforce this tendency.

In these three types of knowledge, which are barely differentiated, the opposition between the mystical form and the rational form is somewhat blurred by the vitalism, but in other respects the speculative, symbolic, and collective, predominate.

(B) *Perceptual knowledge of the external world and common-sense knowledge* are in some way both combined, and subordinated, to magic, mythology, and political knowledge. The external world is placed in projective space, with a tendency towards expansion, and to some extent in time in advance of itself, and under the influence of the vitalist belief of this turbulent society, projected on the space of the external world.

The forms emphasized are the same as in the preceding types of society, but with one exception: because common-sense knowledge penetrates knowledge of the external world, the speculative is considerably limited by the positive form.

(C) *Knowledge of the Other and even of the We* (particularly with regard to groups), must be placed in last position, even though it is supported by the importance of political knowledge and the primordial influence of magic. Yet the groups are so numerous and so often hostile to each other, that it is only within domestico–familial frameworks, magical, and occupational groups, that knowledge of the Other has any opportunity to exist.

Emphasis is on the mystical, empirical, positive, and collective forms.

Finally, it should be noted that among all the types of archaic society just analysed, only the second and fourth (especially) imply the existence of groups based solely on the possession of specific knowledge—associations of priests, magical fraternities, and occupational associations. Yet it is a question of an esoteric knowledge and not an exoteric kind, in that it is not widely diffused, but is transmitted in secret. It is only in historical societies that the situation is different.

*

We are the first to recognize that this attempt at an analysis of the cognitive systems of certain types of archaic society is schematic, 'conjectural', and even somewhat hazardous. Its sole purpose is to show the inadequacy of an over-simplified characterization of the systems of knowledge and mentality of these societies. They are highly complex, and this complexity varies with each of the types, but it is a complexity quite different from that which characterizes various types of historical society. Although Lucien Lévy-Bruhl was right in theory to assert that the system of knowledge of primitive societies is imbued with mysticism, and is related to the affective category of the supernatural, he did not sufficiently appreciate the variety in the degree of intensity of these elements, which vary according to the types of knowledge, and the types of archaic society. And although Lévi-Strauss was wrong to deny that there was a difference between primitive knowledge and the rational knowledge of historical societies, his error becomes even more evident when he is driven to reduce all myths to the same subject-matter, and all knowledge to the same principles of classification, by eliminating from knowledge the various degrees of participation.

All systems of knowledge, archaic and historical, are as complex and variable as the social frameworks to which they correspond. In fact variability is their only common trait. *And if we have trespassed on the territory of ethnology, it is in order to pursue our quest to its conclusion, in such a way as to reveal the relativism and pluralism in the sociology of knowledge.*

We have already emphasized, in connection with archaic societies, the demarcation line which separates them from historical societies, which are imbued with prometheanism to various degrees. It is appropriate to recall here that by using the term promethean with regard to the collective consciousness of these societies (or certain of their constituent groups) we mean the possibility of structural change by the intervention of human will. The tension created attains its paroxysm in revolutions or, at least, in sudden overthrows of established powers.

As soon as we approach the question of the relationship between these historical societies and the types and forms of knowledge, we are faced with two new problems:

(a) The first concerns the case where conflicts between the global structures of these societies, and the subjacent total social phenomena, provokes division in the cognitive systems. Here one witnesses a struggle between two entire cognitive systems, or at least a marked opposition between two different emphases of the same system.

(b) The second problem is concerned with discovering, in the case of a disjunction between cognitive system and social framework, which one of them, in each particular circumstance, plays the causative role.

*

These problems already arise in dealing with the first type of historical society that we shall analyse in the following chapter devoted to 'theocratico-charismatic' societies and their cognitive systems.

CHAPTER THREE

Theocratico-charismatic Societies and their Cognitive Systems

The most striking historical example of a society of this type—which the kings–priests–magicians–living gods incarnated—was Ancient Egypt where one is immediately struck by the frequency of revolutions and the importance of the disjunction between the structure and the total social phenomenon.

The best-known revolutions were those which concerned the rapid democratization of funeral rites, the accession of the common people to the mysteries of Isis–Osiris, the integration of occupational organizations into the state after the end of the Eleventh dynasty in Egypt, and the revolts of the Yellow Turbans[1] and the Red Eyebrows[1] in Imperial China. The presumed eternal nature of the social structures was only an official ideal, which was more of a political than a cosmogonic myth, contradicted by the reality of the historical facts.

As for the disjunction between structure and total social phenomenon, it can be seen that in theocratico-charismatic societies the role of the structure tended to be reduced to that of a convenient, artificial cover. It was as if under cover of this structure, which was but a semi-official, limited expression, the subjacent total social phenomena were leading a much richer, more animated life than a superficial glance would lead one to suppose. Also we know that broad sections of social life developed towards rationalism, the economic calculation of exchange, the individual right to bonds, contracts, loans and credit, and the plurality of particular groups—such as the occupational groups and trade associations in Egypt, and the merchant societies in the Caliphates. Moreover,

---

[1] *Translators' Note:* the reference is to the revolt of the *Yellow Turbans* in China in A.D. 184 (the name is an allusion to a distinctive item of their dress).

The *Red Eyebrows* were involved in a peasant uprising which broke out in China in A.D. 18 (the name came from the distinguishing mark they adopted). Cf. Edwin O. Reischauer and John K. Fairbank, *East Asia: The Great Tradition*, I (Boston, Houghton Mifflin, 1960), 122 and 126.

large heterogeneous, non-integrated masses, made up of conquered peoples and slaves, perpetuated unrest.

Official prometheanism, inherent in the role attributed to the *king–priest–magician–living god*, which amounted to combining *state*, *church* and *magical fraternities* into one supreme being, created strong tensions. The powers possessed by the dynasties and their leaders had a magical, religious and personal character, or rather these three aspects were combined together until there was complete fusion. The dynastic leaders were *demiurges*, according to the official mythological doctrine, but this demiurgy appeared only at the top of the hierarchy: it penetrated the different levels of the official or unofficial hierarchy. These living gods–priests–magicians–kings–demiurges, who were responsible for maintaining and developing the mythologico-cosmogonic order—which included the natural, religious and social orders— were often overwhelmed and immobilized by the burden of their tasks. This was because conflicts between the various orders were inevitable, for the priests, magicians, civil servants of the extensive administrative machine, the scribes, merchant and artisan fraternities, plus the defeated, enslaved peoples, could all be opposed to the dynastic leaders or the dynasties themselves. From their own point of view, the kings–demiurges–living gods ran the risk of (consciously or not) being unfaithful to their ancestors. All these difficulties explain the plurality of dynasties (particularly in Ancient Egypt and China) whose succession of changes brought about breaks in continuity and upheavals, and ran the risk of precipitating real revolutions, resulting directly from eruptions in the subjacent total social phenomenon.

Theocratico-charismatic societies were therefore far from having a calm existence, such as one might have expected from a society ruled by demiurges. As we have seen, they were constantly erupting, for ever undergoing upheavals or revolutions brought about by the action of the total social phenomena where it was in disjunction with the structure.

Apart from Ancient Egypt, one might also cite as examples of charismatic theocracies: Babylon, Assyria, the Hittite kingdom, Persia, China, Ancient Japan, Tibet, the Indies and, in a special form, the Islamic Caliphates in the dynasties of the Umayyads and the Abbasids from the eighth to the thirteenth century, and very probably the Inca Empire. But we shall confine ourselves to the example of Ancient Egypt whose social structure is the most familiar.

The structure of these societies was characterized by:

(a) The predominance of the state–church–magical fraternity and its great economic enterprises (the canals) over other groups, such as the priestly caste, functionaries, public and private scribes (in Egypt and the Indies), military groups, patriarchal families, and occupational fraternities of merchants and artisans. For the most part these groups were very active and inclined to demonstrate their own demiurgical powers.

(b) The predominance of masses over communities and communions (the latter being limited to groups of priests and initiates of particular cults).

(c) Emphasis on large-scale organization, morphological foundations, and techniques, some of which are still unequalled, such as embalming; next came magico-religious symbols and beliefs of a vitalist nature; and finally, related to these and constituting their basis —the official one at least—were the theogonic and political myths.

(d) A highly elaborate division of labour, both technical and social, in some spheres (irrigation, drainage, construction, painting, and embalming in Egypt; woodcarvers and jewellers in China, etc.).

(e) In the hierarchy of social controls, first place was not occupied by religion, magic and myths (contrary to what one might think). They were relegated to a secondary position by *technical knowledge* which was pushed into the foreground by its link with early scientific knowledge, magic, the more pronounced vitalism of religious beliefs, and the creative morality stimulated by the promethean demiurge. The perceptual knowledge of the external world came immediately after technical knowledge. Secular law and art, which largely ignored the myths, further strengthened this situation.

(f) Thus in all the cultural works which cemented the structures, the official, superficial mysticism was very limited. This resulted in an increased rationalism—whence some unexpected findings concerned with the cognitive system of theocratico-charismatic societies.

(A) *Technical knowledge*, having succeeded in dominating and integrating mythologico-cosmogonic knowledge and mythologico-political knowledge, *must be put in first place*. The kings–living

M

gods–magicians–demiurges might be described as the first *technocrats*. But they shared their 'technocratic' power and their technical knowledge with an entourage of civil servants, scribes, priests, magicians and military men. The technical knowledge in different fields varied according to the different artisan and commercial occupations. There were even traces of it among the officials in charge of the irrigation canals and even in the patriarchal agricultural families.

Nevertheless technical knowledge was to a large extent esoteric, in spite of the creation of academic institutions which, however, taught only the semi-official mythology, the art of writing on papyrus, and the rudiments of the burgeoning scientific knowledge. Thus, technical knowledge at its different levels—inasmuch as it could be transmitted—remained limited to circles of initiates; the same phenomenon will be observed in scientific knowledge which, it is true, was still only in its early stages.

Despite the integration of mythology and magic into technical knowledge, its emphasized forms tended towards the rational rather than the mystical; the symbolic, the speculative and naturally the collective predominated over their opposites, whilst the empirical and conceptual forms varied according to the level of the technical knowledge.

(B) *The perceptual knowledge of the external world* was placed immediately after technical knowledge in this cognitive system. Like technical knowledge, it absorbed and incorporated certain elements of the cosmogonic mythology which it completely dominated. One would think that the space in which the external world was placed, encompassing on the ecologico-morphological level the seasonal floods of the Nile, would have been mainly concentric, and that time, for the same reason, would have been mainly cyclical. Yet such conclusions are weakened and shown to be inadequate by the 'demiurgical'[1] techniques, since the canals broke the concentric elements of space, as well as its egocentric nature; other techniques (such as military techniques) and the strength of the administrative and economic organization led to projective space, at some points even pushing towards prospective space (as in the contacts with Babylon and Assyria: commercial and cultural exchanges, alliances and conquests). Cyclical time

[1] *Translators' Note:* 'demiurgical' in the sense of creating or extending the world.

was broken by a vitalist interpretation, which gave renewal and strengthened impetus, and therefore a real acceleration to each cycle; deceptive time, whose underlying pressure caused unusual eruptions in the structures and organizations, benefited from this. Thus, time of irregular pulsations alternating between advance and retardation, which was characteristic of theocratico-charismatic society, was projected on to the movement of the external world. Furthermore, knowledge of the space and time in which the external world was situated benefited directly and as a result of the influence of geometry and astronomy at their inception, and the appearance of calendars; it is not surprising that the rational form of this knowledge was emphasized much more than the mystical form, and, that contrary to what one finds in technical knowledge, the empirical, the positive and the concrete predominated.

(C) *Political knowledge* occupied third place. The entourage of the charismatic leader, along with the civil servants, the military, the priestly caste, the scribes, occupational fraternities, and even the agrarian patriarchal families were its main sources. It used mythology at its higher levels and was combined with common-sense knowledge at almost all its levels. Political knowledge, however, exceeded common-sense knowledge in that it also appeared in relations with the conquered, enslaved peoples. The forms of political knowledge were variously emphasized.

(D) *Common-sense knowledge*, which came in fourth place, varied according to the different ranks, groups, milieux, and conquered peoples. It found its strongest support in the agrarian, patriarchal family.

(E) It was in theocratico-charismatic societies that for the first time there appeared a *scientific knowledge* detached from the cosmologico-theogonic mythology, magic and technical knowledge. From a historical point of view, one can formulate the hypothesis that scientific knowledge was first derived from Assyria and Babylon by Ancient Egypt, which in turn transmitted it to the Greek cities where it was more precisely developed. This knowledge involved mathematics, particularly geometry, and elements of astronomy and biology. Although this scientific knowledge had repercussions on the perceptual knowledge of the external world, it remained essentially esoteric. It was the prerogative of members of the priestly caste and the group of scribes. But,

for the first time in a global society, a *group of scholars* emerged
who, often independently of any religious connections, deliber-
ately assumed the task of maintaining scientific knowledge and,
through education, transmitting it to their successors (even if these
were limited to a small number of initiates).

The forms emphasized in this initial appearance of scientific
knowledge may seem somewhat surprising. In fact, contrary to
what one might have thought, this knowledge was seen to be more
mystical, speculative, symbolic and conceptual than in any other
type! This apparent paradox, which was to be repeated in the
Middle Ages, should be interpreted as the price to be paid for the
new cognitive acquisitions. In any case, it is proven that numbers,
equations, geometric analyses and quantified calendars, which
were the first manifestations of scientific knowledge, can assume
strong mystical forms. Marcel Granet, the late disciple of Durkheim, in his two works: *La pensée chinoise*, 1934, and *Les études
sociologiques sur la Chine*, 1953, stressed the mystical character
which numbers could assume and in this connection recounted
this anecdote: a military leader in Ancient China convened a
council of war to find out if he should attack the enemy or retreat.
Three members pronounced themselves to be for the attack, and
eight against. The leader declares 'the majority is for, therefore
we shall attack'. This is because 3, a mystical number, prevails
over 8.[1]

[1] Cf. Marcel Granet, *La Pensée chinoise*, Paris, A. Michel (1st edn., 1934, 2nd
edn., 1950), pp. 298–9: 'Tso T'ang recounts the proceedings of a council of
war: should we attack the enemy? The leader is keen to fight, but he has to
enlist the responsibility of his subordinates and consider their opinions. Twelve
generals, including himself, are present at the council. The opinions are divided.
Three leaders refuse to engage in combat; eight wish to join battle. The latter
are in the majority and proclaim this to be so. However, the opinion that unites
eight voices never prevails over the opinion that unites three: three is almost
unanimity, which is quite different from the *majority*. The chief general will
not fight. He changes his mind. The opinion with which he concurs is imposed
from then on as a unanimous one.' Cf. also ch. III in this book entitled 'Les
nombres', pp. 148–299, particularly pp. 273 ff.: '*Numbers are not used for
expressing size:* they are used for adjusting concrete dimensions to the proportions of the universe'; pp. 275–6: 'Numbers are but emblems: the Chinese do
not regard them as abstract, restricting signs of quantity'; cf. Marcel Granet,
La civilisation chinoise (Paris, A. Michel, 1st edn., 1929; 2nd edn., 1948),
pp. 351–4; ibid., Preface by Henri Berr, pp. xvii–xviii: 'In sum, a profound
mysticism but, if one dares to say so, a positive mysticism which is oriented
towards the practical . . . enables the society to participate in that which is
regular and fixed in nature'; cf. also Marcel Granet, *Etudes sociologiques sur la
Chine* (Paris, Presses Universitaires de France, 1953), pp. 148–9, 201–213.

Even in Pythagoras one found a mysticism attached to numbers. This observation may seem paradoxical, but it is nevertheless true: stages in scientific thought are not always rational, and, in its beginnings in theocratico-charismatic societies, they were much less so than in any other knowledge.

(F) *Knowledge of the Other and the We, of groups and societies,* is barely perceptible. In the extraordinary chaos of ranks, milieux, groups and conditions, it could not, at the most, go beyond the familial, artisan and commercial circles on the one hand, and the entourage of the king–demiurge, priests and scribes on the other. Elsewhere passive, dispersed masses predominated. Inasmuch as this knowledge succeeded in appearing, its emphasized forms were the speculative, symbolic and conceptual rather than their opposites.

CHAPTER FOUR

Patriarchal Societies and their Cognitive Systems

Max Weber talked about the secularization and routinization of 'charisma' (*Veralltäglichung des Charismus*) in patriarchal societies. Without realizing it, he was thus adopting the evolutionist point of view which he rejected in other respects. I propose an interpretation which seems to be more consistent. In fact, I do not believe that patriarchal societies arose out of theocratico-charismatic societies. They were very similar, and if one considers their prometheanism, i.e. their historicity, or even their cognitive systems, patriarchal societies appeared to be much more backward than theocratico-charismatic societies. Yet, they were different, and should not be classified as archaic societies in the strict sense of the term.

In this type of global society, the structure was based on the exclusive pre-eminence of the large-scale domestico-familial group based on consanguineous kinship, related usually through masculine descent, whether or not it was polygamous. This group incorporated all others, such as those relating to economic activity, locality, neighbourhood (if it was settled), and mystico-ecstatic groups; it predominated over age and sex groups.

All economic, political, and religious activities were brought together in the home of the domestico-conjugal family: the patriarch being father, owner–entrepreneur, priest, and political leader. Thus the family was established as an economic enterprise, a political state and a church simultaneously, although the father and proprietor–entrepreneur aspects were much more prominent than the political leader or priest aspects. Indeed, the gods or God, which the patriarch served, were first and foremost familial or domestic gods. *Religion was completely at the service of the family*; it involved a strongly reduced mysticism, and served as guarantor of traditional morality.

These observations apply as much to the type of structure which emerges from the *Old Testament* as to that which can be gleaned from the *Odyssey* and the *Iliad*, to the Roman family before its integration into the city, and to the German *Haus-genossenschaft* (an association of several patriarchs). It is interesting to note that the remnants of or parallels to this type of society and global structure—such as the *latifundia* of the high Roman Empire, the Slavic *zadrugas*, the patrimonial monarchies (the Frankish monarchies of the sixth to the ninth centuries)—were all linked with very different religions: monotheism, polytheism, paganism, Judaism and Christianity. This shows that in the life of these societies and in the equilibrium of their structure, religion tended to play only a very secondary role. This type of structure was characterized among other things by the absence of power differentiation, the exceptional weakness, if not absence, of particular groups, and the quasi-rational and secular atmosphere of their functioning.

We can draw up the following outline of these global structures:

(a) Complete predominance of the domestico-familial group.

(b) Pre-eminence of the *We* over *relations with the Other*, the *community* over the *mass* and the *communion* which are barely evident, and the passive 'We' over the active 'We'.

(c) At the top of the hierarchy relating to the levels of social reality were various patterns of an extremely routine nature, and the corresponding regular behaviour, preferably *customary* and *traditional* rather than *procedural* or *ritualistic*. An over-generalization about this type of society has led a number of sociologists and philosophers to repeat time and time again that *all societies are routinized, traditional, stagnant, immobilized* and 'closed'. But such statements are true only of patriarchal societies. Second among the depth levels was the morphological and ecological base: the fertility of the domestico-conjugal family, its size, its density, its 'natural environment'. Rational as well as mystical symbols came third; then social roles: the eldest son, the benjamin, the adopted and the slave, etc. All the other depth levels were forced into the background, including organizations.

(d) The division of technical labour was little developed, and the division of social labour was reduced to age and sex groups, and to descendants, adoptees and slaves.

(e) In the hierarchy of social regulations or 'social controls', *traditional morality and the morality of ideal symbolic images* occupied first place.

(f) The non-technical cultural works were limited to *recited epic traditions*, chants, dances and feasts, spoken and written language, cults, rites, revelations, etc. Furthermore, there were no perceptible tensions between the structures and the total global social phenomena.

Knowledge played a very limited role in these societies.

(A) In first place were three closely combined types of knowledge: *common-sense knowledge, the perceptual knowledge of the external world, and knowledge of the Other and the We.* The first was firmly attached to tradition which, dominating all activities of this society, tended to absorb all the other kinds of knowledge. In the perceptual knowledge of the external world, it was the concentric, autistic, projective space which predominated. In this knowledge the external world was placed in the time of slowed down, long duration, as well as cyclical–seasonal time. The knowledge of the Other and the We was based mainly on the microsocial element of the community, although the community was weakened by internal struggles between the eldest and the younger sons. Furthermore, the 'adoptees' were integrated into the community only with difficulty and often their 'Otherness' was resistant to knowledge. We will not labour the fact that slaves (in so far as patriarchal societies possessed them), because they were not considered as the Other, represented an obstacle to this knowledge.

(B) In second place came *political knowledge*, whose manifestations—which were obviously completely spontaneous—in patriarchal societies often assumed the form of intrigues designed to obtain the favours of the leader, or even the succession to the leadership. As a result of the struggles between the eldest and the younger sons, and their respective supporters, as well as the struggles between their mothers and their entourages, this situation gave rise to measures for self-defence. These conflicts were further aggravated by the 'adopted' sons who, by joining in the competition, strived to profit from it.

(C) *Technical knowledge* occupied third place: since it was underdeveloped and rudimentary, it tended to be intermingled with the perceptual knowledge of the external world, and common-sense knowledge.

(D) Fourth and last place was given to a weakly expressed *mythico-theological knowledge.* This no longer concerned theogonico-cosmogonic myths proper but somewhat ineffective theologies which projected the hierarchies arising from the global structure on to the divine level. The fact that the concern for perpetuating the mythico-theological tradition was left to the 'bards', narrators and singers of epic tales, whose position and social role were the least respected ones, is sufficiently eloquent: it proves that the patriarchs and their followers had little time to be concerned with theological knowledge.

It is hardly necessary to recall that in the patriarchal society scientific knowledge was non-existent: it would be difficult to name any group of 'wisemen', 'scholars' or even, in a more general sense, intellectuals.

The emphasized forms in these types of knowledge would tend to be the rational, positive, empirical, and obviously the collective forms. The symbolic and concrete forms were mutually restricting.

In concluding this inevitably very brief analysis, it is essential that we reply to an objection which it probably raises. It might be wondered why, having demonstrated that the patriarchal society's cognitive system was much less advanced than the theocratico-charismatic society's, we do not classify the patriarchal society as an 'archaic society'? We would reply that such a question would mistakenly eliminate all considerations other than the exclusively intellectual one. For, to show that a more mediocre system of knowledge corresponds to a certain type of society than that which can be observed in a different type, is not to make a value judgement on either of these societies. Furthermore, the promethean, historical nature of a society is not always evaluated by the level of its cognitive system; it can be seen in its internal cohesion, its capacity for handling situations, its power for action and its force of resistance, etc. The degree of prometheanism, however weak it may be, is nevertheless dependent on the internal struggles for power. However, the contribution of the patriarchal structure in the sphere of knowledge is insignificant.

CHAPTER FIVE

City-states in the Process of Becoming Empires, and their Cognitive Systems

Despite the historically probable hypothesis that the ancient city-states were born of an osmosis between patriarchal structures and theocratico-charismatic structures—a combination accomplished under different conditions and with varied results—from the point of view of a strictly sociological typology, it would seem more logical to consider first the feudal structures. Indeed, with regard to the principles which govern feudal structures, they are much more removed from our own than those of city-states, especially those which became empires. This is why, in our various writings about the typology of global societies,[1] we thought it necessary to study the feudal structures before those of city-states, and we still see no reason to think we were wrong in this.

But considered from the aspect of formulated and explicit knowledge, the heritage of the ancient city-states has been of such richness and significance that, to omit its important effect on the diverse societies which have succeeded classical antiquity, would be to falsify the relationship between any global social framework and the corresponding cognitive system. Moreover, it is here, for the first time, that we find ourselves facing a concrete case of *disjunction between the social framework and knowledge,* a disjunction to which we referred in the introduction to this book—suggesting that it can not only lead to relationships of polarization, ambiguity, or complementarity, between social framework and cognitive system, but also require us to search for a singular causality of the effects of knowledge on the social framework, or vice versa. This is the reason for studying city-states before feudal structures as social frameworks of knowledge.

---

[1] Cf. *Déterminismes sociaux et liberté humaine* (1955, 2nd edn. revised and corrected 1963), pp. 261 ff.; *La vocation actuelle de la sociologie* (3rd edn., 1963), I, 476 ff.; and *Traité de Sociologie* (1st edn., 1958; 2nd edn., 1963), vol. I, pp. 221 ff.

We have already seen that in theocratico-charismatic society and patriarchal society—the interpenetration of which engendered the city-state—first place was occupied by perceptual knowledge of the external world, which was sometimes combined with cosmogonic and social myths, and at other times was identical with common-sense knowledge. The city-states freed this type of knowledge from involvement with other types and gave it a distinct primacy. One might say that these societies revelled in discovering the external world through disinterested perceptual knowledge. They could be defined as the most *extroverted* global societies ever to exist.

This type of global society is well known. The Greek *Polis* (from the seventh to the fifth century B.C.) and the Roman *Civitas* (from the fifth to the first century B.C.) provide classic examples. Certain characteristics of their cognitive systems are found in the Italian towns of the Renaissance, despite differences in their particular destinies.

The principal characteristic of this type of society is the pre-eminence of a specific territorial group: the city, the town, which symbolizes the principle of locality and neighbourhood, predominant over groups based on kinship (*genos, gentes, curia, phratries*) and religious belief (the church being only one subordinate organ among others), over domestico-conjugal families, to which the slaves are attached, associations, and artisan fraternities (*sodalities* and *collegia*, being as yet little developed), tax-collecting associations and economic strata, etc.

The establishment of the superiority of the city over all other groupings is accompanied by a tendency towards *secularization* and *rationality, differentiation*, and *emancipation of the law, ethics, philosophy, and scientific knowledge, from religion and magic*, which were pushed into the background. In a sense it represents the triumph of the natural over the supernatural, which is strikingly illustrated by the primacy of the natural in perceptual knowledge of the external world. The democratization of the global social structure accompanies the strengthening of the territorial principle and the supremacy gained by human knowledge and reason.

Greco-Roman individualism took the concept of *persona* as formulated by Roman law (in reality the paterfamilias) as the focus of juridical life, family life, and economic exchange as it became increasingly more highly developed. The term *persona* originally meant 'mask';[1] in Rome it took on the double meaning of a person seen under a 'juridical mask' (as distinct from a psychological, religious, or moral agent), and of a will with the power to command. This will can belong to an individual or collective 'person', but the latter is always distinct from other 'persons' to which it is opposed. It is this person, as a single, encompassing unit, which is considered as the foundation and sole agency of all social relationships, ownership, and power. The balance between the *imperium-potestas*, insuring the *dominium* of the private individual, and the limitations imposed by the latter on the former, is the mainspring of this whole social structure, which allows a considerable place to the state, to contract, and to private property—in sum, to juridical individualism. The basis of this social structure remained substantially the same when the democracy of the city gave way to tyrannical régimes in Greece, the Principality, and then the Empire in Rome. The last two were characterized by the development of an imperial bureaucracy, excessive centralization, and Caesarian absolutism.

If individualism triumphed in Rome through the intermediary of Roman law, prompting both *dominium* and *imperium*, it prevailed in Greece not only in the politico-democratic organs and in judicial proceedings, but also in art, philosophy, manners and customs, and in exchanges of all kinds. It prevailed also in the principle of the *dialogue*, and the Greek tragedies, where man struggles against his destiny—his decisions being free, but often thwarted by the *fatum*.

The techniques in operation in economic life were very backward compared with the development of philosophical and scientific knowledge, and even knowledge of the external world (which was more spontaneous and widespread), and art, law, and political organization. It is necessary, however, to distinguish the cities from the country areas. The cities engaged in an international maritime commerce, which penetrated as far as the northern Mediterranean, Asia Minor, Sicily, and the eastern countries. Their citizens, resident aliens, and freedmen, developed fairly refined artisan techniques. The country areas, even those

---

[1] Cf. on this subject the penetrating analysis of Marcel Mauss in his study 'Une catégorie de l'esprit humain: la notion de personne, celle de moi', in *Sociologie et Anthropologie* (2nd edn., 1960, Presses Universitaires de France), pp. 360 ff.

surrounding the towns, were very backward from all points of view, and stagnated in virtual technical poverty. We know that neither the Greeks nor the Romans knew how to harness horses for use in working the land; they used them only in ceremonial displays and cavalry combat.

Agriculture and stock-rearing remained at an extremely low level until the end of the classical era, under both the city-states and the empires. This can be explained partly by the importance of slavery in the country areas, and the consequent lack of honour attached to agricultural labour. Techniques of financial speculation were developed first of all as a result of maritime commerce, and then due to the activities of proconsuls in distant provinces of the Roman Empire. Tax collection, which was monopolized by freed slaves as an occupation, supported the speculations of the proconsuls.

The pronounced economic inequalities, the movements of great masses not integrated in any stable framework, the 'idle proletariat' demanding bread and circuses, and the slave revolts (Spartacus), might give the impression that some social classes were being formed (especially at the time when these societies were beginning to dissolve). However, the similarity remains external and superficial: apart from the fact that these sections offered no effective resistance to the global society, there was an absence of structuration. This was impossible because these groups lacked class-consciousness and ideology and, moreover, did not play any specific role in production, and could not communicate (because they lacked the technical means) with similar social strata in other towns, cities and empires.

We shall now summarize the salient features of this type of social structure and the subjacent global total social phenomenon. The latter, as we have already mentioned, strongly imposed itself and so limited the development of structure.

(a) With regard to the hierarchy of groups: At the head of the state or the Empire was the city-state, which predominated over all other groups, such as domestico-conjugal family groups (including slaves), groups based on common origin or birth (eupatrides, demos, patricians, plebeians), property groups, economic groups, educational groups (the famous academies), and mystico-ecstatic groups (priests, augurs, officials in charge of the mysteries and oracles), which played only a subordinate role and were subject to the secularized city-state. Among these groups, only the domestico-conjugal families and the hereditary groups limited the ascendancy of the city. All other groupings appeared insubstantial compared to the city—it dominated them, just as it dominated the *individus-paterfamilias*.

(b) In the hierarchy of the manifestations of sociality, the 'We' was strongly limited by the relations with the Other. In the end inter-individual and inter-group relations clearly predominated over all partial fusions. From this developed the emphasis on individualism, found in all spheres and in all forms, which provoked the vigorous philosophical reaction of Plato and Aristotle, although the positions they took did not have any direct effect.

Among the various relations with the Other, it was particularly active relationships of a mixed nature—i.e. combining proximity and distance—that were strong. This situation appeared in all types of exchanges, including intellectual exchanges and dialogues, and more particularly, naturally, in commercial contractual relations.

Within the 'We', which mainly existed in the city itself and to some extent in its subordinate groups, *communities* predominated without challenge, and *communions* were limited to narrow circles of philosophers and to the occasional public performances of the mysteries. As for *masses*, they appeared only under tyrannies, the Empire, and Caesarism. Because they were both active and rational, these communities served as a springboard and base for the expansion of the ancient cities. They facilitated relationships with the Other. As we have already pointed out in the first part of this book, it is communities which favour perceptual knowledge of the external world, and also philosophical and scientific knowledge. They also contribute to the development of structuration and organization (the latter being only one of the possible aspects of the former), and the development of juridical regulation. The predominance of the active community in the city provided the milieu from which flowed the 'Greek miracle', marking the birth of autonomous human reason, faith in the unlimited power of man, in the infinite capacity of human knowledge and in humanity's future.

(c) The emphasized depth levels: models, symbols, rules, signs, especially those of an intellectual, juridical, artistic, and moral nature, were particularly strong and dominated the hierarchy of levels of social reality. But they did not have a routine or tradi-tional character. On the contrary, they were often innovative and changing, consciously attached to human reason and will, which invented, created, modified, and used them as points of reference for social change. Moreover, they were supported by a collective mentality which had confidence in man's powers and was favour-ably disposed towards every new undertaking, experience, or initiative. Thus mental acts—judgements and intuitions—were favoured over mental states (memory, representations, affectivity, etc.). Yet the morphological base remained very important, not only in relation to the backward techniques of the country areas, but also in relation to maritime and inland waterway routes, the famous Roman roads of the Imperial era, and especially the factor of mobility and density of population in the city-towns, where citizens, foreigners, merchants, foreign sailors, and free slaves, rubbed shoulders and confronted each other. Social roles and collective attitudes were more emphasized than patterns of con-duct such as rites, procedures, customs, practices. Certain of these social roles—those of tribune, rhetor, demagogue, conspirator, politician, reformer, military leader, pretorian, freeman, wealthy merchant, proletarian (in the Roman sense of the term), were not organized, imposed, or routinized roles. They arose spontaneously and became widely prevalent. Much more than in charismatic theocracies, innovative behaviour was important. In these types of structures and global societies, reforms, revolts, disturbances, coups d'état, and even revolutions, were not at all exceptional.

(d) As we have already emphasized, the technical division of labour was much more backward—particularly in rural areas—than one might be led to expect by reference to the general pro-gress of the civilization, the development of international com-mercial exchanges, the accumulation of wealth, the political and military power. On the other hand, the social division of labour was very advanced, even among slaves, especially in Rome.

(e) Knowledge (particularly knowledge of the external world, philosophical, scientific, and political knowledge), law, and art, occupy a similar position in the hierarchy of social regulation, followed by education and morality; religion, cosmogonic and theogonic mythology occupy last place.

(f) It is possible to speak of a common Greco-Latin civilization, whose heritage was transmitted to feudal societies, whilst at the same time recognizing differences in emphases: it was more humanist, philosophical, and artistic, in Greece; more formalist, juridical, political, and military, in Rome.

*

What was the system of types and forms of knowledge found in this type of society and global structure? More than in charismatic theocracies, and contrary to what we have observed in patriarchal societies, the disjunction between the backward total social phenomenon and the advanced global structure, introduced conflicts between cognitive systems existing within the same society. Moreover, the city-states were the first global frameworks where *philosophical knowledge* can be seen to have been entirely separate from mythologico-cosmogonic knowledge. By acquiring complete autonomy it was able to attain an extraordinary degree of development and vitality, of a kind sufficient to draw into its orbit both *political knowledge* and *scientific knowledge*, whose progress, once begun, was considerable. However, the primacy of philosophical knowledge was seriously challenged by *perceptual knowledge of the external world*, which was very rich, attractive, and widespread, in these essentially extroverted structures. Thus there was rivalry between these two types of knowledge for the ascendancy in the cognitive system. Was it not this unyielding hostility, although often disguised, which had Socrates condemned to death, and on the other hand caused Plato to assert that non-philosophers were 'prisoners chained in a cave'? Aristotle's role was to attempt the reconciliation of perceptual knowledge of the external world and philosophical knowledge.

(A) In order to remain objective, we must affirm that in the cognitive system of the city-states, *perceptual knowledge of the external world, and philosophical knowledge*—the former spontaneous, the latter formulated, but both autonomous—were promoted to first place, without their being able to reach a compromise. Furthermore, one cannot accurately characterize this cognitive system without recognizing this duality and parity, in which each of the two pre-eminent types of knowledge struggled for supremacy at the top of the hierarchy.

We shall begin with philosophical knowledge. For the first time it appears as an independent knowledge, and its brilliance, preserved in the collective memory, illuminated societies which arose in the West after the ancient cities. For it was concerned with an avant-garde knowledge, with all that was most character-istic of the 'Greek miracle', and which was later to be reproduced in Rome.

Philosophical knowledge, as we have defined it in our introduc-tion, is a second-order knowledge; it is grafted retrospectively on to other knowledge or on to already accomplished non-cognitive mental acts, and strives to integrate these as partial manifestations of infinite totalities, in order to justify their veracity. As scientific knowledge and doctrinal political knowledge were greatly depen-dent on philosophical knowledge at their inception, philosophical knowledge was mainly in opposition to perceptual knowledge of the external world. This was a characteristic trait of all the 'philoso-phical schools'. From the beginning, philosophical knowledge showed itself to be a *partisan knowledge*, divided into a number of schools—whose reverberating conflicts won for it much of its prestige and attraction. But the essential object of the debate was, nevertheless, the consideration of knowledge of the external world, including the time in which society and humanity itself moved. The struggles between the Eleatics and the partisans of Heraclitus, between the Sophists of different schools and Socrates, between the Stoics (themselves divided into various tendencies) and the Epicurians who succeeded Democritus, between the Platonists and the Aristotelians, between Pyrrhon and other sceptics and the academicians, these struggles were all concerned primarily with the veracity of perceptual knowledge of the external world and the future of society, and only secondarily with justification of the sciences and the ideals and tactics of political knowledge. From this point of view, all classical philo-sophy was 'realistic', in spite of differences of interpretation.

This enables us to estimate the importance which perceptual knowledge of the external world assumed in this cognitive system, and we will turn to an examination of this knowledge next. How-ever, it is important to note first that, in all of these philosophical orientations, there is posed the problem of time in advance of itself, in which the present is projected into the future, whilst turning its back on the past. This awareness of the future was conceptualized by Greek philosophy, which emphasized the human effort required to master this time. However, this time remained alien to the actual society in which it arose.

N

We have already seen how *perceptual knowledge of the external world* was for Greek philosophy both its main object of consideration and its main rival. Perhaps this esteem and prominence was less marked in Rome than in Greece, due to the fact that in Greece this type of knowledge was related to aesthetic taste and was more independent of political knowledge than in Rome. Nevertheless, it was the Greeks and Romans who finally made clear the independent existence of the external world. They put an end to autistic and egocentric perception of the space in which the world exists. Concentric space and diffuse space gave way to space which could easily both contract and expand. Prospective space was clearly dominant over projective space. This new outlook created conditions favourable to the mastery of space (through extensive maritime transportation required for commercial and military enterprises of an international nature), and to attempts to conceptualize, measure and quantify space, not to mention the power of attraction of concrete, qualitative space. From this came the discovery of the human body and its sublimation in sculpture; the discovery of perspective; the development of biology, physiology, and medicine as sciences; and the progress of mathematics and astronomy.

Thus scientific knowledge (which we shall study separately), required to act as intermediary between perceptual knowledge of the external world and philosophy, began to develop. The awareness of time in advance of itself, with the future dominating the present and separated from the past, engendered the concept of historical reality, which in turn gave rise to an appropriate discipline—historiography or historical knowledge, of which Plutarch and Herodotus were the main promoters, and Aristotle the first philosopher to utilize its findings. The developing philosophy of history was linked to formulated political knowledge (to which we shall return). The mastery of time, its conceptualization and measurement, aided by calendars, posed the question of the relationship between the time in which society evolved and that in which the external world moved; a question to which the various philosophical schools frequently gave contradictory replies.

(B) In second place, behind the competing perceptual knowledge of the external world and philosophical knowledge, one must place *political knowledge*. In the city-states, as in every other society, it originally appeared in a spontaneous form. The struggles between the demos and the eupatrides, the plebeians and the patricians, the citizens, foreigners, and freedmen, senators and pretorians, etc., are sufficiently well known, and the strategies they adopted were so variable, that it would be unprofitable to dwell on them. The important point is that we are faced for the first time with a conscious formulation of political doctrines, which systematized acquired political experience. The fixed goals and the multiplicity of tactics for attaining them were bound up with a particular philosophical tendency, without, however, sacrificing the independence necessary for safeguarding the specificity of political knowledge.

Thus the individualist and contractualist Sophists showed themselves to be strongly democratic in their doctrines, agreeing on this point with their main adversary, Socrates, who based his defence of democracy on the universality of human reason. Plato—friend of tyrants—demanded political power for philosophers, and showed himself to be Statist, totalitarian, and reactionary. Aristotle, being more of a realist, sought for the right setting, and found it in a balance between tyranny, aristocracy, and democracy, whilst excluding ochlocracy. Cicero, the great theorist of republican Rome, also sought for a balance which was closer to Aristotle's than may appear at first sight. Finally, to the sceptical relativism of Pyrrhon and his followers (which may have concealed the revolutionary tendencies of the discontented and disillusioned masses) were opposed the various schools of Stoics, who advocated the virtue of submission to the law in all circumstances and whatever the political régime—an attitude which anticipated that of Christianity.

*

Before leaving the three types of knowledge pre-eminent in the cognitive system of the city-states in the process of becoming empires, it is interesting to note that within these types it was always the same forms of knowledge that were emphasized. In every case the rational, conceptual and concrete forms prevailed over their opposites, whilst the positive and speculative, collective and individual forms had a tendency to balance each other. The mystical form, which was barely perceptible in Plato's philosophy, was stronger in the philosophy of Plotinus and his successors (Denys the Areopagite, etc.); the symbolic and speculative forms at times received greater emphasis in political knowledge, and more especially in scientific knowledge. In these last two types of knowledge, collective knowledge took precedence over individual knowledge.

The advent of autonomous philosophical knowledge, and its apparent dynamism, gave rise to a prejudice in many societies other than that type we are analysing, according to which 'philosophical knowledge' *per se* must be the predominant type of knowledge, and the belief that it would always occupy first place. In fact, such a predominance does not correspond to reality; in the city-states it was greatly restricted, as we have seen, by the esteem in which perceptual knowledge of the external world was held; it has only been really prominent in one other type of society (although with the same limitations)—that of early capitalism, where it served to oppose the last vestiges of the dominance exercised by theological knowledge, and promoted scientific and technical knowledge. In all other types of society and structures philosophical knowledge has occupied different places in the hierarchy of types of knowledge. This demonstrates the impossibility of stating *a priori* that one type of knowledge will be superior to any other.

(C) Third place in this cognitive system goes to *scientific knowledge*, to the extent that it began to detach itself from philosophical knowledge. Indeed, during the classical period science developed to a considerable extent. Of all the ancient philosophers, it was undoubtedly Aristotle and his school who contributed most to its development and towards making it autonomous. The reduction of time to 'quantification of motion' was attractive to the Peripatetics, whether it was concerned with the actions of matter (physics), the actions of living things (biology), or the actions of *Politeias*, in sum of the natural and biological sciences, and even the human sciences—science of the state, science of social relationships (pre-sociology), and the science of history. Plato and his disciples—the predecessors of the Peripatetics—limited themselves, as far as science was concerned, to furthering the development of mathematics, particularly geometry.

The exact sciences also developed outside philosophy: algebra, geometry, and physics, with Pythagorus and Archimedes; physiology and biology with Hippocrates and his disciples; medicine with Esculapius. Historical science, as we have already mentioned, also developed under the influence of Herodotus and Plutarch.

What were the forms of knowledge which received the greatest emphasis in this scientific knowledge, as it began to free itself from the tutelage of philosophy, from which it had gained as much as it had from perceptual knowledge of the external world? Here again, without doubt, the rational, conceptual, and symbolic forms were evident, whilst the speculative and positive forms entered into a reciprocal relationship, complementing and combining with each other. Moreover, the need to increase observation and experimentation, to organize centres of culture and education, and also to create the first laboratories and hospitals, necessarily led to the predominance of the collective over the individual form.

(D) In fourth place in this system are *technical knowledge* and *common-sense knowledge*, which to a large extent were combined. In fact, in these societies technical knowledge was relatively weak, especially during the period of the city-states (in the Empires it was affected by the techniques of conquered lands, especially in the Roman colonies, and thus profited from the far superior technical traditions such as those of Ancient Egypt and the Germanic barbarians). If we exclude maritime navigation, international commerce, techniques of financial speculation, the organization of tax collection in the colonies, the famous Roman roads, and craftsmanship devoted to satisfying the needs of daily life in the cities, it is difficult to find any notable progress in technical knowledge. Its backwardness relative to social structures was very marked, especially in rural life as we have already indicated.

It is clear that no relationship can be established between technical knowledge and the developing scientific knowledge. The techniques did not utilize scientific knowledge. It seems to have been normal in those conditions for technical and common-sense knowledge to converge; it was only in the world of the merchant seaman and craftsmen that technical knowledge predominated.

Obviously common-sense knowledge had a much wider bearing than technical knowledge, in as much as it was strongly politicized in the city-states. Moreover, it varied according to the setting. Thus, it was not the same in the towns as in the country areas, nor for the eupatrides as for the demos, the patricians and plebeians, the sailors and craftsmen, the military men and civilians. It was different inside the domestic family from what it was among the politicians, the members of the Areopagus, the Senate, among the voters, and for full citizens in contrast to foreigners; it varied also depending on whether one was a free man or an emancipated slave, and it varied between emancipated slaves and slaves. Be that as it may, for the majority of the population, which was not affected by philosophical and scientific knowledge, and was deprived of special technical qualifications, and was often illiterate, common-sense knowledge and technical knowledge tended to assume the same forms, combining mysticism and rationality, as well as the conceptual and empirical. Yet the positive, symbolic, and especially the collective forms were strongly emphasized.

(E) In fifth and last place is *knowledge of the Other and the We.* It was limited not only by slavery, but also by the opposition between citizens and foreigners, eupatrides and demos, patricians and plebeians, city dwellers and country dwellers, and finally by the tendency of the non-Statist society to dissolve into a collection of isolated individuals. Elements of this type of knowledge were to be found only within domestico-conjugal families; in groups of philosophers, whether organized into schools and academies, or directing debates in the public squares; among followers of esoteric cults; and lastly, and above all, in the embryonic professional groups (sailors, merchants, craftsmen, etc.). Even then this knowledge was more likely to perceive the Other as a generality than in its concrete individuality. This tendency appears very clearly in Socrates and his adversaries the Sophists, who were less interested in man as a specific individual and distinct from his peers, than they were in man as an undifferentiated and generic representative of rational man in general. We need not dwell on the fact that the forms emphasized in this knowledge are rational, conceptual, speculative, symbolic, and collective. The weakness of this type of knowledge, which was the least important in the cognitive system of the city-states, served to limit the influence of community, and to strengthen that of the mass, in this type of structure and society.

*

To conclude this discussion of the cognitive system inherited from classical antiquity—a system which, with all its strengths and weaknesses, left its mark on Western global societies and structures—one positive point needs to be emphasized: there developed groups of scholars, wise-men, teachers—in other words, a whole group of people responsible for developing, perpetuating, and diffusing knowledge. In this sphere, the establishment of philosophical and scientific schools, the organization of academies, gymnasia and high schools, the activities of Socrates and the Sophists, and particularly that of Aristotle and the Peripatetics, as well as the role played by Greek slaves in the education of the privileged strata of the Roman population, all exercised a considerable influence, which should be noted. These groups, schools, and diverse organizations, which were to spread and develop formulated knowledge, were no longer of an esoteric nature. The custom, begun by Socrates and the Sophists, of taking philosophical and scientific discussions out into the public square, the market place, and the street, was characteristic and significant. As soon as formulated knowledge of whatever kind finds a place in specialized groups, there is a good chance that the cognitive system will be consolidated. This does not mean that the hierarchy of the types of knowledge will remain static, nor that the importance of knowledge in social life will always remain the same. This will be demonstrated in the next part of the book.

CHAPTER SIX

Feudal Societies and their Cognitive Systems

When we move on from city-states–empires to feudal societies the situation changes radically. We are faced not only with an extremely marked disjunction between the subjacent global phenomenon and the corresponding structure (which is new only in its intensity), but also with an unusual pluralism in the structure itself and the cultural works which cement it. Several hierarchies of groups, structures, social regulations, and cultural works were in competition, and reached a very unstable, complex equilibrium. Correspondingly there was a plurality of traditions coming from many different heritages: Greco-Roman, Germanico-barbarian, and the influence of the Moors who invaded part of Europe and transmitted to feudal society the scientific and technical knowledge which had been developed in Egypt and other Arab countries.

European feudalism existed between the tenth and fourteenth centuries, generally referred to as the Middle Ages. Historians have noted that feudalism in France, England, Flanders and Germany had certain special traits which distinguished it from other types of feudalism (such as Japanese, Chinese and Russian feudalism). It was this extreme pluralism which made it distinct.

The feudal global structure was characterized by five different, competing hierarchies.

1. *Hierarchized federation of military groups* based on *vassal fealty*, personal commitment of the vassal to the suzerain, and the system of *fiefs* which required *oaths of fealty* and *military obligations*. One had to be a knight, whose status was obtained through consecration, to enter into this bond of feudal dependency.

2. *Hierarchy of patrimonial groups* whose economic nature was shown in two ways: in the relationship between lords and peasants and the yeomen of the land with differing rights; and in the relationship between suzerains and vassals when the fief became hereditary and passed into the vassal's patrimony. The result was that the hierarchy of suzerains–vassals and that of patrimonial groups became partly parallel and partly divergent.

3. *Hierarchy headed by the monarchic state:* it did not seem to be truly effective either under the form of the Germanic Holy Roman Empire, or under the form of a confederation of *principal suzerains* in a region who are only loosely tied to their feudal king, 'the first among equals'. The very nature of the state as a 'bloc' of local groups, as primarily a territorial unit, was very shaky. It is sometimes claimed that in feudal types of society 'The state was dead'. This is not true: it was merely dormant, and lacking in strength. But all that was needed was a favourable occasion to awaken it. This is what happened at the end of the feudal era, as a result of agreements between the feudal monarchs and the free towns, who bought their freedom from the territorial state.

4. *Ecclesiastical hierarchy of the Roman Church.* This was quite different from all the other groups, federations and hierarchies. This was the largest body to play a part in feudal society, and was the only one to possess a universal character. Although its dignitaries were also part of the vassal and patrimonial structure, they were considered to be dependent on the ecclesiastical hierarchy. This led to disputes concerning investitures (from the eleventh to the thirteenth centuries) and then to tendencies to form a theocratic state. In feudal society, the church was considered above all as the visible incarnation of the *corpus mysticum* integrating into its unity the plurality of groups and their hierarchies. It sought to utilize this position to assert itself as a supra-functional body *par excellence* representing the total global phenomenon. Nevertheless, after numerous conflicts and struggles (for example between Pope Gregory VII and Emperor Henry IV and, later, between the Guelphs and the Gibelins) which led to Marsilius of Padua's political doctrine (proclaiming the sovereignty of the people rather than the church), and the Bologna school of jurists' doctrine (returning to the sovereignty of the state), the church's power was appreciably limited by the military pre-eminence of the feudal bond and by the economic, technical, intellectual pre-eminence of the free towns.

There is no doubt that in the feudal structure the two main sources of the cognitive system were the Roman Church and the free towns. Furthermore, these two rival sources of knowledge could also combine as frameworks of knowledge. This was what happened in the universities, which were very numerous in the Middle Ages. Since they were religious establishments, their teachers belonged to the clergy, and since the universities were all situated in free towns, they were also strongly influenced by the towns. The common saying that 'town air liberates' was confirmed in the teaching of the universities, which disseminated a knowledge which became more and more like that of classical tradition, inherited from the cognitive system of the city-states–empires.

We have already discussed the types and forms of knowledge corresponding to the Roman Church as a group in the second part of this book. It is sufficient to recall the predominance of theologico-philosophical knowledge and political knowledge over the knowledge of the Other, and the unexpected emphasis on rational, conceptual and positive forms of knowledge due to the strength of revealed dogmas and the church's organization. The role of the church in the Middle Ages as the framework for a cognitive system serves to confirm and substantiate our earlier observations.

5. *Federation of free towns and their hierarchies of groups:* masters, craftsmen and apprentice associations, journeymen, merchant guilds. In feudal societies this represented a separate world and a widespread movement for the freedom of the urban communities. This movement attracted the attention of Saint-Simon and his secretary Augustin Thierry, who saw it as the beginning of the industrial era which would progressively eliminate the 'unemployed'. The 'charters of freedom', usually bought from the suzerains, kings and bishops, strengthened the constitution of the towns, which were run by municipal councils where merchant societies and guilds were represented. The corporations of masters, artisans and apprentices were often in conflict, and these antagonisms were complicated by rivalries between the guilds and merchant societies. The bishops and their councils lost all secular power in these towns, which became republics in effect and entered into widespread alliances that sometimes assumed the form of international federations: from Bruges to Novgorod (the Russian urban republic), by way of Cologne, Hamburg and Lubeck. Vast new areas were thus opened up to the perceptual knowledge of the external world which the free towns enjoyed. They alone in the feudal structure showed themselves capable of promoting and extending this type of knowledge. In connection with this flourishing of the free towns, Pirenne spoke of a 'veritable municipal revolution' in that they had established 'provisional

governments'. Perhaps this was overstating the case, but there is no doubt that these centres of industry and commerce were also centres of intellectual inspiration, and the resurrection of Roman law. These centres radiated the perceptual knowledge of the external world, and prepared for the triumph of Thomism over Augustinianism, and later the 'Renaissance'.

Having described the characteristics of the five hierarchies which combined to bring about the complexity of the feudal structure, I shall now attempt to summarize the main traits of feudal structure and society, despite this plurality.

(a) There was competition between the five hierarchies: the church's tendency towards a certain pre-eminence; the importance of the free towns and the somnolence of the state; the considerable profusion of particular non-territorial groups—orders of knights, religious orders, corporations, etc.; the proliferation of narrower conjugal families rather than domestic families.

(b) There was a preponderance of the 'We' over relations with the inter-individual and inter-groupal Other, which however—because of the plurality of groups and varied hierarchies—assumed an unexpected importance. Of the 'We', it was the active communities which had the strongest influence (particularly in the towns, the different corporations, fraternities, orders of knights, etc.); they assumed a passive nature in the manorial, patrimonial and village groups. The passive masses limited communities, not only in the (barely existent) state, but also in the church, where communions occurred only in monasteries, orders, sects, and among supporters of heresies.

(c) The emphasized depth levels of social reality were roles and attitudes. They were not only the privileged, imposed, regular roles, but also the fluctuating, variable, improvised roles. In fact, in each of the five conflicting hierarchies, the roles of groups and individuals were many and various. They overlapped, combined and contradicted each other. The ways of playing these same roles, and their interpretations, were extremely varied. The paradox of a feudal society regulated in a way that was both extremely rigid and pluralist was resolved by this almost infinite variety and flexibility. There were no two lords, two orders of knights, two towns, or two religious orders who conceived their role in the same manner, and this variety was found in each of their members. In second place were the symbols and models which were either mystical or rational, followed by various regulations, rites, procedures, customs, and practices, whose diversity and contradiction favoured innovation. Ideas and values, which in theory were linked to religion, theology, and the art that they inspired, in fact found as much of their support in the diverse social frameworks as in these various spiritual traditions. They found their expression in ethics, law, education, and knowledge. (We shall turn to the types and forms of knowledge in this society soon.) The morphological base played a more important role in the country areas than in the towns, and was related to the rather low level of agricultural techniques, though they were much superior to those of the Ancient World. Finally, despite the predominance of cyclical time, time in advance of itself was experienced not only in the unrest of the free towns, but also in the ruptures between the different conflicting hierarchies, thus providing encouragement for innovative, effervescent behaviour. The Crusades were an example of this.

(d) Despite a more considerable technical development here than in the city-states–empires, not only in the industrial field and the free towns, but also in the military sphere and even, though to a lesser extent, in the agricultural domain, the social division of labour clearly continued to predominate over the technical division of labour.

(e) In the hierarchy of social regulations, law (including common law, law based on precedents, law created *ad hoc*, and statutory law—though not including legislative law) and religion occupied first place, followed by art, morality (traditional morality, morality based on ideal symbolic images, and, in the towns, utilitarian morality), education and knowledge (the importance of which was based on classical tradition) which competed for second place.

(f) I have already described the culture which cemented this structure, and pointed out its complexity. To this should be added the heroic and lyrical epics, historiography, the truce of God, the *aevum* serving as a link between the *aeternitas* and the *tempus*, the tendency towards mastery of time and space, (applicable both to the church and the free towns), and finally the combination of Latin, Greek and the national language.

*

Merely raising the problem of the cognitive system associated with this type of society is sufficient to make us realize that only certain hierarchic groups were in a position to utilize formulated knowledge. (Apart from the church and the free towns, one could make special mention of the hierarchy of military groups.) In the others, as in the subjacent total social phenomenon, there existed only a spontaneous diffuse knowledge. Having said this, let us now try to analyse this cognitive system.

1. *First place* should go to *philosophico-theological knowledge*, for which the Roman Church and its subordinate institutions served as the main social frameworks. An osmosis between the dogmas of the church and classical philosophy was brought about—the philosophy of Plato, Aristotle, Plotinus, Damascius, Denys the Areopagite and so on. As a result the differences between idealist and realist philosophies (relying on Plotinean and Aristotelian traditions), Saint Augustine and Saint Thomas being the protagonists, became also those between mysticism and rationalism, and the opposition between empirical nominalism (represented by British scholars such as Duns Scotus and his followers) and conceptual realism was also translated into theological conflicts. According to Max Scheler's apt remark, it was the influence of the bourgeoisie in the free towns, where the universities were established—which were ecclesiastical institutions but were imbued with the realism and rationalism of their environment—which brought about the victory of Saint Thomas over Saint Augustine.

In the philosophico-theological knowledge, which was influenced by the towns, the empirical, speculative and individual forms were strongly emphasized, whilst in the same knowledge which was based exclusively on the teaching of the church, it was the conceptual, positive, and collective forms which prevailed.

2. In *second place*, as one might have expected, came *political knowledge*, both spontaneous and formulated into doctrines. In such a complex society, which was so fragmented, so divided by the plurality of hierarchies and the number of groups and controls, without political knowledge the social existence of the collective groups and their members, the 'We' and the Other would have become impossible and might have been transformed into a war of all against all. Political knowledge was indispensable in each of the five hierarchies, although it assumed a different

nature in each one. The strategy for relationships between lords and vassals, lords and peasants, the monarch and his peers, the ecclesiastical authorities of different ranks, the free towns, and their internal corporations, etc., was extremely varied and was different in each case. The tactics for relationships between the various orders of knights, religious orders, and even within each monastery also differed.

This spontaneous political knowledge, which was sometimes rather similar to common-sense knowledge but, nevertheless, differed from it by virtue of its complicated etiquette (ceremonies, rules of politeness, marks of respect depending on social and hierarchic rank, rites, etc.), was clearly distinct from the political knowledge formulated into doctrines, whose ideal—a goal to be attained—was often found in complicated relationships with the tactical or strategic means employed. There were different opposing doctrines: those which defended the cause of the church by pushing for a theocratic state, those jurists of Bologna who preached the sovereignty of the territorial state, and those who advocated a strong federalism of completely independent free towns.

What was most striking in the feudal system was that the emphasized forms within political knowledge—whether spontaneous or formulated in doctrines—were the rational, positive, empirical, concrete, and collective which clearly predominated over their opposites. The mystical, speculative, symbolic, conceptual, and individual elements appeared only in some political doctrines which were partly related to the church or one of its orders, or to a heresy.

3. *Third place* in this cognitive system was held by *common-sense knowledge*. It was widespread in all the hierarchies, milieux, and groups, including, naturally, the domestic families, depending on the number of illiterates there were. It was often combined with spontaneous political knowledge and technical knowledge. When common-sense knowledge appeared within organized corporations, it generally assumed the character of 'esprit de corps' which was so prevalent in the Middle Ages.

The forms emphasized in this type of knowledge were mainly empirical, positive and collective. They were more symbolic than concrete, and there was a tendency towards a certain equilibrium of the mystical and the rational, though with a slight emphasis on the latter.

4. In *fourth place* was *knowledge of the Other and the We*. In this social framework it held a specific, complex position. On the one hand, the multiplicity of exclusive groups, whose members lived at close quarters (the court of lords and bishops, orders of knights, convents, trades guilds, companies of artisans and apprentices, to give only a few examples) facilitated the mutual knowledge of participants in their individuality. Furthermore, loyalty, fidelity, devotion, which were highly valued moral virtues, seemed to strengthen and encourage knowledge of the concrete Other and the We, at least among 'equals'. Yet there were serious obstacles to the knowledge of the Other in the feudal structure. One of the two main obstacles lay in the fact that the hierarchical bonds encouraged people in the upper ranks not to consider a serf or even a poor tenant farmer as an 'Other'; this knowledge was therefore impossible on both sides. The second obstacle lay in the fact that the two main sources of knowledge: the universal church and the free towns, did not encourage the knowledge of the Other as such. Added to this was the deficiency of the territorial state which, even when it sufficiently awoke from its torpor to negotiate with, or to ally itself with, the free towns, could scarcely have appeared to be a group or milieu favourable to knowledge of the Other. Furthermore, in the church, the free towns and the state, masses normally predominated over communities and communions: masses were the 'We' which were least favourable to the knowledge of the Other and themselves.

If the many exclusive groups of 'equals' promoted this knowledge, it was impeded by powerful obstacles in the global structure. However, when it did appear, as a function of the nature of the exclusive groups, the mystical, rational, symbolic and concrete forms combined, whilst the empirical, positive and individual forms prevailed over their opposites.

5. In *fifth place* in this cognitive system was *technical knowledge*, which was much more highly developed than one might think. This was so in the country areas where the *harnessing of the horse*, *wind- and water-mills* unleashed new motor forces. After the *trebuchet* and the *harquebus*, military techniques were further improved by *firearms* before the end of the Middle Ages. In the monasteries (especially the Benedictine ones) the *clock* was invented. These early mechanical devices virtually revolutionized the measurement of time, by making it accessible to wide sections

of the population. In the towns, the merchant federations encouraged the development of navigation, and the craftsmen, organized into guilds, owed their development in part to the use of new techniques. Finally, in the field of architecture (cathedrals and castles), and religious art, technical knowledge was considerably deepened and improved.

This development of technical knowledge which was so pronounced in feudal society was, however, slowed down by a twofold deficiency: first, the lack of interest in the perceptual knowledge of the external world, which gave these societies an introverted rather than an extroverted character—which becomes more striking when one compares them with the ancient city-states; second, the absence of juncture between technical knowledge and scientific knowledge, which was at a very low level. These two obstacles will be dealt with when we examine the positions of the perceptual knowledge of the external world and scientific knowledge in the feudal cognitive system.

We must first point out the forms which were emphasized in technical knowledge. They were notable for their rational, empirical, positive and concrete nature, and for the combination of the collective and the individual. Such forms of knowledge would lead one to suppose that this was a much more advanced society from a technical point of view than feudal society actually was! This shows that technical knowledge would have had great opportunities for progress in feudal society had it not encountered obstacles in the very structure of this society.

6. *The perceptual knowledge of the external world* occupied only sixth place. Its low position was peculiar to feudal society which had a system of knowledge strikingly different from that of the city-states. The external world figured so little in the knowledge of this society, at least in its formulated knowledge, that the Renaissance had to return to classical tradition to rediscover the external world.

The suppression of the perceptual knowledge of the space in which the external world was placed was clearly seen in the *absence of perspective* in art, the lay-out of villages, small towns and even large-scale cities in the way that they were turned in on themselves, the phantasmagoric way in which the universe and the earth were represented, and also in the popular saying that 'all roads lead to Rome'.

The external world was placed in autistic, egocentric space which was hardly at all projective. At the same time, concentric space clearly predominated over space which expanded and contracted; to some extent concentric space combined with diffuse space.

In this connection there is no doubt that the perceived and familiar space in feudal society was in conflict with the social and cosmic time of which it was becoming aware. One may suppose that the distinction between *tempus, aevum,* and *aeternitas* established by Catholic theology, represented a much more advanced stage than the knowledge of space which considered it to be infested with dire temptations, as was held by wide sections of the population. Among the times of which the church was the source, only the cyclical time of rites and religious feasts (the 'dance on the spot' time) corresponded to the space familiar to the illiterate, but, nevertheless, it was unable to expand the knowledge of this space.

It is true that the Catholic Church—at least its clergy—was more open than the ordinary people to the perceptual knowledge of the external world. Indeed, for the church, space was co-extensive with its own diffusion, the validity of its dogmas, rites, symbols, and its prospects for converting infidels—whether by arms or peaceful means.

The free towns, their federations, their international commerce, etc., reacted against the introverted character of feudal societies even more than the church. The merchant societies in the free towns, by developing navigation, increased the value of the perceptual knowledge of the external world and enhanced its prestige. It was certainly not coincidence that the Renaissance, which was oriented in the opposite direction to the feudal cognitive system, found its principal support in the free towns. Indeed, their aspirations and knowledge ran counter to this whole system.

When, despite obstacles, the perceptual knowledge of the external world succeeded in reaching an advanced level, it was the rational, empirical, positive, concrete forms which were emphasized on the whole, while the collective and individual forms complemented each other.

7. Surprising though this may seem, *scientific knowledge* occupied last position. The fact that this type of knowledge was the most neglected and the least advanced in the feudal cognitive

o

system calls for an explanation. For, *a priori*, the dual Hellenic and Arab heritage, the development of the universities in the free towns, and the growing technical knowledge should have constituted a particularly good milieu for the blossoming of the sciences. Since this was not so, we must look for the explanation in the fact that the scientific contributions of the Arabs, which complemented those of the Greeks, were known only towards the end of the feudal era. Even in Rome, scientific knowledge had been of little interest and was rather neglected. As for the teaching in the universities, it was concerned only with theology and philosophy. All the currents of opinion and ideas, and the discussions which attracted the attention of the most well-informed minds had nothing to do with scientific knowledge. Technical progress occurred on a different level from that of the sciences, and without the slightest contact with them. Thus the Middle Ages' reputation for obscurantism and the description of it as being 'lost in darkness' as far as knowledge was concerned, was based on too hasty an interpretation and consequently, an inexact one. This error came from failing to distinguish between the different types of knowledge; thus, in the positivist manner, knowledge in general was confused with scientific knowledge, which indeed was then at a very low level.

It was essentially represented by alchemists and astrologers, who were protected by powerful lord-potentates—particularly by alchemists whose function consisted of finding ways of artificially producing much-desired gold. What these protectors failed to discern was that behind the alchemists' attempts to make the precious metal lay chemical experimentation, and that the astrologers' activity served to mask the development of astronomy.

In these circumstances, one should not be surprised that of all the types of knowledge in the feudal cognitive system, it was, paradoxically, in scientific knowledge that one saw the strongest emphasis on mystical, speculative, symbolic, conceptual and individual forms. This explains why the church, its educational establishments—universities, orders and monasteries—the municipalities and the trades guilds, and wide sections of the population, considered the 'scholars' devoted to sciences as heretics or sorcerers (substitutes for the 'magicians' in archaic societies).

We have already mentioned the lack of contact between scientific knowledge and technical knowledge. We should add that the very idea that the sciences could perhaps increase the power of men, groups and societies over nature, social reality, or other men, did not even enter their heads. Not until the Renaissance and especially Francis Bacon's *Novum Organum* (1620),[1] did we see a resurgence of this idea and the promotion of scientific knowledge.

*

Finally we must emphasize the very important role of teaching and non-teaching scholars, their orders, the universities, though situated in the free towns, and the monasteries, in the maintenance, diffusion and development of knowledge and most of its formulated types (with the exception of the sciences). It was therefore mainly the ecclesiastics who constituted the group of *intellectuals* or 'learned men', the possessors of knowledge. Consequently, the theologians obviously exercised control in this sphere, and it is very doubtful that representatives of scientific knowledge (beginning with the alchemists protected by powerful lords) were admitted even with exceptional qualifications. In any case, in this type of society knowledge had well-organized protagonists who were capable of contributing to its progress as well as to its regression.

[1] Cf. on the subject of Bacon's contribution (1561–1626), the fine works of Pierre-Maxime Schuhl, beginning with *Machinisme et Philosophie*, coll. 'Nouvelle Encyclopédie philosophique' (Paris, Alcan, 1937—several editions).

CHAPTER SEVEN

The Cognitive System of Nascent Capitalistic Global Societies

Despite certain traits which are reminiscent of the ancient cities-becoming-empires, this type of society was radically different from them. The beginnings of mechanization and industrialization, the transformation of labour into a commodity, the appearance of real social classes, and a lessening of the disjunction between the global structure and the subjacent total social phenomenon, gave a very special character to this type of society, which was linked to the renascent state. In fact, the state, reactivated by this alliance, assumed the form of an absolute monarchy. It actively participated in the development of nascent capitalism and showed a marked tendency to consider political problems from an economic point of view. This is probably why historians and economists described the political organization of this society as 'enlightened despotism'. In Western Europe, this type of society existed in the seventeenth and eighteenth centuries, although it had already begun to appear in the second half of the sixteenth century, especially in Great Britain.

In the structure of this global society, the vast monarchic territorial state which granted absolute power to the monarch, having made alliances with the bourgeoisie in the towns and the civil nobility, predominated over the church, the military nobility, the clergy, the third estate, the peasantry, and the religious and political factions. It also held sway over the economic, industrial and even commercial enterprises of a new type, at least where it concerned their functions and expansion. These were the enterprises which the state itself created and encouraged (particularly in France where the 'manufacturers' competed with the former 'craftsmen, masters and trade guilds'). The state also dominated the workers in the factories and mills. This working population was recruited from among the most impoverished elements of the towns and rural areas where the extortions of the lords and the extreme poverty compelled some of the peasants to abandon their fields to become workers. The state supported the self-made bourgeoisie, industrial capitalists, international merchants, and bankers particularly (whose wealth was considerably increased after the discovery of the New World and who became the state's creditors) against the military nobility, the workers and the peasants. Thus, without ceasing to recognize the old hierarchy, it brought about its replacement by a new one. In the beginning, the state kept the social classes well under control (at least as well as it kept the official 'orders') and it regarded industrialization (whose progress was particularly striking in metallurgy and textiles) and the promotion of capitalism as ways of strengthening its own prestige—political and military as well as financial and economic. But later it played the role of sorcerer's apprentice and, instead of dominating the social classes, it came to be dominated by them.

The steadily improving technical and economic patterns began to assume great importance in this type of structure. Yet, new inventions and their applications did not follow a regular curve of progress, since the organization of the economy (including vestiges of the guilds) and demographic movement lagged behind technology. Furthermore, the total global social phenomenon—held back by the non-productive 'estates' and the stagnation in the rural areas which changed only under the influence of the towns and the state—impeded technical and industrial development.

We shall try to sketch a brief picture of this type of global social structure.

(a) The territorial monarchic state was completely predominant over the other groups, which, however, possessed much more power and effectiveness than in the ancient city. The official hierarchy of the constituent orders: the nobility, clergy, third estate and peasants (the latter included farmers of different kinds, wage-earning servants who all paid manorial dues: tithes and tolls); the various ranks of the nobility, as well as certain offices which could be bought, and which intruded on the civil nobility; the residue of trades guilds, fraternities, craft unions, etc.—this hierarchy was threatened internally by the nascent social classes which competed with and undermined these groups. The new large-scale economic enterprises, factories, mills, societies of maritime commerce and banks which had been favoured by the monarchy, finally became hostile to it, approving neither the politics of war, nor the maintenance of the nobility's privileges. Finally, traditional groups, such as the church and the conjugal–domestic family, began to lose their influence, despite their resistance.

(b) On the microsocial scale, the passive masses were the most influential of the 'We's. The politics of levelling, combined with the population movement towards the large towns, and the break-down of the feudal–seigneurial structure, created conditions favourable to the development of the masses. On the whole, partial fusions were very limited by the development of relation-ships with the active Other, both between individuals and groups; these relationships favoured all kinds of exchanges and contracts, but further progress in this direction was impeded by vestiges of the privileged estate, the barriers between orders and corporations, and the interference in economic life of 'enlightened' absolutism.

(c) Two types of patterns, relating to juridical rule and technical models, were first among the depth levels of social reality. Both were innovative. The technical patterns which were developed in the factories represented a very important aspect of the upheaval in economic life. The minute and penetrating juridical regulations, issuing from above, contended with the obsolete customs and practices. Next came the morphologico-demographic base. Its importance was increased by the need for manpower and the problem of its recruitment. The third place was occupied by organizations of all kinds, which began to be bureaucratized. Lastly, symbols, innovative and rational ideas and values encour-aged this society to take the initiative in dominating nature and society.

(d) The enormous growth in the division of technical labour, combined with mechanization, led to unprecedented productivity both in quantity and quality. The social division of labour was greatly surpassed by the technical division of labour. The accumu-lation of wealth, accelerated by the discovery of the New World, quickly attained record proportions, which made the contrasts between poverty and opulence even more flagrant.

(e) In the hierarchy of social control, knowledge and law competed for first place. Scientific knowledge and technical knowledge competed with philosophical knowledge, compelling the latter to take into consideration this new situation which we will go on to analyse in detail. Law was mainly legislative or based on royal decrees. Education occupied second place and began to free itself from ecclesiastical tutelage. Morality, art and religion came next.

(f) In the cultural system, one saw the victory of the natural over the supernatural, reason over faith, the increase of individualism in all areas, and the birth of the idea of the 'progress of consciousness'. The civilization and mentality of this global society at the time when it attained its apogee, found their most complete expression in the 'age of enlightenment'. Man felt confident of his success and the success of his technical and economic enterprises. The natural and the rational gradually suppressed the supernatural, allowing it only a narrowly circumscribed, controlled sphere, either limited to the individual conscience (Protestantism), or considered subordinate to national life (Gallicanism). Before this period, some thinkers had already expressed the same intellectual tendency, though with different nuances and emphases: Francis Bacon, Rabelais, Montaigne, Descartes, Hobbes, Locke, Spinoza, Montesquieu, Voltaire, Rousseau, Condillac, Diderot, d'Alembert, d'Holbach, Condorcet. . . . The *Encyclopédie,* which characteristically bears the subtitle of *Rational Dictionary of Sciences, Arts and Crafts,* was the most representative expression of this movement.

We are now in a position to attempt an outline of the cognitive system associated with this type of structure and global society.

(A) First place was shared between *philosophical* and *technical knowledge.* Sometimes they were in competition, and sometimes they complemented each other. Nevertheless, philosophical knowledge still tended to surpass its rival, though it did rely on the discoveries of science which, since the Renaissance, had developed prodigiously. After the revolution brought about in astronomy by Copernicus (1473–1543), Kepler (1571–1630), and Galileo (1564–1642), differential and integral calculus was invented by Newton (1643–1727) and at the same time, under another form, by Leibniz (1646–1716), the joint founders of mechanical physics. Modern chemistry began with Lavoisier (1743–94); physiology with Priestley (1733–1804), followed up in France by Bichat, Dr. Burdin and many others. The human sciences developed by dividing into several branches: political economics was created by Smith and Ricardo and, under another form, by the Physiocrats; the political sciences grew with Hobbes, Spinoza, Locke, Montesquieu, Rousseau, the Encyclopédistes, Condorcet and Destut de Tracy. Certain of these, particularly Montesquieu, anticipated the emergence of sociology.

The development of scientific knowledge was accelerated by the reform of education which became increasingly secularized. Continuing and intensifying the movement which had begun in 1529 by the foundation of the Collège de France to compete with the Sorbonne, the academies, founded in the seventeenth and eighteenth centuries,[1] the Royal Society of Science, l'École des Mines, l'École des Ponts et Chaussées, l'École d'Artillerie, etc., had the same tendencies and thus strove to free education from its scholastic and rhetorical nature.

The development of scientific knowledge is all the more striking when one recalls the obstacles which impeded its progress during the Middle Ages. All the great philosophers adopted a position in scientific discussions which stimulated their thought, even if, like Pascal and Malebranche, they had certain reservations. The secularization of philosophical knowledge, which became increasingly independent of theology, encouraged their tendency to make the sciences the basis of their thought. However, these two types of knowledge did not relate to each other in the same way. For, if philosophical knowledge tended to make scientific knowledge the main object of its reflection, most scientists showed little interest in philosophical knowledge as such. It was generally acknowledged that it was possible to be a scientist without being a philosopher, but a philosophy which neglected scientific knowledge did not merit consideration. However, philosophical knowledge maintained its prestige, first because it was the best placed to defend science against theology, and second because it was often the philosophers themselves who expressed hypotheses that were truly scientific, such as Descartes and Leibniz for example.

With regard to the emphasized forms of knowledge, philoso-

---

[1] Here let us recall the dates of their successive foundations, which were mentioned above (Part II, ch. 6, pp. 77–78) in this book: *Académie française*: 1634, founded by Richelieu in the reign of Louis XIII; *Académie des Inscriptions et Belles-Lettres*: 1663, founded by Colbert in the reign of Louis XIV, who gave his approval, though reluctantly, in 1669; *Académie des Sciences morales et politiques*, founded by the Revolution in 1795; *Académie des Beaux-Arts*, founded by the Revolution in 1795; and *Académie de Médecine*, founded in the period of the Restoration in 1820.

phical knowledge was characterized (to different degrees) by the predominance of the rational over the mystical (with rare exceptions such as Pascal, Malebranche to a certain extent, and Spinoza —that mystic of rationality), the concrete over the symbolic, the combination of the conceptual and the empirical, the speculative and the positive, and the predominance of the individual form over the collective form—which was very little in evidence.

In scientific knowledge, the emphasis on the rational was exclusive; the conceptual predominated over the empirical, and the collective form was preponderant; the positive and the speculative, as well as the symbolic and the concrete tended to be in equilibrium.

(B) *Second place* in this cognitive system went to the *perceptual knowledge of the external world.* Technical knowledge followed it very closely, though without attaining such a high level. The knowledge of the external world owed its rapid promotion to the creation of new means of communication. The discovery of the New World and the extension of commerce on a world scale which resulted from it, involved knowledge of oceans and continents previously unknown. The extension and improvement of roads which crossed the Western countries, and an increasing number of coaches, allowed relatively rapid communications.

Even more important were the new perceptions and conceptualizations of the space and time in which the external world was placed. Freed from its autistic, concentric character, space became both projective and prospective. Expanding and contracting with ease, it also appeared to be infinite, and began to transcend the limits of a particular society. In the time scale of this society, the competition between time in advance of itself and retarding time, which corresponded to a structure that was both innovative and anachronistic, introduced a time in which the past, the present and the future was rapidly to enter into conflict, a situation that was ultimately explosive and advantageous for controlling the future. In addition, we must take into consideration erratic time which threatened to disturb those powerful organizations which existed near the surface of the total social phenomenon. This situation explains the paradox with regard to the time in which the subjacent total social phenomenon evolved in this structure: a time which was partially in advance and partially retarded in relation to the structure. Knowledge of the external world, economic life, industrial techniques, international commerce, philosophical knowledge, the bourgeoisie and its ideology, were all basically advanced, whereas the nobility, the clergy, agrarian life, and the peasantry lagged behind. The absolute monarchy itself was advanced with respect to its initiatives, and retarded where it concerned its organization and actions. The breakdown of the Ancien Régime, which was much more spectacular than the English and Dutch revolutions, or the religious and civil wars (including the American War of Independence), was never to be eradicated from the collective memory of later societies, and led to a series of various types of capitalism and then to various types of collectivism. The complex time in which this society existed was projected on to the external world, which was as rich in unpredictable, new possibilities as the time and space in which it was placed.

Time and space became, at least partly, effectively measurable in this society. Everyone is familiar with the famous saying of the incipient bourgeois class: 'Time is money'. One might add to this a second saying: 'All roads lead to gold or at least to silver'. Space was evaluated less by means of the metric system than by the time taken to cover it. To the degree that it assumed its place in quantified space and time, the external world, in all its aspects, became an object for scientific study. It was here that the perceptual knowledge of the external world and scientific knowledge were united. It was this which gave greater importance to the respective positions of these two types of knowledge in this society's cognitive system than in many others. Scientific knowledge was here being prepared for its accession to first place in the next stage of capitalism.

The emphasized forms of knowledge were the same as in scientific knowledge, with the minor difference that the empirical and collective were more strongly emphasized here.

(C) In *third place* in this system was *technical knowledge*, which made considerable progress particularly in industry, navigation, and military art. Yet, in all these fields, the perfection of technical knowledge was directly related not to the findings of science, but to improvements of a practical nature, as both Adam Smith and Karl Marx observed. In the classic spheres of textiles and metallurgy, this process was especially notable in England. Thus it was that spinning and weaving quickly passed from the small domestic workshop to the factory, and the technical division of labour created conditions favourable to the invention of the spinning machine as devised by J. Wyatt in 1738, from which developed the famous 'Mule-Jenny'. But it was only in 1785 when Cartwright succeeded in synchronizing the weaving and spinning processes in a single machine that the textile industry became the most advanced of all. Likewise, in metallurgy (iron and coal) it took centuries to bring the iron and coal mines into joint production, but, once accomplished, this combination rapidly led to the production of steel through the use of blast furnaces. Also, it was from the wooden rails used in the mines to bring the coal extracted from the galleries up to the surface, that the railways developed, which, in the nineteenth century, completely revolutionized the means of transport. Finally, the steam engine (its precursor was invented by a Frenchman, Denis Papin (1647–1714)) took almost a century to be perfected, and, thanks to Watt in 1769, rendered usable in the factories.

Karl Marx was therefore right to emphasize, in the first volume of *Das Kapital* (fourth section, chs. XIV and XV), that it was not the technical inventions which brought about the growth of factories, but that, on the contrary, the technical division of labour in the many large factories created the need for mechanized techniques, and thus prompted the introduction of machines. He wrote, 'The workshop, the product of the division of labour in manufacturing, gives birth to machines.' In addition, the appearance of machines created a new industry, devoted to the production of the machines themselves. What we know of industrial techniques in the seventeenth and eighteenth centuries confirms this assertion, which might also be applied to techniques of war, for it was the standardization and reorganization of armies which led to the creation and diffusion of new armaments.

In fact, the new military art resulted from the unification of an increasingly state controlled army. The provision of standardized uniforms and equipment, the formation of clearly defined units, the foundation of provision stores, barracks and military hospitals, the creation of a body of military engineers, the establishment of rules for military tactics, such was the achievement of Louvois (1639–91) in France, and also Vauban (1633–1707), who was a specialist in fortification and a military genius in general. It was a result of their initiative that artillery was developed into a French specialty in the seventeenth and the beginning of the eighteenth century. The use of the musket, a German invention, became more general in France; it was then replaced by the rifle, where the spark was produced by the impact of a flint on a piece of steel. The rifle, adopted in Germany in 1689, was introduced into France, where a bayonet was added by Vauban in 1703. Its use permitted infantrymen to get closer to each other, which facilitated tactical manoeuvres. Not only was artillery used in the infantry, but it was introduced into the navy too. Furthermore, Vauban was the great promoter of the military engineering corps, the precursor of the *École polytechnique*, which was founded during the Revolution, and produces the best qualified technicians for industry while remaining a military school. This development of military techniques had repercussions in metallurgy and textiles, of which the army was the biggest consumer.

The emphasized forms within technical knowledge were not very different from those which characterized the perceptual knowledge of the external world. It is therefore not necessary to repeat them.

(D) *Political knowledge*, both implicit and explicit, occupied fourth place in this cognitive system.

Implicit political knowledge was naturally particularly widespread at court; it was also related to the rivalry between the military nobility and the civilian nobility, the nobility and the rising bourgeoisie, within the third estate, and between the different segments of the bourgeoisie: industrial, commercial and financial. On the other hand, the lower classes, confused by the structural changes from which they received no benefit, tended to be devoid of spontaneous political knowledge; they did not know how to handle it or what tactics to adopt in situations which were altogether unfavourable to them. Their 'class-consciousness' and their 'ideology' appeared only in the nineteenth century, long after the upheavals of the French Revolution.

It might seem surprising that we give a relatively low position to the spontaneous political knowledge of the privileged groups under the Ancien Régime, since they constituted such a fertile source of intrigues. To understand the reason, one should bear in mind that, compared with absolutism or even enlightened absolutism, political quarrels and consequently political knowledge of the subjects, however high their ranks might have been, were only of secondary importance. The Ancien Régime, while it existed, necessitated politics which did not take account of group interests, however privileged they might have been.

These groups, especially the ones with a promising future—at least the most advanced, clear-sighted ones—found compensation in the formulation of 'political doctrines'. These proliferated during this period both in England and France, and neighbouring countries (Holland and Germany). In England during the Renaissance, Thomas More with his *Utopia* (1516) and Francis Bacon with the *New Atlantis* (unfinished) initiated a series of political writings. In the seventeenth and eighteenth centuries, the writings of Hobbes and Locke reflected the aspirations of the rising bourgeoisie which eventually triumphed. In France, the doctrines of the Physiocrats were succeeded by the Encyclopédistes, Turgot, Jean-Jacques Rousseau, who were influential both before and during the Revolution. All of these doctrines dealt with the final ideal goal and the tactics to be used to attain it. In Holland, Spinoza's *Traité politique* (1675–77) anticipated certain elements of Rousseau's thought. We can now mention the forms emphasized in this knowledge—spontaneous and formulated.

In spontaneous political knowledge, the rational form was combined with the empirical form; the positive and the speculative, the symbolic and the concrete, the collective and the individual were equal. In the formulated political knowledge, represented by political doctrines, the rational, conceptual and speculative forms predominated; the symbolic and individual forms were emphasized much more than their opposites. The symbolic, speculative and conceptual were always very prominent in political doctrines (and in the 'ideologies' which inspired them), even those most concerned with rationality, empiricism, objectivity, and concretization.

(E) *Common-sense knowledge* occupied next to last place. This was because it was considerably disturbed by a somewhat new and unforeseen situation, the advent of capitalism and mechanization, the discovery of the New World, the politics of reducing absolute monarchy, the weakening of the church, and the flow of large masses of people into the towns, etc. It took refuge mainly in rural life and the limited circles of the domestico-conjugal family. Yet, it was dispersed among the most varied settings. It was obviously not the same knowledge among the various groups:

the courtiers, the representatives of the military and civil nobility, the different groups in the bourgeoisie, the new professional army, the sailors, and the workers in the factories. There were perhaps increasing contradictions between the different possessors of common-sense knowledge which prompted Descartes to say that this faculty was the most widespread. But in making this observation, perhaps this great philosopher was simply seeking reasons for resisting the temptation to deny the very existence of this type of knowledge.

The forms emphasized in this knowledge were as varied as the settings which acted as its frameworks. This multiplicity excuses us from studying them in detail. We note only that the mystical and the rational forms were closely related, particularly among the clergy and the peasantry.

(F) *Knowledge of the Other and the We* came in last place in this cognitive system: from this a new parallel can be drawn with the ancient cities-becoming-empires. The dispersion of this knowledge in the different settings was related to the materialization of manifestations of sociality that we have termed masses, the politics of reducing the absolute monarchy, and the disintegration of groups left by feudal society. The conjunction of all these elements considerably militated against knowledge of the Other and the We ('esprit de corps' clearly declined). We shall not dwell on the fact that in the developing social classes—the proletarian class and the rising bourgeois class—which were imbued with the ideology of competition and economic profit, knowledge of the Other was practically non-existent. It was found rarely, except in the limited circles of the domestico-rural family, particularly among the peasantry.

This decline in the knowledge of the Other as a concrete individual was in part compensated for by the tendency to universalize the human person. Rousseau, with his theory of the 'general will common to all', then Kant, with his concept of the 'transcendental consciousness' and 'practical reason' (which led to the recognition of the same moral dignity in all men) were the main representatives of this. But this was a general concept of the Other, unrelated to effective concretization and individualization.

This new knowledge of the Other emphasized particularly the rational, conceptual, speculative and symbolic forms. The collective and the individual sought—without success—to combine in the 'general' or the 'universal'.

*

To conclude the analysis of this cognitive system, we must stress that the intellectual strata, responsible for maintaining, developing and diffusing it, were enriched by new groups and new members. In addition to the philosophers, the scientists, the teaching professors, and the academicians one also found representatives of the humanities, writers, political theorists, and inventors of new techniques.

CHAPTER EIGHT

The Cognitive System of Democratic–Liberal Societies

This was the type of structure and global society that dominated Europe and America in the nineteenth century and the beginning of the twentieth century. Following the British, American, and particularly the French revolutions, this society developed parliamentary régimes and customs in most Western countries, especially in England, Holland, the Scandinavian countries, and finally in France. This society was characterized by the principles enunciated in the *Declaration of the Rights of Man and Citizen* (1789). These were combined with universal suffrage, the predominance of legislative power over executive power, most often by 'parliamentarianism' (i.e. government responsible to and dependent on a parliamentary majority); the freedom and influence of a plurality of political parties; the freedom of workers and employers to organize; the freedom of joint-stock companies, trusts and cartels; and the separation of church and state.

The democratic and secular territorial state remained at the apex of all functional groupings. In certain areas it extended its power by interfering in economic life—through its colonial policies, which opened up new markets; its often desperate efforts to combat unemployment and economic crises; its social legislation, which protected the economically weak and dispossessed; and by seeking to bring about conditions that would facilitate work agreements between employers and trade unions. In cultural life its efforts were directed to the development of free public education at all levels.

Yet the democratic–liberal state succeeded much less than the old régime in dominating economic life and restricting the influence of the powerful economic organizations. There were several reasons for this. First, the state was often dominated by the industrial, financial and commercial bourgeoisie, sometimes alone, sometimes in combination with the middle classes and wealthy farmers. Their particular economic interests pressed heavily on the state. Second, private disciplinary and regulatory power was always exercised internally by the management or owners of these great factories and enterprises, to which millions of workers were submitted in their daily life. This private, arbitrary power limited the authority of the state and threatened to become a kind of economic feudalism ('industrial feudalism' in Proudhon's words). Third, the jurisdiction and power of the state was reduced considerably by the rise of trusts and cartels—the first manifestations of organized capitalism—on the one hand, and trade unions and employers' organizations on the other, not to mention the strikes, lock-outs, and the resulting joint agreements, which engendered autonomous juridical regulations. It is possible to refer to this as a tendency toward the 'dismembering of the sovereignty of the state'. The intense activity of political parties— which increasingly brought the social classes into confrontation and conflict—in practice resulted in a weakening of the state's authority and pre-eminence. Thus the hierarchy of functional groupings, headed by the state, was severely shaken, and the social class hierarchy tended to take its place, which further aggravated the instability of the state. The latter—the executive organ of the bourgeois class or, at times, the result of a compromise between different social classes—depended more on its formidable bureaucratic–military machinery than on its moral prestige, or even its juridical and economic power.

Technical or economic patterns (organization of business and labour) played a decisive role in this type of structure and global society. The triumph of mechanization and mass production in the major industries, the use of coal, hydro-electric power, and steam-power, electrification, the spectacular progress brought about by motorization, particularly the automobile and the aeroplane, along with the rapid development in communications (telegraph, telephone, and the beginning of radio)—all these established technical equipment as the very foundation of social life. Those who affirm the 'pre-eminence of technology in social life' (such as Mumford, and before him Ogburn and Veblen) are correct to some extent, but only with regard to this type of structure and society, and only in part, for social structures continued to predominate over techniques. The latter became effectively independent and began to constitute a disruptive danger for the

P

social structure only when organized capitalism began to develop in the direction of technocracy (cf. below).

In order to analyse the structure of democratic–liberal society we do not think it is necessary to enumerate in detail its principal characteristics, since the memory of it is still present today. We shall confine ourselves to discussing in brief only a few aspects.

First, with regard to the manifestations of sociality, we must emphasize the general tendency towards the predominance of active masses, which were sometimes dispersed and at other times assembled together. Active communities were found pre-eminently in the bourgeois class: for example, employer organizations. Active communions were accentuated in the militant proletarian class (during strikes, for example), as well as in trade unions and in political parties representing labour. Otherwise the 'We' was strongly limited by relations with the Other, both inter-groupal and inter-individual, which were of an active nature. The competitive character of the social structure was extremely marked.

Next, we need to discuss the full effects of the division of labour, which was both technical and social in this case. The development of mechanization led to a redistribution of labour and a greater intensification of the two types of division of labour, which had to find a new equilibrium. Moreover, it should be noted that there was a significant predominance of the towns over the country areas, of large urban conglomerations over medium size and small towns, and of industry over agriculture. Likewise, we can observe an extraordinary increase in the accumulation of wealth, almost exclusively in a financial form, and in investment in technology, due to the importance of production, the exploitation of large numbers of wage-earners, the unprecedented amount of world commerce, and the flow of raw materials from the colonies.

Finally, concerning the hierarchy of social control, our discussion of the corresponding cognitive system will show that knowledge played a dominant role (especially scientific, technical and political knowledge). It is enough to recall how important education became as it was rendered progressively more secular, public, and even compulsory at the lower levels. There was a consequent decline in the influence of religion, and a weakening of the church's power.

To end this analysis of the democratic–liberal social structure, we should emphasize the fact that nations competed over equipment and industrial profits. Also, within each nation there was intense competition for modernization between capitalist enterprises. The investment of capital in more efficient machinery finally leads to a considerable reduction in profits. In spite of economic crises on a world-wide scale, periodic unemployment, increasingly bitter class conflict, the development of the labour movement and its organization in political parties and trade unions, the Socialist Internationale and an event such as the Paris Commune, and despite the threat of imperialist and colonial wars, *this is the finest epoch of capitalism.* Competitive capitalism seemed, indeed, to stimulate production and technical invention, and consequently to raise the standard of living of the population, even that of the proletariat. This orientation was so marked that capitalism was assured not only of the colonial markets but also the markets of technologically underdeveloped countries.

*

We now come to the question of primary interest: What is the cognitive system corresponding to the democratic–liberal type of structure and society? This question raises another, in some ways complementary: What effect does this cognitive system have on its global social framework?

The cognitive characteristic which appears most striking is the obvious decline of philosophical knowledge, not only in comparison to the rapidly developing scientific knowledge, with which we saw it in competition in early capitalist society, but also in comparison to technical knowledge, political knowledge, and perceptual knowledge of the external world. Thus we are led to the conclusion that the decline of philosophy begins in developed competitive capitalism, the cognitive system of which we are about to analyse. This decline is continued and accentuated in several other types of structure and society which we will be studying—organized capitalism, technocratic fascism, and centralized collectivism. This observation raises the following question: In what type of structure and society would philosophical knowledge have some chance of rising again from its ashes and occupying once more an important position in the cognitive system? We shall try to answer this question at the end of this book.

(A) There is no doubt that *scientific knowledge* occupied *first place* in democratic–liberal societies. Clearly the natural and exact sciences had primacy. However, the 'human sciences', among which we can now include sociology, also began to develop in effectiveness.

The promotion of scientific knowledge to first place can be confirmed in several ways. First, it was generally acknowledged that all technical knowledge was but a practical application of science. The same thesis was advanced with regard to political knowledge, particularly that which was formulated in doctrine, or at least in party programmes. We shall observe, when we analyse these two types of knowledge, that this almost unanimous conviction is far from being verified by the facts, and that we should see in it merely the expression of the exceptional prestige enjoyed by the sciences in this cognitive system.

In reality, vast areas of technical knowledge, including inventions and innovations, remained on the periphery of scientific knowledge. As for political knowledge, even the most elaborate and best formulated doctrines, the claim to be related to scientific knowledge (which would include a developing sociology), was pure fantasy. Nevertheless, all political doctrines, whether they were reactionary, conservative, liberal, radical, collectivist, or communist, insisted on invoking the human and social sciences. Just how much this was the case can be seen in the fact that various socialist doctrines were opposed to each other in the name of 'scientific socialism', which each one claimed to draw upon (for example, those of the Saint-Simonians, Proudhon—the inventor of the term—and Marx), with the sole intention of hurling at the others the charge of utopianism.

In fact it was a case in which value judgements were substituted for factual judgements—a substitution that could be camouflaged only by the unconscious prior introduction into the social reality of values, which were the very values they would later claim to discover there. Therein lies the problem posed by the human or 'ideological' factor inherent in the social sciences (including sociology): *How can the human sciences be freed from dogmatism?* The problem remains unsolved to this day.

The privileged position of scientific knowledge in this cognitive system was confirmed by the very attitudes of the philosophers themselves, whatever their orientation. 'Positivist philosophy', which, after several false starts, was brought to full development by Auguste Comte, saw in philosophical knowledge only a generalization of the results of scientific knowledge, for which it proposed a fixed hierarchy ranging from astronomy to sociology. On the other hand, it considered sociology to be a pre-eminent type of philosophy, but this was transformed by successive stages into 'sociocracy' first of all, then 'sociolatry', and finally 'Religion of Humanity'. 'Positivist politics', which at first aimed to be nothing more than a practical application of sociology, evolved in the same way. At the end of this evolution it reached the point of affirming the primacy of 'order'—and the most reactionary order possible—over 'progress', which came to constitute a threat to society and reason. Now the fact that Comte's system continued to exalt scientific knowledge at the same time that it was subordinating it to a new religion at the service of politics, was truly a sign of the times. It matters little that certain of his successors, such as Littré and Mill, rejected Comte's conclusions as mere digressions. What does matter, and this was symptomatic, is that in this democratic–liberal society and its cognitive system, nothing was possible without a preliminary recognition of the pre-eminence of science!

The fiercest opponents of Comte's positivism, Proudhon and Marx, despite their pragmatist, dialectical philosophy, differently interpreted, believed not only in the undisputed primacy of scientific knowledge but also in 'scientific socialism', on which they themselves placed a high value. Marx, particularly, maintained that once communism was set up, scientific knowledge would guide disalienated society without difficulty.

Philosophers of a different orientation to that of Positivism and Marxism, such as the various neo-Kantians who gained philosophical prominence during the later phases of democratic–liberal society, acknowledged the superiority of scientific knowledge over all other types. They considered the goal of philosophy to be exclusively the *justification of the validity of the conceptual apparatus of the sciences*. The famous Marburg School, led by the philosophers Hermann Cohen and Paul Natorp, typified this point of view. All that should properly be called knowledge was to be found solely in scientific knowledge, and philosophy was reduced to reflection on that knowledge. The *a priori* sought for were exclusively those of science, and man, as such, was reduced to one who possessed scientific knowledge. Moreover, these philosophers considered themselves to be the representatives of the new scientific rationalism.

Finally, even philosophers who revolted against the reigning 'scientism', such as Bergson in France, and William James and Dewey in the United States, yielded more than they would admit to the primacy of scientific knowledge. Thus Bergson, after having succeeded in *Les données immédiates de la conscience* and in *Matière et mémoire*, in preserving 'qualitative time' and 'concrete space' from being destroyed by scientific conceptualization and spatialization (a point to which he returned in his book against Einstein), nevertheless in *Évolution créatrice* placed his philosophy under the exalted patronage of biological science, from which he drew the vitalism that enabled him to proceed to the pronounced spiritualism of his last book: *Les deux sources de la morale et de la religion*. Likewise, William James and then John Dewey regarded pragmatism as a science based on the scientific and experimental psychology of their time.

One might say that in the cognitive system of democratic–liberal society, philosophical knowledge abdicated its primacy and accepted without effective resistance the promotion of scientific knowledge to the top of the hierarchy of the types of knowledge.

The rational, empirical, and positive forms were the most emphasized in scientific knowledge; the symbolical and conceptual combined together and were indispensable to scientific knowledge, in which they occupied a prominent position; the collective and individual forms succeeded in attaining an equilibrium.

(B) In this cognitive system *technical knowledge* ascended to *second place*. We have already mentioned the importance of technical patterns in the democratic–liberal structure and society. To the developments in mechanization, organization of labour, radio-telephony, radio broadcasting, film, and aviation, should be added the wider application of chemistry in industry.

But, important as these results were, technical knowledge was faced with three serious limitations. First, the threat of over-production and declining profits as a result of heavy investment on the basis of private initiative, periodic economic crises, policies of colonial expansion which provided an outlet for obsolete industrial products, all inevitably impeded the development of technical knowledge.

Second, technical knowledge and scientific knowledge still remained in large part independent of each other in this type of society, as was pointed out by the great British physicist J. D. Bernal in his book *Science and Industry in the Nineteenth Century* (1953). Bernal also noted that, contrary to what might logically be expected, the majority of the main technical inventions were due to foremen, engineers, and sometimes even amateurs, as in the previous type of society discussed. The inventors drew only indirectly on scientific knowledge, gleaning their information from manuals or popular scientific works (Bernal, op. cit., p. 151). This was due to the simple fact that even the large firms still did not possess research laboratories, which had to be created later by private trusts or the government, with a view to stimulating intercommunication between science and industry (ibid., p. 151). This contrasts with the situation today, where the nuclear and electronics industries would be impossible without scientific laboratories for technical research, thus bringing the two types of knowledge into close collaboration (ibid., p. 133).

Finally, the pace of development of technical knowledge was slowed down by its uneven distribution and level of attainment in different sections of society. Indeed, the great mass of workers engaged in production lacked any training or professional qualification. Their technical knowledge was acquired on the job, and it was at an extremely low level. This was still more true for that unskilled section of the population employed neither in industry nor agriculture. The level of technical knowledge was higher among supervisory personnel, who might combine professional qualifications with experience. But only engineers with diplomas from special schools attained a level of technical knowledge in which science could be used to some extent. This applied also to the army. It was only the higher ranks from specialized schools who were capable of combining military knowledge with scientific knowledge.

A great many of Bernal's observations that we have mentioned concern twentieth-century society which, as we shall see, can no longer be described as democratic–liberal. He came to the conclusion that: 'This large-scale scientific industry was in turn to produce economic social strains which were to threaten the system that gave them birth. Twentieth-century science, now integrated with industry, is proving too big for the system of private enterprise that gave birth to it two hundred years ago' (ibid., p. 176). Obviously he is referring here either to organized capitalism or to collectivism, in which scientific knowledge and technical knowledge enter into an effective combination which, for the reasons indicated, was lacking in democratic–liberal society.

As for the forms emphasized within technical knowledge, they depend on the level of knowledge. At the lowest level, the empirical, positive, concrete, and collective forms predominate. At the highest level, it is, on the contrary, the conceptual, speculative, symbolic, and individual forms which prevail.

(C) *Perceptual knowledge of the external world* and *political knowledge* (mainly of a formulated sort) both occupy third place in this cognitive system. As a result they could peacefully co-exist, harmonize, even fuse, or else enter into competition.

Knowledge of the external world was extended and enriched by the profusion of improved and more rapid means of transport, and the more widespread means of communication and broadcasting. This development was not entirely spontaneous. It was also due to the influence of scientific knowledge, particularly that of physical and human geography, which permeated wide sections of the population, even among those who had not gone beyond elementary education. For it was not only attendance at school, but also the development of the press, the reading of daily newspapers by great masses, that contributed to its diffusion. At the same time the different levels of technical knowledge benefited from increased knowledge of the external world.

The space in which the world was placed was not reduced to quantified space. Concrete space became essentially prospective, not only from the economic and occupational point of view, but also from the point of view of aesthetic pleasure, relaxation and leisure. It could expand and contract easily according to need; its diffuse and concentric aspect declined.

However, this enlargement of space encountered two limitations. The first was bound up with modes of transport and the vehicles available to the persons involved—space was enlarged or reduced according to the mode of transport used. The origin of the second limitation was quite different and more unfortunate. It concerned the influence of political knowledge, both spontaneous and formulated, on knowledge of the space in which the external world was placed. For conflicts of interest between states, nations, governments, international blocs, not to mention social classes and political parties, often transformed space into hostile and friendly zones; which ran the risk of re-introducing diffuse and even concentric space. The competition which existed in the cognitive system of democratic–liberal societies between perceptual knowledge of the external world and political knowledge is here clearly apparent. However, political knowledge did not succeed in gaining the higher position that it attained, as we shall see, in other types of society, such as organized, directed capitalism, technocratic fascism, and centralized communism.

Living in precipitate time, in advance of itself, which was combined with an erratic time of irregular and arhythmic pulsations appropriate to economic crises and political difficulties, and also explosive time of creation, democratic–liberal society tended to project this time in which it lived onto the external world. No conceptualization, measure or quantification, social time, time of the external world, could succeed completely in eliminating these qualitative elements. Mechanical physics gradually had to abandon its claim.

As for the forms emphasized in perceptual knowledge of the external world, the intervention of scientific, technical, and political knowledge, modified its specificity.

This is the point when we can examine closely the knowledge that competed with knowledge of the external world—the all-pervasive *political knowledge* of democratic–liberal society. One of its characteristics was to be simultaneously spontaneous and formulated on all occasions. In fact, the freedom and multiplicity of political parties, which through their very diffuse programmes sought to address masses of electors who did not belong to any party, led to the interpenetration of tactics, moods, *ad hoc* reactions, and definite goals. Furthermore, political knowledge in its various manifestations was stimulated as much by class struggles as by the often surprising parliamentary and electoral alliances.

Besides, it was still activated in the bourgeois class by the need for intellectual resistance to large-scale working-class movements. From this point of view, the Commune of 1871—the first manifestation of the social revolution—acted as an alarm signal. In the proletariat, strike action, the trade union movement, as well as the 'collective labour agreements', gave rise to intense, spontaneous political knowledge, which was not contained in any precise doctrine. Finally, even the peasant class in democratic–liberal society had access to spontaneous and precise political knowledge, especially in France under the Third Republic, of which it was the principal supporter.

It goes without saying that in such an atmosphere, in addition to party programmes and spontaneous political knowledge of social classes and their leaders, many *political doctrines* were systematized. In France, for example, various doctrines co-existed in democratic–liberal society: the reactionary royalist doctrine of Charles Maurras, the radical socialist doctrine based on the solidarism of Léon Bourgeois, the moralistic socialist doctrine of Jaurès, which prevailed over the more leftist tendencies of Guesdes and over the really reformist tendencies, the doctrine of revolutionary syndicalism, and finally, from 1920, communist doctrine. Collectivist doctrines of different countries confronted each other in the Socialist Internationals, particularly the Second International and, after the advent of communism, in the Third International. It is hardly necessary to point out that in these Internationals, as in the national congresses of different parties, programmes, doctrines, and spontaneous political knowledge were all combined.

As for the emphasized forms of knowledge, it was the formulated, and especially doctrinal, manifestations of political knowledge that were most clearly evident. The rational form remained predominant, but not without some early signs of a certain mystical aura (the 'miracles of the general strike', *'le grand soir'*, etc., for the extreme left; the dream of 'solidarity' in the centre; the belief in the benefits of a return to monarchy, on the extreme right). Otherwise, the conceptual, speculative, symbolic (even myth), and collective forms prevailed over their opposites.

(D) *Philosophical knowledge* not only yielded its place to scientific knowledge, but was relegated to fourth position. We have already pointed out that philosophical knowledge, whether it was dominated by positivism, neo-Kantianism, or Marxism, found itself pushed into an inferior position by science, technical knowledge, and political knowledge. Thus its social role was considerably reduced compared to what it was at the beginning of capitalism. Essentially an academic and university subject, philosophical knowledge was henceforth addressed to an increasingly limited number of groups. It attracted the attention of the wider public only very occasionally, and exclusively through the mediation of those somewhat rare political doctrines that sought to utilize it.

As for the forms emphasized in this type of knowledge, we have already referred to them in connection with the promotion of scientific knowledge to first place. We need only emphasize that in the philosophical knowledge of this cognitive system, the individual form totally dominated the collective form.

(E) *Knowledge of the Other and the We* was in *last position* in the hierarchy of types of knowledge corresponding to democratic–liberal society. However, relative to what it was under the old order of society, it became slightly more marked. This was because new perspectives on knowledge of the Other and the We were opened up by the profusion of political parties and their local organizations, the development in the factories of trades unionism and its cells (due to the collective labour agreements), and the formation of teams of workers to carry out mass production in heavy industries. Moreover, the household family resisted dissolution and continued to assert itself as a source of knowledge. It is also possible to observe the appearance of such knowledge in administrative offices, and in school classes.

However, for different reasons, knowledge of the Other and the We remained slight and without real importance in this cognitive system. This was due to the fact that the Other and the We were less appreciated as unities or totalities as a result of their specialized and fragmented activities. Also, the scientific psychology of this period favoured a theory of closed consciousness, turned in on itself, and tended to deny the possibility of knowing the Other. This individualist psychology found support in the idea expressed and constantly reaffirmed by most of the philosophical schools, of a generic 'Me' (usually derived from a subject or a transcendental consciousness) identical for all.

In actual knowledge of the Other, based on its limited activities, it was the empirical, positive, and fairly concrete forms which were emphasized. On the other hand, with regard to knowledge of the Other taken in its generic sense, the rational, speculative, and symbolic forms triumphed. In both cases the individual form suppressed the collective form.

(F) *Common-sense knowledge* occupied *last position*. The conditions of life, techniques and patterns changed so rapidly in democratic–liberal society that this type of knowledge was disrupted. Except within domestico–conjugal families, country areas, and some traditional circles (such as the Jockey Club in France) and among the remnants of the nobility steeped in it from the beginning, common-sense knowledge steadily disappeared, especially in urban life. However, it tended to reappear in sections of political parties and trades unions, but this was exceptional.

The channels devoted to the maintenance and diffusion of knowledge in this cognitive system were becoming increasingly dispersed to the point where they lost contact with each other.

CHAPTER NINE

Knowledge Corresponding to the Managerial Society of Organized Capitalism

This type of global society acquired greatest prominence in the U.S.A., in Germany before Nazism (and after it in West Germany), and also in France in recent years, particularly under the Fifth Republic. Likewise, Great Britain, Italy, and other European countries are proceeding in the same direction. In the Far East the same structure has been established in Japan, partly under the pressure of the United States.

The economy is no longer left to free competition but is planned both by the state itself—in the interest of the reigning industrial and financial upper middle classes—and by private trusts and cartels (national and international), often with the support of the state, which puts its vast bureaucratic administrative machinery at their service.

Let us try to summarize briefly the structure of this global society.

(a) The state, and the trusts and cartels, whether they work together or separately, in their capacity as planning agencies serving the interests of the upper middle class, predominate over all other groups, which they seek to undermine. Political parties, the free play of constitutional institutions, democratic and civil liberties, are all dangerously compromised. The whole of political and economic life is dominated and perverted by directed capitalism. In the United States the workers' trades unions are often demoralized, if not undermined from the inside, by their adversaries. Organized capitalism will go to any lengths to break any collectivity or force which is not entirely subject to it. This is particularly easy in countries where the press, radio, television, and most universities and research institutes are dominated by private interests.

Roosevelt's New Deal represented a desperate attempt, with the help of an unprecedented crisis, to wrest economic planning from the hands of trusts and cartels by committing it to tripartite agencies—state, employers, and trades unions (freed from direct or indirect employer interference). But this experiment failed.

(b) From the microsocial point of view passive masses predominate in organized and directed capitalism. They limit active communities to public or private planning agencies, and passive communities to local groups.

(c) Organizations for economic domination and planning (utilizing automation and electronic machines) occupy first place among the depth levels. Next comes the army, whose leadership is made supremely powerful by the possession of nuclear bombs, intercontinental and interplanetary rockets, and the secret information for their operation. Workers' organizations, even when they succeed in remaining independent at the cost of constant struggle and effort (as in France and England), cannot avoid intense bureaucratization of their managerial élites. The technological patterns, as well as advertising and political slogans, are diffused by steadily improving techniques, which creates a tendency towards uniformity of manufactured goods, and especially consumer goods. (In this field the U.S.A. is unequalled.)

(d) The onset of automation slows down the technical division of labour, and consequently also the social division of labour.

(e) We shall discuss further how technical knowledge takes the lead both in the cognitive system and in the hierarchy of social regulation, when we consider education, leisure activities, morality, and law.

(f) Technicization affects not only all kinds of knowledge and social regulation, but also 'human relations' in all their diversity. Americans consider themselves to be great experts in this field by virtue of having created a specialized occupation devoted to it.

We might briefly recall that it was in the United States that the famous doctrine of the 'Managerial Society' arose, from which a new régime emerged—a 'technocracy', whose structure and cognitive system we shall analyse in the next chapter. James Burham, apart from the example of fascist societies (which he tried to make acceptable to the average American), drew mainly on the study by Berle and Means, *The Modern Corporation and Private Property* (1933), which suggested that 65 per cent of the stocks of the largest American industrial companies were divided among their managers, who thus formed a new ruling class. These findings have subsequently been disputed by numerous researchers. They have demonstrated that the data on which these conclusions were based related to only a single, short-lived economic situation, because some years later a new concentration of the stocks of these industrial companies were in the hands of large banks, which could impose their will on the managers.

Moreover, in a more recent work entitled *The Twentieth Century Capitalist Revolution* (1954), Berle himself states that the crucial element is not the transfer of stocks into the hands of the managers of trusts, but the fact that the corporate power of trusts and cartels in the United States is as strong as, if not stronger than, that of the state. The trusts and cartels account for approximately 65 per cent of all industrial ownership in the United States, and plan the economy in their own way, which consists of being in accord with the national and international politics of the state.

It is not their very debatable statement that this structure is 'ineluctable' that explains our interest in Burnham and other theorists (the so-called 'liberals' of technocracy), but their implicit suggestion that managerial capitalism leads to a variously interpreted techno-bureaucratic fascism, without necessarily desiring it or knowing it. Apparently this is the only way it can maintain itself and provide a defence against the increasingly powerful threats to its existence. In fact, the essential point is that without the elimination of capitalism democracy cannot survive.

Certainly, organized capitalism strives to conceal its intention. In the United States it works hard at improving working conditions in the factories, by combating noise and poor ventilation, remedying the discomfort of harsh lighting, and creating homogeneous work teams. Soon all workers will be working to the sound of music, with the two-fold aim of giving them satisfaction and increasing their productivity to the maximum.[1]

---

[1] Another means of pacification, this time directed at the middle classes, is the development of higher education and campuses (Cités Universitaires) during the last two decades. There are approximately 3,800,000 students and 2,000 universities across the country. The author from whom we took these figures predicts 7 million students in 1970, and a proportionate increase in faculty (cf. Jacques Lusseyran, 'L'Étudiant américain', in *Esprit* (April, 1965), pp. 646–7). Although viewing this favourably, this author does not omit to point out that the universities, called 'colleges', are at a level corresponding to the highest classes in the grammar schools (*lycées*) in France, and that the higher education in the graduate schools corresponds to what until recently was called the *propédeutique* [the preparatory first year at a French university—Translator].

In France, under the Fifth Republic, triumphant directed capitalism and its techno-bureaucrats hoped to conceal the fascist tendencies of an increasingly authoritarian régime by the theatricals of a referendum and direct election of an all-powerful president. Another disguised feature is the so-called independent foreign policy, which is in fact profitable exclusively to the industrial and financial upper middle classes, and especially to the national and international trusts and cartels. Also discussed is 'the workers' share in the profits of the enterprise', which in fact is never really accomplished under a capitalist régime, and arises from what is in fact a process of mystification.

All these façades simply bear witness to the incapacity of the ruling classes and their representatives to discern the dangers that organized capitalism presents to humanity—the enslavement of men and groups to machines, the destruction of social structures and cultural works by increasingly autonomous techniques, progressive denial of workers' rights and those of their organizations, and, more generally, of the rights of all citizens (producers and consumers) to govern themselves and to control whatever power seeks to impose itself on them. The authoritarianism of the 'sorcerer's apprentices', whether they be political rulers, employers, their trusts and cartels, or the technocrats in their service, is increasingly acknowledged. And yet the explosive forces that it unleashed go uncontrolled. Thus organized and directed capitalism moves steadily towards the type of structure and society characteristic of technocratic fascism—which we shall discuss in the next chapter.

Let us first examine the corresponding cognitive system.

(A) In *first position* is *technical knowledge*. It seems to have a logical and ineluctable primacy in the era of automation and electronic machinery. It asserts itself at all levels and to such a degree that all other aspects of knowledge are influenced by it to

Most of these students could not be compared to those who are working for a degree in France. As for the university teachers, he states that the higher the reputation of the establishment, the less it participates in education proper, but rather operates technical laboratories. However, the number of teachers is considerable (thus Harvard University numbers 4,840 faculty for 11,400 students—i.e. a ratio of 1 to 3; ibid., p. 648). Any unbiased person will recognize the public relations bluff which lies behind this information. Above all it is a matter of satisfying the middle classes, who nevertheless pay a lot for it, given the exorbitant cost of higher education in the United States (cf. ibid., pp. 649–50), particularly at the prestigious universities.

the point of being technicized as far as possible. Neither scientific knowledge, philosophical knowledge, nor knowledge of the external world can effectively resist this all-pervasive ascendancy of the technical.

Science is encroached upon by technical knowledge and in some respects disorganized by it. This phenomenon is particularly evident in the field of the exact and natural sciences. Doubtless it is inevitable that in the age of atomic energy, industrial automation, television, and intercontinental and interplanetary rockets, technical knowledge will tend to absorb science. Even in mathematics and biology all work is related to the improvement of industrial, medical, and agricultural techniques.

In addition, scientific experimentation in its present stage presupposes vast technical apparatus and organization, which is found mainly in the form of the various public or private 'laboratories'.

Technicization also invades the human sciences, often almost to the point of parody. The representatives of the human sciences, particularly those of psychology (individual, 'social', and collective) and sociology, want to be technicians of psychic and social life, and increasingly lay claim to the title of 'technocrats'. Also, their alleged skill in the different branches of the public services is frequently called upon, by the holders of economic and public power, with the sole aim of justifying unreasonable, unpopular, and autocratic measures.

These psychologists and sociologists thus stand revealed in reality as 'straw technocrats', acting as a screen to conceal the arbitrary and authoritarian nature of public power-holders, and also the private, national, and international trusts and cartels. These pseudo-scientists, who have no connection with true science, which they claim to represent (such as the organizers of public opinion polls and market research, etc.), succeed only in compromising the human sciences. They merely bring about the mechanization and technicization of 'human relationships' and the real problems of present-day mental and social life, with the sole aim of reducing them to preconceived formulae. This state of affairs is particularly flagrant in the United States (where it is beginning to provoke justifiable reactions), and is spreading to all those countries financially dependent on America. Unfortunately, France has been impressed by this process, although it is contrary

Q

to its intellectual tradition, and resorts to it more and more—thus providing further evidence of the attraction that fascist, techno-bureaucratic control has for France today.

(B) *Political knowledge*, which is significantly promoted to *second place* in this system, is also very much under the influence of technical knowledge; an influence perceptible both in spontaneous forms and in the most elaborate party programmes and political doctrines. In this case it is more a question of techniques for handling men rather than machines. They are required as a result of the combination of political power at all levels of social life; the impairment of the freedom of action of workers' organizations by trusts and cartels with the concurrence of the state; and the struggle between the two centres of power—the state on the one hand, and trusts and cartels on the other—not to mention competition between the trusts themselves. Besides this route by which the technical penetrates political knowledge, a further consideration is the position which politically-minded groups take up with regard to planning and automation.

Whether it is a question of political doctrine, or simply party programmes adopting new political slogans and symbols, their relationship with technical knowledge or its distorting influence can be observed, not only in their organizations and techniques, but also in their very ideals.

The political myopia of those who hold power in this society is shown in their failure to discern the increasingly obvious threat of destruction presented to all social structures by uncontrolled techniques. They act like 'sorcerer's apprentices'—a role we have already criticized.

(C) *Perceptual knowledge of the external world*, which comes in *third place*, also bears the marks of technicization, as a result of television and even more from the opening up of space by the use of machines—although space becomes concentric or diffuse again as soon as the technical means are lacking.

(D) *Philosophical knowledge*, relegated in this system to a much lower position than in the previous type of society (in view of the fact that scientific knowledge is combined with technical knowledge), undergoes an almost complete technicization. Indeed, 'symbolic logic' and 'logical positivism' tend to suppress all other philosophical orientations. The various types of existentialism, which caused such a stir for a short time before rapidly collapsing, simply represented an attempt to resist the technicization of philosophy in the name of the Self, the Other, and concrete collectivities. In the face of symbolic logic—itself increasingly reduced to a technique—only Marxism, dialectical empiricism, and the religious philosophies managed to maintain themselves, although none of them could succeed in blocking this trend.

(E) Technical knowledge appears even in *common-sense knowledge*, which consists above all in knowing how to manipulate household equipment (washing machines, vacuum cleaners, etc.), and also in the limited circles of administrative committees of trusts and cartels, and in the managing committees of trades unions and parties, etc. However, it is seldom located in the family group, except in fairly isolated country areas.

(F) Only *knowledge of the Other and the We* resists being penetrated by technical knowledge (despite the contrary statements of psychoanalysts and proponents of psychodrama). It is for this reason that it is relegated to last position in this cognitive system. However, it is not altogether excluded from it, due to the existence of work teams, business committees, groups of political associates, and friends, etc., as well as families and isolated villages. Still, these vestiges of knowledge of the Other and the We are constantly threatened under directed capitalism—as can be seen in the mechanization of human relations, so dear to the heart of American managers.

We shall now try to specify the emphasized forms in the different types of knowledge in this cognitive system.

The pervasiveness of technical knowledge requires that we first of all distinguish its various levels. In common-sense knowledge it accentuates the positive and collective forms. The workers' knowledge, whether they are semi-skilled or unskilled, simultaneously emphasizes the empirical, concrete, partly-collective and partly-individual forms. At the level of foremen and engineers it is the rational, conceptual, partly-symbolic and partly-concrete, and individual forms which appear most favoured. On the level of experts and inventors, the symbolic, speculative and individual forms triumph.

Political knowledge allows some mystical coloration to appear, although under cover of rational aspects. The other emphasized forms are the conceptual, symbolic, and collective.

In perceptual knowledge of the external world the empirical, positive, concrete, and individual are particularly marked, although to some extent they are limited by the symbolic and collective, either because of the utilization of technical apparatus, such as television, or by an often unavoidable politicization.

In philosophical knowledge the rational takes the form of a combination of technical and symbolic, along with the conceptual. Philosophical orientations that are opposed to 'symbolic logic' and its technicization of philosophy, emphasize the speculative, concrete, and empirical forms. In both cases the individual form predominates.

The problem of emphasized forms of knowledge does not arise for common-sense knowledge, since it is technicized and politicized to such an extent. Knowledge of the Other and the We, to the extent that it exists, adopts any form that permits it to maintain itself.

CHAPTER TEN

The Knowledge of Fascist Techno-Bureaucratic Society

We now turn to techno-bureaucratic societies and the corresponding cognitive system. This type of structure and society was first experienced before the Second World War in Italy, Germany, and then Argentina. Neither the military victory of the Allies, nor the later fall of Perón in Argentina cut short these structural tendencies.

Techno-bureaucratic fascism can assume very different forms, as is shown by a comparison of Franco's régime in Spain, Salazar's in Portugal, and that dreamt of by supporters of the O.A.S. in France.

As we have pointed out, those Western countries under organized capitalistic régimes are threatened by it, especially in so far as it constitutes their only defence against social revolutions. This applies as much to the United States as to Federal Germany (full of memories of Nazism), and to France, particularly under the Fifth Republic which, from one point of view, represents a stage somewhere between directed capitalism and one form of technocratic fascism.

The rise of Pan-Arabism may also favour technocratic fascism. The dictatorship of Nasser in Egypt, that of Ben Bella after Algeria gained independence, and the régimes of Iraq and Iran, are reminiscent of that type of society, although with different nuances. It is striking that countries that are clearly 'underdeveloped' technically and economically should strive to by-pass these stages in order to take from directed capitalism its tendency towards fascism.

We shall content ourselves with a short discussion of this type of structure and its corresponding cognitive system, leaving aside most of its nuances[1] and keeping to broad generalizations, in order

---

[1] Thus, we make an exception of the régime established by Bourguiba in de-colonized Tunisia. However, the efforts at planning and improving the

to extract the basic characteristics of techno-bureaucratic fascism in its various aspects.

It consists essentially of a complete fusion between the totalitarian state, the economic planning agencies, and the army organization, managed by technocratic groups. These come both from the army itself, and from the top administrative personnel, and also, should the need arise, either from trusts, cartels and banks, or from veterans of 'national liberation' organizations (for example, the leaders of the F.L.N.), etc. The dictatorship and subjection are such that, even when publicity is given to notions of worker and peasant self-management (as in the Arab countries), this is transformed into a form of subjection of those groups, who are thus the dupes and victims of a bluff.

Political parties and worker organizations are forbidden, with the exception of the one official party directed by the head of state himself. This semi-charismatic leader, who is the figurehead, can be no more than a straw man of the technocrats, or of the interests of foreign capital and trusts (Franco, Salazar), or a man who plays at being the demagogic leader of the poverty-stricken masses (Hitler, Mussolini); but he can also, as with Nasser, Ben Bella, and many other dictators, gain support from the impatience of the 'young nations' to by-pass the various stages of capitalism by any means.

One of these means is arbitrary and absolutist planning, in which profiteers charge what they can get in different situations, but the victims of which are always either the workers and peasants, or minority ethnic groups (such as the Kabyls in Algeria, the Kurds in Iraq, the Jews, etc.). Chauvinistic racial mythology is only one of the masks behind which the various kinds of fascist authoritarianism hide. The importance of mythology, fanaticism, and slogans, are characteristic of the general atmosphere of this régime.

Here briefly are the essential characteristics.

(a) The subjection of all social classes and all particular groupings to the state, which is itself dominated by cliques, whether they are techno-bureaucrats, the military, or 'national liberators';

standard of living of the working population are not taken as far as allowing for effective control by the interested parties themselves. In the interesting work of Jean Duvignaud *Tunisie* (Lausanne, Rencontre, 1965) it is impossible to fail to see the threat that government authoritarianism, however mild, presents to a developing trade unionism.

this can also conceal the process of submission and resistance to large capital, either national or international.

(b) The development of large communions, based on an often artificially inspired hate or ecstasy. These are rivalled by large-scale passive masses, who are depressed and confused.

(c) The organized apparatus of the state is in the hands of the leader's immediate followers, the single party, and the all-powerful police (such as the Nazi Gestapo). Techniques, combined with myths, slogans and delusions, can create highly developed methods of extermination. The morphological, ecological base, which is essentially politicized and imbued with fanaticism and mythology (the famous *Lebensraum*—living space—of the Nazis). Accumulation of wealth accompanies the confiscation of the goods of the enemy, and those of persecuted or exterminated ethnic groups.

(d) Law and morality fall into last place in the hierarchy of social regulation; education is reduced to drill, except in Islamic fascism, which places traditional religious education in first place, whilst maintaining the universities founded by the colonizers, provided that they go along with the illusions, fantasies and slogans of the new régime, and assist in their diffusion. If one considers the general climate, one can easily imagine at what point, under these conditions, the cognitive system corresponding to these structures collapses into confusion.

In concluding this brief analysis, we note only that this type of structure is much more detached from the subjacent total social phenomenon than was organized and directed capitalism. In spite of all the efforts of technocratic fascism to integrate and dominate the entire global society, it does not succeed in reducing the disjunction between its structure and the society as a whole. The subjacent total social phenomenon includes not only all those who resist, and those who are persecuted, but also all those groups and parties that are officially forbidden; moreover, it includes the great mass of the population who, escaping from the hold of the frenzied delusions of the fascist leaders, continue as far as possible to lead a family life and to carry on their daily work. As we shall see, it is there that the remainder of the types and forms of knowledge that the structure of technocratic fascism did not succeed in corrupting, are concentrated.

*

We can now seek to analyse the cognitive system corresponding to this structure.

(A) The most salient characteristic is the *complete fusion of political, technical, and scientific knowledge*. But this fusion is brought about in conditions such that the term 'knowledge' is not applicable to any of these types. Scientific knowledge is certainly the one which appears to be most deformed and stifled. It has lost all trace of being independent knowledge. As for what would properly be called technical knowledge, it is also profoundly affected, and survives only to the extent that it remains subject to the politics of the government, and when required it can be used for such purposes as extermination and war. One can no longer talk of a political knowledge worthy of that name, as real knowledge is practically excluded. Obviously there exists a spontaneous political knowledge—it is manifested in the artificial excitation of the people. (It appears even more in the disappointment and anguish felt by foreign countries that are not fooled by the alleged 'peaceful goals' proclaimed by the régime's representatives merely to give themselves time to increase their arms.)

A certain spontaneous political knowledge is still discernible in the intrigues that centre around the leader or within the single party. But since it is reduced to the art of manipulating delusions, more or less consciously, it has no other role than that of exalting political doctrines based on the systematization of clichés, slogans, grossly false and aberrant myths, and fanaticism. In so far as it can still be considered as a type of knowledge, this is the one which predominates in total fusion with 'technical knowledge' and a degenerate 'scientific knowledge'.

As German and Italian colleagues have testified, it was not necessary to be either resistant or Jewish in order to be dismissed from the universities under Nazism or Fascism. It was sufficient to want to pursue the teaching of technical or scientific knowledge —even technicized scientific knowledge—without acknowledging the slogans, myths, and delusions of the dominant clique.

(B) In these conditions it is not surprising that *perceptual knowledge of the external world*, which occupies second place, is itself profoundly imbued (in so far as it corresponds to the structure) with elements alien to knowledge, and entirely politicized. Not only is the space in which the external world is placed concentric and diffuse (concentric for the home country, and diffuse with respect to all others), and time made to appear cyclical or deceptively precipitate, but one might conclude that this knowledge appears to be beset with a kind of blindness which largely conceals from it the reality of the external world.

(C) *Philosophical knowledge*, which is both technicized and politicized, comes in third place in this cognitive system. It is only tolerated in so far as it offers justifications for all aspects of the régime's politics. Thus, the philosophy of Heidegger, under the Nazi régime, despite its apparent existentialism, became a glorification of man who is guided, in the depths of ignorance, by the illumination provided by the Fuhrer and his followers. However, Nazism preferred simpler and more straightforward justifications directly based on racist positivism.

The position of philosophical knowledge in the Arab fascist dictatorships seems more complex. This is not to say that it does not also contribute to the justification of governmental measures, but its greater complexity derives from the fact that it is combined with Islamic theology, and the interpretation of this is beyond our field of competence.

(D) *Common-sense knowledge*, the last in the cognitive system corresponding to this structure, nevertheless plays a considerable role in the subjacent total social phenomenon. For all the elements of society not integrated by the régime, even if they are not directly threatened, have recourse to this kind of knowledge in order to preserve all the other types from the degeneration into which the régime leads them. Technical knowledge, scientific knowledge, political knowledge, perceptual knowledge of the external world, and knowledge of the Other and the We, in the proper sense, are non-existent in the official cognitive system. Thus, the underlying total social phenomena become the real carriers of knowledge, while awaiting liberation from the state of delusion created by the official cognitive system.

As for the forms of knowledge emphasized in the hierarchy corresponding to this structure, they are identical for all that remains of the types of knowledge. A thick cloud of false myths and artificially imposed collectivism hangs over the whole cognitive system.

However, the various types of knowledge that are able to escape the régime's control, due to the underlying total social phenomenon, and which are in disjunction with the structure, accentuate the rational, empirical, positive, concrete, and mainly individual, forms. They do not succeed, however, in freeing themselves from a certain mystical tinge, which must be attributed to the despair of groups of the persecuted, believers, resisters, and those threatened with extermination.

The fascist régimes of the West and of Arab dictatorships have been experienced for only a relatively short time. One cannot contemplate without fear the terrifying 'dark night of knowledge' into which humanity would plunge, if the structures that we have just briefly analysed were successfully maintained for a long period.

CHAPTER ELEVEN

The Cognitive System of Centralized State Collectivism

Examples of this type of society are provided by Soviet Russia since the October 1917 Revolution (despite its changes at different stages of the régime's development), China since 1949, both before and after it came into conflict with the U.S.S.R., and the 'people's democracies', the tendencies of which have often varied (but excepting Yugoslavia which, since 1949–50, has been moving towards decentralized collectivism). This structure is not considered permanent by those most qualified to speak for it, but as a necessary stage towards the 'second phase of communism'. Furthermore, it has not been clearly defined, either by Marx or his followers, who foresaw the disappearance of social classes and the 'dissolution of the state into the society', but refused to specify how this society should be structured and organized.

The first phase of communism is regarded as arising out of a social revolution—which was clearly the case in Russia. The capitalist enterprises and the bourgeois class were eliminated. The 'absolutism of private profit' and 'industrial feudalism' disappeared. The proletarian class alone, or united with the peasant class, is officially proclaimed as 'dictator' in this social structure. This dictatorship is not, however, exercised by the people themselves, but by the Communist Party, which becomes the supreme organ of the state, responsible for controlling all economic planning, the execution of the plans, the 'political line' and the 'ideological line' of all public services, including state trades unions and approved associations, such as the writers' association, for example. The economic planning agencies, which formulate the plans and supervise their execution, have great importance, but neither the workers and peasants, nor in fact the great mass of consumers, are directly represented in this process.

The industrial, administrative, military, and planning, techno-bureaucracies became extremely powerful under the personal dictatorship of Stalin, although since his death and the liquidation of his myth[1] they have been kept in submission by the state and its highest organ the Communist Party, as well as by the trade unions. Regional decentralization of the economic planning agencies, which began some years ago, democratization of the Supreme Soviet of the U.S.S.R. and of the Communist Party itself (the membership of which is steadily increasing), and the foreign policy of 'peaceful coexistence', are precursory signs of the profound changes that are occurring in this structure. Only the pressure of China (very backward in every respect compared to the U.S.S.R.), can retard this process. The problems posed in China are less concerned with social revolution than with an Asiatic nationalistic revolution, in which the elements of social revolution are but secondary.

It is far from being our intention to suggest that direct control by the workers has already come about in the U.S.S.R. (with the exception of the *kolkhozes*), when the very organs of the Communist Party have to struggle against the still exorbitant power of the *apparatchiki* within the party. It is simply that real freedom and democracy in the field of economic planning and work in industry, and in the political and cultural sphere, seem less distant. Their complete realization is promised only for the 'second phase of communism', which is proclaimed as the next stage. Yet the twenty-second Party Congress, whose decisions were not annuled by Khrushchev's downfall, called for 'direct self-government by the masses' and 'periodic changes in leadership' which one would hope to see brought about in more direct forms where there would be control by all. But one must be patient. . . .

We shall briefly summarize this structure.

The state, dominated by the Communist Party, is deeply involved in the whole of economic life and rules over all the other particular groupings, whether official or merely sanctioned. Examples of the first type are factories and businesses, trade unions, shops, youth groups (*komsomols*), local groups, *sovkhoses*, etc., and as examples of the second type there are scientific and cultural groups, the writers' association, and also the Orthodox Church, its monasteries and seminaries, as well as the other confessional bodies (including those of the Islamic faith). The state

---

[1] The Khrushchev period represents but one important stage in this liquidation.

rules equally over the three main social classes—the proletariat, peasantry (60 per cent of the population), and the techno-bureaucratic class, with its many and varied sections. The peasant class is the least subject of the three. This is due to the fact that it is by far the most numerous, that the majority are organized in *kolkhozes* that are self-managing, that it predominates in all ranks of the Red Army, and that it remains the most faithful to Orthodox religious beliefs.

The proletarian class, on the contrary—which constituted the main support of the October Revolution, due to the local soviets seizing power in the factories (only to be dissolved later)—although the state still speaks in its name, finds itself in a situation of unexpected frustration. The trade unions have insufficient freedom of action, and the more recently introduced 'workers' committees' exercise only 'informative functions'. The improvement in their situation as far as the proletariat is concerned means simply the possibility, open to the most obedient and gifted, of ascending the educational ladder free of charge, which enables them to leave the working class; or the obligation of the state to find employment for every worker, and freedom from the possibility of being dismissed without serious justification by the factory or enterprise; to this should be added the newly introduced right of every worker to refer to court any abuse of power committed against him by the factory management.

With regard to the microsocial, the We is much more strongly emphasized than relationships with the Other. In the population as a whole the We is sometimes passive, at other times active, depending upon the circumstances. In the proletarian class, masses tend to be active, as do the communities which are emphasized in factories, trades unions, and by workers' committees and their wall-newspapers. As for the peasant class, to the extent that it finds expression in *kolkhozes*, active communities predominate. Active communions can be observed in the different groups of the techno-bureaucratic class, and in certain sections of the Communist Party, especially in certain specific circumstances.

As for the depth levels, it is centralized or decentralized planning, dealing not only with the economy, but with the creation of the 'new man', and constituting a system of specific symbols and ideals, that is at the top of the hierarchy. Next comes the organized apparatus of the party, the state, the planning organs, etc. Finally, the demographico-ecological foundation plays an important role, although it varies according to different regions of the U.S.S.R., and has also been extended towards cosmic space in the last decade.

The technical division of labour and the social division of labour are both highly developed, and as a consequence the considerable progress in industrialization and automation is carried still further by being combined with planning. This is particularly cumulative in heavy industry, atomic energy, electronic and space equipment.

In the hierarchy of social regulation first position is occupied by knowledge of various types (philosophical and political first, scientific and technical next, as will be seen), then the morality of ideal symbolic images and creativity, next education, and finally law and the arts—mainly literary art.

This new culture seeks to synthesize, as far as possible, human-ism and technology, which proves to be an extremely difficult task and would require for its success enormous and unswerving effort.

*

We can now begin the analysis of the cognitive system corre-sponding to this type of structure and global society.

(A) In first place is *doctrinal political knowledge* and *philosophical knowledge,* an effort being made to combine the two. This com-bination is facilitated by the dominance of the Marxist–Leninist tradition of thought. But Marxism, both in its philosophical and its socio-political aspects, allows for the most varied interpretations, and it has never been possible to avoid a multiplicity of philo-sophical and politico-doctrinal orientations, despite the efforts of the Party. In fact, it can be observed that in the U.S.S.R. in different periods and circumstances, varying interpretations of Marxist–Leninism are emphasized and it is not as dogmatic as its reputation would suggest, despite the obligatory teaching of the 'Diamat' (dialectical materialism) to all first-year students in the universities. However, we obviously cannot enter into details here. What is of interest is the fact that the need for philosophical knowledge is so vital and deep in this cognitive system (even if one denies that dialectical materialism constitutes such knowledge).

This tendency to combine philosophical and socio-political knowledge, formulated in doctrines, requires special analysis. Philosophical knowledge, even if it seeks to be detached (involving 'neither laughter nor tears' according to Spinoza), is nevertheless a partisan knowledge, as we have shown. In this cognitive system, this partisan character is linked with a political position. But because socio-political knowledge, whether formulated or spontaneous, is influenced in its concerns by this same position, an extreme politicization of philosophical knowledge ensues. The problems facing the U.S.S.R. today were not foreseen by Marx or Lenin, and in consequence socio-political knowledge tends to become detached from philosophical knowledge. Attempts to combine the two at any price tends to result in a dogmatism that destroys them both. From this point of view, spontaneous political knowledge, which varies from one group to another in the Communist Party and different social classes, and depending on the circumstances, acquires an unexpected primacy.

Political knowledge and philosophical knowledge are also made less dogmatic as a result of the conflict with China, the movement towards final de-Stalinization and democratization, and the passionate desire in communist society to maintain peace in the world. This intellectual atmosphere is the opposite of that which characterizes fascist totalitarianism, including that of the recently liberated Arab states. In this respect at least, any attempt to equate the knowledge of centralized collectivist states and that of totalitarianism is fundamentally mistaken.

(B) *Scientific knowledge* comes in second place, and in contrast to that of directed capitalist societies it is not identical with technical knowledge. This can be explained by the fact that Russia, at the time of the October Revolution of 1917, was an underdeveloped country, technically speaking, and that the exact and natural sciences and their laboratories received special aid and support from the Soviet Government. This support has become a tradition and is maintained still. The sciences are considered to be essentially apolitical. It should be noted that, despite the enormous development in both numbers and quality of universities spread throughout all the regions of the U.S.S.R., the exact and natural sciences have maintained their primacy in education and research, not only ahead of the human sciences (where only history and ethnology have progressed), but also over technical knowledge. Though this may seem paradoxical, the cognitive system of communist societies more closely resembles democratic–liberal societies than directed capitalist societies. It is not inconceivable that, as it is now reaching the technical level of western societies, the combination and fusion of scientific and technical knowledge may follow. But such is not the case at present.

(C) Thus, in the U.S.S.R. and other communist societies, *technical knowledge* occupies only *third position*, and remains subordinate to science. This characteristic is strikingly evident even in the field where the U.S.S.R. is considered to be most advanced, such as that of space satellite communications, space equipment and operating skills, intercontinental rockets and missiles. Astronomy, physics, chemistry, etc., remain in control. Moreover, the number of qualified engineers turned out by institutions of higher education, with a view to raising industrial productivity, is impressive and increases considerably each year. But, even in the training of engineers, scientific knowledge plays a much more important role than in the Western countries.

(D) In *fourth place* is *perceptual knowledge of the external world*, the importance and extent of which is much greater than in most other societies. This is because it is also concerned with Asia, America, Europe, and Africa, and because its attraction is much stronger than elsewhere. Consequently, it is less self-interested and politicized than under organized capitalist régimes, and certainly more so than under fascist régimes.

(E) *Knowledge of the Other and the We* comes next. Knowledge of the We is clearly more widespread than that of the Other. It asserts itself particularly in workshops and factories, in the planning and Party agencies, as well as in warring factions. It is also evident in trade unions, workers committees, and in the *kolkhozes*.

On the other hand, knowledge of the Other takes refuge in the intimacy of the family, which remains strongly integrated, with a patriarchal head. One finds it also in the small *kolkhozes*. In all other groups, public services, army units, different milieux and social classes, knowledge of the Other is kept secret when it exists, as stereotypes of the Other are officially imposed—such as that of the soviet man, completely dedicated to the régime, the party, the communist cause, and full of enthusiasm for all that is established. One may well wonder what resemblance that bears to the concrete, individualized Other.

(E) *Common-sense knowledge* in this cognitive system must be placed in last position. It is nevertheless widely diffused, particularly among the rural population and peasant families. Common-sense knowledge has a certain intensity in the *kolkhozes*, where it often combines with elements of technical knowledge and spontaneous political knowledge. It hardly exists at all in other groups and settings, except families.

Concerning the emphasized forms of knowledge in this cognitive system, mystical elements appear in philosophical and politico-doctrinal knowledge, despite its militant rationalism. It nevertheless favours the conceptual, symbolic, and collective forms, although these are sometimes limited by the empirical and a tendency towards the concrete. In scientific knowledge, the rational form easily predominates, whilst the conceptual and the empirical, the positive and speculative, the symbolic and adequate, collective and individual, appear to be complementary. In technical knowledge and perceptual knowledge of the external world, the situation is the same. Knowledge of the Other owes its emphasis on the symbolic and conceptual forms to the imposed, artificial stereotypes that we mentioned. As for common-sense knowledge the positive, empirical, symbolic, and collective, predominate as a general rule.

*

To summarize the cognitive system corresponding to societies whose structure takes the form of a centralized collectivist state, one can say that the hierarchy of types of knowledge (provided the stereotyped knowledge of the Other is omitted) offers hope of a constant and rapid advance in most branches of knowledge, especially in view of the fact that they are being carefully taught and widely diffused. Yet this system admits of a grave shortcoming, which is located in the combination of a particular political doctrine with a specific philosophical orientation—both of which are artificially imposed, and under a form that is at the same time crystallized and changing. These two types of knowledge are therefore seriously distorted and compromised by obvious dogmatism, which makes them submit to slogans dictated from above. It is relevant to ask the question whether a differently arranged collectivist structure could not lead to a cognitive system free of such shortcomings and entirely independent, in the not-too-distant future. This would be decentralized collectivism, based on the self-management of all the interested parties.

R

CHAPTER TWELVE

The Cognitive System of Decentralized Pluralist Collectivism

For us this is not an idealized type of structure and society. Nor is it necessarily the 'second phase of communism', as the question of whether all countries have to experience the 'first phase of communism' in order to arrive as this stage lies outside our subject. However, in order to pass from organized and directed capitalism, and even more so from fascist technocracy, to decentralized, pluralist collectivism, based on the self-government of those involved, it would seem difficult to avoid social revolutions. The structures would also assume different forms in various countries. Certainly they would not have the same character in the Nordic states or in Great Britain (where socio-political development has always followed a unique course), in the United States, in France, in Latin America, etc. The differences would be still more pronounced between the Asiatic countries, such as India, Japan, North and South Vietnam, or Indonesia, not to mention China, where centralized communism and militant Asiatic nationalism are triumphant for the time being. However, there is no doubt that if the countries of the 'Third World', which face so many problems, were to succeed by some extraordinary chance in bypassing stages, whilst freeing themselves from the economic hold of Western countries, they would accomplish their own forms of social revolution and arrive at their own particular interpretations of 'decentralized collectivism'.

It cannot be denied that this type of structure and society, which also suggests a multiplicity of secondary types, has never yet been experimented with fully and effectively, even in Europe, where several very limited attempts in this direction have appeared.

Yet it would be inaccurate to view decentralized collectivism as nothing more than an arbitrary mental construction or a mere ideal, stemming from Proudhon (who was actually much more realistic than is generally thought). It systematizes and carries through to their logical conclusion actual tendencies observable today in certain 'popular democracies', principally in Yugoslavia (since de-Stalinization in 1948) where, in spite of a series of obstacles and difficulties, worker self-management and decentralized collectivism have obtained important results. Recently, Poland and Hungary have begun to follow a fairly similar path, which, very recently seems to have begun to tempt Czechoslovakia. Even in the U.S.S.R., after the twenty-second Party Congress, under Khruschev's leadership and after his fall, the same tendency seems to be asserting itself, although it is still tentative. Finally, in certain Nordic countries which have not yet passed through social revolutions, such as Sweden, Norway, and particularly Finland (where the influence of the U.S.S.R. makes itself more strongly felt, because of its close proximity), they have bettered centralized communism by a combination of planning and direct participation in control by those involved.

Let us briefly specify the characteristics of decentralized pluralist collectivism, such as can be discerned in the many tendencies that are beginning to take shape at present.

It is essentially a question of effecting a balance—which would constantly need to be re-established—between the democratized collectivist state and economic planning, which would allow for the direct participation of all those concerned. The so-called technicians would be subject to the dual control of the state and the independent economic organizations, managed by the workers themselves. This is what Proudhon foresaw in an inspired way in seeking to discover how 'economic democracy' and the 'new political democracy' could both collaborate and 'mutually balance each other'. It is clear that democratization of the collectivist state presupposes a return to at least two, if not several, political parties, reinforced by being linked to the new divisions of 'economic democracy'. The latter would require the setting up of an economic federalism providing at least four different methods to ensure effective participation and control by all those concerned. These would be:

(1) a federalism of workshops, factories, and whole industrial enterprises, along with all the agricultural organizations ('agricultural co-operatives', '*kolkhozes*', '*zadrugas*', etc.), which would themselves be grouped in federations;

(2) an economic federalism based on regionalism in industry and agriculture;

(3) a federalism in planning by enterprises and localities, leading up to a unifying federalism that would accomplish its function by producing a total economic plan for the country;

(4) a federal ownership of the means of production in industry and agriculture—all levels would participate in ownership: society as a whole, each region, each branch of industry and agriculture, each particular group of workers, and every individual who participates in the economic process. Individual or group withdrawals from this collective ownership obviously would not be able to dissolve it, and the effects would be confined to those who brought them about. This federal ownership could not be dissolved, it would be guaranteed by the collectivist state, which would also remain the guarantor of a complete economic plan, even though the planning process was federalized.

The organs of worker and peasant self-management begin with *councils of control*, complemented by *councils of management and productivity*, to which the managers of an enterprise would be responsible, as well as being liable to dismissal by these councils. Next come the *regional economic councils*, responsible for planning, and composed of representatives from the management and productivity councils, along with smaller numbers of representatives of technical managers, consumers, and the political government. Finally, there is the *central economic councils of the country*, on which all the regional councils are represented, and where decision-making would again be in the hands of the workers and peasants—delegated by the management and productivity councils—who would constitute the majority. Representatives of the political government and of the technicians would be in a minority on this central economic council, where the most general economic planning would take place.

The difficulties encountered by Yugoslavia in self-management and planning are often attributed to the indifference or resistance of agricultural enterprises (*zadrugas*), but in our opinion the real reason is the failure to integrate the planning organs and the organs of self-management. In fact, in the central planning authority, set up by the political government, there are only a few worker and peasant representatives, and they are not regularly elected by the councils of control and management of the industrial and agricultural enterprises.

The same situation can be seen in the regional planning councils.

We believe that only a profound reform of the composition of the planning organs would enable decentralized collectivism, at present in its initial states in Yugoslavia, to be fully realized, first on the economic level, and then at the level of the whole social structure.

From all that we have just portrayed, it is clear that there is no question of the political state disappearing in this type of society. But because it would be highly decentralized and, in theory at least, limited in its functions, it would be possible to balance it with the independent economic organization, based on the federalized ownership of the means of production.

Now the question arises as to what would be the form of organization of the political government under such a régime. Several solutions seem possible, depending on the circumstances and traditions of the countries involved. One might envisage political representation based on municipalities and regions; or again, a representation of occupations and functions. One might also keep to the formula of parliamentarianism, with a government responsible to an assembly elected on the basis of universal suffrage without any other specification. In any case, what is essential is a profound reform of collectivist political government, so that it would be restricted in certain of its former functions by a parallel economic government based on self-management and federalized ownership, although the political government would have final control in foreign policy and military matters.

Impartial judicial bodies to regulate possible conflicts between the two organizations would be indispensable to the proper functioning of this régime.

Let us summarize briefly the main characteristics of decentralized, pluralist collectivism.

(a) Parity of the economic planning organization and the collectivist political state, each responsible only for itself and mutually balancing one another, and both highly democratized.

(b) Disappearance of the old social classes and the appearance of new social classes, tending to correspond to the various functions or occupations, and receiving different kinds of benefits, designed to strengthen and maintain their equality. The existence of two or more political parties, linked to the new social classes, or to localities and regions.

(c) From the microsocial point of view, communities and active communions would predominate, thus suppressing as far as possible the importance of masses.

(d) Among the depth levels would come first of all the plans, drawn up by those directly involved and imbued with creative ideas and values; next would follow the innovative, unpredictable social roles, economic and political organizations open to all, juridical regulations based not on established patterns or rules, but drawing mainly upon the living, spontaneous law. The ecologico-morphological base, which would be profoundly transformed by all these elements, as well as by the development of constantly improving techniques, would have only secondary importance.

(e) The cognitive system, which we intend to analyse in detail after this brief summary of the structural characteristics, would be de-politicized as far as possible. Knowledge, education, morality (creative morality, the morality of virtues, and imperative morality), art and law, would all struggle to establish their pre-eminence in the hierarchy of social regulation. It would seem, moreover, that in this competition, the numerous possibilities for conflict between the economic and political organizations, as well as the federal character of the ownership of the means of production, would tend to assure the predominance of law.

(f) A new civilization would emerge, in which men, the We, groups, and structures, succeed in appropriating and mastering the most advanced techniques and the most powerful machines. The threat of technocracy would be avoided, not only because of the direct participation in control of all those concerned, and the strength that such a structure would possess, but also due to the ascendancy of *humanism over technology. To humanize every technique to the utmost would be the vocation of decentralized collectivism.*

*

We can now trace the main outlines of the cognitive system that would correspond to this type of structure and society.

First of all, in addition to the previously mentioned de-politicization of most types of knowledge, this cognitive system is essentially characterized by the unprecedented promotion of knowledge of the Other and the We; the de-dogmatization of philosophical knowledge which, freed from all restrictions, becomes once more pluralistic in its orientation; finally, scientific knowledge is more independent of technical knowledge, which it helps to humanize, whilst the human sciences are raised to an equal, if not superior, position relative to the natural sciences.

(A) In the hierarchy of types of knowledge, *philosophical knowledge* and *knowledge of the Other and the We* occupy first place, entering into dialectics of complementarity, and sometimes mutual implication, but rarely competition and polarization, with the result that any artificial barrier between human science and philosophy is impossible.

Philosophical knowledge, whatever its viewpoint, is no longer reduced to mere consideration of scientific knowledge or any other single type of knowledge. Its subject matter is now every type of mental act and mental state, all individual and collective consciousness, penetrating into the very core of reality—especially the social reality of which it is a part. Finally, it is concerned with creativity, decision-making, choice, innovation, and therefore with every transformation of the social world, as well as the world of nature. Thus the fact of being a second-order or sometimes even third-order knowledge would no longer deflect philosophy from its primordial vocation—that of commitment to a profound humanism, concerned with the infinite and real totalities in which men, the various We's, groups, classes, and global societies, are all involved, whilst at the same time playing a part in their transformation and continuous creation. One can give different interpretations of this realist humanism, but it is not possible to eliminate it from any philosophical doctrine that rejects the pursuit of shadows or illusions. Thus the way is clear not only for epistemology, but also ontology and de-ontology, provided only that they renounce naturalism, spiritualism, materialism and positivism. Philosophical knowledge exists to discover new perspectives in human knowledge, not to shut off access to them.

Knowledge of the Other and the We, which is favoured by the very existence of worker participation in management and control, and by the pluralism of groups and the equal benefits enjoyed by all classes, starts from a spontaneity of outlook and a refusal to be bound by stereotypes. It seeks for, and finds, concrete, individual Others and We's. But in order to transform this impression into coherent images, it is necessary for concepts and judgements to be introduced—without which no real knowledge is possible—as this knowledge allows for neither exclusive nor excessively vague generalizations.

In order to gain an understanding all of that is human, and its place in the world, one must begin with knowledge of the Others among whom one works, and the We's in which one participates, and combine this with philosophy and knowledge of the relationship between singularity and the infinite global totality—hence the complementarity of philosophical knowledge and knowledge of the Other, which is so indispensable to decentralized collectivism that it promotes a tendency towards their reciprocal integration. The more they succeed in attaining this integraton, the greater are the chances that these two types of knowledge will flourish. And this development is accompanied by humanization of both science and technology.

(B) *Scientific knowledge* must be placed in second position in this cognitive system. Not only are the sciences humanized and maintain their autonomy vis-à-vis technical knowledge, but also the human sciences rival the natural sciences and sometimes even dominate them. This cognitive system is in fact the only one in which sociology, history, psychology (individual, social and collective), economics, 'political science', etc., are effectively de-politicized and freed from their ideological fetters, and so can at last attain maximum results.

(C) *Technical knowledge* would occupy third place. Despite its continuing development, it would be subject to control from four quarters—philosophical knowledge, knowledge of the Other and the We, scientific knowledge, and human science especially. Creative morality, the morality of virtues, imperative morality, as well as all kinds of law, would collaborate with these types of knowledge to humanize technical knowledge and to preserve it from the abuse of technicism.

(D) *Perceptual knowledge of the external world* is placed in fourth position, as in the cognitive system of societies planned according to the principles of the centralized collectivist state, but with this one difference, that it is much more de-politicized and even broader in its purview, since it would be completely open.

(E) *Political knowledge* is relegated to next to last position because it is not envisaged that there would be any need to elaborate this type of knowledge or to formulate political doctrines. Here, the divorce between political knowledge, philosophy, and science, and even techniques, appears complete. Certainly, spontaneous political knowledge would exist: it has its contribution to make and appears in mutual relationships between the many groups functioning under the federalized ownership of the means of production; it would also be exercised in the economic organization and the political organization, where it would be required in maintaining a balance between the two. But this strategic political knowledge tends to combine with knowledge of the Other and the We, and common-sense knowledge, which we have still to discuss.

At the risk of stating a paradox, it might be suggested that, in this cognitive system, even political knowledge is very much de-politicized in normal circumstances. However, in the case of crises and difficulties, which can occur in decentralized collectivism just as in any other type of structure (although more rarely), the political knowledge of groups, classes, planning agencies, and local and state organizations, can still manifest itself in an intense form. But if it were to succeed in becoming crystallized into opposing, rival doctrines, this would be a symptom of destructuration—even a warning sign of the breakdown of this structure, since no type of structure is eternal, and historical reality pursues its course by substituting new types of society for old.

(F) As in several other cognitive systems already considered in this work, *common-sense knowledge* comes in last position, given the great diffusion of philosophical, scientific and technical knowledge, by compulsory secondary education for all. Normally common-sense knowledge would seldom play a role except in the education of pre-school children. However, it would still be visible in certain circumstances and turning points, and to the extent that it partly combined with knowledge of the Other and spontaneous political knowledge. In any case, it does not entirely disappear from this cognitive system.

As for the forms emphasized within this system, they mark the complete triumph of the rational. It could be said that it is now a question of a completely rationalist hierarchy of knowledge. With regard to the other emphasized forms there is a balance between the empirical and conceptual, positive and speculative, symbolic and concrete, collective and individual, although with the possibility of slight variations according to circumstances.

It might be objected that in describing a cognitive system that has never yet functioned effectively, we have not escaped the temptation to assert our ideal as to the hierarchy of the types and forms of knowledge. Now we insist on showing that such is not the case, and for this purpose we do not hesitate to stress all the faults and uncertainties in this system. First, *it suffers from an excessive rationalism, which could enter into conflict with its realist humanism.* Then, and this is its principal fault, it runs the risk of arresting or retarding the progress of most types of knowledge, in order to avoid unsettling their hierarchy and equilibrium, having attained them with great difficulty. In view of this it might be said that this cognitive system and social structure risks sinking into a new kind of conservatism.

It might also be wondered whether technical knowledge, so tightly controlled by other types of knowledge, is not going to lose its dynamism. These doubts and criticism are further confirmed by the fact that law, morality (especially the morality of virtues and imperative morality), and socialization, seem to occupy a high position in this cognitive system, and thus might have a tendency to slow down the progress of knowledge.

Also, it is not a question of denying these faults and uncertainties but rather of remembering that there is no type of society and global structure that does not have qualities and faults, which inevitably have repercussions in the corresponding cognitive system. It is because of this that they all eventually become corrupt and disappear. But we have simply sought to demonstrate that the structure of societies planned according to the principles of decentralized collectivism, based on participation in control by all those involved, is infinitely more favourable to knowledge than that of organized capitalism, fascist technocracy, and centralized communism. It is not impossible that some time in the future other types of society, with other cognitive systems, will arise in their turn, but we are not in a position to foresee their characteristics or their effects.

Supplement

SUPPLEMENT

Sociological Inquiry into Knowledge of the Other

By *Jean Cazeneuve, Paul Maucorps and Albert Memmi, with an introduction by Georges Gurvitch*
The problem of knowledge of the Other has occupied many minds since the second quarter of the twentieth century, as a reaction against the rationalism and idealism that had been predominant for several centuries. Previously, even those who did not follow Kant in identifying the Other with generic representations of a universal human reason, at least posited a closed consciousness, turned in on itself, with the implication that it was possible and necessary to know one's self first in order to know others. And even those who rejected the appeal to analogy and the notion of direct projection of our own states on to others, resorted either to empathy (Einfühlung), such as Lipps advocated, or in the case of the Freudian school, to heteropathic or idiopathic identification, which did not allow them to grasp the concrete reality of the Others and the active resistance that they present to acts of the individual self (of which only Fichte had any real understanding in the nineteenth century).

Scheler provided a new approach by emphasizing the specificity of knowledge of the Other, its parity with—or even superiority to—knowledge of the self, and the fact that it is integrated in social reality. But having done this, he then proceeded to block any further progress; for, by seeking to base this knowledge almost exclusively on sympathy and love, conceived as direct intuitive apprehension, he committed several errors. He ignored the great variety in the concrete manifestations by which the Other appears in social reality. The Other can appear as father, brother, stranger, companion, rival, friend, foe, comrade, inferior, superior, help, embarrassment, protection, threat, centre of attraction, repulsion or indifference; it can also assume an ambivalent nature by combining opposing traits. In view of this we should not be surprised to find that to apprehend the Other can involve the intellect, emotions, or will, and that it can be either rational or mystical, etc.

Moreover, Scheler confused direct intuitive apprehension and elaborated knowledge of the Other—the second presupposing systematized conceptual images of the Other, based on judgements that claim to be true. Since he also ignored perception of the external aspect of the Other, he both disembodied the Other and suppressed the complex dialectic between apprehension of and knowledge of the Other, which may involve complementarity, mutual implication, or polarization. The same dialectic is lacking in the analysis of variations in transcendence or immanence, homogeneity or heterogeneity between the self, the Other, and the We, and the degree of their integration in particular groups, social classes, and global societies. Furthermore, it seems clear to us that in cases of conceptualized knowledge of the Other, the criteria supplied by large supra-functional entities tend to limit the spontaneity of the images arising in more restricted circles.

Mead's conceptions with regard to knowledge of the Other seem even more dogmatic and restrictive than those of Scheler, and yet Mead was more of a psycho-sociologist than a philosopher. In his book, *Mind, Self and Society* (1934), Mead suggests that knowledge of the Other is based on the capacity for assuming different roles and for taking the role of the Other. This exchange of roles provides the basis for communication by signs and symbols, which would be necessary for knowledge of the Other, and the end product would be reason, which is identified with society, both simply representing the generalized Other. In fact, this strange combination of pragmatism and rationalism does not take into account, to any extent, the variability of social frameworks and their effective reality, or the many aspects of the Other and variations in the character of knowledge of the Other. In contrast to Scheler, Mead completely eliminates direct apprehension of the Other. Mead based his ideas on sports teams and children's play groups, where the roles are effectively interchangeable; he thus forgets that in most other collectivities they are not interchangeable (not to mention the case of privileged roles), and that, furthermore, communication, signs and symbols are not essential for knowledge of the Other, and even when they are involved their importance varies.

From these two examples of recent theories concerning knowledge of the Other (several other examples could have been given), it should be clear that all these theories need to be made less dogmatic. It is the task of the sociology of knowledge to refute a whole series of untenable positions in epistemology—without, however, claiming to take its place.[1]

This is especially the task of the sociology of knowledge of the Other, and it is facilitated by the fact that, more than any other type of knowledge, it is in close or direct functional correlation with the specific social reality in which it resides. This is why empirical research seemed to be easier to carry out in this field than anywhere else.

In proposing to undertake an inquiry into variations in the apprehension and knowledge of the Other as a function of different social frameworks, it seemed that the types of groups best suited for an initial study were those specific groups that possessed a definite structure. There are several reasons for this: from the technical point of view, all participants of the selected groups could be questioned, which obviated the use of samples and polling procedures; from the theoretical point of view, we were dealing with groups which were integrated into the same global society, and strongly influenced by it; furthermore, the groups studied represented both microcosms of the manifestations of sociality, and were also real units forming a part of macrocosmic groups.

Our research revealed considerable variations in the nature of the apprehension and knowledge of the Other, and confirmed the hypothesis that there would be a strong positive correlation between the latter and the types of social frameworks—a result that should encourage the pursuit of further empirical investigations in the field of the sociology of knowledge.

G.G.

*

The 'Groupe de Recherches Sur la Sociologie de la Connaissance et la Sociology de la Vie morale,' working under the direction of Georges Gurvitch, carried out a series of investigations into the apprehension and knowledge of the Other in different structured groups. After a pre-test, conducted in a senior class in the Lycée Louis-le-Grand, which enabled us to make refinements in the interview, the research proper was carried out on eight groups. They can be broken down into four categories:

(1) Two groups that we agreed to call *intellectuals:* a philosophy

[1] Cf. my contribution in vol. II of the *Traité de Sociologie*, section vii, ch. ii: 'Problèmes de la sociologie de la connaissance', pp. 103–36.

class in the Lycée Turgot, and a company of actors called *Theâtre d'aujourd'hui*, under the direction of Michel de Ré;

(2) Four groups from the *industrial* sector: a group of assembly line workers in the Régie Renault plant (making gear-boxes); a group of semi-assembly line workers in the same plant; a group working in a foundry (Aciéries Legenisel–Blanchard); and a group of research engineers, chemists and their assistants working in a laboratory concerned with the use of plastics at the Centre de Recherches Péchiney;

(3) A group of *administrators* working in a department concerned with the inspection of technical education;

(4) A *rural* group made up of the inhabitants of a small village, Seine-et-Marne.

The interview method was used, with two special features:

(a) The instructions to the investigators were clearly defined, so as to avoid too great a dispersion in the responses, and to eliminate as far as possible the 'subjective factor' that might be introduced by each investigator.

(b) However, it was understood that these instructions were simply starting points, and a certain spontaneity was encouraged, enabling the interviewer to assess the individual personality factors (see the details of the questionnaire in Appendix 1).

The interviews were organized around four topics. Topic 1 was directed towards getting the subject to make explicit what he found most striking about people in his group (i.e. with regard to direct apprehension or intuition of the Other). Topic 2 centred on the following question: 'Upon reflecting further what enables you to arrive at a more precise image of the Other?' Its purpose was to determine the role played by ideal images and stereotypes, social prestige and standing in the group, conversations with fellow members and common work, in the formulation of actual knowledge of the Other. Topic 3 was oriented in such a direction as to discover how, once a person believes that he has a precise image of the Other, this is modified (by intuition or knowledge), and to what extent the subjects think they know their colleagues and are known by them. Topic 4 dealt with communication and knowledge, and aimed to discover the relative ease and rapidity according to which knowledge was communicated between the subjects, and the role of verbal, and even non-verbal, communication.

For each investigation, the reports of the interviewers were compared and a separate, detailed account was written. Then the eight dossiers were combined for a total analysis and, in order to enable us to arrive at general conclusions from our investigation of knowledge of the Other, we prepared the data for two types of treatment: one based on a careful quantitative analysis; the other based on a qualitative analysis. The present report deals with the results from the quantitative analysis. The results from the qualitative analysis will be reported in a later publication. Of course, these two aspects of the results of our investigations have been separated simply to attain greater clarity, and they are in fact interdependent and complementary.

For the quantitative analysis of the results of the investigations on the eight groups, the method adopted was mainly the analytic technique known as *analysis of variance*, according to the principles formulated by Sir R. A. Fisher in 1936. Also, the eight groups have been classified into the four categories discussed above, and the analysis has been carried out on the four types of groups, designated as follows: intellectuals (I); factory workers and employees (W); employees in the administrative department (A); rural (R). Although the results of the investigation fit together as a whole, it is convenient to present them here in terms of the four topics.

TOPIC I

For reasons of convenience, the responses, despite their complexity (which will no doubt appear in the qualitative analysis), have been grouped into three categories: physical appearance of the Other, behaviour of the Other, and social attitudes of the Other. What importance do members of the different groups interviewed attach to these three elements in apprehending the Other? It should be said at the outset that all the data collected in response to this question was highly significant in probability terms. Indeed, if one considers the positive and negative responses to the question as to the importance of the three elements in apprehension of the Other, it is observed that the replies vary according to the type of group. The breakdown of positive and negative responses is clearly not distributed according to chance (the calculations show that the hypothesis that the positive and

S

negative responses would divide according to chance is refuted at the 0.02 level of probability), but rather depends on the joint action of the experimentally introduced variables. On the other hand, the distribution of the variance (according to Fisher's technique), which enables us to assign to each factor or combination of factors its share of responsibility for the observed phenomena, shows that the factual reality is highly complex. Indeed, the responses vary as a result both of the type of group and of the specificity of the perception. The results obtained on this aspect have a certain value for sociology. Finally, as Figure 1 shows, the positive response curves as to the importance of the three elements (physical, behaviour, social attitudes) in perception of the Other, are the direct opposite of the negative response curves, for each of the four types of groups. This shows that the unclassifiable responses (whether evasive or ambiguous), in spite of their relative frequency, especially in the rural group and to a lesser degree among the factory workers (the intellectuals were clear and firm in their reponses), did not upset the internal logic of the design of the investigation, and did not falsify the general interpretation of the results.

The significance and validity of these results having been established, what indications do they give concerning the central question of Topic 1?

(1) Comparing the curves for *factory groups* and *administrative groups*, they appear somewhat similar with regard to the importance of the physical appearance and the behaviour of the Other. But the importance attached to social attitudes is greater for the administrative groups than for the factory workers.[1] This difference seems to reflect the conditions under which these two categories of subjects carry out their work. Increasing mechanization in the industrial sector results in the workers being increasingly isolated from each other. It is natural that the administrative employees should attach greater importance to interpersonal contacts, whether between equals, or with superiors or inferiors (cf. Fig. 1).

(2) The *intellectual groups* are clearly differentiated from the former groups by virtue of attaching special importance to the physical appearance and social attitudes at the expense of overt behaviour, whereas, in the eyes of subjects in other groups, these

[1] It is true that in this respect we did not take account of the part played by union affiliations in the perception of the Other characteristic of worker groups.

play a minor role in perception of the Other. The fact that intellectuals are more impressed than the others by the physical appearance of the Other is remarkable, and it suggests various hypotheses. Could it be due to a more pronounced development of the aesthetic sense, or else to a greater freedom with regard to

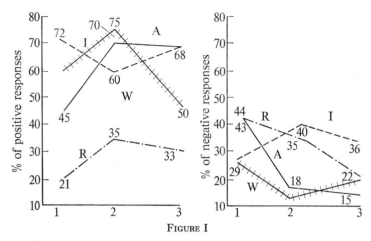

FIGURE I

The Interaction of the Options (Yes and No) and Certain Elements in Apprehending the Other

Legend: The figure at the left represents the percentage of positive responses (concerning the relative importance of the factors dealing with the knowledge of the Other) and is marked by the numbers on the vertical line; the figure on the right represents the percentage of negative responses.

The numbers under the horizontal line represent the three factors considered: (1 = physical, 2 = behaviour, 3 = social attitudes).

The intellectuals (I) are represented by dashes (– – –).

The administrators (A) by an unbroken line (———).

The workers (W) by a plus sign (+ + +).

The rural (R) by dots and dashes (– · –).

For example, the rural curve has a maximum positive response towards behaviour of 35%. The same holds for the workers; but their percentages for positive responses in favour of behaviour are considerably greater (75% in terms of the behaviour of the Other).

certain conventions that devalue the role of physical appearance compared to that of moral behaviour? As for the marked interest of the intellectuals in social attitudes of the Other, it may be that this is the result of a more imaginative, refined, and changeable awareness.

(3) The *rural group* is very clearly differentiated from the three

other types of groups. None of the elements of direct apprehension seem to be really important to rural people. What is said and what is done were relatively highly favoured in their answers, but only received limited approval. The importance given to social attitudes in relationships with the Other was clearly much less than that accorded to them by other groups; the importance attached to physical appearance was extremely low. One might deduce that the social isolation and exploitation in which agricultural workers and small farmers exist would not be conducive to direct apprehension of the Other. Moreover, rural groups are local groups, and so like all others they are susceptible to criteria coming from the global society.

(4) Apart from the relative similarity of the responses given by the industrial and administrative subjects, as opposed to the intellectual groups, and apart from the special case of the rural group in its perception of the Other, it should be noted that there is a certain tendency towards a general convergence with regard to social attitudes of the Other, or more exactly, less marked divergence in the responses of all groups in this regard, than with regard to physical appearance, for example, which produced the maximum disagreement.

TOPIC 2

It should be remembered that this second part of the interview was attempting to determine what it was that enabled the subject to arrive at a carefully considered, more precise image of the Other, i.e. his knowledge based on reflection. Quantitative analysis of the responses provides information on two aspects of this process of knowledge.

(1) *The importance given by subjects to the similarities or differences between others and themselves* in the process leading to a carefully considered image of the Other. First, it should be noted that if all the different types of groups were taken as a whole the opinions given were divided equally between these two possibilities. In other words, if one takes all the subjects who were questioned together, almost equal importance was attached to similarities as to the differences to be observed between oneself and one's colleagues, in the elaboration of an image of the Other. The process that consists of comparison and consideration of the Other as a non-

self, and the process that consists of projecting one's own image on to the Other, are equally widespread according to these responses, if one takes into consideration only the subjects as a whole rather than the specific groups to which they belong.

On the other hand, if one takes these groups separately, it is

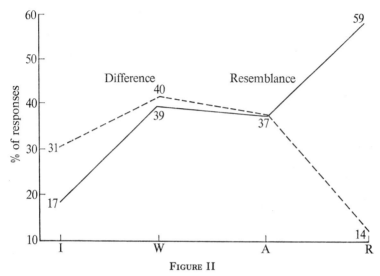

FIGURE II

The Interaction of the Options 'Difference–Resemblance' and the Collectivities

Legend: The horizontal line carries the four types of collectivities. The vertical line represents the percentages of responses. Resemblance with the Other is represented by an unbroken line; difference by dashes.

This shows very clearly that the greatest difference between the two curves is in relation to the responses of the rural group (R). Considerable importance is given to resemblance and little to the differences between them and the Other. At the left of the table the two curves are noticeably separated. Such is the case of the intellectuals (I). In the centre, the opposite holds for the factory groups (W) and the administration (A). The curve of responses in favour of resemblance and the curve of responses insisting on differences are at just about the same level.

perceived that the relative importance of similarity or difference in knowledge of the Other is not the same in all cases. With regard to variation between the different types of groups, three character-istics can be observed (see Fig. II):

(a) The workers, and particularly administrative employees, consider similarity and difference to be equally important as factors facilitating knowledge of the Other;

(b) By contrast, the intellectuals are clearly differentiated by virtue of the very low percentage employing similarity and the rather high percentage of responses attaching greater importance to difference from the Other;

(c) The rural group on the whole adopts an attitude exactly opposite to that of the intellectuals, and know the Other only in terms of similarity.

These differences are so clear and leave such a small place for chance that one is compelled to seek an explanation. Doubtless the intellectual is more inclined to notice in the Other that which surprises and seems unusual to him, and that which he does not find in himself. On the other hand, the suspicious peasant only recognizes an Other by identifying him with himself. Perhaps it is also due to a less developed imagination that he tends to perceive the Other in this way much more than the intellectual.

(2) *Comparative importance of specific aspects of life in the group* (ideal companion, role in the group, conversations and co-operation). Here again the type of group clearly exercises a differentiating influence. In fact, in contrast to factory and administrative workers, the intellectuals seem much less preoccupied with these aspects, and evidence individualistic reactions (see Fig. III). This observation does not contradict the results on the first topic, where the intellectuals showed themselves to be particularly sensitive to the social attitudes of the Other. For an individual to perceive the Other in terms of his attitudes towards others is something quite different from the individual formulating a cognitive image by allowing himself to be guided by criteria imposed by the group. The integration of intellectuals in group life was relatively slight.

Furthermore, the four factors specially considered with regard to knowledge of the Other (apart from similarity and difference), i.e. the stereotype of the ideal companion, the degree of influence possessed, common conversations and co-operation in work, do not assume the same importance in the eyes of members of different types of groups. On this point, a consensus was established and a hierarchy emerged from the responses given by members of all the groups taken as a whole, on these questions (see Fig. IV). The most effective source of real knowledge of the Other, in the opinion of the respondents, was conversation or verbal exchanges. Next came common work and the role played by the Other in the group. The ideal that one has of a colleague or work-mate comes in last position. It might be questioned whether the stereotypes relating to what the work-mate in each group should be are really ineffectual, or whether it is rather that

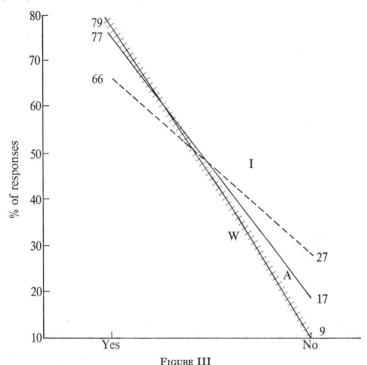

FIGURE III

The Interaction of Options and Types of Collectivities

Legend: Below the horizontal line, the options 'yes' and 'no' are given; the vertical line gives the percentages of responses. Dashes = intellectuals; straight line = administration; pluses = workers.

The 'yes' and 'no' here correspond to Topic 2. The difference between the positive responses and the negative ones is less prominent on the intellectual curve than the others.

The rural curve is missing from this figure. For particular reasons the rural group was not questioned on this point.

the subjects are not aware of them and do not perceive them because they have never thought about the problem. But if the responses on this particular point do not always seem to express very clear opinions, on the other hand those that concern the primacy of verbal exchanges and the relatively important role of common work in knowledge of the Other, are very clear and yield very suggestive percentages (cf. Appendix II, paragraph (2), items *a* and *e* of the table).

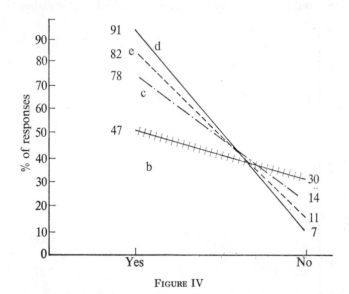

FIGURE IV

The Interaction of Options and Certain Factors in the Knowledge of Others

Legend: Conversations (d) straight line; work in common (e) dashes; role in group (c) dashes and dots; ideal companion (b) pluses. Below the horizontal line, the responses 'yes' and 'no'; the vertical shows the four factors in knowing the Other envisioned in Topic 2 (the factor 'resemblance–difference' has been envisioned in part).

The percentages of responses are for each collectivity as a whole.

Clearly the curve of response dealing with the importance of conversations (d) denotes the maximum approbations (91%) and the minimum of negative responses (7%) while the ideal companion reveals on the contrary the minimum of 'yes' (47%) and the maximum of 'no's' (30%).

TOPIC 3

(1) Knowledge of the Other is modified over time and according to circumstances. It is a common observation, if not a truism, that we not only do not have a single view of the Other, but also that our knowledge of the Other is uncertain, and often questioned or contradicted. Do these modifications, however frequently they occur, happen suddenly (because of the influence of changed circumstances, for instance), or steadily? In all the groups investi-

gated, the majority of responses favoured a slow evolution in knowledge of the Other. The variations in the response percentages that occurred between the different groups within a single category (e.g. between the various industrial groups) were relatively high, so that the differences between the categories could not assume any significance in a purely quantitative analysis. In other words, the internal variations within each category override the differences between the different categories of groups. These differences are seen to be very slight, as the table below indicates:[1]

Suddenly				Slowly			
I	W	A	R	I	W	A	R
30%	30%	40%	24%	33%	49%	57%	42%

At the most, it can be noted (although without statistical significance reaching a probability level that would permit firm conclusions) that the intellectuals are less inclined than others to accept slow modification rather than sudden change and, inversely, that the rural group exercises greater restraint than the others in allowing unexpected circumstances to rapidly change their image of the Other. But we repeat that despite these differences between the groups, all believed in a slow modification rather than sudden changes in this matter, i.e. they give primacy to knowledge over direct apprehension. Clearly the investigation has produced here a finding that transcends particular groups.

(2) The rhythm of changes is obviously not the only important question posed by fluctuations in knowledge of the Other. The interviewers were also instructed to ask the subjects about the feeling of confidence that they possessed, or lacked, with regard to their own judgements about the Other, and the judgements of their comrades about them. The analysis of all the data on this matter leads to the following conclusions (cf. Fig. V):

(a) The data as a whole are highly significant and do not result from a chance distribution.

(b) If one takes the results from all those questioned, it can be said that for all groups the salient fact is the confidence that the subjects have in their knowledge of the Other.

(c) However, there are degrees and subtle variations in this self-confidence. Examination of results according to the type of

[1] Legend: I = Intellectuals; W = Workers; A = Administrative employees; R = Rural.

group allows us to note variations in their different tendencies. On the one hand, the intellectuals, in contrast to the industrial and administrative workers and also the rural group, state their

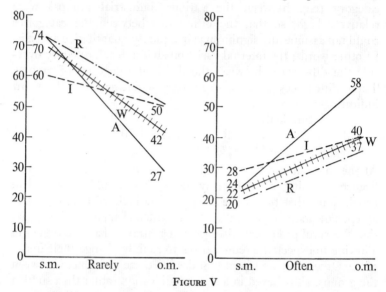

FIGURE V

The Interaction of Options (Rarely–Often), Propositions (Lack of confidence in his own judgements of the Other; lack of confidence in the judgements of the Other of himself), *and the Types of Collectivities* (represented by the same symbols as in Figs. I and III).

Legend: Below the horizontal line the propositions: s.m.—self mistaken (lack of confidence in terms of himself, formulated in this question, 'Do you believe you are often wrong in your impression of others?') and o.m.—others mistaken (lack of confidence in the judgement of the Other formulated in the question: 'Do you consider that others are often mistaken in their judgement of you?'); the vertical line gives the percentages of responses.

For example, the curve of administrators (A = straight line) reveals a great confidence in their own judgements of others and a considerable lack of confidence in the estimations of others of themselves.

confidence in their judgements about their colleagues only very hesitantly and with reticence.

(d) In contrast, the workers, especially administrative employees, while claiming to be relatively certain in their estimate of the Other, showed themselves to be clearly the most distrustful about others' judgements of them. They tended to regard themselves as being quite often misunderstood.

These results reveal two major facts. First, intellectuals often question their own knowledge of the Other, and their former certainty often turns to uncertainty. Sudden modifications in their image of the Other are not unusual. Second, factory workers, and administrative employees even more, consider that they are misjudged, and share with the rural group a firm confidence in their method of attaining knowledge of the Other.

TOPIC 4

Communication and knowledge of the Other. The quantitative analysis of the data resulting from the interviews allow for firm conclusions on this topic:

(1) The majority of subjects questioned, regardless of group affiliation, thought that they entered into relationships with their work-mates easily and quickly. The group factor did not seem to play a decisive role. However, the rural subjects, whilst not experiencing difficulty in communicating with their neighbours, entered rather slowly into such communication. Contrary to other groups, their responses were exactly divided, as percentages, between the options 'rapidly' and 'slowly' (cf. Appendix II, paragraph 4). One might compare this result with the finding above concerning the first question in Topic 3, where the same conclusions could be drawn.

(2) The results obtained from the interviews on Topic 4 were related to the results obtained from certain questions on previous topics, and a statistical comparison was made with regard to the role of verbal exchanges in knowledge of the Other. These data, taken as a whole, clearly establish the emphasis that is generally given to conversations in the formulation of this knowledge. In summary: 83 per cent of the subjects affirmed the great importance of conversation in this regard, only 7 per cent denied its importance, though often equivocally, and 10 per cent did not reply or gave ambiguous responses.

(3) But, having clearly established this general result, one can observe very significant differences on this subject (cf. Fig. VI) between types of groups. The rural subjects accord much less importance to oral communications than others. In order to explain this fact, several hypotheses might be suggested. First, as previously indicated, the rural group live in a situation characterized by a certain amount of social isolation. On the other hand,

the members have confidence only in overt behaviour; as far as they are concerned, the most eloquent words carry little weight. Finally, they are the most conformist with regard to the criteria provided by the global society.

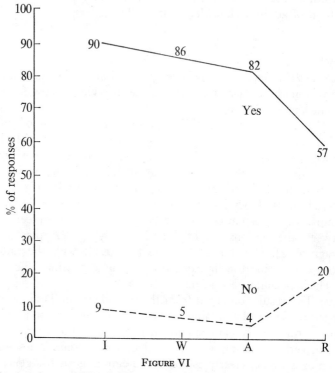

FIGURE VI

Conversations and Knowledge of the Other. The Interaction of the Option (Yes–No) and the types of Collectivities

Legend: Below the horizontal line, the type of collectivity is represented; the vertical line gives the percentages of responses.

The 'yes' curve is shown as a straight line, that of 'no' as dashes. The question posed was that of the importance of conversations in the knowledge of the Other. A minimum separation exists between the two curves when considering the rural group, while the distinction is uniformly quite sharp for the other three types of collectivities.

(4) The interviews were organized in such a way as to bring out the types of conversation that seemed most suitable for facilitating knowledge of the Other. The responses obtained reveal more to a qualitative analysis. From a purely quantitative view-

point, the nuances are too numerous, and the complexity of the forms too great for a systematic classification. However, it might be mentioned that the administrative employees and the rural

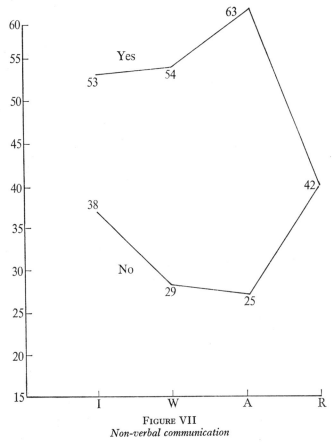

FIGURE VII
Non-verbal communication

Legend: Below the horizontal the different types of groups; the vertical represents the percentages of responses (*positive* = yes; *negative* = no) to the question: 'Does non-verbal communication with your fellow workers permit you to know them better?'
The maximum separation between Yes and No is clearly evident at the administrative level, while with the rural group the two curves are joined.

group attach most importance to conversations about work in developing knowledge of the Other. Conversations about cultural subjects are, as might have been expected, cited more often by the intellectuals than by others.

(5) The last part of the inquiry was concerned with discovering whether non-verbal communication with colleagues facilitated a better knowledge of them. The analysis shows first of all that positive replies prevailed to a statistically significant degree over negative replies (34 per cent). Although the responses of the intellectual groups, and the rural group especially, produced almost equal percentages of positive and negative replies, administrative employees, on the other hand, were exceptional in giving a substantial number of positive replies. The industrial groups, although less clearly, also attributed fairly considerable importance to non-verbal communications. It can be imagined that in noisy factories, gestures often replace words. In the case of offices, however, it is possible that it may be the respect for silence, which is necessary for work, that produces the same result. When machines drown voices, or when noise has to be avoided, there is recourse to non-verbal communication.

CONCLUSIONS

From all these results, which will be complemented and refined by the qualitative analysis, some general conclusions can be drawn.

First, the respective importance of the factors that affect the apprehension and knowledge of the Other often varies according to the type of group. This variation is particularly evident in the results from the first topic. Indeed the statistical data reveal a strong contrast between the responses of the intellectual groups on the one hand, and the administrative and worker groups on the other, and also show the special position occupied by the rural group regarding the nature of apprehension of the Other.

On other topics the specificity of the groups is less pronounced, but it is revealed in some rather clear trends. For example, the intellectual and rural groups differ greatly with regard to the role played by resemblance and difference in the knowledge of the Other, whilst the other group take a median position in this respect. Also, we have seen that different types of groups diverge in the amount of confidence they have in judgements made by the Other, and judgements about the Other. Finally, their estimates of the importance of conversations and non-verbal communication are similar on the whole, but clearly differ in degree.

Thirdly, certain results of the inquiry show general agreement on several questions. We have just suggested that this is so with regard to verbal exchanges and silent communication. This is also true for the classification in order of importance of the factors that deepen knowledge of the Other, and also for the rate at which modifications are made in this knowledge—slow rather than rapid. It seems quite possible that in those cases where different types of groups make similar responses, it is the influence of the global society that is being revealed.

Briefly, the results of the purely quantitative analysis of this inquiry offer precise answers to some important questions posed by the sociological problem of the apprehension and knowledge of the Other; they show the impossibility of maintaining over-general theories in these areas, whilst revealing distinct variations that exist as a function of particular groups within the framework of the same type of global society.

Finally, if one considers the results on the different topics in such a way as to form an over-all view about each of the four types of group, it can be seen that the characteristics of each are clearly reflected in the manner by which the members know each other. For example, it can be seen that *members of the intellectual groups* are immediately struck by the physical appearance and social attitudes of the other, and are somewhat insensitive to overt behaviour; they specify their image of the Other by noting what differentiates their neighbour from themselves, by attaching only moderate importance to factors related to group life, and without being too fearful that their view of the Other might suddenly change. They are never very sure that they know others well. The *members of factory groups* first notice the overt behaviour of their work-mates, and only slightly their physical appearance. Their responses with regard to the role of resemblance and difference in knowledge of the Other, and the rate of modification of the Other's image, are rather indecisive on the whole. They have more confidence in their own judgement about others than in the judgements of others about them. The *members of administrative groups* are like factory workers in being primarily sensitive to overt behaviour, and attaching little importance to physical appearance; but they take social attitudes into consideration. They are similar to the workers in their responses with regard to the role of resemblance and difference, about which they are indecisive. They are strongly influenced by specific aspects of group life; but they rarely modify their image of the Other. Like the workers they have more confidence in their own estimates than in those of others. Finally, they are characterized by the special importance that they attach to conversations about work, and non-verbal communication.

The *rural group members* evidence specific characteristics in their apprehension and knowledge of the Other. Apprehension proper is practically non-existent here, and knowledge is based on resemblance, similarity to oneself, and to a stereotype usually derived from the global society. In the rural group, only the women feared that they might not be truly known by others. Finally, while attaching a certain importance to conversation for knowledge of the Other, the members of this group were less positive in their responses on this point than those of other groups, as they attached most importance to overt behaviour and resemblance to a stereotype.

In conclusion, it can be observed that groups of workers and administrative employees evidenced similarities in their formulation of knowledge of the Other; the intellectual and rural groups, on the other hand, showed opposite tendencies in this respect. In any case, as we have suggested, the statistics reveal important specific differences in the apprehension and knowledge of the Other in different types of groups.

C.N.R.S.
École Pratique des Hautes Études
(*Section VI*).

APPENDIX I

Instructions Given to the Interviewers

Topic 1.—What strikes you about your work partner?
(a) His physical appearance.
(b) His facial expressions.
(c) What he says.
(d) What he does.
(e) His attitudes towards you.
(f) His attitudes towards other fellow workers.
(g) His spirit of co-operation within the group.
(g') His spirit of co-operation within your particular work team.
(h) His attitude towards his superiors.
(i) His attitude towards his subordinates.

Rank the above statements.

Topic 2.—On reflecting further, what helps you to reach a more precise image of the Other? Is it:
(a) His resemblance or difference in terms of yourself?
(b) Because he had to be, or chose to be, your work partner?
(c) The degree of his influence in your group?
(c') The degree of his influence outside work?
(d) The conversations that you have with him?
(e) The work you do in common with him?

Rank the above statements.

Topic 3.—When you believe you possess a precise image of the Other, how is this knowledge modified?
(a) Does it change slowly or rapidly?
(b) Under the influence of what circumstances?
(c) Do you believe you are often wrong in your impression of others?
(d) Do you consider your comrades are often wrong in their estimations of you?
(e) Which is more frequent: that others are wrong about you, or that you are wrong about them?

T

Topic 4.—Communication and knowledge.

(*a*) Do you enter rather easily or with difficulty into congenial relation-ships with your fellow workers?

(*a'*) Rapidly or slowly?

(*b*) Does the exchange of words always help you know your fellow workers better?

(*c*) If not, give example(s) of cases where verbal communication did not aid in this knowledge, or even undermined it.

(*d*) If yes, give example(s) of conversations or discussion with your fellow workers which helped you to know them better.

(*d'*) Classify in a hierarchy the subjects of the conversations and dis-cussions which were most revealing for this knowledge.

(*e*) Does non-verbal communication with your fellow workers permit you to know them better?

(*f*) If yes, what forms of non-verbal communication?

(*g*) Under what circumstances?

NOTE.—As we have already said, these questions did not constitute a stereotyped questionnaire, but merely a framework within which the interview might freely evolve.

APPENDIX 2

Here are some results, expressed as a percentage of the affirmative (Y = Yes) and negative responses (N = No), obtained in the different items figuring in the instructions given to the interviewers.

(1) For Topic 1, here are the percentages of positive and negative responses concerning the importance of the different items in the topic (e.g. a = physical appearance, b = facial expression, etc.) in the industrial groups:

Industrial enterprises

	a	b	c	d	e	f	g	h	i	
Renault semi-assembly line	57	70	70	57	57	41	33	33	0	
Renault assembly line	27	90	63	51	27	90	51	63	27	
Péchiney	34	46	66	52	71	66	52	63	56	YES
Fonderie	24	46	59	59	56	48	46	48	50	
Renault semi-assembly line	33	22	22	22	33	49	49	57	49	
Renault assembly line	39	0	27	27	51	0	0	27	27	
Péchiney	49	43	22	31	4	4	24	19	28	NO
Fonderie	56	40	18	22	24	32	32	27	32	

(2) For Topic 2, here are the quantitative data concerning, for item a, Difference (D) or Resemblance (R); and for the other items, the affirmative (Y) or negative (N) responses about their importance in the formulation of a more precise image of the other:

		Turgot	Théâtre	Renault 2	Renault 1	Péchiney	Foundry	Admin.	Rural
a	D	37	30	35	51	40	33	37	12
	R	27	21	41	39	31	39	37	53
b	Y	33	30	57	63	40	39	42	
	N	53	45	22	0	38	29	42	
c	Y	75	45	68	51	55	53	57	45
	N	15	30	0	27	31	24	29	32
c'	Y			32	27	47	33	42	
	N			32	27	29	43	46	
d	Y	74	60	68	90	80	61	75	53
	N	16	30	22	0	10	14	10	29
e	Y	41	72	68	90	66	53	75	
	N	37	18	22	0	19	24	14	

(3) For Topic 3—here are the percentages for responses about items (*c*) and (*d*):

	Intellectual		Industrial		Administrative		Rural	
	c	*d*	*c*	*d*	*c*	*d*	*c*	*d*
Rarely	41	43	49	41	59	31	59	45
	60	45	63	39				
			54	31				
			63	48				
Often	36	41	41	41	29	49	26	37
	30	37	27	39				
			24	39				
			18	38				

(4) For Topic 4—the following table gives the percentages for responses to the questions expressed in items *a* and *a'*:

	Intellectual		Industrial		Administrative		Rural	
	a	*a'*	*a*	*a'*	*a*	*a'*	*a*	*a'*
Easily	57	40	57	75	59	51	63	45
and			63	51				
rapidly	60	60	42	51				
			69	54				
Slowly	27	15	33	24	31	39	27	45
and			0	39				
with	30	30	40	31				
difficulty			21	33				

And here are the percentages for responses to the question in item *e* about non-verbal communication:

YES				NO			
Intel-lectual	Indus-trial	Admin.	Rural	Intel-lectual	Indus-trial	Admin.	Rural
45	57	63	42	45	33	25	42
60	63			30	27		
	52				33		
	45				21		

Bibliography of the Sociology of Knowledge

ACKERMANN (W.). — Étude sur la diffusion et la représentation sociale des connaissances scientifiques, *Sociologie du Travail*, 1963, *5*, pp. 415-417.
ACKERMANN (W.), ARCHAMBAUD (J.), RIALAN (B.). — Transmission et assimilations de notions scientifiques, *Rapport au Commissariat Général au Plan et à la Productivité*, 1963, Doc. 5, 80 p.
ADLER (Franz). — A quantitative study in the sociology of knowledge, *American sociological review*, 1954, *19*, 1, pp. 42-48.
ADLER (Franz). — The sociology of knowledge since 1918, *Midwest sociologist*, 1955, *17*, Spring, 3 ff.
ADLER (Franz). — The value concept in sociology, *American journal of sociology*, 1956, *62*, 3, pp. 272-279.
ADLER (Franz). — The range of sociology of knowledge, in *Modern sociological theory in continuity and change*, ed. by Howard Becker and Alvin Boskoff. New York, Dryden Press, 1957, pp. 398-423.
ADLER (Franz). — Werner Stark's sociology of knowledge. A critique. — Werner Stark: Reply, *Kyklos* (Bâle), 1959, *12*, 2, pp. 216-226.
ADLER (Max). — Soziologie und Erkenntniskritik, *Jahrbuch für Soziologie*, 1925, Erster Band, pp. 4-34.
ADORNO (Theodor W.), HORKHEIMER (Max). — *Dialektik der Aufklärung.* Amsterdam, Querido Verlag, 1949, 310 p.
ADORNO (Theodor W.). — Beiträge zur Ideologienlehre, *Kölner Zeitschrift für Soziologie*, 1953-1954, *6*, 3-4, pp. 360-375.
ADORNO (Theodor W.). — Das Bewusstsein der Wissenssoziologie, in *Prismen*, Kulturkritik und Gesellschaft. Berlin und Frankfurt/Main, Suhrkamp Verlag, 1955, pp. 32-50.
ADORNO (Theodor W.). — Zur Metakritik der Erkenntnistheorie. Stuttgart, W. Kohlhammer, 1956, 251 p.
AHLBERG (René). — « *Dialektische Philosophie* » *und Gesellschaft in der Sowjetunion.* Philosophische und soziologische Veröffentlichungen des Osteuropa-Instituts an der Freien Universität Berlin, hrsg. von Hans-Joachim Lieber, Bd. 2, Berlin, 1960, 135 p.
ALBERT (Hans). — Zur Logik der Sozialwissenschaften: Die These der Seinsgebundenheit und die Methode der kritischen Prüfung, *Archives européennes de sociologie*, 1964, *5*, 2, pp. 241-254.
ALDRICH (Charles Roberts). — *The primitive mind and modern civilization*, with an introduction by Bronislaw MALINOWSKI and a foreword by C. G. JUNG. London, Kegan Paul, Trench, Trubner, New York, Harcourt, Brace, 1931, XVII-249 p.
ALLEN (V. L.). — Valuations and historical interpretation: a case study, *The British journal of sociology*, 1963, *14*, 1, pp. 48-58.
ALLIOTT (Michel). — Coutume et mythe, *Année sociologique*, 1953-54, vol. 3, pp. 369-383.
ALLPORT (Floyd H.). — *Theories of perception and the concept of structure*, review and critical analysis with an introduction to a dynamic-structural theory of behavior. New York, J. Wiley, London, Chapman and Hall, 1955, XXII-709 p.
ANSART (Pierre). — Les cadres sociaux de la doctrine morale de Saint-Simon, *Cahiers internationaux de sociologie*, 1963, *34*, pp. 27-46.

ARON (Raymond). — Compte rendu des ouvrages de Weber Mannheim, Hartmann, dans « Philosophie de l'histoire et sociologie », *Annales sociologiques*, série A, fasc. I, 1934, pp. 197-200.

ARON (Raymond). — L'idéologie, *Recherches philosophiques*, 1936-37, *6*, pp. 65-84.

ARON (Raymond). — *L'opium des intellectuels*. Paris Calmann-Lévy, 1955, 337 p.

ARON (Raymond). — La société américaine et sa sociologie, *Cahiers internationaux de sociologie*, 1959, *26*, pp. 55-80 (discussion).

ARON (Raymond). — *Dimensions de la conscience historique*. Paris, Plon, 1960, 313 p.

ARON (Raymond). — Sociologie allemande sans idéologie?, *Archives européennes de sociologie*, 1960, *1*, 1, pp. 170-175.

ARREAT (Lucien). — Signes et symboles, *Revue philosophique*, 1913, *75*, pp. 51-70.

ASCOLI (Max). — On Mannheim's 'Ideology and utopia', *Social research*, 1938, Feb., pp. 101-106.

AUBENQUE (Pierre). — Philosophie et idéologie, *Archives de philosophie*, 1959, *22*, 4, Oct.-Dec., pp. 483-520.

AXELOS (Kostas). — *Marx, Penseur de la technique*. Paris, Éd. de Minuit, 1961, 324 p.

AYMARD (André). — L'idée de travail dans la Grèce archaïque, *Journal de psychologie*, 1948, *41*, 1 (*Le travail et les techniques*), pp. 29-50.

BACON (Francis). — *Novum organum*, ed. by J. DEWEY. London, Bell & Sons, 1891.

BAHRDT (H. P.), KRAUCH (H.), RITTEL (H.). — Die wissenschaftliche Arbeit in Gruppen, *Kölner Zeitschrift für Soziologie und Sozialpsychologie*, 1960, *12*, 1, pp. 1-40.

BAIN (Read). — Technology and state government, *American sociological review*, 1937, *2*, 6, Dec. pp. 860-874.

BAIN (Read). — Our schizoid culture and sociopathy, *Sociology and social research*, 1958, *42*, 4, pp. 263-268.

BARBER (Bernard). — *Science and the social order*. Preface by Robert K. MERTON. Glencoe, Ill., The Free Press, 1952, XXIV-288 p.

BARBER (Bernard), MERTON (Robert K.). — Brief bibliography for the sociology of science, *Proceedings of the American Academy of Arts and Sciences*, 1952, *80*, 2, pp. 140-154.

BARBER (Bernard). — Sociological aspects of anti-intellectualism. *Journal of social issues*, 1955, *11*, 3, pp. 25-30.

BARBER (Bernard). — Sociologie de la science, tendances actuelles de la recherche et bibliographie/Sociology of science: a trend report and bibliography, *La sociologie contemporaine/Current sociology*, 1956, *5*, 2, pp. 91-153.

BARBER (Bernard). — Sociology of knowledge and science, 1945-1955, in *Sociology in the United States of America; a trend report*, ed. by Hans Lennart ZETTERBERG. Paris, U.N.E.S.C.O., 1956, 156 p.

BARBER (Bernard). — The sociology of science, in *Sociology to-day*, ed. by MERTON. New York, Basic Books, 1959, XXIV-623 p.

BARBER (Bernard), HIRSCH (Walter) ed. — *The sociology of science. The role and responsibilities of the scientist — discussed as a social phenomena*. New York, The Free Press of Glencoe, 1962, VIII-662 p.

BARBICHON (Guy), MOSCOVICI (Serge). — Diffusion des connaissances scientifiques, *Social sciences / Information / sur les sciences sociales*, 1965, *4*, 1 (March), pp. 7-22.

BARKLEY (R.). — The theory of the elite and the mythology of power, *Science and society*, 1955, *19*, 2, pp. 97-106.

BASSOUL (R.), MAUCORPS (P.-H.). — Jeux de miroirs et sociologie de la connaissance d'autrui, *Cahiers internationaux de sociologie*, 1962, *32*, pp. 43-60.

BASTIDE (Roger). — Groupes sociaux et transmission des légendes, *Psyché*, 1949, 34, August, pp. 716-755.

BASTIDE (Roger). — Contribution à l'étude de la participation, *Cahiers internationaux de sociologie*, 1953, *14*, pp. 30-40.

BASTIDE (Roger). — Sociologie et littérature comparée, *Cahiers internationaux de sociologie*, 1954, *17*, pp. 93-100.

BASTIDE (Roger). — Les cadres sociaux de l'anthropologie culturelle américaine, *Cahiers internationaux de sociologie*, 1959, *26*, pp. 15-26.

BASTIDE (Roger). — Mythes et utopies, *Cahiers internationaux de sociologie*, 1960, *28*, Jan.-June, pp. 3-12.

BAUER (Arthur). — La transformation des idées et le public. *Revue philosophique*, 1907, *63*, pp. 383-408.

BAUMGARTEN (A.). — *Bemerkungen zur Erkenntnistheorie des dialektischen und historischen Materialismus.* Berlin, Akademie Verlag, 1957, VIII-181 p.

BECK (Hubert Park). — *Men who control our universities.* New York, King's Crown Press, 1947, X-230 p.

BECKER (Hellmut). — Bildung und Gesellschaft, *Offene Welt*, 1958, *53*, pp. 55-67.

BECKER (Howard). — Review of *Social and cultural dynamics* by Sorokin, *Rural sociology*, 1938, *3*, p. 356 ff.

BECKER (Howard), DAHLKE (Otto Helmut). — Max Scheler's sociology of knowledge, *Philosophy and phenomenological research*, 1942, 2, March, pp. 310-322.

BECKER (Howard). — Science, culture and society, *Philosophy of science*, 1952, *19*, 4, Oct., pp. 272-287.

BELAVAL (Yvon). — Pour une sociologie de la philosophie, *Critique*, 1953, *9*, 77, pp. 852-865.

BELIN-MILLERON (Jean). — Les expressions symboliques dans la psychologie collective des crises politiques, *Cahiers internationaux de sociologie*, 1951, *10*, pp. 158-167.

BELIN-MILLERON (Jean). — Ethnologie et psychologie de la connaissance, *Ethnographie*, 1957, *52*, pp. 142-154.

BELL (Daniel). — *The end of ideology. On the exhaustion of political ideas in the fifties.* Glencoe, The Free Press, 1960, 416 p.

BELOFF (M.). — Intellectual classes and ruling classes in France, *Occidente*, 1954, *10*, 1, pp. 54-60.

BENDIX (Reinhard). — A study of managerial ideologies, *Economic development and cultural change*, 1957, *5*, 2, pp. 118-128.

BENDIX (Reinhard). — Industrialization, ideologies and social structure, *American sociological review*, 1959, *24*, 5, pp. 613-623.

BERELSON (B.). — *Content analysis in communication research.* Glencoe, Ill., The Free Press, 1952, 220 p.

BERGMANN (Gustav). — Ideology, *Ethics*, 1951, *61*, 3, April, pp. 205-218.

BERKNER (L. V.). — *The scientific Age. The impact of science on society.* New Haven and London, Yale University Press, 1964, 137 p.

BERNAL (John Desmond). — *The social function of science.* 1st edn. London, G. Routledge, 1939, XVI-482 p.; latest edn.: London, G. Routledge, 1944, XVI-482 p.

BERNAL (John Desmond). — Science, industry and society in the XIXth century, *Centaurus*, 1953, *3*, 1-2, pp. 138-165.

BERNAL (John Desmond). — *Science and industry in the nineteenth century.* London, Routledge and Kegan Paul, 1953, XII-230 p.

258   *Bibliography*

BERNAL (John Desmond). — *Science in history.* London, Watts, 1954, XXIV-967 p.
BERNAL (John Desmond). — Vlijanie ekonomiceskih i tehniceskih faktorov na sovremennuju nauku (The influence of economic and technical factors on contemporary science), *Vestnik Akademii nauk SSSR*, 1958, *28*, 1, pp. 25-38.
BERNARD (Michel). — *Introduction à une sociologie des doctrines économiques, des physiocrates à Stuart Mill.* Paris, La Haye, Mouton & Co., 1963, 270 p.
BERNSDORF (Wilhelm). — Primitive Gruppe, primitive Mentalität und Traumstruktur, in *Die Einheit der Sozialwissenschaften...* Stuttgart, F. Enke, 1955, pp. 160-185.
BETTELHEIM (Charles). — *Initiation aux recherches sur les idéologies économiques et les réalités sociales.* Paris, Tournier & Constans, 1948, 66 p.
BETTELHEIM (Charles). — Idéologie économique et réalité sociale, *Cahiers internationaux de sociologie*, 1948, *4*, pp. 119-134.
BIANCA (Omero). — Intorno alla sociologia della conoscenza, *Quaderni di sociologia*, 1952, *3*, pp. 103-116.
BIERSTEDT (Robert). — The logicomeaningful method of P. A. Sorokin, *American sociological review*, 1937, Dec., pp. 813-823.
BIRNBAUM (Norman). — The sociological study of ideology (1940-1960): A Trend Report and Bibliography, *Current Sociology / La sociologie contemporaine*, 1960, *9*, 2, pp. 91-172.
BIRNBAUM (Norman). — Ideologiebegriff und Religionssoziologie, *Kölner Zeitschrift für Soziologie und Sozialpsychologie*, 1962, supplement 6, pp. 78-86.
BLAHA (I. A.). — Social psychology of the intelligentsia, *Social sciences*, 1936, Summer, pp. 196-201.
BLOCH (Marc). — Technique et évolution sociale. A propos de l'histoire de l'attelage et de celle de l'esclavage, *Revue de synthèse historique*, 1926, *41*, pp. 91-99.
BLOCH (Marc). — Avènement et conquêtes du moulin à eau, *Annales d'histoire économique et sociale*, 1935, 7, 36, pp. 538-563.
BLOCH (Marc). — Les inventions médiévales, *Annales d'histoire économique et sociale*, 1935, 7, 36, pp. 634-643.
BLOCH (Marc). — Les transformations des techniques comme problème de psychologie collective, *Journal de psychologie*, 1948, *41*, 1, pp. 104-119.
BLOUNT (B. K.). — Die Wissenschaft wird die politische Welt verändern, *Zeitschrift für Sozialreform*, 1958, *4*, 4, pp. 256-261.
BOAS (Franz). — *The mind of the primitive man.* New York, Macmillan, 1911, X-294 p. Reviewed by Émile DURKHEIM, *Année sociologique*, 1909-1912, *12*, pp. 31-33.
BOAS (Marie). — Quelques aspects sociaux de la chimie au XVIII⁰ siècle, *Revue d'histoire des sciences*, 1957, *10*, 2, April-June, pp. 132-147.
BODIN (Louis), TOUCHARD (Jean). — Les intellectuels dans la société française contemporaine. Définitions, statistiques et problèmes, *Revue française de science politique*, 1959, *9*, 4, pp. 835-859.
BOGDANOW (A.). — *Entwicklungsformen der Gesellschaft und die Wissenschaft.* Berlin, 1924.
BONNOT (R.). — Sur les modes et les styles, *Année sociologique*, vol. 3, 1949-1950, pp. 3-32.
BORKENAU (Franz). — Zur Soziologie des mechanistischen Weltbildes, *Zeitschrift für Sozialforschung*, 1932, *1*, pp. 311-335.
BORKENAU (Franz). — *Der Übergang vom feudalen zum bürgerlichen Weltbild.* Studien zur Geschichte der Philosophie der Manufakturperiode. Paris, F. Alcan, 1934, XX-559 p.

Bose (D. M.). — Science and mythological thinking, *Man in India*, 1954, *34*, 3, July-Sept., pp. 187-193.

Bottomore (T. B.). — Some reflections on the sociology of knowledge, *The British journal of sociology*, 1956, 7, 1, March, pp. 52-58.

Bouglé (Célestin). — *Les idées égalitaires, étude sociologique.* 1st edn. Paris, F. Alcan, 1899, 249 p. 2nd edn.: Paris, Alcan, 1925, 251 p.

Bourdier (Frank). — La connaissance liée a la technique, *Revue de synthèse*, 1953, *32*, Jan.-June, pp. 5-17.

Bramson (Leon). — *The political context of sociology.* Princeton, N. J., Princeton University Press, 1961, xi-164 p.

Bridgman (Percy W.). — Science and its changing social environment, *Science*, 1943, *97*, pp. 147-150.

Brill (A. A.). — The universality of symbols, *The psychoanalytic review*, 1943, *30*, pp. 1-18.

Brown (H.), ed. — *Science and the creative spirit: Essays on humanistic aspects of science.* Toronto, University of Toronto press, 1958, xxvii-165 p. Reviewed B. Barber, *American sociological review*, 1958, *23*, 4, Aug, pp. 448-449.

Bryson (Lyman Lloyd), Finkelstein (Louis), Hoagland (Hudson), Mac Iver (R. M.). — *Symbols and society.* New York, Harper and brothers, 1955, xi-611 p.

Bunzel (J. H.). — The general ideology of American small business, *Political science quarterly*, 1955, *70*, 1, pp. 87-102.

Burlingame (Roger). — *The American conscience.* New York, Alfred A. Knopf, 1957, ix-420-xv p.

Busia (K. H.). — La conception africaine du monde, *Le monde non chrétien*, 1956, 38, pp. 165-174.

Caillois (Roger). — *Le mythe et l'homme.* Paris, Gallimard, 1938, 223 p. (Les Essais, VI).

Camichel (Charles). — Les caractères des techniques modernes et leurs effets. *Journal de psychologie*, 1948, *41*, 1 (*Le travail et les techniques*), pp. 120-126.

Caplow (Theodore), McGee (Reece J.). — *The academic marketplace*, with a foreword by Jacques Barzun. New York, Basic Books, 1958, 262 p.

Carleton (W. G.). — American intellectuals and American democracy, *Antioch review*, 1959, *19*, 2, pp. 185-204.

Carrouges (Michel). — Le vrai mythe du xx⁰ siècle, *Vie intellectuelle*, 1953, *24*, 8-9, pp. 102-111.

Cassirer (Ernst). — *Philosophie der symbolischen Formen.* Berlin, B. Cassirer, 3 vol.: «Die Sprache», 1923; «Das mythische Denken», 1928; «Phänomenologie der Erkenntnis», 1929. English Translation by Ralph Mannheim, *The philosophy of symbolic forms*, introduction by Charles W. Hendel. New Haven, Yale University Press, 1953-1957, 3 vol.

Cassirer (Ernst). — *Sprache und Mythos, ein Beitrag zum Problem der Götternamen.* Leipzig, Berlin, B. G. Teubner, 1925, 87 p. English translation by Suzanne K. Langer, *Language and myth.* New York, Dover publications, 1946, 103 p.

Cassirer (Ernst). — *An essay on man, an introduction to a philosophy of human culture.* Garden City, N.Y., Doubleday, 1st edn: 1944, 298 p.

Cassirer (Ernst). — *The myth of the state.* Garden City, N.Y., Doubleday, 1946, 382 p.

Cazeneuve (Jean). — La connaissance d'autrui dans les sociétés archaïques, *Cahiers internationaux de sociologie*, 1958, *25*, pp. 75-99.

Cazeneuve (Jean). — La connaissance technique dans l'Égypte ancienne, *Cahiers internationaux de sociologie*, 1960, *28*, pp. 23-32.

CAZENEUVE (Jean), MAUCORPS (Paul-H.), MEMMI (Albert). — Enquête socio-logique sur la connaissance d'autrui. Avant-propos de Georges GURVITCH, *Cahiers internationaux de sociologie*, 1960, *29*, pp. 137-156.

CAZENEUVE (Jean). — *La mentalité archaïque*. Paris, A. Colin, 1961, 204 p.

CAZENEUVE (Jean). — Les cadres sociaux de la morale stoïcienne dans l'Empire romain, *Cahiers internationaux de sociologie*, 1963, *34*, pp. 13-26.

CAZENEUVE (Jean). — La perception des étendues dans les sociétés archaïques, *Cahiers internationaux de sociologie*, 1964, *37*, pp. 107-117.

CHACON (Vamireh). — Sociologia marxista e sociologia do conhecimento, *Sociologia*, 1958, *20*, 2, May, pp. 248-254.

CHALL (Leo P.). — The sociology of knowledge, in *Contemporary sociology*, ed. by Joseph S. ROUCEK. New York, Philosophical Library, 1958, p. 285 ff.

CHAPOT (V.). — Sentiments des anciens sur le machinisme, *Revue des études anciennes*, 1938, *40*, 1, Jan.-March, pp. 158-162.

CHATELAIN (Abel). — Pour une géographie sociologique de la culture intel-lectuelle, *Revue de géographie de Lyon*, 1958, *33*, 2, pp. 201-208.

CHATELET (Fernand). — *Logos et Praxos*. Recherches sur la signification théorique du Marxisme. Paris, Sedes, 1962, 205 p.

CHILD (Arthur). — The problem of imputation of the sociology of knowledge, *Ethics*, 1941, *51*, Jan., pp. 200-219.

CHILD (Arthur). — The theoretical possibility of sociology of knowledge, *Ethics*, 1941, *51*, July, pp. 392-418.

CHILD (Arthur). — The existential determination of thought, *Ethics*, 1942, *52*, Jan., pp. 153-185.

CHILD (Arthur). — The problem of imputation resolved, *Ethics*, 1944, *54*, Jan., pp. 96-109.

CHILD (Arthur). — The problem of truth in the sociology of knowledge, *Ethics*, 1947, *58*, Oct., pp. 18-34.

CHILDE (Vere Gordon). — *Social worlds of knowledge*. London, Oxford Univer-sity Press, 1949, 26 p. (L. T. Hobhouse memorial trust lecture, 19).

CHILDE (Vere Gordon). — *Society and knowledge*. New York, Harper and brothers, 1956, XVII-131 p. (World perspectives, vol. 6).

CHOMBART DE LAUWE (P.-H.), MENDRAS (H.) et TOURAINE (A.). — Sociologie du travail sociologique, *Sociologie du Travail*, 1965, 7th year, 3 (July-September), pp. 273-294.

CHU WANG (Y.). — The intelligentsia in changing China, *Foreign affairs*, 1958, *36*, 2, Jan., pp. 315-329.

COHEN (Marcel). — *Le système verbal sémitique et l'expression du temps*. Paris, Imprimerie Nationale, 1924, XXVIII-317 p. (Conclusion).

COHEN (Marcel). — Langage et transfusions de civilisation, *Annales sociologiques*, E series, 1942, 3-4, pp. 1-15.

COHEN (Marcel). — Faits linguistiques et faits de pensée, *Journal de psychologie*, 1947, *4*, Oct.-Dec., pp. 385-402.

COHEN (Marcel). — *Linguistique et matérialisme dialectique*. Gap, Ophrys, 1948, 19 p.

COHEN (Marcel). — *Le langage, structure et évolution*. Paris, Éditions Sociales, 1950, 144 p.

COHEN (Marcel). — *Pour une sociologie du langage*. Paris, A. Michel, 1956, 396 p.

COHEN (Marcel). — Structure sociale et structure linguistique, *Diogène*, 1956, *15*, pp. 46-57.

CONANT (James Bryant). — *On understanding science, an historical approach*. New Haven, Yale University Press, 1947, XV-146 p.

CONANT (James Bryant). — The role of science in our unique society, *Science,* 1948, *107*, pp. 77-83.
CONANT (James Bryant). — *Science and common sense.* London, G. Cumberledge, 1951, XII-371 p.
CONANT (James Bryant). — *Modern science and modern man.* New York, Columbia University Press, 1952, 111 p.
COOLEY (Charles Horton). — The roots of social knowledge, in *Sociological theory and social research,* being selected papers of Charles HORTON COOLEY, with an introduction and notes by Robert COOLEY ANGELL. New York, H. Holt, 1930, pp. 287-312.
COSER (Lewis A.), ROSENBERG (Bernard). — *Sociological theory;* a book of readings. New York, Macmillan, 1957, 578 p. (chap. 15: 'Sociology of knowledge', pp. 557-574).
COWELL (Frank Richard). — *History, civilization and culture,* an introduction to the historical and social philosophy of Pitirim A. Sorokin. London, A. & C. Black, 1952, XII-259 p.
CROWTHER (James Gerald). — *Science and life.* London, V. Gollancz, 1938, 96 p.
CROWTHER (James Gerald). — *The social relations of science.* New York, Macmillan, 1941, XXXII-665 p.
CUNNINGHAM (H. E.). — Intelligence and social life, *American journal of sociology,* 1922, *28*, 1, July, pp. 67-75.
CURY (Gilbert). — Le savant, le mythe et le philosophe, *Revue philosophique,* 1960, *150*, 1, pp. 49-64.
CUVILLIER (Armand). — Sociologie de la connaissance et idéologie économique, *Cahiers internationaux de sociologie,* 1951, *11*, pp. 80-111.
DAHLKE (H. Otto). — The sociology of knowledge, in: *Contemporary social theory,* ed. by H. E. BARNES, H. BECKER and F. B. BECKER. New York, D. Appleton Century, 1940, pp. 64-89.
DAHLKE (H. Otto). — Max Scheler's sociology of knowledge, *Philosophy and phenomenological research,* 1942, March, pp. 310-332.
DAHRENDORF (Ralf). — *Gesellschaft und Freiheit.* München, R. Piper, 1961.
DAMLE (Y. B.). — Communication of modern ideas and knowledge in Indian villages, *Public opinion quarterly,* 1956, *20*, 1, Spring, pp. 257-270.
DANTZIG (D. V.). — The function of words in ideological conflicts, in *Democracy in a world of tensions,* ed. by Richard McKEON and Stein ROKKAN. Chicago, University of Chicago Press, 1951.
DARDEL (Éric). — Le mythique d'après l'œuvre ethnologique de Maurice Leenhardt, *Diogène,* 1954, 7, pp. 50-71.
DAVIS (Allison). — *Social class influences upon learning* (The Inglis Lecture, 1948). Cambridge, Mass., Harvard University Press, 1948, 100 p.
DAVY (Georges). — La psychologie des primitifs d'après Lucien Lévey-Bruhl, *Journal de psychologie,* 1930, *27*, 15 Jan.-15 Feb., pp. 112-176.
DAVY (Georges). — Pour le centième anniversaire de la naissance de Lucien Lévey-Bruhl, *Revue philosophique,* 1957, *82*, 4, Oct.-Dec., pp. 468-493.
DE BIE (Pierre). — Situation de la sociologie. Contribution à une sociologie de la sociologie, *Bulletin de l'Institut de recherches économiques et sociales,* 1955, *21*, 7, Nov., pp. 693-707.
DE FLEUR (Melvin Lawrence), LARSEN (Otto N.). — *The flow of information; an experiment in mass communication.* New York, Harper, 1958, 301 p.
DEGRÉ (Gérard). — The sociology of knowledge and the problem of truth, *Journal of history of ideas,* 1941, *2*, Jan., pp. 110-115.
DEGRÉ (Gérard). — *Society and ideology, an inquiry into the sociology of knowledge.* New York, Columbia University Bookstore, 1943, IV-114 p.

DEGRÉ (Gérard). — *Science as a social institution*, an introduction to the sociology of science. Garden-City, N.Y., Doubleday, 1955, 48 p.

DELANGLADE (J.), SCHALENBACH (H.), GODET (P.), LEUBA (J. L.). — *Signe et symbole*. Neuchâtel, Éd. de La Baconnière, 1946, 176 p.

DEWEY (John). — The role of philosophy in the history of civilization, *Philosophical review*, 1927, *36*, 1, pp. 1-9.

DEWEY (John). — Peirce's theory of linguistic signs, thought and meaning, *Journal of philosophy*, 1946, *43*, pp. 85-95.

DIBBLE (Vernon K.). — Occupations and ideologies, *American journal of sociology*, 1962, *68*, 2, pp. 229-241.

DIETERLEN (Germaine). — Les correspondances cosmobiologiques chez les Soudanais, *Journal de psychologie*, 1950, *43*, 3, pp. 350-366.

DUCASSE (C. J.). — Symbols, signs and signals, *Journal of symbolic logic*, 1939, *4*, pp. 41-52.

DUFRENNE (Mikel). — Pour une sociologie du public, *Cahiers internationaux de sociologie*, 1949, *6*, pp. 101-112.

DUFRENNE (Mikel). — Coup d'œil sur l'anthropologie culturelle américaine. *Cahiers internationaux de sociologie*, 1952, *12*, pp. 26-46.

DUMÉZIL (Georges). — Temps et mythes, *Recherches philosophiques*, 1935-36, *5*, 4 (Le mythe et l'histoire), pp. 235-251.

DUMONT (Fernand). — Idéologie et savoir historique, *Cahiers internationaux de sociologie*, 1963, *35*, pp. 43-60.

DUNCAN (Hugh, Dalziel). — *Language and literature in society; a sociological essay on theory and method in the interpretation of linguistic symbols, with a bibliographical guide to the sociology of literature*. Chicago, University of Chicago Press, 1953, XV-262 p.

DUPRÉEL (Eugène). — La sociologie et les problèmes de la connaissance, *Revue de l'Institut de Sociologie*, Université de Bruxelles, 1925, March-May, pp. 161-183.

DURAND (Gilbert). — *Les structures anthropologiques de l'imaginaire*. Paris, Presses Universitaires de France, 1960, 512 p.

DURKHEIM (Émile), MAUSS (Marcel). — De quelques formes primitives de classification. Contribution à l'étude des représentations collectives, *Année sociologique*, 1901-1902, *6*, pp. 1-72.

DURKHEIM (Émile), BOUGLÉ (Célestin). — Les conditions sociologiques de la connaissance, *Année sociologique*, 1906-1909, *11*, pp. 41-48.

DURKHEIM (Émile). — Sociologie religieuse et théorie de la connaissance, *Revue de métaphysique et de morale*, 1909, *17*, 6, Nov., pp. 733-758.

DURKHEIM (Émile), MAUSS (Marcel). — Note sur la notion de civilisation, *Année sociologique*, 1909-1912, *12*, pp. 46-50.

DURKHEIM (Émile). — « Les fonctions mentales dans les sociétés inférieures de Lucien Lévy-Bruhl », *Année sociologique*, 1909-1912, *12*, pp. 33-37.

DURKHEIM (Émile). — *Les formes élémentaires de la vie religieuse. Le système totémique en Australie*. 1st ed.: Paris, F. Alcan, 1912, 647 p.

DURKHEIM (Émile). — *Sociologie et philosophie*, preface by Célestin BOUGLÉ, 1st edition: Paris, F. Alcan, 1924, XVI-143 p.

DUVIGNAUD (Jean). — Problèmes de sociologie de la sociologie des arts, *Cahiers internationaux de sociologie*, 1959, *26*, pp. 137-148.

DUVIGNAUD (Jean). — *L'Acteur. Esquisse d'une sociologie du Comédien*. Paris, Gallimard, 1965, 304 p.

DUVIGNAUD (Jean). — *Sociologie du Théâtre*. Paris, Presses Universitaires de France, 1965, 588 p.

DYCKMANS (Gommaire). — Les types d'intégration socio-culturelle selon Pitirim Sorokin, *Revue des sciences économiques*, 1939, April, pp. 82-87.

EISENSTADT (S. N.). — The perception of time and space in a situation of culture-contact, *Journal of the royal anthropological institute*, 1949, *79*, pp. 63-68.

EISERMANN (Gottfried). — Ideologie und Utopie, *Kölner Zeitschrift für Soziologie*, 1952-1953, *5*, pp. 528-534.

EISERMANN (Gottfried). — La sociologie de la connaissance et la théorie économique, *Cahiers internationaux de sociologie*, 1955, *28*, Jan.-June, pp. 17-34.

ELEUTHEROPULOS (A.). — Sozialpsychologie und Wissenssoziologie, *Zeitschrift für Volkerpsychologie und Soziologie*, 1927, *3*, 2, pp. 197-215.

ELIADE (Mircea). — *Le mythe de l'éternel retour. Archétypes et répétition*, Paris, Gallimard, 1949, 254 p.

ELIADE (Mircea). — *Images et symboles. Essai sur le symbolisme magico-religieux.* Paris, Gallimard, 1952, 238 p.

ELIADE (Mircea). — Die Mythen in der modernen Welt, *Merkur*, 1954, *8*, 78, pp. 724-735.

ELIADE (Mircea). — *Mythes, rêves et mystères.* Paris, Gallimard, 1957, 310 p.

ELIADE (Mircea). — Prestiges du mythe cosmogonique, *Diogène*, 1958, *23*, July-Sept., pp. 1-17.

ELLIOT (W. Y.). — Ideas and ideologies, *Confluence*, 1953, *2*, 3, pp. 127-141.

ELLUL (Jacques). — *La propagande*, volume I. Bordeaux, Ed. Tex, 1951-1952, 197 p.

ELLUL (Jacques). — *La technique ou l'enjeu du siècle.* Paris, A. Colin, 1954, 402 p.

ELLUL (Jacques). — Information et propagande, *Diogène*, 1957, *18*, pp. 69-90.

ELLUL (Jacques). — Mythes modernes, *Diogène*, 1958, *23*, pp. 29-49.

ÉMERY (Léon). — L'université française et l'idéologie politique, *Contrat social*, 1958, *2*, 1, pp. 1-8.

ENGELS (Friedrich). — *Herrn Eugen Dührings Umwälzung der Wissenshaft (Anti-Dühring). Philosophie. Politische Œkonomie. Sozialismus.* Leipzig, Genossenschaftsbuchdruckerei, 1878, VIII-274 p.

ENGELS (Friedrich). — Ludwig Feuerbach und der Ausgang der klassischen deutschen Philsophie, *Die neue Zeit*, 1886, *4*, pp. 145-157 and 193-209.

ENGELS (Friedrich). — Letter to Starkenburg, 25 January 1894, in *Dokumente des Sozialismus*. Berlin, 1903.

ESPINAS (Alfred). — *Les origines de la technologie*, étude sociologique. Paris, F. Alcan, 1897, 295 p.

ESSERTIER (Daniel). — *Les formes inférieures de l'explication.* Paris, F. Alcan, 1927, 359 p.

FAIRBANK (John King), ed. — *Chinese thought and institutions.* Chicago, University of Chicago Press, 1957, XIII-438 p.

FALK (Werner). — The sociological interpretation of political ideas, *The sociological review*, 1934, *26*, 3, July, pp. 268-287.

FALLOT (Jean). — *Prestiges de la science.* Neuchâtel, Éd. de La Baconnière, 1960, 295 p.

FANFANI (Amintore). — *Catholicism, protestantism and capitalism.* London, Sheed and Ward, 1935, V-224 p.

FAUCHER (Daniel). — Routine et innovation dans la vie paysanne, *Journal de psychologie*, 1948, *41*, 1, pp. 89-103.

FAUL (Erwin). — Wissenssoziologie, in *Einführung in die Soziologie*, publ. under the direction of Alfred WEBER. München, R. Piper, 1955, pp. 358-390.

FEBVRE (Lucien), TONNELAT (Émile), MAUSS (Marcel), NICEFORO (Alfredo), WEBER (Louis). — *Civilisation: Le mot et l'idée.* Paris, La Rennaissance du Livre, 1930, XV-144 p.

FEBVRE (Lucien). — Réflexions sur l'histoire des techniques, *Annales d'histoire économique et sociale*, 1935, *7*, 36, Nov., pp. 531-535.

FEBVRE (Lucien). — Techniques, sciences et marxisme, *Annales d'histoire économique et sociale*, 1935, *7*, 36, Nov., pp. 615-624.

FEBVRE (Lucien). — Les techniques la science et l'évolution humaine, *Europe*, 1938, pp. 494-514.

FEBVRE (Lucien). — Travail: évolution d'un mot et d'une idée, *Journal de psychologie*, 1948, *41*, 1, pp. 19-28.

FEIBLEMAN (James). — *The theory of human culture.* New York, Duell, Sloan and Pearce, 1946, XIV-361 p.

FELDKELLER (Paul). — Die Rolle der « Ideologie » im Leben der Völker, *Sociologus*, 1953, *3*, 1, pp. 1-14.

FERBER (Christian von). — Der Werturteilsstreit 1909-1959. Versuch einer wissenschaftsgeschichtlichen Interpretation, *Kölner Zeitschrift für Soziologie und Sozialpsychologie*, 1959, *11*, 1, pp. 21-37.

FESTINGER (Leon). — *A theory of cognitive dissonance.* Evanston, Ill., Row, Peterson, 1957, 291 p.

FEUER (Lewis S.). — The sociology of philosophical ideas, *Pacific sociological review*, 1958, *1*, 2, pp. 77-80.

FEUER (Lewis S.). — *The scientific intellectual: The psychological and sociological origins of modern science.* New York, Basic Books, 1963, XII-441 p.

FILIASI (Carcano Paolo). — Il contributo della socilogia odella conoscenza all'analisi della crisi, *Scritti di sociologia e politica in onore di Luigi Sturzo.* Bologna, Nicola Zanichelli, 1953, *2*, pp. 193-206.

FILLIOZAT (Jean). — Les origines d'une technique mystique indienne, *Revue philosophique*, 1946, *136*, 4-6, pp. 208-220.

FIRTH (J. R.). — Personality and language in society, *Sociological review*, 1950, *42*, 2, pp. 1-16.

FISCHER (Karl Anton). — *Kultur und Gesellung, ein Beitrag zur allgemeinen Kultursoziologie.* Köln, Westdeutscher Verlag, 1951, 266 p.

FONDANE (Benjamin). — Lévy-Bruhl et la métaphysique de la connaissance, *Revue philosophique*, 1940, *129*, 5-6, May-June, pp. 289-316 et 1940, *130*, 7-8, July-August, pp. 29-54.

FORTUIT (M.). — Le mythe moderne. *Confluences*, 1941, *1*, Oct., pp. 446-453.

Fox (Dixon Ryan). — *Ideas in motion.* New York, London, D. Appleton Century, 1935, 126 p.

FRANCASTEL (Pierre). — Technique et esthétique, *Cahiers internationaux de sociologie*, 1948, *5*, pp. 97-116.

FRANCASTEL (Pierre). — Naissance d'un espace: mythes et géométrie du Quattrocento, *Revue d'esthétique*, 1951, *4*, 1, Jan.-March, pp. 1-45.

FRANCASTEL (Pierre). — Techniques et arts, *Revue de synthèse*, 1953, *32*, June, pp. 89-120.

FRANK (Philipp). — The logical and sociological aspects of science. *Proceedings of the American Academy of Arts and Sciences*, 1951, *80*, 1, pp. 16-30.

FRENKEL-BRUNSWICK (Else). — Social tensions and the inhibition of thought, *Sociological problems*, 1954, 2, pp. 75-81.

FREUD (Sigmund). — *Das Unbehagen in der Kultur.* Wien, Internationaler psychoanalytischer, Verlag, 1930, 136 p.

FRUMKIN (R. M.). — Dogmatism, social class, values, and academic achievement in sociology, *Journal of educational sociology*, 1961 (May), *34*, 9, pp. 398-403.

GAMSON (William A.), SCHUMAN (Howard). — Some undercurrents in the prestige of physicians, *The American journal of sociology*, 1963, *68*, 4, pp. 463-470.

GANDILLAC (Maurice de). — Rôle et signification de la technique dans le monde médiéval, *Diogène*, 1964, *47*, pp. 135-149.

GEIGER (George Raymond). — *Philosophy and the social order, an introductory approach*. Boston, Houghton, 1947, III-407 p.

GEIGER (Theodor). — An historical study of the origins and structure of the Danish intelligentsia, *British journal of sociology*, 1950, *1*, 3, Sept., pp. 209-220.

GEIGER (Theodor). — *Ideologie und Wahrheit*, Stuttgart-Wein, Humboldt, Verlag, 1953, 193 p.

GEIGER (Theodor). — Der Intellektuelle in der europäischen Gesellschaft von heute, *Acta sociologica*, 1955, *1*, 1, pp. 62-74.

GEIGER (Theodor). — Intelligentsia, *Acta sociologica*, 1955, *1*, 1, pp. 49-61.

GERNET (Louis). — Le temps dans les formes archaïques du droit, *Journal de psychologie*, 1956, *53*, 3, pp. 379-406.

GHURYE (G. S.). — Vidyas, Indian contribution to sociology of knowledge, *Sociological bulletin*, 1957, *6*, 2, Sept., pp. 29-70.

GILFILLAN (S. C.). — *The sociology of invention*, Chicago, 1935, XIII-185 p.

GILLE (Bertrand). — Lents progrès de la technique, *Revue de synthèse*, 1953, *32*, Jan.-June, pp. 69-88.

GINZBERG (Eli), ed. — *Technology and social change*. New York, Columbia University Press, 1964, X-158 p.

GIROD (Roger). — Cadres sociaux et orientation de la recherche sociologique, *Cahiers internationaux de sociologie*, 1959, *26*, pp. 39-53.

GITTLER (J. B.). — Possibilities of a sociology of science, *Social Forces*, 1940, March, pp. 350-359.

GLASER (Barney G.). — The local-cosmopolitan scientist, *The American journal of sociology*, 1963, *69*, 3, pp. 249-259.

GLUCK (Samuel E.). — The epistemology of Mannheim's sociology of knowledge, *Methodos*, 1954, *6*, 23, pp. 225-234.

GOLDMANN (Lucien). — *Mensch, Gemeinschaft und Welt in der Philosophie Immanuel Kants, Studien zur Geschichte der Dialektik*. Zürich, New York, Europa Verlag, 1945, 247 p.

GOLDMANN (Lucien). — Matérialisme dialectique et histoire de la philosophie, *Revue philosophique*, 1948, *138*, 4-6, April-June, pp. 160-179.

GOLDMANN (Lucien). — Matérialisme dialectique et histoire de la littérature, *Revue de métaphysique et de morale*, 1950, 3, pp. 283-301.

GOLDMANN (Lucien). — *Le dieu caché. Étude sur la vision tragique dans les Pensées de Pascal et dans le théâtre de Racine*. Paris, Gallimard, 1955, 454 p.

GOLDMANN (Lucien). — Sociologie du roman, *Cahiers internationaux de sociologie*, 1962, *32*, pp. 61-72.

GOLDMANN (Lucien) — *Problèmes d'une sociologie du Roman*. Bruxelles, Institut de sociologie, 1963, 467 p.

GOLDMANN (Lucien). — *Pour une sociologie du Roman*. Paris, Gallimard, 1964, 229 p.

GOLDSCHMIDT (W.). — Ethics and the structure of society, an ethnological contribution to the sociology of knowledge, *American anthropologist*, 1951, *54*, 4, pp. 506-524.

GOODMAN (P.). — The human uses of science, *Commentary*, 1960, *30*, 6, pp. 461-472.

GORDON (Pierre). — *L'image du monde dans l'Antiquité*. Paris, Presses Universitaires de France, 1949, 216 p.

GORIELY (Georges). — Les cadres sociaux de la pensée biologique, *Cahiers internationaux de sociologie*, 1959, *27*, pp. 85-94.

GOTESKY (R.). — The nature of myth and society, *American anthropologist*, 1952, *54*, 4, pp. 523-531.

GOTTINSCHAW (Virgil). — The epistemological relevance of Mannheim's sociology of knowledge, *The journal of philosophy*, 1943, *40*, pp. 57-72.

GRANAI (Georges). — Communication, langage, société, *Cahiers internationaux de sociologie*, 1957, *23*, pp. 97-110.

GRANET (Marcel). — Quelques particularités de la langue et de la pensée chinoises, *Revue philosophique*, 1920, *89*, 1-2, pp. 98-128, and 3-4, pp. 161-195.

GRANET (Marcel). — *La civilisation chinoise, la vie publique et la vie privée.* 1st edn.: Paris, La Renaissance du Livre, 1929, XXI-524 p.

GRANET (Marcel). — La droite et la gauche en Chine, *Bulletin de l'Institut Français de Sociologie*, 1933, 3, pp. 87-116.

GRANET (Marcel). — *La pensée chinoise.* 1st edn.: Paris, La Renaissance du Livre, 1934, XXIII-614 p.

GRANT (Marcel). — *Études sociologiques sur la Chine.* Préface de Louis GERNET, introduction de R. A. STEIN. Paris, Presses Universitaires de France, 1953, XX-304 p.

GRÉGOIRE (Franz). — Constantes et tendances de la mentalité technicienne, *Journal de psychologie*, 1953, 4, Oct.-Dec., pp. 429-464.

GRIAULE (Marcel). — Nouvelles recherches sur la notion de personne chez les Dogons (Soudan français), *Journal de psychologie*, 1947, *40*, 4, Oct.-Dec., pp. 425-431.

GRIAULE (Marcel). — *Dieu d'eau. Entretiens avec Ogotemmeli.* Paris, Éd. du Chêne, 1948, 266 p.

GRIAULE (Marcel). — L'image du monde au Soudan, *Journal de la Société des Africanistes*, 1949, *19*, 2, pp. 81-87.

GRIAULE (Marcel). — Connaissance de l'homme noir, in *La connaissance de l'homme au XXe siècle*, Neuchâtel, 1951, pp. 11-24, discussion: pp. 148-166.

GRIAULE (Marcel). — Réflexions sur les symboles soudanais, *Cahiers internationaux de sociologie*, 1952, *23*, pp. 8-30.

GROSS (F.), ed. — *European ideologies; a survey of 20th century political ideas*, with an introduction by R. M. MACIVER. New York, Philosophical Library, 1948, XV-1075 p.

GRUENBERG (Benjamin Charles). — *Science and the public mind.* Preface by John C. MERRIAM. New York, London, McGraw-Hill Book, 1935, XIII-196 p.

GRUNWALD (Ernst). — *Das Problem der Soziologie des Wissens, Versuch einer kritischen Darstellung der wissenssoziologischen Theorien.* Wien-Leipzig, W. Braumüller, 1934, VIII-279 p.

GURIN (G.). — *The relation of social class ideology to attitudes in an industrial organization.* Ann Arbor, Mich., University Microfilms, 1957, collation of the original: VIII-337 p.

GURVITCH (Georges). — *Les tendances actuelles de la philosophie allemande, E. Husserl, M. Scheler, E. Lask, N. Hartmann, M. Heidegger.* Liège, Paris, J. Vrin, 1930, 235 pp.

GURVITCH (Georges). — Sociologie de la connaissance et psychologie collective, *Année sociologique*, 3rd series, 1940-48, *1*, 2nd part, 4th section, pp. 463-486.

GURVITCH (Georges). — La vocation actuelle de la sociologie, *Cahiers internationaux de sociologie*, 1946 *1*, 3, pp. 3-22.

GURVITCH (Georges) — *Initiation aux recherches sur la sociologie de la connaissance.* Paris, Tournier & Constans, 1948, 65 p. (mimeographed).

GURVITCH (Georges). — La sociologie du jeune Marx, *Cahiers internationaux de sociologie*, 1948, 4, pp. 3-47 (cf.: *La vocation actuelle de la sociologie*, 1st edn. Paris, Presses Universitaires de France, 1950, pp. 568-602).

GURVITCH (Georges). — La technocratie est-elle un effet inévitable de l'industrialisation?, in *Industrialisation et technocratie*, publ. under the direction of Georges GURVITCH. Paris, A. Colin, 1949, pp. 179-199.

GURVITCH (Georges). — *La vocation actuelle de la sociologie*. 1st edn.: Paris, Presses Universitaires de France, 1950, 608 p.; 2nd edn., vol. 1, Paris, Presses Universitaires de France, 1957, VIII-508 p.

GURVITCH (Georges). — Réflexions sur les rapports entre philosophie et sociologie, *Cahiers internationaux de sociologie*, 1957, *22*, pp. 3-14.

GURVITCH (Georges). — Philosophie et sociologie, *Encyclopédie française*, 1957, *19*, pp. 19, 26, 15-19, 28, 4.

GURVITCH (Georges). — Structures sociales et systèmes de connaissances, in *La notion de structure et structure de la connaissance*. Paris, A. Michel, 1957, pp. 291-342.

GURVITCH (Georges). — Le problème de la sociologie de la connaissance, *Revue philosophique*, 1957, *147*, 4, pp. 494-502; 1958, *148*, 4, pp. 438-451; 1959, *149*; 2, pp. 145-168 (and in *Traité de sociologie*, vol. II, 1960, and 1963).

GURVITCH (Georges). — Structures sociales et multiplicité des temps, *Bulletin de la Société Française de Philosophie*, 1958, 3, pp. 99-142; and *Cahiers de l'Institut de Science Économique Appliquée*, 1960, 99, March (series M, 7), pp. 37-53.

GURVITCH (Georges). — Wissenssoziologie in *Die Lehre von der Gesellschaft, ein Lehrbuch der Soziologie*, under the direction of G. EISERMANN. Stuttgart, F. Enke Verlag, 1958, pp. 408-451.

GURVITCH (Georges). — Les cadres sociaux de la connaissance sociologique, *Cahiers internationaux de* sociologie, 1959, *26*, pp. 165-172.

GURVITCH (Georges). — Problèmes de la sociologie de la connaissance, dans *Traité de sociologie*. Paris, Presses Universitaires de France, 1960, vol. 2, pp. 103-136; 2nd edn.: 1963, id.

GURVITCH (Georges). — *Dialectique et sociologie*. Paris, Flammarion, 1962, 242 p.

GURVITCH (Georges). — *The spectrum of social time*. Dordrecht (Netherlands), D. Reidel Publishing, 1964, XXVI-152 p.

GURVITCH (Georges). — La sociologie de Karl Marx, in *La Vocation Actuelle de la Sociologie*, vol. II, 2nd edn., Paris, Presses Universitaire de France, 1963, pp. 220-322.

GURVITCH (Georges). — Les variations des perceptions collectives des étendues, *Cahiers internationaux de sociologie*, 1964, *37*, pp. 79-106.

GURVITCH (Georges). — Sociologie de la connaissance et épistémologie, in *Actes du Ve Congrès Mondial de Sociologie* (2-8 September 1962), vol. IV, Washington, 1964, pp. 193-207.

GURVITCH (Georges). — La sociologie de la connaissance, *Revue de l'Enseignement Supérieur*, 1965, 1-2, pp. 43-52.

GURVITCH (Georges). — *Les cadres sociaux de la connaissance*. Paris, Presses Universitaires de France, 1966.

GUSDORF (Georges). — *Mythe et métaphysique*. Paris, Flammarion, 1953, 294 p.

GUYAU (Jean-Marie). — *La genèse de l'idée du temps*. Paris, F. Alcan, 1890, XXX-142 p.

HACKER (Andrew). — In defence of utopia, *Ethics*, 1955, *65*, 2, pp. 135-138.

HALBWACHS (Maurice). — *Les cadres sociaux de la mémoire*. 1st edn.: Paris, F. Alcan, 1925, XII-404 p.

HALBWACHS (Maurice). — La mémoire collective chez les musiciens, *Revue philosophique*, 1939, March-April, pp. 136-165.

HALBWACHS (Maurice). — *La topographie légendaire des Évangiles en Terre*

U

Sainte, étude de mémoire collective. Paris, Presses Universitaires de France, 1941, 212 p.

HALBWACHS (Maurice). — *Psychologie collective.* Paris, Tournier & Constans, 1942, 144 p. (mimeo.).

HALBWACHS (Maurice). — *La mémoire collective.* Paris, Presses Universitaires de France, 1950, 171 p.

HALL (A. R.). — The rise of the West, in *A History of Technology,* ed. by Ch. SINGER, E. J. HOLMYARD, A. R. HALL, T. I. WILLIAMS. Oxford, The Clarendon Press, vol. III, 1957, pp. 709-721.

HALL (E. W.). — *Modern science and human values; a study in the history of ideas.* Princeton, N. J., Van Nostrand, 1956, 483 p.

HALLOWELL (John H.). — *The decline of liberalism as an ideology,* with particular reference to German politico-legal thought. 1st edn.: London, Kegan Paul, Trench, Trubner, 1946, XIII-141 p.

HARTUNG (Frank E.). — The sociology of positivism, *Science and society,* 1944, *8,* pp. 328-341.

HARTUNG (Frank E.). — Sociological foundations of modern science, *Philosophy of Science,* 1947, *14,* pp. 68-95.

HARTUNG (Frank E.). — Problems of the sociology of knowledge, *Philosophy of science,* 1952, *19,* Jan., pp. 17-32.

HAUDRICOURT (A. G.), GRANAI (G.). — Linguistique et sociologie, *Cahiers internationaux de sociologie,* 1955, *19,* pp. 114-129.

HAVIGHURST (Robert James). — *Human development and education.* New York, Longmans, Green, 1953, 338 p.

HENLE (P.). ed. — *Language, thought and culture.* Ann Arbor, Mich., University of Michigan Press, 1958, VI-273 p.

HERMAN (T.). — Pragmatism: a study in middle class ideology, *Social forces,* 1944, *22,* pp. 405 sq.

HERTZLER (Joyce Oramel). — *The history of utopian thought.* New York, Macmillan, London, G. Allen & Unwin, 1923, 321 p.

HERTZLER (Joyce Oramel). — *The social thought of the ancient civilizations.* New York, London, McGraw-Hill Book, 1936, XV-409 p.

HERTZLER (Joyce Oramel). — Toward a sociology of language, *Social forces,* 1953, *32,* Dec., pp. 109-120.

HINSHAW (Virgil G.). — The epistemological relevance of Mannheim's sociology of knowledge, *The journal of philosophy,* 1943, *40,* Feb., pp. 57-72.

HIRSCH (W.). — The autonomy of science in totalitarian societies, *Social Forces,* 1961, 40, 1, pp. 23-30.

HOBART (Charles W.), FAHLBERG (Nancy). — The measurement of empathy, *The American journal of sociology,* 1965, *70,* 5, pp. 595-603.

HODGES (H. A.). — *Wilhelm Dilthey: an introduction.* London, Routledge & Kegan Paul, 1944, X-174 p.; 2nd edn.: 1949.

HOGGART (Richard). — *The uses of literacy; aspects of working-class life with special reference to publications and entertainments.* London, Chatto and Windus, 1957, 319 p.

HOIJER (Harry). — The relation of language to culture, in *Anthropology to-day,* edited by A. L. KROEBER and others. Chicago, University of Chicago Press, 1953, pp. 554-573.

HOIJER (Harry), ed. — *Language in culture.* Menasha, Wisc., American Anthropological Association, 1954, XII-286 p.; and *The American anthropologist,* 1954, *56,* 6, Dec., part 2.

HOLTON (G.), ed. — *Science and the modern mind; a symposium.* Boston, Beacon Press, 1958, IX-110 p.

HONIGMANN (John J.). — Interpersonal relations and ideology in a Northern Canadian community, *Social forces*, 1957, *35*, 4, pp. 365-370.

HONIGSHEIM (Paul). — Soziologie der Mystik, in *Versuche zu einer Soziologie des Wissens*, publ. under the direction of M. SCHELER. München, Leipzig, Duncker u. Humblot, 1924, pp. 323-346.

HONIGSHEIM (Paul). — Soziologie der Scholastik, in *Versuche zu einer Soziologie des Wissens*, publ. under the direction of M. SCHELER. München, Leipzig, Duncker u. Humblot, 1924, pp. 302-307.

HONIGSHEIM (Paul). — Soziologie des realistischen und des nominalistischen Denkens, in *Versuche zu einer Soziologie des Wissens*, publ. under the direction of M. SCHELER. München, Leipzig, Duncker u. Humblot, 1924, pp. 308-322.

HORKHEIMER (Max). — Ein neuer Ideologiebergriff?, *Archiv für die Geschichte des Sozialismus und der Arbeiterbewegung*, 1930, *15*.

HORKHEIMER (Max). — Bemerkungen über Wissenschaff und Krise, *Zeitschrift für Sozialforschung*, 1932, *1*, pp. 1-7.

HORKHEIMER (Max). — Bemerkungen zur philosophischen Anthropologie, *Zeitschrift für Sozialforschung*, 1935, 4, pp. 1-25.

HORKHEIMER (Max). — Zum Problem der Wahrheit, *Zeitschrift für Sozialforschung*, 1935, 4, pp. 321-363.

HORKHEIMER (Max). — *Eclipse of reason*. New York, Oxford University Press, 1947, VII-187 p.

HORKHEIMER (Max). — Ideologie und Wertgebung, in *Soziologische Forschung in unserer Zeit, Leopold von Wiese zum 75. Geburtstag*. Köln, Opladen, Westdeutscher Verlag, 1951, pp. 220-227.

HORKHEIMER (Max). — Philosophie und Soziologie, *Kölner Zeitschrift für Soziologie und Sozialpsychologie*, 1959, 1, pp. 154-164.

HOROWITZ (Irving Louis). — Science, criticism, and the sociology of knowledge, *Philosophy and phenomenological research*, 1960 (Dec.), *21*, 2, pp. 173-186.

HOROWITZ (Irving Louis). — *Philosophy, science and the sociology of knowledge*. Springfield, Ill., Charles C. Thomas, 1961, XIV-169 p.

HUBERT (Henri). — Étude sommaire de la représentation du temps dans la religion et dans la magie, *Annuaire de l'École pratique des hautes études, Section des sciences religieuses*, 1905, p. 29.

HUBERT (R.). — Réflexions sur les rapports actuels de la sociologie et de la philosophie, *Revue internationale de philosophie*, 1950, 4, 13, pp. 251-267.

HUGHES (H. Stuart). — Is the intellectual obsolete? the freely speculating mind in America, *Commentary*, 1956, *22*, 4, Oct., pp. 313-319.

HUGHES (H. Stuart). — *Consciousness and society. The orientation of European social thought 1890-1930*. London, MacGibbon & Kee, 1959, 433 p.

HUNTINGTON (S. P.). — Conservatism as an ideology, *American political science review*, 1957, *51*, 2, June, pp. 454-473.

HUSZAR (George B. de), ed. — *The intellectuals, a controversial portrait*. Glencoe, Ill., The Free Press, 1960, 543 p.

Ideologie, *Frankfurter Beiträge zur Soziologie*, 1956, 4, pp. 162-181.

Les intellectuels dans la société française contemporaine, *Revue française de science politique*, 1959, *9*, 4, pp. 831-1081.

JAMES (Arthur), MALINOWSKI (Bronislaw), SINGER (Charles) et al. — *Science, religion and reality*, publ. under the direction of Joseph NEEDHAM. New York, Macmillan, 1925, 396 p.

JANET (Pierre). — *Les débuts de l'intelligence*. Paris, Flammarion, 1934, 261 p.

JANKÉLÉVITCH (S.). — Du rôle des idées dans l'évolution des sociétés, *Revue philosophique*, 1908, *66*, July-Dec., pp. 256-280.

JANNE (Henri). — Notes critiques relatives à la sociologie de la technique, *Revue de l'Institut de Sociologie Solvay*, 1952, 4, pp. 532-652.

JANNE (Henri). — Les cadres sociaux de la sociologie, *Cahiers internationaux de sociologie*, 1959, *26*, pp. 3-13.

JANOWITZ (Morris). — Some observations on the ideology of professional psychologists, *American psychologist*, 1954, *9*, 9, Sept., pp. 528-538.

JAYASWA (S. R.). — Language structure and social group, *Shiksha*, 1955, *7*, 2, April, pp. 125-135

JERUSALEM (Wilhelm). — Soziologie des Erkennens, *Die Zukunft*, 1909, *67*, May, pp. 236-246; and *Kölner Vierteljahrshefte für Sozialwissenschaften*, 1921, *1*, p. 28 ff.

JERUSALEM (Wilhelm). — Die soziologische Bedingtheit des Denkens und der Denkformen, in *Versuche zu einer Soziologie des Wissens*, publ. under the direction of Max SCHELER. München, Leipzig, Duncker u. Humblot, 1924, pp. 182-207.

JORDAN (L.), La logique et la linguistique, *Journal de psychologie*, 1933, 1-4 (*Théorie du langage*), pp. 45-56.

KAHN (Paul). — Les symboles dans la psychologie sociale de M. Mead, *Cahiers internationaux de sociologie*, 1949, *6*, pp. 134-149.

KAHN (Paul). — Idéologie et sociologie de la connaissance, *Année sociologique*, 1949-50, pp. 203-217.

KAHN (Paul). — Idéologie et sociologie de la connaissance dans l'œuvre de K. Mannheim, *Cahiers internationaux de sociologie*, 1950, *8*, pp. 147-168.

KAHN (Paul). — Mythe et réalité sociale chez Georges Sorel, *Cahiers internationaux de sociologie*, 1951, *11*, pp. 131-154.

KARDINER (Abram). — *The individual and his society; the psychodynamics of primitive social organization* ... with a foreword and two ethnological reports by Ralph LINTON. New York, Columbia University Press, 1939, XXVI-503 p.

KARDINER (Abram). — The concept of basic personality, in *Science of man in the world crisis*, edited by Ralph LINTON. New York, Columbia University Press, 1945, pp. 107-122.

KATZ (Robert L.). — *Empathy: Its nature and uses.* London, Free Press of Glencoe, 1963, XII-210 p. (pp. 1-54).

KECSKEMETI (Paul). — *Meaning, communication and value.* Chicago, University of Chicago Press, 1952, VIII-349 p.

KECSKEMETI (Paul). — Introduction to the *Essays on sociology and social psychology*, of Karl Mannheim. London, Routledge & Kegan Paul, 1953, pp. 1-11; 2nd edn. 1959.

KELSEN (Hans). — *Aufsätze zur Ideologiekritik.* Neuwied/Rh, Berlin, Hermann Luchterhand, 1963, 368 p.

KEMPSKI (J. von). — Wissenschaft als freier Beruf, *Kölner Zeitschrift für Soziologie*, 1953-1954, *6*, 3-4, pp. 423-434.

KILZER (Ernest), Ross (Eva). — The sociology of knowledge, *American catholic sociological review*, 1953, *14*, 4, pp. 230-233.

KLUCKHON (Clyde). — Myths and rituals: a general theory, *Harvard theological review*, 1942, *35*, pp. 45-79.

KLUCKHOHN (Clyde). — Recurrent themes in myths and myth-making, *Daedalus*, 1959, *88*, 2, pp. 268-279 (Bibliography).

Knowledge and society: a philosophical approach to modern civilization, by G. P. ADAMS, W. R. DENNES, J. LOEWENBERG, D. S. MACKAY, P. MARHENKE, S. C. PEPPER, E. W STRONG. New York, London, D. Appleton Century, 1938, XIII-417 p.

KÖNIG (René). — *Soziologie* (Lexikon). Frankfurt/Main Fischer Bücherei K.G.,

1958, 364 p. (articles: « Intelligenz », pp. 140-147; « Kultur », pp. 151-156; « Mentalität und Ideologie », pp. 180-184; « Technik », pp. 291-296; « Wissen », pp. 320-327).

KORNHAUSER (Arthur). — *The politics of mass society.* Glencoe, Ill., The Free Press, 1959, 256 p.

KORNHAUSER (William). — *Scientists in industry: Conflict and accommodation.* Berkeley, University of California Press, 1962, 230 p.

KOROL (Alexander G.). — *Soviet education for science and technology.* Cambridge, Mass., The Technology Press of Massachusetts Institute of Technology, 1957, XXV-513 p.

KOYRÉ (A.). — Les origines du machinisme, *Critique*, 1948, *4*, pp. 610-629.

KRAFT (Julius). — Soziologie oder Soziologismus? Zu Mannheims Ideologie und Utopie, *Zeitschrift für Völkerpsychologie und Soziologie*, 1929, pp. 406-417.

LACROIX (Jean). — *Marxisme, existentialisme, personnalisme, présence de l'éternité dans le temps.* Paris, Presses Universitaires de France, 1950, 123 p. (Reviewed by Georges GURVITCH: *Cahiers internationaux de sociologie*, 1950, *9*, pp. 186-187).

LANDHEER (Barth). — Presupposition in the social sciences, *American journal of sociology*, 1932, *37*, 4, Jan., pp. 539-546.

LANDSBERG (Paul Ludwig). — Zur Soziologie der Erkenntnistheorie, *Schmollers Jahrbuch für Gesetzgebung, Verwaltung und Volkswirtschaft*, 1931, *55*, 2, pp. 772 sq.

LANE (Robert E.). — *Political ideology.* New York, Free Press of Glencoe, 1962, XI-509 p.

LANGER (Suzanne K.). — *Philosophy in a new key, a study in the symbolism of reason, rite and art.* 1st ed.: Cambridge, Mass., Harvard University Press, 1942, XIV-313 p.

LASSWELL (Harold D.), and associates. — *Propaganda, communication and public opinion: a comprehensive reference guide.* Princeton, Princeton University Press, 1946.

LASSWELL (Harold D.), LEITES (Nathan), and associates. — *Language of politics, studies in quantitative semantics.* New York, G. N. Stewart, 1949, VII-398 p. Chap. I: The language of power, chap. II: Style in the language of politics.

LAUWERYS (J. A.). — Science as medium for the synthesis of school and society, *Sociological review*, 1946, *38*, 1, pp. 19-22.

LAVINE (Thelma Z.). — Sociological analysis of cognitive forms, *Journal of philosophy*, 1942, *39*, June, pp. 342-356.

LAVINE (Thelma Z.). — Naturalism and the sociological analysis of knowledge, in *Naturalism and the human spirit*, ed. by Yervant H. KRIKORIAN. New York, Columbia University Press, 1944, pp. 184 sq.

LAZARSFELD (Paul Felix), BERENSON (Bernard), GAUDET (Hazel). — *The people's choice; how the voter makes up his mind in a presidential campaign.* New York, Duell, Sloan & Pearce, 1944, 178 p.; 2nd ed.: New York, Columbia University Press, 1948, XXXIII-178 p.

LAZARSFELD (Paul Felix), THIELENS (Wagner). — *The academic mind*, with a field report by David RIESMAN. Glencoe, Ill., The Free Press, 1958, XIII-460 p.

LE CHATELIER (Henry). — *L'industrie, la science et l'organisation au XXᵉ siècle.* Paris, Dunod, 1935, 82 p.

LECLERCQ (Jacques). — La sociologie de la philosophie, *Bulletin de l'Institut de Recherches Économiques et Sociales*, 1955, *21*, 7, Nov., pp. 677-692.

LEENHARDT (Maurice). — Ethnologie de la parole, *Cahiers internationaux de sociologie*, 1946, *1*, pp. 82-105.

LEENHARDT (Maurice). — *Do Kamo.* Paris, Gallimard, 1947, 259 p.

272   *Bibliography*

NHARDT (Maurice). — Les carnets de Lucien Lévy-Bruhl, *Cahiers internationaux de sociologie*, 1949, *6*, pp. 28-42.

LEFEBVRE (Henri), GUTERMAN (N.). — *La conscience mystifiée*. Paris, Gallimard, 1936, 285 p.

LEFEBVRE (Henri). — *Critique de la vie quotidienne*. I: *Introduction*. 1st ed.: Paris, Grasset, 1947, 251 p.; 2nd ed.: Paris, L'Arche, 1958, 271 p. (chap. II: « La connaissance de la vie quotidienne », pp. 143-150; chap. III: « Le marxisme comme connaissance critique de la vie quotidienne », pp. 151-188). II: *Fondements d'une sociologie de la quotidienneté*, Paris, L'Arche, 1961, 360 p.

LEFEBVRE (Henri). — La notion de totalité dans les sciences sociales, *Cahiers internationaux de sociologie*, 1955, *18*, pp. 55-77.

LEFEBVRE (Henri). — *Problèmes actuels du marxisme*. Paris, Presses Universitaires de France, 1958, 128 p.

LEFEBVRE (Henri). — Retour à Marx, *Cahiers internationaux de sociologie*, 1958, *25*, pp. 20-37.

LEFEBVRE (Henri). — Les cadres sociaux de la sociologie marxiste, *Cahiers internationaux de sociologie*, 1959, *26*, pp. 81-102.

LEFEBVRE (Henri). — Les mythes dans la vie quotidienne, *Cahiers internationaux de sociologie*, 1962, *33*, pp. 67-74.

LEFORT (Claude). — L'aliénation comme concept sociologique, *Cahiers internationaux de sociologie*, 1955, *28*, pp. 35-54.

LENK (Kurt). — *Ideologie. Ideologiekritik und Wissenssoziologie*. Neuwied/Rh., Berlin, Hermann Luchterhand, 1960, 350 p.

LENK (Kurt). — Soziologie und Ideologienlehre, *Kölner Zeitschrift für Soziologie und Sozialpsychologie*, 1961, *13*, 2, pp. 227-237.

LENK (Kurt). — Dialektik und Ideologie. Zum Ideologieproblem in der Philosophie Hegels, *Archiv für Rechts- und Sozialphilosophie*, 1963, *49*, 2-3, pp. 303-318.

LENK (Kurt). — Die Rolle der Intelligenzsoziologie in der Theorie Mannheims, *Kölner Zeitschrift für Soziologie und Sozialpsychologie*, 1963, *15*, 2, pp. 323-337.

LEONARDI (F.). — Sociologia della conoscenza e planificazione sociale. Note su K. Mannheim, *Rassegna italiana di Sociologia*, 1960, *1*, 2, pp. 25-44.

LERNER (D.), POOL (Ithiel de Sola), LASSWELL (Harold D.). — Comparative analysis of political ideologies: a preliminary statement. *Public opinion quarterly*, 1951-52, *15*, 4, pp. 715-733.

LERNER (Marx). — *Ideas are weapons; the history and the uses of ideas*. New York, The Viking Press, 1939, XIV-553 p.

LERNER (Max). — *America as a civilization, life and thought in the United States to-day*. New York, Simon & Schuster, 1957, XIII-1036 p.

LEROI-GOURHAN (André). — *Milieu et techniques*. Paris, A. Michel, 1945, 512 p.

LEROI-GOURHAN (André). — Origine et diffusion de la connaissance scientifique. Extract from the *Revue S.E.T.*, 1953, 33-34, Jan.-June, 20 p.

LEROI-GOURHAN (André), *Le geste et la parole*. Paris, A. Michel, 1965.

LÉVI-STRAUSS (Claude). — Langage et société, in *Anthropologie structurale*. Paris, Plon, 1958, chap. III, pp. 63-75.

LÉVI-STRAUSS (Claude). — Linguistique et anthropologie, in *Anthropologie structurale*. Paris, Plon, 1958, chap. IV, pp. 77-91.

LÉVI-STRAUSS (Claude). — L'efficacité symbolique, in *Anthropologie structurale*. Paris, Plon, 1958, chap. X, pp. 205-226.

LÉVI-STRAUSS (Claude). — *La pensée sauvage*. Paris, Plon, 1962, 11-397 p.

LÉVI-STRAUSS (Claude). — *Le totémisme aujourd'hui*. Paris, Presses Universitaires de France, 1962, 154 p.

Bibliography 273

LÉVI-STRAUSS (Claude). — *Mythologiques. Le Cru et le Cuit.* Paris, Plon, 1964, 402 p.
LEVIN (H.). — Some meanings of myth, *Daedalus*, 1959, *88*, 2, pp. 223-231.
LÁVY-BRUHL (Lucien). — *Les fonctions mentales dans les sociétés inférieures.* Paris, F. Alcan, 1910, 455 p.
LÉVY-BRUHL (Lucien). — *La mentalité primitive.* 1st ed.: Paris, F. Alcan, 1922, 537 p.
LÉVY-BRUHL (Lucien). — *L'âme primitive.* 1st ed.: Paris, F. Alcan, 1923, 537 p.
LÉVEY-BRUHL (Lucien), AUPIAIS (R. P.), BOAS (F.), BRUNSWICG (L.), LENOIR (R.), MAUSS (M.), RIVET (P.), MEYERSON (E.). — Discussion sur l'âme primitive, *Bulletin de la Société Française de Philosophie*, 1929, *29*, pp. 105-139.
LÉVY-BRUHL (Lucien). — *Le surnaturel et la nature dans la mentalité primitive.* Paris, A. Colin, 1931, 526 p.
LÉVY-BRUHL (Lucien). — *La mythologie primitive. Le monde mythique des Australiens et des Papous.* Paris, F. Alcan, 1935, XLVII-336 p.
LÉVY-BRUHL (Lucien). — *Morceaux choisis.* Paris, Gallimard, 1936, 255 p.
LÉVY-BRUHL (Lucien). — *L'expérience mystique et les symboles chez les primitifs.* Paris, F. Alcan, 1938, 316 p.
LÉVY-BRUHL (Lucien). — *Les carnets de Lucien Lévy-Bruhl.* Preface by Maurice LEENHARDT. Paris, Presses Universitaires de France, 1949, XXI-259 p.
LEWALTER (Ernst). — Wissenssoziologie und Marxismus. Eine Auseinandersetzung mit Karl Mannheims Ideologie und Utopie von marxistischer Position aus, *Archiv für Sozialwissenschaft und Sozialpolitik*, 1930, *64*, pp. 63-121.
LEWIS (Clarence Irving). — *An analysis of knowledge and valuation.* La Salle, Ill., The Open Court Publishing, 1946, XXI-567 p.
LEWIS (Lionel & S.). — Knowledge, danger, certainty, and the theory of magic, *The American journal of sociology*, 1963, *69*, 1, pp. 7-12.
LEWIS (Morris Michael). — *The importance of illiteracy.* London, G. Harrap, 1953, 187 p.
LIEBER (Hans-Joachim). — Sein und Erkennen, *Zeitschrift für philosophische Forschung*, 1948, *3*, 2, pp. 249-264.
LIEBER (Hans-Joachim). — *Wissen und Gesellschaft. Die Probleme der Wissenssoziologie.* Tübingen, Max Niemeyer, 1952, 166 p.
LIEBER (Hans-Joachim). — Ideologische Elemente in der Sozialkritik der Gegenwart, in *Festgabe für Friedrich Bülow zum 70. Geburtstag.* Berlin, 1960, pp. 223-235.
LINS (Mario). — The sociology of knowledge, aspects of its problematics, *Revue internationale de sociologie*, 1958, *1*, 2-3, pp. 3-10.
LINTON (Ralph). — *The cultural background of personality.* New York, D. Appleton Century, 1945, XIX-157 p., London, Kegan Paul, Trench, Trubner, 1947, XII-102 p.
LITT (Theodor). — *Mensch und Welt.* München, Federmann, 1948, 336 p.
LITT (Theodor). — *Die Selbsterkenntnis des Menschen.* Hamburg, Richard Meiner Verlag, 1948, 89 p.
LITT (Theodor). — *Technisches Denken und menschliche Bildung.* Heidelberg, Quelle und Meyer, 1957, 95 p.
LOEWENSTEIN (K.). — L'influence des idéologies sur les changements politiques, *Bulletin international des sciences sociales*, 1953, *5*, 1, pp. 53-79.
LOEWENTHAL (Leo). — Das Individuum in der individualistischen Gesellschaft, *Zeitschrift für Sozialforschung*, 1936, *5*, 1, pp. 321-363.
LOEWENTHAL (Leo). — *Literature, popular culture, and society.* Englewood Cliffs, N.J., Prentice Hall, 1961, XXIV-169 p.
LOMBARDI (Franco). — Philosophie und Gesellschaft, *Frankfurter Beiträge zur Soziologie*, 1955, *1*, pp. 211-218.

274 *Bibliography*

Lovejoy (O. Arthur). — Reflections on the history of ideas, *Journal of the history of ideas*, 1940, *1*, 1, Jan., pp. 3-23.

Luchtenberg (Paul). — *Uebertragungsformen des Wissens*, in *Versuche zu einer Soziologie des Wissens*, publ. under the direction of M. Scheler, München, Leipzig, Duncker u. Humblot, 1924, pp. 151-181.

Luebbe (H.). — Die Freiheit der Theorie. Max Weber über Wissenschaft als Beruf, *Archiv für Rechts- und Sozialphilosophie*, 1962, *48*, 3, pp. 343-365.

Lukács (Georg). — *Geschichte und Klassenbewusstsein, Studien über marxistische Dialektik*. Berlin, Malik Verlag, 1923, 341 p.

Lukács (Georg). — Marx und das Problem des ideologischen Verfalls, dans *Karl Marx und Friedrich Engels als Literaturhistoriker*. Berlin, Aufbau Verlag, 1948.

Lukács (Georg). — *Existentialisme ou marxisme?*, Paris, Nagel, 1948, 317 p.

Lukács (Georg). — *Die Zerstörung der Vernunft, der Weg des Irrationalismus von Schelling zu Hitler*. Berlin, Aufbau Verlag, 1955, 692 p.

Lukács (Georg). — *Schriften zur Literalursoziologie*. Neuwied/Rh., Luchterhand, 1961, 568 p.

Luthy (Herbert). — « Calvinisme et capitalisme », *Preuves*, 1964, July, 161, pp. 3-22.

MacClung Lee (Alfred). — *How to understand propaganda*. New York, Rienhart, 1953, 281 p.

MacDonagh (E. C.). — Social myths in Soviet communism, *Sociology and social research*, 1952, *36*, 5, pp. 369-376.

MacDonald (H. Malcolm). — The revival of conservative thought, *Journal of politics*, 1957, *19*, 1, Feb., pp. 66-80.

MacDougall (William). — *World chaos: the responsibility of science*. London, Kegan Paul, Trench, Trubner, 1931, VI-119 p.

Machlup (Fritz). — *The production and distribution of knowledge in the United States*. Princeton, New York, Princeton University Press, 1962, XIX-416 p.

MacKeen (Cattell J.). — Science and democracy, *Scientific monthly*, 1938, *46*, 1, Jan., pp. 80-88.

MacKenzie (Dan). — *The infancy of medicine: an inquiry into the influence of folklore upon the evolution of scientific medicine*. London, Macmillan, 1927, XIV-421 p.

MacKenzie (Donald Alexander). — *The migration of symbols and their relations to beliefs and customs*. London, Kegan Paul, Trench, Trubner, New York, A. A. Knopf, 1926, XVI-219 p.

MacKinney (John C.). — The contribution of G. H. Mead to the sociology of knowledge, *Social forces*, 1955, *34*, 2, Dec., pp. 144-149.

MacLuhan. — Myth and mass media, *Daedalus*, 1959, *88*, 2, pp. 339-348.

MacRae (Donald G.). — Class relationships and ideology, *Sociological review*, 1958, *6*, 2, pp. 261-272.

MacRae (Donald G.). — *Ideology and society*. Papers in sociology and politics. London, Melbourne, Toronto, Heinemann, 1961, XII-231 p.

Malgaud (Walter). — Le rôle de la logique dans la sociologie, *Revue de l'Institut de Sociologie*, 1923-1924, *1*, 2, Sept., pp. 183-204.

Malinowski (Bronislaw). — The problem of meaning in primitive languages, in C. K. Ogden and I. A. Richards, *The meaning of meaning*, a study of the influence of language upon thought and of the science of symbolism, with supplementary essays by Malinowski (B.) and Crookshank (F. G.). 1st ed.: New York, London, 1923.

Malinowski (Bronislaw). — *Myth in primitive psychology*. New York, W. W. Norton, 1926, IX-11-94 p., and London, Kegan Paul, Trench, Trubner, 1926, 128 p.

Bibliography 275

MALINOWSKI (Bronislaw). — Article "Culture", in *Encyclopaedia of the social sciences*. Edwin R. A. SELIGMAN and Alvin JOHNSON ed., New York, Macmillan, 1931, vol. IV, pp. 621-646.

MALINOWSKI (Bronislaw). — *A scientific theory of culture and other essays*, with a preface by Huntington CAIRNS. Chapel Hill, The University of North Carolina Press, 1944, 228 p.

MALINOWSKI (Bronislaw). — Magic, science and religion, in *Magic, science and religion, and other essays*. Glencoe, Ill., The Free Press, 1948, pp. 1-71.

MALRIEU (Philippe). — *Les origines de la conscience du temps. Les attitudes temporelles de l'enfant*. Paris, Presses Universitaires de France, 1953, 158 p.

MALRIEU (Philippe). — Aspects sociaux de la construction du temps chez l'enfant, *Journal de psychologie*, 1956, *53*, 3, pp. 315-332.

MANDELBAUM (Maurice). — *The problem of historical knowledge: an answer to relativism*. New York, Liveright publishing Co., 1938, X-340 p.

MANNHEIM (Ernst). — Karl Mannheim, 1893-1947, *The American journal of sociology*, 1947, *52*, May, pp. 471-474.

MANNHEIM (Karl). — *Die Strukturanalyse der Erkenntnistheorie*. Berlin, Reuther & Reichard, 1922, 80 p.

MANNHEIM (Karl). — Zum Problem einer Klassifikation der Wissenschaften, *Archiv für Sozialwissenschaft und Sozialpolitik*, 1923, *50*, pp. 230-237.

MANNHEIM (Karl). — Ideologische und soziologische Interpretation der geistigen Gebilde, *Jahrbuch für Soziologie*, 1926, *2*, pp. 424-440.

MANNHEIM (Karl). — Die Bedeutung der Konkurrenz im Gebiete des Geistigen, *Schriften der deutschen Gesellschaft für Soziologie*, 1929, *6*, pp. 35-83.

MANNHEIM (Karl). — *Ideologie und Utopie*. Bonn, F. Cohen, 1929, IX-XV-250 p. English trs.: *Ideology and utopia; an introduction to the sociology of knowledge*, with a preface by Louis WIRTH. London, Kegan Paul, Trench, Trubner, New York, Harcourt, Brace, 1936, XXXI-318 p.

MANNHEIM (Karl). — *Rational and irrational elements in contemporary society*. London, Oxford University Press, H. Milford, 1934, 36 p. (L. T. Hobhouse, memorial trust lectures).

MANNHEIM (Karl). — The crisis of culture in the era of mass-democracies and autarchies, *The sociological review*, 1934, *26*, 2, April, pp. 105-129.

MANNHEIM (Karl). — *Mensch und Gesellschaft im Zeitalter des Umbaus*. Leiden, A. W. Sijthoff, 1935, XVIII-208 p. English translation by E. SHILS, modifications and additions by K. MANNHEIM: *Man and society in an age of reconstruction; studies in modern social structure, with a bibliographical guide to the study of modern society*. London, Kegan Paul, Trench, Trubner, 1940, XXII-3-469 p.

MANNHEIM (Karl). — Article "Utopia", in *Encyclopaedia of the social sciences*, Edwin R. A. SELIGMAN and Alvin JOHNSON ed. New York, Macmillan, 1935, vol. 15, pp. 200-203.

MANNHEIM (Karl). *Diagnosis of our time*. London, Kegan Paul, Trench, Trubner, 1943, XI-180 p.

MANNHEIM (Karl). — *Essays on the sociology of knowledge*, edited by Paul KECSKEMETI. London, Routledge & Kegan Paul, 1952, VIII-327 p.

MANNHEIM (Karl). — *Essays on sociology and social psychology*, ed. by Paul KECSKEMETI. London, Routledge & Kegan Paul, 1st ed.: 1953, VIII-319 p.

MANNHEIM (Karl). — Towards the sociology of the Mind; an introduction, in *Essays on the sociology of culture*, ed. by Ernest MANNHEIM in co-operation with Paul KECSKEMETI. New York, Oxford University Press, London, Routledge & Kegan Paul, 1956, Part I, IX-253 p.

MAO TSE TUNG. — *Über die Praxis. Über den Zusammenhang von Erkenntnis und Praxis, von Wissen und Handeln*. Berlin/Ost, Dietz, 1952, 26 p.

MAQUET (J.). — *Sociologie de la connaissance*, sa structure et ses rapports avec la philosophie de la connaissance. Étude critique des systèmes de Karl Mannheim et de Pitirim A. Sorokin. Preface by F. S. C. NORTHROP. Louvain, Institut de Recherches Économiques et Sociales, 1949, 360 p.

MAQUET (Jacques). — Le conditionnement social de l'anthropologie culturelle, *VIe Congrès international des sciences anthropologiques et ethnologiques*, Paris (30 July-6 Aug), 1960. Musée de l'Homme, tome II (1), 1963, pp. 191-197.

MAQUET (Jacques). — Some anthropological contribution to the sociology of knowledge, *Information sur les sciences sociales/Social Sciences Information*, 1962, *1*, 3, pp. 5-20.

MARCHI (E.). — Thought and political practice in Italy, *Occidente*, 1954, *10*, 1, pp. 60-72.

MARCSON (Simon). — *The scientist in American industry*. Princeton, Princeton University (Industrial relations section), 1960, vol. IX, 158 p.

MARCUSE (Herbert). — Zur Wahrheitsproblematik der soziologischen Methode Karl Mannheims Ideologie und Utopie. *Die Gesellschaft*, 1929, *6*, Oct., pp. 356-369.

MARCUSE (Herbert). — *One dimensional man: studies in the Ideology of advanced Industrial Society*. Boston, Beacon Press, 1964, XVII-260 p.

MARTIN (Alfred Wilhelm Otto von). — *Soziologie der Renaissance; zur Physiognomik und Rythmik bürgerlicher Kultur*. Stuttgart, F. Enke Verlag, 1932, XII-135 p. English translation: *Sociology of the Renaissance*. London, Kegan Paul, Trench, Trubner, New York, Oxford University Press, 1944, X-100 p.

MARTIN (Alfred Wilhelm Otto von). — *Geist und Gesellschaft*. Frankfurt/Main, Knecht, 1948, 258 p.

MARX (Karl). — *Kritik des Hegelschen Staatsrechis* [unedited 1843]. Moscow and Frankfurt/Main, M.E.G.A. 1927, I, 1/1, pp. 401-553.

MARX (Karl). — Zur Kritik der Hegelschen Rechtsphilosophie, Einleitung. *Deutsch-französische Jahrbücher*, I-II, Paris, February 1844; and Moscow and Frankfort, M.E.G.A., 1927, I, 1/1, pp. 607-621.

MARX (Karl). — *Nationalökonomie und Philosophie* [unedited 1844]. Berlin, M.E.G.A., I, 3, 1932, pp. 33-172 (Œkonomisch-philosophische Manuskripte aus dem Jahre 1844); re-ed. by E. TIER: Köln, Berlin, Kiepenheur, 1950; and S. LANDSHUT, in *Die Frühschriften*. Stuttgart, A. Kröner, 1953, pp. 225-316.

MARX (Karl). — *Zur Kritik der Nationalökonomie mit einem Schlusskapitel über die Hegelsche Philosophie* [unedited 1844]. Moscow and Berlin, M.E.G.A., I, 3, pp. 33-172 and 589-596.

MARX (Karl). — *Die heilige Familie oder Kritik der kritischen Kritik, gegen Bruno Bauer und Consorten*. Frankfurt/Main, Literarische Anstalt (J. Rütten), 1845, VIII-336 p.; Moscow and Berlin, M.E.G.A., I, 3, 1932, pp. 173-388.

MARX (Karl). — *Die deutsche Ideologie. Kritik der neuesten deutschen Philosophie in ihren Repräsentanten, Feuerbach, B. Bauer und Stirner, und des deutschen Sozialismus in seinen verschiedenen Propheten* [unedited 1845-1846]. Moscow, Vienna-Berlin, M.E.G.A., 1932, I, 5, pp. 3-528 et 536-537.

MARX (Karl). — *Thesen über Feuerbach* [unedited 1845], published by F. ENGELS in appendix to *Ludwig Feuerbach und der Ausgang der klassischen deutschen Philosophie*, 1886, Moscow, Vienna-Berlin, M.E.G.A., I, 5, pp. 533-535.

MARX (Karl). — *Misère de la philosophie. Réponse à la « Philosophie de la misère »* de M. Proudhon. Paris, A. Franck, 68, rue Richelieu; Bruxelles, C. G. Vogeler, 1847, 8-178 p.

MARX (Karl). — *Die Klassenkämpfe in Frankreich*, series of articles in *New

Rheinische Zeitung. Politisch-ökonomische Revue, 1850, 1, March 2, March 3, April.

MARX (Karl). — *Der 18te Brumaire des Louis-Bonaparte*, preface by WEYDE-MEYER. *Die Revolution*, 1st May 1852; 2nd ed. With foreword by MARX: Hambourg, Meissner, 1869, VI-98 p.

MARX (Karl). — [*Gundrisse der Kritik der politischen Œkonomie*], [unedited 1857-1858]. Publ. from the German manuscripts by the Institute of Marx-Engels-Lenin, Moscow. Moscou, Verlag für fremdsprachige Literatur, vol. I, XVI-764 p.; vol. II, 339 p.

MARX (Karl). — *Zur Kritik der politischen Œkonomie. Erstes Heft.* Berlin, Franz Duncker, 1859, VII-170 p.

MARX (Karl). — *Der Bürgerkrieg in Frankreich*, German version by F. ENGELS. *Volksstaat*, Leipzig, 26 June to 29 July 1871.

MASSON-OURSEL (Paul). — La magie comme technique. De la magie à la religion, *Revue de synthèse*, 1953, *32*, Jan.-June pp. 41-53.

MASSON-OURSEL (Paul). — Mythes et métaphysique, *Revue de synthèse*, 1953, *32*, Jan.-June, pp. 55-67.

MAUCORPS (Paul-H.). — Empathie et compréhension d'autrui, *Revue française de sociologie*, 1960, *1*, 4, Oct.-Dec., pp. 426-444.

MAUCORPS (Paul-H.), BASSOUL (R.). — *Emphathes et connaissance d'autrui*. Paris, C.N.R.S., 1960, 93 p.

MAUSS (Marcel), DURKHEIM (Émile). — De quelques formes primitives de classifications, *Année sociologique*, 1901-1902, *6*, pp. 1-72.

MAUSS (Marcel). — Esquisse d'une théorie générale de la magie, *Année sociologique*, 1902-1903, *7*, pp. 1-146, and in *Sociologie et anthropologie*. Paris, Presses Universitaires de France, 1950 and 1960, pp. 3-138.

MAUSS (Marcel), HUBERT (Henri). — *Mélanges d'histoire de la religion. De quelques résultats de la sociologie religieuse, le sacrifice, l'origine des pouvoirs magiques, la représentation du temps.* Paris, F. Alcan, 1909, XLII-236 p.

MAUSS (Marcel). — Rapports réels et pratiques de la psychologie et de la sociologie, *Journal de psychologie*, 1924, *21*, 10, Dec., pp. 892-922, and in *Sociologie et anthropologie*. Paris, Presses Universitaires de France, 1950 and 1960, pp. 283-310.

MAUSS (Marcel). — Les civilisations. Éléments et formes, in *Civilisation, le mot et l'idée*, Paris, La Renaissance du Livre, 1930, pp. 81-109.

MAUSS (Marcel). — Les techniques du corps, *Journal de psychologie*, 1936, *32*, 3-4, and in *Sociologie et anthropologie*. Paris, Presses Universitaires de France, 1950, pp. 363-386.

MAUSS (Marcel). — Une catégorie de l'esprit humain, la notion de personne, celle de « moi », un plan de travail, *Journal of the royal anthropological institute*, 1938, *68*, pp. 263-281.

MAUSS (Marcel). — Les techniques et la technologie, *Journal de psychologie*, 1948, *41*, 1, pp. 71-78.

MAVALANKAR (N. A.). — The role of science in modern society, *Sociological bulletin* (Bombay), 1956, *5*, 1, March pp. 1-8.

MEAD (Georges Herbert). — *Mind, self and society*, from the standpoint of a social behaviorist. Chicago, The University of Chicago Press, 1934, 400 p.

MELZER (Leo). — Scientific productivity in organizational settings, *Journal of social issues*, 1956, *12*, 2, pp. 32-40.

MEMMI (Albert). — Cinq propositions pour une sociologie de la littérature, *Cahiers internationaux de sociologie*, 1959, *26*, pp. 149-159; and *Traité de sociologie*, publ. under the direction of G. GURVITCH, vol. II. Paris, Presses Universitaires de France, 1960, pp. 299-314.

MERLEAU-PONTY (Maurice). — La philosophie et la sociologie, *Cahiers internationaux de sociologie*, 1951, *10*, pp. 50-69.

MERTON (Robert K.). — Science and military technique, *Scientific monthly*, 1935, *41*, pp. 542-545.

MERTON (Robert K.). — Civilization and culture, *Sociology and social research*, 1936, pp. 103-113.

MERTON (Robert K.). — Puritanism, pietism and science, *The sociological review*, 1936, *28*, 1, Jan., pp. 1-30.

MERTON (Robert K.). — Science, population and society, *Scientific monthly*, 1937, *44*, 2, Feb., pp. 165-171.

MERTON (Robert K.). — The sociology of knowledge, *Isis*, 1937, 75, *27*, 3, Nov., pp. 493-503.

MERTON (Robert K.). — Science and the social order, *Philosophy of science*, 1938, July, pp. 321-337.

MERTON (Robert K.). — Science, technology and society in seventeenth century England, *Osiris*, 1938, *4*, 2, pp. 360-632.

MERTON (Robert K.). — Science and the economy in the seventeenth century England, *Science and society*, 1939, pp. 3-27.

MERTON (Robert K.). — Karl Mannheim and the sociology of knowledge, *The journal of liberal religion*, 1941, Winter, pp. 125-147.

MERTON (Robert K.). — Review of F. Znaniecki's "The social role of the man of knowledge", *American sociological review*, 1941, *6*, 1, Feb., pp. 111-115.

MERTON (Robert K.). — Role of intellectuals in public bureaucracies, *Social forces*, 1945, *23*, 4, May, pp. 405-415.

MERTON (Robert K.). — The sociology of knowledge, in *Twentieth century sociology*, ed. by G. GURVITCH and W. E. MOORE. New York, The Philosophical Library, 1946, pp. 366-405.

MERTON (Robert K.). LAZARSFELD (Paul). — Mass communication, popular taste and organized social action, in *Communication of ideas*, ed. by Lyman BRYSON. New York, Institute for religious and social studies, 1948.

MERTON (Robert K.). — A paradigm for the study of the sociology of knowledge, in *The language of social research*, ed. by Paul F. LAZARSFELD and Morris ROSENBERG. Glencoe, Ill., The Free Press, 1955, pp. 498-511.

MERTON (Robert K.). — Priorities in scientific discoveries: a chapter in the sociology of science, *The American sociological review*, 1957, *22*, 6, Dec., pp. 635-659.

MERTON (Robert K.). — Singletons and multiples in scientific discovery; a chapter in the sociology of science, *Proceedings of the American Philosophical Society*, 1961, *105*, pp. 471-486.

MERTON (Robert K.). — Resistance to the systematic study of multiple discoveries in science, *Archives européennes de sociologie*, 1963, *4*, 2, pp. 237-282.

MÉTAIS (Élyane). — Étude comparative d'expressions graphiques d' « étendues concrètes » canaques, *Cahiers internationaux de sociologie*, 1953, *15*, pp. 115-131.

MEYERHOFF (H. A.). — Social implications of scientific progress. *Social science*, 1950, *25*, 3, pp. 177-187.

MEYERSON (Ignace). — Le temps, la mémoire, l'histoire, *Journal de psychologie*, 1956, 3, pp. 333-354.

MICHEL (Andrée). — Les cadres sociaux de la doctrine morale de Frédéric Le Play, *Cahiers internationaux de sociologie*, 1963, *34*, pp. 47-68.

MICHELS (Roberto). — Article "Intellectuals", in *Encyclopaedia of the social sciences*, Edwin R. A. SELIGMAN and Alvin JOHNSON ed. New York, Macmillan, 1932, vol. 8, pp. 118-126.

MILHAUD (G.). — *Études sur la pensée scientifique chez les Grecs et les Modernes.* Paris, Société Française de Librairie et d'Imprimerie, 1906, 275 p.
MILHAUD (G.). — *Nouvelles études sur l'histoire de la pensée scientifique.* Paris, F. Alcan, 1911, 237 p.
MILLER (Perry). — *The New England mind; the seventeenth century.* New York, Macmillan, 1939, XI-3-528 p.
MILLIOUD (Maurice). — La propagation des idées, *Revue philosophique,* 1910, *69,* pp. 580-600, 1910, *70,* pp. 168-191.
MILLS (C. Wright). — Language, logic and culture, *American sociological review,* 1939, *4,* Oct., pp. 670-680.
MILLS (C. Wright). — The language and ideas of ancient China: *Marcel Granet's Contribution to the Sociology of Knowledge.* Madison, University of Wisconsin, 1940, (mimeographed).
MILLS (C. Wright). — Methodological consequences of the sociology of knowledge, *American journal of sociology,* 1940, *46,* 3, Nov., pp. 316-330.
MILLS (C. Wright). — The professional ideology of social pathologists, *The American journal of sociology,* 1943-44, *49,* 2, pp. 165-180.
MILLS (C. Wright). — The powerless people. The role of the intellectual in society, *Politics,* 1944, *1,* 3, April, pp. 68-72.
MILLS (C. Wright). — *The new men of power. America's labor leaders,* with the assistance of Helen SCHNEIDER. New York, Harcourt, Brace, 1948, 324 p.
MILLS (C. Wright). — *The sociological imagination.* New York, Oxford University Press, 1959, 234 p.
MITRANI (Nora). — Réflexions sur l'opération technique, les techniciens et technocrates, *Cahiers internationaux de sociologie,* 1955, *19,* July-Dec., pp. 158-170.
MITRANI (Nora). — Les mythes de l'énergie nucléaire et la bureaucratie internationale, *Cahiers internationaux de sociologie,* 1956, *21,* pp. 138-148.
MITRANI (Nora). — Attitudes et symboles techno-bureaucratiques: réflexions sur une en enquête, *Cahiers internationaux de sociologie,* 1958, *24,* pp. 148-166.
MITRANI (Nora). — Ambiguïté de la technocratie, *Cahiers internationaux de sociologie,* 1961, *30,* pp. 101-114.
MITTENZWEY (Kuno). — Zur Soziologie der psychoanalytischen Erkenntnis, in *Versuche zu einer Soziologie des Wissens,* publ. under the direction of Max Scheler. München/Leipzig, Duncker u. Humblot, 1924, pp. 365-375.
MOLNAR (Thomas). — *The decline of the Intellectual.* Cleveland, World Publishing Co., 1961, 369 p.
MONRO (D. H.). — The concept of myth, *Sociological review,* 1950, *42,* 6, pp. 1-20.
MONTEL (Paul). — Le nombre et la civilisation, *Sciences,* 1951, *78,* 70, pp 337-349.
MORGENTHAU (Hans J.). — *Scientific man and power politics.* Chicago, University of Chicago Press, 1946, 245 p.
MORIN (Edgar). — Intellectuels: critique du mythe et mythe de la critique, *Arguments,* 1960, 4, 20, pp. 35-40.
MORRIS (Charles W.). — *Signs, language and behavior.* New York, Prentice-Hall, 1946, XIII-365 p.
MORRIS (Charles W.). — Foundations of the theory of signs, in *International encyclopedia of unified science,* vol. I, 2. Chicago, University of Chicago Press, 1953, VIII-59 p.
MORTON (A. L.). — Utopias yesterday and to-day, *Science and society,* 1953, *17,* 3, pp. 258-263.
MUELLER-FREIENFELS (Richard). — Zur Soziologie und Sozialpsychologie der

Wissenschaft, *Zeitschrift für Völkerpsychologie und Soziologie*, 1931, *7*, 4, pp. 401-419.

MUELLER-FREIENFELS (Richard). — Zur Soziologie der Wahrheit, *Zeitschrift für Völkerpsychologie und Soziologie*, 1932, *8*, 3, pp. 310-323.

MUELLER-FREIENFELS (Richard). — Zur Soziologie des wissenschaftlichen Menschen, *Kölner Vierteljahreshefte für Soziologie*, 1933-34, *12*, pp. 375-389.

MUENKE (St.). — Die Rolle der Soziologie in der modernen Gesellschaft, *Schmollers Jahrbuch*, 1959, *79*, 4, pp. 79-95.

MUHLMANN (W. E.). — Soziologie des Genie Mythos. Zur Neuauflage des Werkes von Lange-Eichbaum, *Kölner Zeitschrift für Soziologie*, 1957, *9*, 1, pp. 118-125.

MUIRHEAD (John H.). — The place of philosophy in American universities, *Philosophical review*, 1927, 36, 3, May, pp. 209-215.

MUKERJEE (Radhakamal). — *The symbolic life of man*. Bombay, Hind Kitabs, 1959, XII-294 p.

MUKERJI (D.). — The intellectuals in India, *Confluence*, 1956, *4*, 4, pp. 443-455.

MUMFORD (Lewis). — *The story of utopias*, with an introduction by Hendrick Willem VAN LOON. New York, Boni and Liveright, 1922, XII-11-315 p.

MUMFORD (Lewis). — *Technics and civilization*. New York, Harcourt, Brace, 1934, 506 p.

MUMFORD (Lewis). — Authoritarian and democratic technics, *Technology and Culture*, 1964, *5*, 1, pp. 1-8.

MURRAY (H. A.). — Introduction to the issue "myth and myth making", *Daedalus*, 1959, *88*, 2, pp. 211-222.

MUS (Paul). — La mythologie primitive et la pensée de l'Inde, *Bulletin de la Société Française de Philosophie*, 1937, *37*, 3, May-June, pp. 83-126.

NEEDHAM (Joseph). *Science and civilization in China*, Cambridge University Press, 1954, 2 volumes.

NEF (John Ulric). *Cultural foundations of industrial civilization*. Cambridge, Cambridge University Press, 1958, XIV-163 p.

NETTLER (Gwynne). — A test for the sociology of knowledge, *American sociological review*, 1945, *10*, 3, June, pp. 393-399.

NEWCOMB (Theodore M.). — *The acquaintance process*. New York, Holt, Rinehart and Winston, 1961, XV-303 p.

NICHOLAS (A. G.). — Intellectuals and politics in U.S.A., *Occidente*, 1954, Jan.-Feb.

NILSSON (Martin P.). — *Primitive time-reckoning*, a study in the origin and first development of the art of counting time among the primitive and early culture peoples. Lund, G. W. K. Gleerup, 1920, XIII-384 p.

NISBET (Robert A.). — The French Revolution and the Rise of Sociology, *The American journal of sociology*, 1943, *49*, 2, pp. 156-164.

NORTHROP (Filmer Stuart Cuckow). — *The logic of the sciences and the humanities*. New York, Macmillan, 1947, XIV-402 p.

NORTHROP (Filmer Stuart Cuckow). — *Ideological differences and world order*, studies in the philosophy and science of the world's cultures. New Haven, Yale University Press, 1949, XI-486 p.

OPPENHEIMER (J Robert). — Meditationes sobre la ciencia y la cultura, *Revista mexicana de sociologia*, 1962, *24*, 2, pp. 567-585.

ORNSTEIN (Martha). — *The role of scientific societies in the seventeenth century*. Chicago, University of Chicago Press, 1938, VII-XVIII-308 p.

OSSOWSKI (Stanislas). — Les différents aspects de la classe sociale chez Marx, *Cahiers internationaux de sociologie*, 1958, *24*, pp. 65-79.

Bibliography 281

PARETO (Vilfredo). — *Trattato di Sociologia Generale*, 3 vols., Florence, 1916. English edn., *The Mind and Society*, 4 vols., New York and London, 1935.

PARK (Robert E.). — Review of Pitirim A. Sorokin: "Social and culture dynamics", *American journal of sociology*, 1938, *43*, 5, March, pp. 824-832.

PARSONS (Howard). — *Myth and religious knowledge*. Chicago, University of Chicago Press, 1946.

PARSONS (Talcott). — The place of ultimate values in sociological theory, *The international journal of ethics*, 1934-1935, *45*, April, pp. 282-316.

PARSONS (Talcott). — Review of Alexander von Schelting's *Max Webers Wissenschaftslehre*, *American sociological review*, 1936, *1*, 4, Aug., pp. 675-681.

PARSONS (Talcott). — The role of ideas in social action, *American sociological review*, 1938, *3*, 5, Oct., pp. 652-664.

PARSONS (Talcott). — Struktur und Funktion der modernen Medizin, eine soziologische Analyse, *Zeitschrift für Soziologie und Sozial-psychologie*, 1958, 3, pp. 10-57.

PELSENEER (Jean). — *L'évolution de la notion de phénomene physique, des primitifs à Bohr et Louis de Broglie*. Bruxelles, Office International de Librairie, 1947, 178 p.

PELSENEER (Jean). — Les dangers de la prolétarisation de la science, *Revue de l'Université de Bruxelles*, 1956, *8*, 2, pp. 167-172.

PEMBERTON (H.). — The effect of a social crisis on the curve of diffusion, *American sociological review*, 1937, *2*, 1, Feb., pp. 55-61.

PEREIMAN (Ch.). — Le statut social des jugements de vérité, *Revue de l'Institut de Sociologie*, 1933, *1*, pp. 17-23.

PERELMAN (Ch.). — Sociologie de la connaissance et philosophie de la connaissance, *Revue internationale de philosophie*, 1950, *4*, 13, pp. 309-317.

PERELMAN (Ch.). — Les cadres sociaux de l'argumentation, *Cahiers internationaux de sociologie*, 1959, *26*, pp. 123-135.

PERROUX (François). — L'information, facteur de progrès économique dans les sociétés du xxᵉ siècle, *Diogène*, 1958, *21*, pp. 32-60.

PERRY (Ralph Barton). — Is there a social mind?, *American journal of sociology*, 1922, *27*, 5, March, pp. 561-572; 1922, *27*, 6, May pp. 721-736.

PIAGET (Jean). — *La représentation du monde chez l'enfant*. Paris, F. Alcan, 1926, XLIII-425 p.

PIAGET (Jean). — *La construction du réel chez l'enfant*. Paris, Neuchâtel, Delachaux & Niestlé, 1937, 398 p.

PIAGET (Jean). — *La formation du symbole chez l'enfant, imitation, jeu et rêve, image et représentation*. Neuchâtel, Delachaux & Niestlé, 1945, 310 p.

PIAGET (Jean). — *Le développement de la notion de temps chez l'enfant*. Paris, Presses Universitaires de France, 1946, VIII-299 p.

PIAGET (Jean), INHELDER (Bärbel). — *La représentation de l'espace chez l'enfant*. Paris, Presses Universitaires de France, 1948, 581 p.

PIAGET (Jean). — *Introduction à l'épistémologie génétique*. Paris, Presses Universitaires de France, 1950, vol. III: « La pensée biologique, la pensée psychologique et la pensée sociologique », 345 p.

PIAGET (Jean). — Pensée égocentrique et pensée sociocentrique, *Cahiers internationaux de sociologie*, 1951, *10*, pp. 34-49.

PIAGET (Jean). — Les opérations logiques et la vie sociale, in: *Études sociologiques*. Genève, Librairie Droz, 1965, pp. 143-171. (1st ed.: in *Publications de la Faculté des Sciences économiques et sociales de l'Université de Genève*, Geneve, Georg, 1945).

PICAVET (F.). — *Les idéologues, essai sur l'histoire des idées et des théories scienti-*

fiques, philosophiques et religieuses en France depuis 1789. Paris, F. Alcan, 1891, XII-628 p.

PIERIS (Ralph). — Speech and society, a sociological approach to language, *American sociological review*, 1951, *16*, 4, Aug, pp. 499-505.

PIERIS (Ralph). — Ideological momentum and social equilibrium, *American journal of sociology*, 1957, *52*, 4, pp. 339-346.

PLESSNER (Helmut). — Zur Soziologie der modernen Forschung und ihrer Organisation, in *Versuche zu einer Soziologie des Wissens*, publ. under the direction of Max Scheler. München, Leipzig, Duncker u. Humblot, 1924, pp. 407-425.

PLESSNER (Helmut). — Abwandlungen des Ideologiegedankens, *Kölner Vierteljahreshefte für Soziologie*, 1931, *10*, pp. 147-170.

PLESSNER (Helmut). — *Das Schicksal des deutschen Geistes im Ausgang seiner bürgerlichen Epoche.* Zürich und Leipzig, M. Niehans, 1935, II-190 p.

PLESSNER (Helmut). — *Zwischen Philosophie und Gesellschaft;* ausgewählte Abhandlungen und Vorträge. Bern, Francke, 1953, 334 p.

PLESSNER (Helmut). — Zur Lage der Geisteswissenschaften in der industriellen Gesellschaft, *Schweizer Monatshefte*, 1958, *38*, 8, pp. 647-656.

POYER (Georges). — Le délire et les sept univers de la pensée, *Cahiers internationaux de sociologie*, 1948, *5*, pp. 38-65.

PRALL (D. W.). — Sorokin and the dangerous science, *Harvard guardian*, 1937, Nov., pp. 8-13.

PROESLER (Hans). — Chladenius als Wegebereiter der Wissenssoziologie, *Kölner Zeitschrift für Soziologie*, 1954, *6*, 3-4, pp. 617-622.

PROESLER (Hans). — Zur Genesis der wissenssoziologischen Problemstellung, *Kölner Zeitschrift für Soziologie und Sozialpsychologie*, 1960, *12*, 1, pp. 41-52.

PYKE (Magnus). — *The Science Myth.* New York, Macmillan, 1962, 179 p.

RAEYMACKER (Louis de), MUND (Walter), LADRIÈRE (Jean). — *La relativité de notre connaissance.* Louvain, Institut supérieur de philosophie, 1948, 156 p.

RANDALL (John Herman jr). — *Our changing civilization. How science and the machine are reconstructing modern life.* New York, Frederick A. Stokes, 1929, VII-362 p.

RAPHAEL (Max). — *Zur Erkenntnistheorie der konkreten Dialektik.* French translation by L. GARA : *La théorie marxiste de la connaissance.* Paris, Gallimard, 1937, 267 p.

RAUP (Robert Bruce). — *Education and organised interests in America.* New York, G. P. Putnam's sons, 1936, VI-238 p.

RECORD (Wilson). — Intellectuals in social and racial movements, *Phylon*, 1954, *15*, 3, Sept., pp. 231-242.

RECORD (Wilson). — Social stratification and intellectual roles in the Negro community, *British journal of sociology*, 1957, *8*, 3, pp. 235-255.

REDFIELD (R.). — Social science in our society, *Phylon*, 1950, *11*, 1, pp. 31-41.

REISER (O. L.). — *The integration of human knowledge. A study of the formal foundations and the social implications of unified science.* Boston, P. Sargent, 1958, 478 p.

RENAN (Ernest). — L'islamisme et la science, *Journal des Débats*, 1883, 30 March.

REY (Abel). — De la pensée primitive à la pensée actuelle. *Encyclopédie française*, publ. under the direction of A. de MONZIE, 1937, vol. I, section A: « La pensée primitive ».

REY (Abel). — L'outillage mental, *Encyclopédie française*, publ. under the direction of A. de MONZIE, 1937, vol. I, section B: « La pensée logique ».

Bibliography 283

REZNIKOV (L. O.). — Langage et société, *Cahiers internationaux de sociologie*, 1949, *6*, pp. 150-164.

REZSOHAZY (Rudolf). — La notion sociale du temps: Les facteurs socio-culturels du développement. L'exemple de la notion socialedu temps, *Esprit*, 1965, 33rd year (July-Aug.), 340, pp. 21-44.

RIES (Raymond E.). — Social science and ideology, *Social Research*, 1964, *31*, 2, pp. 234-243.

RIESMAN (David). — Some observations on community and utopia, *Yale law journal issue*, 1947, *57*, Dec., pp. 174-200.

RIESMAN (David), GLAZER (Nathan). — The intellectuals and the discontented classes, *Partisan review*, 1955, *22*, 1, Winter, pp. 47-72.

RILEY (Matilda White), FLOWERMAN (Samuel H.). — Group relations as a variable in communications research, *American sociological review*, 1951, *16*, 2, April, pp. 174-180.

RILEY (Matilda White), RILEY (John W.). — A sociological approach to communication research, in *The process and effects of mass communication*, ed. by Wilbur Lang SCHRAMM. Urbana, Ill., University of Illinois Press, 1960, pp. 389-401.

ROBERTY (Eugène de). — *Sociologie de l'action. La genèse sociale de la raison et les origines rationnelles de l'action*. Paris, F. Alcan, 1908, XI-355 p.

ROBERTY (Eugène de). — *Les concepts de la raison et les lois de l'Univers*. Paris, F. Alcan, 1912, 179 p.

ROBIN (Léon). — *La pensée grecque et les origines de l'esprit scientifique*. Paris, La Renaissance du Livre, 1st ed.: 1923, XXI-480 p.

ROBINSON (Daniel S.). — Karl Mannheim's sociological philosophy, *Personalist*, 1948, *29*, Spring, pp. 137-148.

ROSENBERG (Bernard). — Thorstein Veblen. Portrait of the intellectual as a marginal man, *Social Problems*, 1955, *2*, 3, pp. 181-187.

ROSSI (Pietro). — Scientific objectivity and value hypotheses, *International social science journal/Revue internationale des sciences sociales*, Unesco, 1965, *17*, 1, pp. 64-70.

ROUCEK (Joseph S.). — La ideología como elemento componente en la sociología del conocimiento, *Revista mexicana de sociología*, 1956, *18*, 1, Jan.-April, pp. 37-50.

ROUCEK (Joseph S.). — Historia del concepto de ideologia, *Revista mexicana de sociología*, 1963, *25*, 2, pp. 665-694.

ROUMEGUERE-EBERHARDT (Jacqueline). — *Pensée et société africaine, essais sur une dialectique de complémentarité antagoniste chez les Bantu du Sud-Est*. Paris, La Haye, Mouton, 1963, 99 p.

ROUMEGUERE-EBERHARDT (Jacqueline). — Sociologie de la connaissance et connaissance mythique chez les Bantu, *Cahiers internationaux de sociologie*, 1963, *35*, pp. 113-125.

ROY (G. Francis). — *The rhetoric of science*. Minneapolis, University of Minnesota Press, 1961, 183 p.

RÜSCHEMEYER (Dietrich). — *Probleme der Wissenssoziologie*. Eine Kritik der Arbeiten K. Mannheims und M. Schelers und eine Erweiterung der wissenssoziologischen Fragestellung durchgeführt am Beispiel der Kleingruppenforschung. Köln, Diss., 1958, II-367 p.

RUSSELL (Bertrand). — The role of the intellectual in the modern world, *American journal of sociology*, 1939, *44*, 4, Jan., pp. 491-498.

RUSSELL (Bertrand). — *The impact of science on society*. New York, Columbia University Press, 1951, 114 p.

RUSSELL (E. J.). — *Science and modern life*. New York, Philosophical Library, 1955, 171 p.

X

RUSSEL (P.). — The social control of science, *New Left Review*, 1962, *16*, pp. 10-20.

RUYSSEN (Théodore). — Technique et religion. *Revue philosophique*, 1948, *138*, 10-12, pp. 427-458.

SABINE (George H.). — Logic and social studies, *The philosophical review*, 1939, *48*, n° 2, pp. 155-176.

SABINE (George H.). — Beyond ideology, *Philosophical review*, 1948, *57*, 1, Jan., pp. 1-26.

SAINT-SIMON (C.-H. de). — *La Physiologie sociale, Œuvres choisies*. Introduction and notes by Georges Gurvitch. Paris, Presses Universitaires de France, 1965, 160 p.

SALANT (W.). — Science and society in ancient Rome, *Scientific monthly*, 1938, *47*, 6, Dec., pp. 525-535.

SALOMON (Albert). — Karl Mannheim, *Social research*, 1947, *14*, 3, Sept., pp. 350-364.

SALOMON (Gottfried). — Historischer Materialismus und Ideologienlehre, *Jahrbuch für Soziologie*, 1926, pp. 386-423.

SALOMON-DELATOUR (G.). — Politik als Wissenschaft, in *Politische Soziologie*. Stuttgart, F. Enke Verlag, 1959, pp. 249-256.

SAMUELSSON (Kurt). — *Religion and economic action: The Protestant Ethic, the rise of capitalism, and the abuses of scholarship*. Edited and with an introduction by D. C. Coleman, translated from the Swedish by E. Geoffrey French. New York, Basic Books, 1961, XII-157 p.

SANTUCCI (Antonio). — Forme e significati dell'utopia in Karl Mannheim, *Filosofia e sociologia*, 1954, pp. 238-248.

SANTUCCI (Antonio). — Karl Mannheim e la sociologia americana. *Filosofia e sociologia*, 1955, 4, pp. 1027-1051.

SAPIR (Edward). — *Language, an introduction to the study of speech*. New York, Harcourt, Brace, 1921, VII-258 p.

SAPIR (Edward). — Communication, *Encyclopaedia of the social sciences*, publ. under the direction of Edwin R. A. SELIGMAN and A. JOHNSON. New York, Macmillan, 1949, vol. 4, pp. 78-80.

SARAN (A. K.). — Sociology of knowledge and traditional thought, *Sociological Bulletin*, 1964, *13*, 1, pp. 33-46; *ibid.*, *13*, 2, pp. 36-48.

SARTON (George). — *The history of science and the new humanism*. New York, H. Holt, 1931, XVII-178 p.

SARTON (George). — *The history of science and the problems of to-day*. Washington, Carnegie Institution of Washington, 1936, III-30 p. (On the influence of science and research on current thought.)

SARTON (George). — *The life of science*. Essays in the history of civilization. New York, Henry Schuman, 1948, 197 p.

SARTON (George). — *Science, religion and reality*. New York, G. Braziller, 1955, 355 p.

SAURAMIS (Demosthenes). — Soziale Utopien, *Soziale Welt*, 1957, *8*, 4, pp. 294-310.

SCHAAF (Adam). — « Sociologie de la connaissance » de Mannheim et le problème de la vérité objective, *Voprosi filozofii*, 1956, 4, pp. 118-128.

SCHAAF (Julius Jacob). — *Über Wissen und Selbstbewusstsein*. Stuttgart, Schmiedel, 1947, 176 p.

SCHAAF (Julius Jacob). — *Grundprinzipien der Wissenssoziologie*. Hamburg, Felix Meiner, 1956, XII-216 p.

SCHAUB (Edward L.). — A sociological theory of knowledge, *The philosophical review*, 1920, 4, July, pp. 319-339.

SCHELER (Max Ferdinand). — *Vom Umsturz der Werte.* Leipzig, Der neue Geist, 1919.

SCHELER (Max Ferdinand). — *Wesen und Formen der Sympathie. Die Phänomenologie der Sympathiegefühle.* Bonn, F, Cohen, 1923, XVI-312 p.

SCHELER (Max Ferdinand). — *Schriften zur Soziologie und Weltanschauungslehre.* Leipzig, Der Neue Geist Verlag-P. Reinhold, 1923-1924, 4 vol. : I « Moralia », XI-175 p. ; II « Nation und Weltanschauung », 174 p. ; III « Christentum und Gesellschaft », (1) « Konfessionen », VIII-233 p., (2) « Arbeits- und Bevölkerungs probleme », 175 p.

SCHELER (Max Ferdinand). — Probleme einer Soziologie des Wissens, in *Versuche zu einer Soziologie des Wissens,* publ. under his direction, München, Leipzig, Duncker u. Humblot, 1924, pp. 5-146.

SCHELER (Max Ferdinand). — Wissenschaft und soziale Struktur, in *Verhandlungen des vierten deutschen Soziologentages 1924 in Heidelberg.* Tübingen, J. C. B. Mohr, 1925, pp. 118-212.

SCHELER (Max Ferdinand). — *Die Wissensformen und die Gesellschaft.* Leipzig, Der neue Geist, 1926, XI-565 p.

SCHELER (Max Ferdinand). — *Philosophische Weltanschauung.* Bonn, F. Cohen, 1929, 158 p. English translation by Oscar A. HAAC: *Philosophical perspectives.* Boston, Beacon Press, 1958, 144 p.

SCHELSKY (Helmut). — Bildung in der wissenschaftlichen Zivilisation, *Soziale Welt,* 1962-63, *13,* 3-4, pp. 193-208.

SCHELTING (Alexander von). — Zum Streit um die Wissenssoziologie, *Archiv für Sozialwissenschaft und Sozialpolitik,* 1929, *62,* pp. 1-66.

SCHELTING (Alexander von). — *Max Weber's Wissenschaftslehre. Das logische Problem der historischen Kulturerkenntnis; die Grenzen der Soziologie des Wissens.* Tübingen, J. C. B. Mohr, 1934, pp. 94-100 and 117-167.

SCHELTING (Alexander von). — Review of « Ideologie und Utopie » by K. Mannheim, *American sociological review,* 1936, *1,* 4, Aug. pp. 664-674.

SCHILPP (Paul A.). — The formal problems of Scheler's "Sociology of knowledge", *The philosophical review,* 1927, *36,* March, pp. 101-120.

SCHOEK (Helmut). — Der sozialökonomische Aspekt in der Wissenssoziologie Karl Mannheims, *Zeitschrift für die gesamte Staatswissenschaft,* 1950, *106,* I.

SCHOEK (Helmut). — Soziologie, in *Die Wissenssoziologie und ihre Entwicklung.* Freiburg, München, Karl Alber, 1952, pp. 1-17.

SCHORER (M.). — The necessity of myth, *Daedalus,* 1959, *88,* 2, pp. 359-362.

SCHRAMM (Wilbur Lang), ed. — *Communications in modern society; fifteen studies of the mass media.* Urbana, University of Illinois Press, 1948, VI-252 p.

SCHRAMM (Wilbur Lang), ed. — *Mass communications,* a book of readings. Urbana, Ill., University of Illinois Press, 1949, XI-552 p.

SCHÜCKING (Levin Ludwig). — *Die Soziologie der literarischen Geschmacksbildung.* 1st ed. : München, Rösl, 1923, 150 p. 2nd ed. : Leipzig und Berlin, B. G. Teubner, 1931, IV-119 p. English translation by E. W. DICKES: *The sociology of the literary taste.* London, Kegan Paul, Trench, Trubner, 1944, V-78 p.

SCHUHL (Pierre-Maxime). — *Essai sur la formation de la pensée grecque,* introduction historique à une étude de la philosophie platonicienne. Paris, F. Alcan, 1934, 2 vol. ; 2nd ed. : Paris, Presses Universitaires de France, 1949, XXXIII-482 p.

SCHUHL (Pierre-Maxime). — *Machinisme et philosophie.* Paris, F. Alcan, 1938, 110 p. ; 2nd ed. : Paris, Presses Universitaires de France, 1947, XV-132 p.

SCHUMPETER (Joseph Alois). — Science and ideology, *American economic review*, 1949, March, pp. 345-359; and in *Essays of Joseph Schumpeter*, ed. by Richard V. CLEMENCE. Cambridge, Addison-Wesley Press, 1951, 327 p.

Science and the creative spirit; essays on the humanistic aspects of science, ed. by Harcourt Brown for the American Council of Learned Societies. Toronto, University of Toronto Press, 1958, XXVII-165 p.

SCOTT (Harry F.) and associates. — *Language and its growth*. Chicago, Scott, Foresman, 1935, VII-389 p.

SCOTT (William A.). — Empirical assessment of values and ideologies, *American sociological review*, 1959, *24*, 3, pp. 299-310.

SEELY (F. A.). — The development of time-keeping in Greece and Rome, *The American anthropologist*, 1888, *1*, pp. 25-50.

SHLAKMAN (Vera). — Status and ideology of office workers, *Science & Society*, New York, 1951-52, *16*, 1, pp. 1-26.

SILBERMANN (Alphons). — *Musik, Rundfunk und Hörer*, die soziologischen Aspekte der Musik am Rundfund. Köln, Westdeutscher Verlag, 1959, 214 p.

SINGER (Charles Joseph). — *From magic to science; essays on the scientific twilight*. New York, Dover publications, 1958, 253 p.

SMALL (Albion W.). — Review of Scheler's « Versuche zu einer Soziologie des Wissens », *The American journal of sociology*, 1925, *31*, 2, Sept., pp. 262-264.

SMITH (Bruce Lannes), LASSWELL (Harold D.) et CASEY (R. D.). — *Propaganda, communication and public opinion*, a comprehensive reference guide. Princeton, Princeton University Press, 1946, IX-435 p.

SMITH (William C.). — The rural mind: a study in occupational attitude, *The American journal of sociology*, 1927, *32*, 5, March, pp. 771-786.

SMITH (W. S.). — Communication, the function of symbols in society, *Society under analysis*, ed. by E. PENDOLL, Lancaster, 1942, pp. 290-323.

Social class and educational opportunity, by J. E. FLOUD, ed., A. H. HASEY and F. M. MARTIN. London, William Heinemann, 1956, XIX-152 p.

Sociétés, traditions et technologie, Paris, U.N.E.S.C.O., 1953, 407 p.

Society and sociological knowledge. Transactions of the Fourth World Congress of Sociology; vol. I: *Sociology in its social context;* vol. II: *Applications and research;* vol. III: *Abstracts of Papers and Discussions;* vol. IV: *The sociology of knowledge*. Louvain, International Sociological Association, 1959-1961, IX-204 p.; 289 p.; V-429 p.; XI-115 p.

Sociology and education, addresses given at the Winter school of sociology and civics organised by the Institute of Sociology, Le Play House, Oxford, ed. by Miss D. M. E. DYMES. Malvern, Le Play House Press, 1944, 96 p.

SOMBART (Werner). — Technik und Kultur, in *Verhandlungen des 1. deutschen Soziologentages, 1910 in Frankfurt/M.* Tübingen, J. C. B. Mohr (Paul Siebeck), 1911, pp. 63-83.

SOMBART (Werner). — *Noo-Soziologie*. Berlin, Duncker u. Humblot, 1956, 123 p.

SOMMERFELT (Alf.). — *La langue et la société. Caratères sociaux d'une langue de type archaïque*. Oslo et Paris, Belles-Lettres, 1938, 233 p.

SONDEL (Bess Seltzer). — *Speak up! A new approach to communication*. Chicago, University of Chicago Press, 1944, VI-70 p.

SOREL (Georges). — Y a-t-il de l'utopie dans le marxisme? *Revue de métaphysique et de morale*, 1899, 7th year, 2, pp. 152-175.

SOREL (Georges). — *Réflexions sur la violence*. Paris, Librairie de « Pages Libres », 1908, XLIII-257 p.

SOREL (Georges). — *Les illusions du progrès*, Paris, M. Rivière, 1908, 283 p.

SOROKIN (Pitirim A.), MERTON (Robert K.). — The course of Arabian intellectual development 700-1300 A.D., a study in method, *Isis*, 1935, 64, *22* (2), Feb., pp. 516-524.

Bibliography 287

SOROKIN (Pitirim A.), LOSSKY (N. O.), LAPSHIN (I. I.). — The fluctuation of idealism and materialism in the Greco-Roman and European cultures from 600 B.C. to 1920 A.D., in *Reine und angewandte Soziologie*, eine Festgabe für Ferdinand Tonnies zu seinem achtzigsten Geburtstag am 26 July 1935. Leipzig, H. Buske, 1936.

SOROKIN (Pitirim A.). — *Social and cultural dynamics*. Vol. II: *Fluctuations of systems of truth, ethics and law*. New York, Cincinnati American Book, 1937, XVII-727 p.

SOROKIN (Pitirim A.), MERTON (Robert K.). — Social time, a methodological and functional analysis, *American journal of sociology*, 1937, *42*, March, pp. 615-629.

SOROKIN (Pitirim A.). — Review of "The concept of time" by Louise Robinson Heath, and of "The problem of time" (University of California publication in philosophy, 18), *American journal of sociology*, 1938, *43*, 6, May, pp. 1016-1018.

SOROKIN (Pitirim A.). — *Sociocultural causality, space, time;* a study of referential principles of sociology and social science. Durham, N.C., Duke University Press, 1943, IX-246 p.

SOROKIN (Pitirim A.). — *Society, culture and personality*, their structure and dynamics, a system of general sociology. New York, Harper and brothers, 1947, XIV-742 p.

SOROKIN (Pitirim A.). — Notes on the interdependance of philosophy and sociology, *Revue internationale de philosophie*, 1950, *4*, 13, July, pp. 268-277.

SOROKIN (Pitirim A.). — *Fads and foibles in modern sociology and related sciences*. Chicago, Henry Regnery, 1956, 357 p.

SOUSTELLE (Jacques). — *La pensée cosmologique des anciens mexicains*. Paris, Hermann, 1940, 91 p.

SPEIER (Hans). — Review of E. Grunwald's « Das Problem einer Soziologie des Wissens », *American sociological review*, 1936, *1*, 4, Aug. pp. 681-682.

SPEIER (Hans). — The social determination of ideas, *Social research*, 1937, May, pp. 182-205.

SPEIER (Hans). — Review of « Ideologie und Utopie » by K. Mannheim, *American journal of sociology*, 1937, *43*, 1, July, pp. 155-166.

SPEIER (Hans). — The sociological ideas of P. A. Sorokin, an integralist sociology, in *An introduction to the history of sociology*, Harry Elmer BARNES ed. Chicago, University of Chicago Press, 1948, pp. 884-901.

SPIER (Leslie), HALLOWELL (A. Irving), NEWMAN (Stanley S.), ed. — *Language, culture and personality*, essays in memory of Edward SAPIR. Menasha, Wis., Sapir memorial publication fund, 1941, X-298 p.

SPIRKINE (A.). — Formation de la pensée abstraite au premier stade du développement humain, *Recherches soviétiques*, Philosophie, cahier I. Paris, Édition de la Nouvelle Critique, 1956, 155 p.

STARK (Werner). — Towards a theory of social knowledge, *Revue internationale de philosophie*, 1950, *4*, 13, pp. 287-308.

STARK (Werner). — *The sociology of knowledge*. London, Routledge and Kegan Paul, 1958, XII-356 p.

STARK (Werner). — The conservative tradition in the sociology of knowledge, *Kyklos* (Bâle), 1960, *13*, 1, pp. 90-101.

STARK (Werner). — *Die Geschichte der Volkswirtschaftslehre in ihrer Beziehung zur sozialen Entwicklung*. Dordrecht, D. Reidel, 1960, 86 p.

STARK (Werner). — Die idealistische Geschichtsauffassung und die Wissenssoziologie, *Archiv für Rechts- und Sozialphilosophie*, 1960, *46*, 3, pp. 355-374.

STARK (Werner). — *Montesquieu: Pioneer of the sociology of knowledge*. Toronto, University of Toronto Press, 1961, XII-214 p.

STAUFFER (Robert C.), ed. — *Science and civilization*. Madison, University of Wisconsin Press, 1949, XIII-212 p.

STEMBER (Herbert). — Why they attack intellectuals, *The journal of social issues*, 1955, *11*, 3, pp. 22-24.

STERN (Bernhard Joseph). — *Social factors in medical progress*. New York, Columbia University Press, London, P. S. King, 1927, 136 p.; Princeton, Princeton University Press, 1941, XVII-264 p.

STOLTENBERG (H. L.). — Kundnehmen und Kundgeben, dans *Versuche zu einer Soziologie des Wissens*, publ. under the direction of MAX SCHELER. München, Leipzig, Duncker u. Humblot, 1924, pp. 208-218.

STOVER (Karl), ed. — *The technological order; The Proceedings of the "Encyclopedia Britannica" Conference*. Detroit, Wayne State University Press, 1963, 280 p.

STRAUSS (A. L.). RAINWATER (L.). — *The professional scientist, A study of American chemists*. Chicago, Aldine, 1962, 282 p.

SZCZEPANSKI (J.). — Problems of sociological research on the Polish intelligentsia, *Polish sociological bulletin*, 1961, 1-2 (June-Dec.), pp. 33-41.

SZENDE (Paul). — Eine soziologische Theorie der Abstraktion, *Archiv für Sozialwissenschaft und Sozialpolitik*, 1923, *50*, pp. 407-485.

TARDE (Gabriel de). — *La logique sociale*. Paris, F. Alcan, 1895, XIV-464 p.

TARDE (Gabriel de). — *L'opposition universelle, essai d'une théorie des contraires*. Paris, F. Alcan, 1897, VIII-451 p.

TARDE (Gabriel de). — *L'opinion et la foule*. Paris, F. Alcan, 1901, VII-226 p.

TATON (René). — The French revolution and the progress of science, *Centaurus*, 1953, *3*, 1-2, pp. 73-89.

TAWNEY (Richard Henry). — *Religion and the rise of capitalism*, a historical study. 1st ed.: New York, Penguin books, 1926, X-3-337 p., and London, J. Murray, 1926, XIII-339 p.

TAYLOR (S.). — *Conception of institutions and the theory of knowledge*. New York, Bookman Associates, 1956, 175 p.

TAYLOR (S.). — Social factors and the validation of thought, *Social Forces*, 1962 (Oct.), *41*, 1, pp. 76-82.

The teacher and society, ed. by William H. KILPATRICK. The first yearbook of the John Dewey Society. New York, London, D. Appleton Century, 1937, VII-360 p.

Technology and social change, by Francis R. ALLEN, Horner HART, Delbert C. MILLER, William F. OGBURN and Meyer F. NIMKOFF. New York, D. Appleton Century, 1957, XII-529 p.

THOMAS (L. V.). — *Les idéologies négro-africaines d'aujourd'hui*. Dakar, Université de Dakar, 1965, 81 p.

THOMPSON (David). — Scientific thought and revolutionary movements, *Impact of science on sociology*, 1955, *6*, 1, pp. 3-29.

THORNDIKE (Lynn). — *Science and thought in the fifteenth century*. New York, Columbia University Press, 1929, XII-387 p.

TILLICH (Paul). — Ideologie und Utopie, *Die Gesellschaft*, 1929, *6*, Oct., pp. 348-355.

TILLICH (Paul). — *Politische Bedeutung der Utopie im Leben der Völker*. Vorträge. Berlin, Weiss, 1951, 64 p. (Schriftenreihe der Deutschen Hochschule für Politik, Berlin).

TOMASIC (D.). — Ideologies and the structure of eastern European society, *American journal of sociology*, 1948, *5*, March, pp. 366-375.

TOPITSCH (Ernest). — The sociology of existentialism, *Partisan review*, 1954, *21*, 3, pp. 289-304.

TOPITSCH (E.). — World interpretation and self-interpretation: some basic patterns, *Daedalus*, 1959, *88*, 2, pp. 312-325.
TOPITSCH (Ernst). — *Sozialphilosophie zwischen Ideologie und Wissenschaft.* Neuwied/Rh., Luchterhand, 1961.
TOULEMONT (René). — Review of J. MAQUET: *Sociologie de la connaissance, Année sociologique*, 3rd series, 1952, pp. 256-258.
TOULEMONT (René). — *Sociologie et pluralisme dialectique. Introduction à l'œuvre de Georges Gurvitch.* Louvain, Paris, Nauwelaerts, 1955, 276 p.
TOURAINE (Alain). — Review of MANNHEIM: *Essays on the sociology of knowledge, Année sociologique*, 3rd series, 1952, pp. 251-256.
TREVES (Renato). — Karl Mannheim, *Rivista di filosofia*, 1948, *39*, 2, pp. 165-172.
TREVES (Renato). — *Politica della cultura e sociologia della conoscenza. Spirito critico e spirito dogmatico.* Milano, Nuvoletti, 1954.
TREVES (Renato). — Sociologia della conoscenza e politica della cultura, *Filosofia e sociologia*, 1954, pp. 137-144.
TUCHTFELDT (Egon). — Zur heutigen Problemstellung der Wissenssoziologie, *Zeitschrift für die gesamte Staatswissenschaft*, 1951, *107*, 4, pp. 723-731.
UBBELOHDE (A. R. J. P.). — The beginnings of the change from craft mystery to science as a basis for technology, in *A History of Technology*, ed. by Ch. Singer, E. J. Holmyard, A. R. Hall, T. I. Williams. Oxford, The Clarendon Press, vol. IV, 1958, pp. 663-681.
URBAN (Wilbur Marshall). — *Language and reality; the philosophy of language and the principles of symbolism.* London, G. Allen and Unwin, 1939, 755 p.
VAN GENNEP (Arnold). — *La formation de légendes.* Paris, Flammarion, 1910. 318 p. Reviewed by Marcel MAUSS: *Année sociologique*, 1909-1912, *12*, pp, 296-297.
VARAGNAC (André). — *Civilisation traditionnelle et genres de vie.* Paris, A. Michel, 1948, 403 p.
VEBLEN (Thorstein). — *The higher learning in America*, a memorandum on the conduct of universities by business men. New York, B. W. Huebsch, 1918, VII-286 p.
VEBLEN (Thorstein). — *The place of science in modern civilization and other essays.* New York, B. W. Huebsch, 1919, 509 p.
VERNANT (Jean-Pierre). — Du mythe à la raison. La formation de la pensée positive dans la Grèce archaïque, *Annales, Économies, Sociétés, Civilisations*, 1957, *12*, 2, pp. 183-206.
VERNANT (Jean-Pierre). — *Mythe et pensée chez les Grecs, Étude de psychologie historique.* Paris, F. Maspero, 1965, 331 p.
VIANO (Carlo Augusto). — L'analisi del linguaggio e la conoscenza degli altri, *Rivista di filosofia*, 1954, *45*, 1, Jan., pp. 48-54.
VINCENT (C. E.). — The sociology of knowledge in critiques of family sociology, *Research studies of State college of Washington*, 1953, *21*, 3, pp. 252-257.
WAGNER (Helmut R.). — Mannheim's historicism, *Social research*, 1952, *19*, 3, pp. 300-321.
WAGNER (Helmut R.). — The scope of Mannheim's thinking, *Social Research*, 1953, *20*, 1, pp. 100-109.
WALLER (Willard). — *The sociology of teaching.* New York, John Wiley, 1932, XIV-467 p.
WALLON (Henri). — *Les origines de la pensée chez l'enfant.* Vol. I: Les moyens intellectuels, XVI-307 p., vol. II: Les tâches intellectuelles, XI-449 p. Paris, Presses Universitaires de France, 1945.
WALLON (Henri). — L'étude psychologique et sociologique de l'enfant, *Cahiers internationaux de sociologie*, 1947, *3*, pp. 3-23.

WALLON (Henri). — Sociologie et éducation, *Cahiers internationaux de sociologie*, 1951, *10*, pp. 19-33.

WALLON (Henri). — Les milieux, les groupes et la psychogenèse de l'enfant, *Cahiers internationaux de sociologie*, 1954, *16*, pp. 2-13.

WALLON (Henri). — La mentalité primitive et la raison, *Revue philosophique*, 1957, *148*, 4, pp. 461-467.

WARNER (William Lloyd). — *The living and the dead, a study of the symbolic life of Americans.* New Haven, Yale University Press, 1959, XII-528 p.

WEBER (Alfred). — Der soziologische Kulturbegriff, in *Verhandlungen des zweiten Soziologentages 1912 in Berlin.* Tübingen, J. C. B. Mohr (Paul Siebeck), 1913, pp. 1-20.

WEBER (Alfred). — *Ideen zur Staats- und Kultursoziologie.* Karlsruhe, G. Braun, 1927, 142 p.

WEBER (Alfred). — *Kulturgeschichte als Kultursoziologie.* Leiden, A. W. Sijthoff's uitgeversmaatschappij, 1935, X-423 p.; München, R. Piper, 1950, 479 p.

WEBER (Alfred). — *Prinzipien der Geschichts- und Kultursoziologie.* München, R. Piper, 1951, 176 p.

WEBER (Louis). — *Le rythme du progrès, étude sociologique.* Paris, F. Alcan, 1913, XIV-311 p.

WEBER (Louis). — La civilisation. Civilisation et technique, in *Civilisation: le mot et l'idée.* Paris, La Renaissance du Livre, 1930, pp. 131-143.

WEBER (Max). — Die « Objektivität » sozialwissenschaftlicher und sozialpolitischer Erkenntnis, *Archiv für Sozialwissenschaft und Sozialpolitik*, 1904, *19*, pp. 22-87; and in *Gesammelte Aufsätze zur Wissenschaftslehre.* Tübingen, J. C. B. Mohr, 1922, pp. 146-214.

WEBER (Max). — Die protestantische Ethik und der « Geist » des Kapitalismus, I, II, in *Archiv für Sozialwissenschaft und Sozialpolitik* (de Jaffé), 1905, *20*, pp. 1-54, and *21*, pp. 1-110, and Die protestantische Ethik und der Geist des Kapitalismus, in *Gesammelte Aufsätze zur Religionssoziologie*, vol. I. Tübingen, J. C. B. Mohr, 1922, pp. 1-206, and *Die protestantische Ethik und der Geist des Kapitalismus.* Tübingen, J. C. B. Mohr, 1934, 206 p. English trs. by Talcott PARSONS: *The protestant ethic and the spirit of capitalism*, with a foreword by R. H. TAWNEY, London, Allen & Unwin, 1930, 292 p.; New York, C. Scribner's sons, 1956, VII-XI-2-292 p.

WEBER (Max). — Die sogenannte « Lehrfreiheit » an den deutschen Universitäten, *Frankfurter Zeitung* vom 20. September 1908.

WEBER (Max). — Antikritisches Schlusswort zum « Geist » des Kapitalismus, *Archiv für Sozialwissenschaft und Sozialpolitik*, 1910, *31*, pp. 554-599.

WEBER (Max). — Wissenschaft als Beruf (zuerst bei Duncker u. Humblot, 1919), in *Gesammelte Aufsätze zur Wissenschaftslehre.* Tübingen, J. C. B. Mohr, 1922, 579 p., and in *Max Weber, Soziologie, Weltgeschichtliche Analysen, Politik*, publ. under the direction of J. WINCKELMANN, Stuttgart, A. Kröner, 1956, XXXV-576 p.

WEBER (Max). — *Gesammelte Aufsätze zur Wissenschaftslehre.* Tübingen, J. C. B. Mohr, 1922, 579 p.; 1951, VIII-688 p.

WEIDLE (Wladimir). — Sur le concept d'idéologie, *Contrat social*, 1959, *3*, 2, pp. 75-78.

WEILLER (Jean). — Les cadres sociaux de la pensée économique contemporaine, *Cahiers internationaux de sociologie*, 1959, *26*, pp. 103-118.

WELTER (Gustave). — Le mécanisme de la pensée primitive, *L'ethnographie*, 1955, *50*, pp. 36-41.

WEST (S. S.). — Class origin of scientists, *Sociometry*, 1961, *24*, 3, pp. 251-269.

WESTERMANN (Dietrich). — Kulturelle Wandlungen und Anpassungen in Westafrika, *Sociologus*, 1951, *3*, 1, pp. 96-115.

WESTFALL (Richard S.). — *Science and religion in seventeenth century England.* New Haven, Yale University Press, 1958, IX-235 p.

WHITE (Lynn Jr.). — *Medieval technology and social change.* New York, Oxford University Press, 1962, XII-194 p.

WHORF (Benjamin Lee). — *Language, thought and reality (selected writings of Benjamin Lee Whorf)*, ed. by John B. CARROLL, foreword by Stuart CHASE. Cambridge, Mass., Technology Press of Massachusetts Institute of Technology, 1956, XI-278 p.

WIENER (P. P.), NOLAND (A.), éd. — *Roots of scientific thought, a cultural perspective.* New York, Basic Books, 1957, 677 p. (Selections from the first eighteen volumes of the *Journal of the history of ideas*).

WIESE (Leopold von). — Einsamkeit und Geselligkeit als Bedingungen der Mehrung des Wissens, dans *Versuche zu einer Soziologie des Wissens*, publ. under the direction of Max SCHELER. München, Leipzig, Duncker u. Humblot, 1924, pp. 218-229.

WIESE (Leopold von). — Florian Znaniecki's « Cultural sciences », *Kölner Zeitschrift für Soziologie*, 1951-1952, *4*, pp. 524-532.

WIESE (Leopold von). — *Das Soziale im Leben und Denken.* Köln, Opladen, Westdeutscher Verlag, 1956, 79 p.

WILLENER (Alfred). — *Images de la société et classes sociales*, une étude de la perception et des représentations des différences sociales. Berne, Imprimerie Stämpfli, 1957, 228 p.

WILLIAMS (E.). — Sociologists of knowledge, *Philosophy of science*, 1947, *14*, July, pp. 224-230.

WILSON (F. G.). — Public opinion and the intellectuals, *American political science review*, 1954, *48*, 2, pp. 321-339.

WILSON (F. G.). — The social scientist and his values, *Thought*, 1958, *33*, 128, pp. 21-42.

WILSON (Logan). — *The academic man*, a study in the sociology of a profession. New York, London, Oxford University Press, 1942, VI-3-248 p.

WIRTH (Louis). — Preface to Karl Mannheim's *Ideology and utopia.* London, Kegan Paul, Trench, Trubner, New York, Harcourt, Brace, 1936, pp. I-XXXI.

WIRTH (Louis). — Ideological aspects of social disorganization, *American sociological review*, 1940, *5*, 4, pp. 472-482.

WIRTH (Louis). — Karl Mannheim, 1893-1947, *American sociological review*, 1947, *12*, 3, June, pp. 356-357.

WITHEY (B.). — Public opinion about science and scientists, *Public Opinion Quarterly*, 1959, *23*, pp. 382-388.

WITTFOGEL (K. A.). — Wissen und Gesellschaft, *Unter dem Banner des Marxismus*, 1931, *4*.

WOLFF (Kurt H.). — The sociology of knowledge, emphasis on an empirical attitude, *Philosophy of science*, 1943, *10*, pp. 104-123.

WOLFF (Kurt H.). — *The sociology of intellectual behaviour*, a survey and appraisal of sociology of knowledge. Ohio State University, 1947-1948 (mimeographed).

WOLFF (Kurt H.). — A preliminary inquiry into the sociology of knowledge from the standpoint of the study of man, *Scritti di sociologia e politica in onore di Luigi Sturzo*, Bologna, Nicola Zanichelli, 1953, *3*, pp. 583-622.

WOLFF (Kurt H.). — The sociology of knowledge and sociological theory, in *Symposium on sociological theory*, ed. by Llewellyn GROSS. Evanston, Ill., Row, Peterson, 1959, pp. 567-602.

WOOLSTON (Howard B.). — American intellectuals and social reform, *The American sociological review*, 1936, *1*, 3, June pp. 363-372.

WORSLEY (P. M.). — Emile Durkheim's theory of knowledge, *Sociological review*, 1956, *4*, 1, pp. 47-62.

ZAHAN (Dominique). — Aperçu sur la pensée théogonique des Dogons, *Cahiers internationaux de sociologie*, 1949, *6*, pp. 113-133.

ZAHAN (Dominique). — *La dialectique du verbe chez les Bambara.* Paris, La Haye, Mouton, 1963, 207 p.

ZAZZO (René). — *Le devenir de l'intelligence.* Paris, Presses Universitaires de France, 1946, VIII-160 p. (chap. III: « Du primitif au civilisé », pp. 43-71).

ZEUTHEN (H. G.). — Quelques traits de la propagation de la science de génération en génération, *Rivista di scienza*, 1909, *5*, 9.

ZIELINSKI (Arno R. F.). — Der Einfluss des technischen Apparates, in *Abhängigkeit und Selbständigkeit im sozialen Leben.* Herausgegeben im Auftrag des Forschungsinstituts für Sozialund Verwaltungswissenschaften in Köln von Leopold von Wiese. Köln u. Opladen, Westdeutscher Verlag, 1951, pp. 282-294.

ZILSEL (Edgar). — The sociological roots of science, *American journal of sociology*, 1942, *47*, Jan., pp. 544-562.

ZNANIECKI (Florian). — *The social role of the man of knowledge.* New York, Columbia University Press, 1940, 212 p.

ZNANIECKI (Florian). — The present and the future of sociology of knowledge, *Soziologische Forschung in unserer Zeit, Leopold von Wiese zum 75. Geburtstag.* Köln, Opladen, Westdeutscher Verlag, 1951, pp. 248-257.

ZNANIECKI (Florian). — *Cultural sciences, their origin and development.* Urbana, University of Illinois Press, 1952, VIII-438 p., reprinted., 1963.

ZNANIECKI (Florian). — Should sociologists be also philosophers of values?, *Sociology and social research*, 1952, *37*, 2, Nov.-Dec., pp. 79-84.

ZOLTOWSKI (Victor). — Les fonctions sociales du temps et de l'espace, contribution à la théorie expérimentale de la connaissance, *Revue d'histoire économique et sociale*, 1940-1947, *26*, 2, pp. 113-137.

ZOLTOWSKI (Victor). — La théorie de la connaissance et le rythme de l'histoire, *Année sociologique*, 3rd series, 1949-1950, pp. 533-535.

ZOLTOWSKI (Victor). — Les cycles de la création intellectuelle et artistique, *Année sociologique*, 3rd series, 1952, pp. 163-206.